Out of Darkness

Out of Darkness

*Exploring Satanism and
Ritual Abuse*

David K. Sakheim and Susan E. Devine

LEXINGTON BOOKS
An Imprint of Macmillan, Inc.
NEW YORK

Maxwell Macmillan Canada
TORONTO

Maxwell Macmillan International
NEW YORK OXFORD SINGAPORE SIDNEY

Library of Congress Cataloging-in-Publication Data

Out of darkness: exploring satanism and ritual abuse/edited by David K. Sakheim and
Susan E. Devine.
    p. cm.
    Includes index.
    ISBN 0-669-26962-X
    1. Satanism—Controversial literature. 2. Child abuse.
I. Sakheim, David K. II. Devine, Susan E.
BF 1548.D37 1992
616.85'822—dc20   72219   91–27670
                                              CIP

Lexington Books
An Imprint of Macmillan, Inc.
866 Third Avenue, New York, N.Y. 10022

Maxwell Macmillan Canada, Inc.
1200 Eglinton Avenue East
Suite 200
Don Mills, Ontario M3C 3N1

Macmillan, Inc. is part of the Maxwell Communication Group of Companies.

Printed in the United States of America

printing number

   2   3   4   5   6   7   8   9   10

This book is dedicated to all who have experienced trauma in their lives. We honor those who were able to survive and mourn the loss of those who were not. Specifically, this volume is lovingly dedicated to Melissa Barstow, to Arthur and Anuta Sakheim, and to Kurt and Sophie Oschinsky.

Contents

Acknowledgments

The authors wish to acknowledge the tremendous assistance in editing portions of this book provided by Ms. Kay Adams, Ms. Margaret Zusky, and Mr. Andrew B. Lewis. Ms. Lorraine Stanek also contributed to this volume by sharing her many insights and ideas about what is healing in psychotherapy with traumatized individuals.

Introduction: The Phenomenon of Satanic Ritual Abuse

W e have assembled this material on the phenomenon of satanic ritual abuse in the hope that the more therapists understand about the history, beliefs, and practices of satanic religion, about the patients who present as cult survivors, and about the treatment approaches that are being attempted, the better they will be able to help their patients understand and come to terms with their lives. This field is in its infancy, and future work will likely clarify and change much of what is presented here.

Working as a professional in this area one often feels alone and in the dark. We hope the more the area is explored, the less this will be the case. It is not enough, for example, just to know something about the satanic calendar in order to better anticipate patients' possible anniversary reactions; it is also necessary to know something about how other professionals are approaching the spiritual, ethical, legal, historical, therapeutic, and credibility issues of this phenomenon. By opening the discussion to specialists in many different disciplines, we hope to facilitate further exploration and dialogue.

Patients presenting and being labeled by therapists as ritually abused and/or "satanic cult survivors" is fairly new. Obviously, it is very important to be clear about what such terms signify. In the first two chapters Martin Katchen examines the history as well as the beliefs and practices of groups labeled "satanic." He makes it clear that not only are these groups heterogeneous and complex, but that "satanism" as a religion does not necessarily imply illegal activities. Since there are groups that practice satanism without committing crimes, it is very important to be careful in how one uses the term "satanism." Members of any religious group can abuse a child just as systematically and cruelly as any satanist. It is therefore important to be able to talk about both the specifics of what happened to the patient as well as the motives of the perpetrators. Discussing only crimes of severe child abuse committed by satanists is arbitrary and limiting. Kenneth Lanning (1989) points out that when a murder is committed by someone who believes that Jesus told him to do it, we do not label it a "christian crime" and it would not be helpful to do so. As much as it may help us to understand the perpetrator's motives, we must separate his or her idiosyncratic beliefs from mislabeling an entire religion. Since satanist belief does not require criminal action, we must be very precise about how we label what our patients are presenting. "Ritual abuse" is probably a better generic term. In a recent paper the Los Angeles County Commission for Women (1989) defined *ritual abuse* as follows:

> A brutal form of abuse of children, adolescents, and adults, consisting of physical, sexual, and psychological abuse, and involving the use of rituals. Ritual does not necessarily mean satanic. However, most survivors state that they were ritually abused as part of satanic worship for the purpose of indoctrinating them into satanic beliefs and practices. Ritual abuse rarely consists of a single episode. It usually involves repeated abuse over an extended period of time.

Clearly, there appear to be two major aspects to what our patients are disclosing. One is a history of extreme, overwhelming, and debilitating abuse. The other is that the abuse occurred in a context in which it was justified as an essential part of the perpetrators' religious beliefs. Although these beliefs are usually satanic in nature, both aspects are important and they need to be understood separately. These patients' experiences clearly represent the far end of the emotional, sexual, and physical abuse continuum. To understand the resulting reactions, one must understand the severity of what was endured and the motives of the perpetrators. Accidental, random, deliberate, sanctioned, and religious abuse all have different impacts. It probably makes the most sense to classify patients by the severity of what they experienced as well as by the context in which the abuse occurred. "Ritual abuse" seems a useful way to describe the most severe repetitive types of trauma. One can then specify the context by stating, for example, that the patient was ritually abused as part of a Satan-worshiping group, as part of a multidimensional child-sex ring, or by a psychotic parent.

As we attempt to understand *post-traumatic stress disorder* (PTSD), this subgroup of patients will teach us a lot about reactions to the extremes of abuse and torture. However, by defining the terms we use we are also choosing the factors that will guide our research and thinking. The two factors described above will focus our attention on the severity of abuse as well as its context. These are likely to be important. However, as Lisa McCann and Laurie Pearlman point out in Chapter 8, there are also many other factors that influence how a person is affected by trauma. We must be careful not to narrow our focus prematurely.

In Chapter 2, Martin Katchen and David Sakheim provide some insight into the significance that these groups attribute to various rituals, symbols, objects, numbers, and dates. This information can give a therapist a clearer understanding of what a patient is describing, as well as a better sense of how the groups themselves view their actions. It would be an error to assume that every group attaches the same meanings to all symbols. However, a basic understanding of how such thinking can operate is very helpful in putting together the fragmentary memories that emerge during treatment. It is also interesting to see that the types of indoctrination and specific attempts at mind control described by these patients are very similar psychologically to those that have been developed by other "totalist" groups, which have been studied in other contexts.

At present the most common area for discussion about satanic cults is the reality of their existence. Opinions vary from total acceptance to total disbelief. In Chapter 3, George Greaves presents an excellent overview of the issues involved in this debate, a useful typology of the positions taken by experts in the fields, and a helpful integration of these seemingly divergent perspectives. Without more investigative work there can be no definitive answer to this question. It seems likely that there will never be one single answer. Patients will probably range from those malingering for secondary gain, to those who are delusional, to still others for whom descriptions of satanism are screen memories, to those who have truly experienced ritualized abuse. All of these patients need to be understood and treated, but probably not all in the same fashion. Unfortunately, our field has a tendency to become polarized with some clinicians claiming that every patient's story is true and that the rest of the field is heartless, and others claiming that every patient is delusional and the rest of the field is merely too gullible. Neither of these positions takes into account all of the data, and neither really furthers the understanding of this complex group of patients. We have tried to present the range of views in this volume in the hope that doing so may bring some integration to this area as well as some sensitivity to the complexities involved. Each "side" in this debate has many valid and worthwhile points to make. Each could learn from the other. It may even be the case that the two sides are focusing on different patient groups erroneously classified together under the catchall heading of "satanic cult survivors."

To understand this area we must maintain scientific skepticism and clinical empathy. We need to avoid the hysteria of overreaction and the denial mechanisms triggered when one is confronted with horrible material. Despite humanity's history of interpersonal violence, and despite our psychological understanding of post-traumatic stress reactions, we tend to disbelieve most victims. We preferred not to believe the reports of incest and other forms of child abuse for years. In general, we demand tremendous amounts of proof before we are willing to believe that people can be horrible to one another. Although we know that this has occurred throughout history, each time such practices come to light we try to avoid the pain of knowledge. Recent history is full of killing fields. A list of them could go on for pages. However, these events are not only examples of the extremes of human cruelty, but also examples of the extremes of human denial. We do not want to know how sadistic our species can be.

It is also easy to point to hysterical overreactions throughout our history. Hysteria can be as dangerous as denial. Widespread hysteria—"witch hunt"—is all too common in history. Allegations of the ritual abuse and murder of children have sparked pogroms against the Jews from the beginning of the Christian era to this century. As the days of Senator Joseph McCarthy show us, no group is too "enlightened" or too "sophisticated" to succumb to the witch-hunting hysteria.

As we researched this book, we were distressed to see that such strong hysterical reactions are apparent even today. Some of the people contacted for interviews were far too quick to label someone who expressed skepticism about cults as a cult member or cult apologist. Such labeling and counterlabeling is very dangerous before we have sufficient data to know with what we are dealing. All that will do is divide the field further and decrease our chances for understanding.

Over the years the mental health profession has indulged both in hysterical overreaction to and denial of interpersonal violence. It will be very sad if the internal disagreements about how to approach the area of ritual abuse force therapists to take sides before the information is available to do so intelligently. If that occurs, each side will misdiagnose important clinical situations. "Believing" a delusional patient can be as destructive as "disbelieving" a traumatized one. It would be a major loss to our field if hysteria tempts us to go beyond our data. It would be equally tragic if our field repeats its handling of incest allegations and we end up blaming the victims and dismissing their stories as fantasy rather than confronting the horrors of their experiences.

This is not to imply that a therapist must believe every word of a survivor's descriptions, even if we know for a fact that he or she was abused. Research has shown that people in general are usually not very accurate witnesses even under ideal circumstances. Clearly, the observations of a young child who is deliberately being tortured, confused, drugged, and terrorized will be distorted. This is even more likely when the survivor is trying to reconstruct events that occurred twenty or more years in the past. However, in therapy it is not necessary to verify every detail. In therapy it may be enough to accept that a patient's post-traumatic stress reactions indicate a history that must be explored—with the therapist present as an ally. However, the therapist must not be seduced by his or her own needs. The compelling material and the intensely projected affects must not be allowed to make the therapist into an advocate for either side of the patient's ambivalence. The therapist's role is to help the patient to better understand his or her own doubts and uncertainties. It is the patient's struggle to sort out what is real.

A fascinating phenomenon about which little is yet understood involves cases of "pseudo PTSD." Such cases have been documented clinically. For example, there are instances of patients who believe they have combat-related PTSD, but never were in a war zone. There is a clear need for further study in this area. Until we know more about such behavior, it will be difficult to know if any of the patients alleging ritual abuse are clinically similar to this group. Can completely fantasized trauma (as opposed to real trauma or a screen memory that does, in fact, have a traumatic etiology) produce a PTSD syndrome? What treatment approaches are appropriate for such a population? Clearly, as we learn more about the subtypes of patients who present with PTSD symptoms, as well as about the prevalence, symptom pictures, and course of treatments for each type of subgroup, we will be able to make more credible assessments and design more effective treatment approaches.

At present we do not have this information. It is interesting that we have such a difficult time believing that patients have been severely traumatized even when there *is* corroborating data. This is especially striking since nothing ritual abuse survivors describe is really unknown to us. Taken separately, the crimes that ritually abused patients report (child abuse, torture, infanticide, cannibalism, child pornography, drug abuse, cruelty to animals, and murder) are all known to occur. It is probably our own difficulty imagining the combination of horrors that makes us so skeptical. It is important to realize that working to understand this far end of the continuum of human cruelty through research and treatment with survivors, we will probably be far better able to understand and treat less severe forms of abuse and trauma. A focus on the mystical and sensational aspects of this phenomenon can distract us from the sad reality of the extreme sadism and cruelty truly behind the problems that these patients experience. As Walter Young and Catherine Gould make clear in their chapters on assessment and treatment, the pathology of the ritual abuse survivor is not significant because it is so different from other types of psychopathology, but rather because it contains the extremes of human coping responses to the extremes of potential stressors. As we begin to understand that the etiologies of many diagnostic syndromes are based in defense against trauma (PTSD, borderline personality disorder, the dissociative disorders, adjustment disorders, as well as some brief psychotic reactions, anxiety disorders, and paraphilias), we gain insight from the therapy of ritually abused persons that is tremendously helpful. For example, in Chapter 8, Lisa McCann and Laurie Pearlman discuss the ways that severe early traumatic stress can influence a person's emotional and cognitive processes and give some excellent insights into the implications that this has for the treatment of all traumatized patients.

While reading the various chapters of this volume, it is important to keep in mind that there are strong disagreements among individuals who work both within the field and across subspecialties. Catherine Gould's methods of evaluating and treating ritually abused children, for example, have been viewed by some clinicians as controversial. (See Chapter 5, by Kenneth Lanning.) Because most children are unwilling or unable to disclose their experiences with ritual abuse, Gould suggests asking the child more structured questions rather than neutral, open-ended questions. She also suggests encouraging the child to act out with toys and dolls that symbolize situations of ritual abuse. Clinicians caution that an impressionable child may be led to invent situations that otherwise would never occur to him, and that "leading the witness" can damage the child's testimony in court. Another controversial aspect of Gould's methods is her list of symptoms of ritual abuse. Clinicians argue that many of the symptoms are associated with normal childhood development or are symptoms of less severe forms of abuse.

By offering a variety of perspectives on the topic of ritual abuse, we hope to encourage a critical evaluation. Many strong positions have been taken concerning this phenomenon, often with a lack of empirical data for support. It is hoped that through exposure to a diversity of views, the reader will gain the necessary facts to critically evaluate contrasting perspectives.

At present, the degree to which intergenerational satanic cults exist, conspire, and are organized is not at all clear. There is strong disagreement about this issue. However, there is no disagreement about the fact that many of the patients in question have experienced severe forms of abuse and that as therapists we will need to find ways to help them to heal. The chapter by Linda Stone was included in this book in order to give the reader a sense of how devastating such abuse can be, not only for the victim, but for anyone who is close to him or her as well. Whether or not one accepts the idea of well-organized cults, her testimony demonstrates the degree of distress involved for the individuals who present for treatment. As she makes clear, even if we discover that there is no such conspiracy, we still need to develop ways to investigate and prosecute the criminal acts that do occur, as well as to develop and provide treatment for the victims in such cases. At present, there is no question that the existing mental health system often revictimizes patients and their families through our lack of understanding about their disclosures.

Professionals of varying specialties have a need for differing degrees of skepticism when it comes to these cases. Courts are on one end of this continuum. They need "proof beyond a reasonable doubt" before they convict anyone. This approach is clearly needed to protect the accused. Police officers probably do best when they are somewhere in the middle of the skepticism scale, in that they need to be wary of jumping to conclusions in their investigations, yet open-minded enough not to miss important facts. Robert Kinscherff and Richard Barnum describe the complexities involved in attempting to sort out some of these issues within the criminal justice system. Researchers in this field clearly need to keep an open mind about both sides of the continuum while maintaining a close tie to the empirical data. Richard Mangen's chapter on psychological assessment is an important step in this direction. He describes findings from the use of a variety of validated instruments that may eventually help us to better screen such patients as well as to understand the importance of early trauma in explaining the psychodynamics of this population. As this work progresses, the use of such instruments will be critical in the planning and implementation of treatment. The variety of testing data he presents makes clear that in order to successfully work with a ritual abuse survivor it is very important for a therapist to understand how completely the survivor's world was devastated and shattered by abuse. The presenting complaints may be any of a variety of symptoms or problems but it is critical to understand the connection of any such symptom to its traumatic origins.

Therapists probably do best to lean toward the acceptance end of the skepticism continuum once they have moved beyond the assessment phase and have ruled out malingering or clear delusional disorders. A therapist may be more skeptical in the assessment phase, but while doing treatment needs to be emphathic in order to understand the patient's experiences and to help the patient to work through the feelings that are associated with these memories. Of course, the therapist must be careful not to encourage one type of memory over another, but for therapy to proceed, the accuracy of the memory is usually less important than its emotional impact. A therapist must attend to the pain of the survivor despite the possibility of some distortion in the memories. However, an empathic stance is not the same thing as a leading one. The therapist must allow the patient to struggle with his or her own doubts and must be able to acknowledge that only the patient can know what really occurred.

Interestingly, exacting accuracy is usually more important to the patient, who will often go to great lengths to try to find "proof" that these events did in fact occur precisely as remembered. This is usually a way for the patient to overcome his or her own denial processes and sort out what is accurate from what is not.

Once it has been ascertained that a patient has been traumatized there is less need for a therapist to focus on the specific details than to understand that this is a person in severe pain with extreme PTSD who can only begin to heal by remembering as best they can the traumatic events that led to the creation of their symptoms. To hold a patient to rules of evidence will only inhibit the process of recovery. This is especially true since so much of the treatment is geared toward helping the patient to deal with his or her own skepticism and denial. Even when confronting a blatant screen memory it is usually the case that the patient must first "remember" it in order to see that it doesn't really hold together. Only after the screen memory is fully "uncovered" can the patient move beyond it to the underlying events, which are usually more difficult to accept emotionally. It is important to realize that a major part of the trauma involved for these patients is the very fact that their perceptions and memories have been so distorted by abuse. Healing is made far more difficult and painful by the confusion, dissociation, and nonsequential memories that the abuse created. It does not help this process for the therapist to add to the patient's already profound distrust of his or her own perceptions.

In Chapter 11, we propose a view of therapy that strives to create a safe environment where the therapist acts as consultant, ally, and witness to the patient. We discuss differences between such a relationship-centered orientation and more traditional approaches to treatment. It is clear that at this stage in our knowledge it is essential that we listen to those who are undergoing this process rather than assuming that we have all of the answers ourselves. One cannot know beforehand what will help or harm. This can really only be ascertained by being a supportive ally during each patient's process of recovery. Therapy can be tremendously helpful when early abuse is uncovered in a safe and supportive environment; however, therapy also has the potential to be revictimizing, especially when the underlying traumatic material is not properly understood or addressed.

The question of skepticism versus acceptance is further complicated when specialists from various professions must work together as in an investigation. Therapists and investigators, lawyers, police, and other officers of the court have to develop ways of working together so that the goals of one discipline do not interfere with the needs of another. For example, initial evidence-gathering interviews will have to be developed with an understanding that the abused child needs support but that his or her testimony may be used in a court case where the rights of others are also at stake. Thus, the interviewer (often a therapist) will have to learn to interview without "leading the witness" while still supporting and assisting a traumatized child. Similarly, police and lawyers need to develop interviewing techniques that do not retraumatize the child and make subsequent treatment that much more difficult. It is also critical that no one from any of these disciplines make public statements not based in the data. It does no one any good to discuss "the international satanic conspiracy" as if its existence were a certainty. If we do not stick to the data, we will lose the credibility that this field has enjoyed and the backlash will likely harm our patients as well.

We hope an integration will occur among the disparate reports of clinical observations and experiences in working with ritually abused patients. We hope too that some light will be shed on the people and practices involved in ritual abuse. This process should help us to assist all people who are trying to recover from the effects of extreme trauma. We also hope nothing in this volume will contribute to the development of a witch hunt or an Inquisition. Such activity is usually more violent and abusive than the actions it intends to impede. The defenders of "right" can be as cruel as any satanist. We must keep in mind that it is exactly such activities that create the problems we are trying to solve. History is full of examples of "good" triumphing over "evil" by simply being more powerful, coercive, and violent.

It may be the case that we will never be able to see, much less stop, such victimization by either side until we truly comprehend the human capacity for violence. This will probably only happen if we are willing to look at our own darker sides. As long as we collude in the belief that this is a battle between good and evil and that we must avoid the complexity of human emotion by choosing one side or the other, we will probably always need to deny the reality when "evil" gets too close to home.

David K. Sakheim, Ph.D
Susan E. Devine, R.N., M.S.N.

References

Lanning, K.V. 1989. *Satanic, Occult, Ritualistic Crime: A Law-Enforcement Perspective.* Quantico, Va.: FBI Academy.
Ritual Abuse Task Force. Los Angeles County Commission For Women. 1989. *Ritual Abuse: Definitions, Glossary, The Use Of Mind Control.* September 15.

1

The History of Satanic Religions

Martin H. Katchen, M.A.

The figure of Satan is an ancient one. A figurine depicting a man with a goat's head, seated cross-legged, surrounded by worshiping animals, was found in the Indus valley. It was made in 3000 B.C.

Later, the goat-headed Baphomet figure appears in Babylonian art. Practices such as ritualistic sex to promote fertility and child sacrifice were quite common in early Semitic religion. The name *Satan* possibly came from Egypt, in which the forces of disharmony and disorder are represented by Set, killer of Osiris and disturber of the order of *maat* or harmony. The worship of Set has been associated with the semitic Hyksos invaders of Egypt (Raschke 1990 141–142).

True dualism, however, awaited the growth of Zoroastrianism in Persia and the Jewish civilization in ancient Israel. Zoroastrianism teaches that the world is a battleground between the forces of light, and their god Ahura Mazda or Ormuzd, and the forces of darkness led by their god, Angya Mangu or Ahriman. Zoroastrianism supplanted the worship of the Vedic gods among the Persians in the eighth century B.C. and was to have a profound influence on western religion.

Judaism traditionally did not accept the legitimacy of evil as an opposing force to good. God, according to the Jewish conception, chose the Jewish people to inhabit the land of Canaan, which became the land of Israel, and to live by a set of commandments that would bring them closer to Him. These commandments include prohibitions against the worship of any other deities and some of the ritual practices of other peoples. These commandments were honored in the breach during the period of the First Temple, and when the Temple was destroyed by Nebuchadnezzar in 587 B.C., prophets such as Jeremiah preserved the Jewish people and religion by teaching that the destruction was the fault of the people. By teaching that conquest was the result of the people failing God, rather than the god failing the people (as almost any other conquered people would have concluded), the tendency for the conquered to adopt the religion of the conqueror was averted and the Jewish religion was preserved during the time of exile.

It was in exile that Judaism came to be heavily influenced by Zoroastrian

1

dualism in a way that made it possible for offshoots of Judaism to develop along very unorthodox lines. While the mainstream of Jewish history developed around the return of Jews to the land of Israel, the building of the Second Temple, and the recovery of independence under the Hasmonean Dynasty, the Jewish community that had developed in Egypt following the destruction of the First Temple evolved on a much different path. Under the Persians and particularly the Ptolemaic Greeks, the Jews prospered as a privileged class, intermediate between the Greek overlords and the Egyptian population (Green 1985). With the coming of the Romans, however, these privileges were swept away. Faced with the unwillingness of Jews, even highly hellenized Jews, to make obeisances to Roman gods, the Romans began to eliminate Jewish rights. In addition, the privatization of property in Egypt eliminated the peculiar niche that Jews had enjoyed (ibid.). As a result, particularly after the destruction of the Second Temple in A.D. 70, Jews in Egypt began to see the world as hostile in a theological sense.

From this negative world view the theological conception known as *Gnosticism* began. Gnosticism teaches that the creator of the world, although good, has withdrawn from the world, leaving it in the hands of evil or incompetent forces known as *archons,* which together make up the *demiurge.* Thus subordinated to the control of evil forces, humanity has the choice of two paths. One can attempt either to transcend the world through the practice of asceticism or to control the world and take the pleasant things from it through the practice of magic. Both paths involve a highly individualistic path of attainment of esoteric and arcane knowledge known as *gnosis.* The individual who attains this gnosis is to be considered superior to the one who has not.

Thus, two essential elements of satanism, the conception of the world as being ultimately controlled by evil or hostile forces and the figure of the magician as a hero who can control these hostile forces entered the consciousness of late antiquity. As belief in the gods and goddesses of Classical Greece and Rome collapsed, the destruction of the Second Temple split Judaism into three factions. Rabbinic Judaism affirmed the supremacy of one God even in the face of destruction. Gnosticism affirmed the supremacy of hostile forces. Christianity took a middle ground, affirming the existence and power of evil forces in the world, which can be conquered and transcended, but only through faith in Christ and membership in the Church.

Needless to say, Christianity was far more successful than the other two alternatives. Rabbinic Judaism codified its paradigms of behavior in the Talmud, and ultimately grappled with the question of God's relationship with this world in Merkava mysticism, which developed into Kabbalah. Christianity became very popular and, under Constantine and Theodosius, the state religion of the remnants of the Roman Empire. The Gnostic paradigm also survived in heretical sects and cults through the Middle Ages.

In the third and fourth centuries A.D., Epiphanius, an Egyptian monk and later a bishop, uncovered one such group, the Phibionites. Unlike the inquisitors of the Middle Ages, who were barred from "undercover" operations by doctrinal and legal considerations, Epiphanius had no compunctions about infiltrating the Phibionites. He reports a group that practiced promiscuity, used semen as a sacrament, and sanctified abortion (Hill and Goodwin 1989); Sally Hill and Jean Goodwin remark that such early Gnostic rituals share certain elements with the satanic mass, namely a secret feast, a sexual orgy, reversals of the Christian mass, ritual use of blood, semen, and other excretions, and the practices of infant sacrifice and cannibalism (ibid.).

Sally Hill and Jean Goodwin (ibid.) see variations on the satanic mass persisting throughout the Dark Ages. The proscriptions against dancing and incantations by the Synod of Rome and the laws of Charlemange that punished sacrificing to demons with death are probably in reaction to such groups.

Other dualistic sects appeared in Europe during this time and led up to the medieval vogue of satanism. The first of these was the Paulician heresy, which arose in the sixth century in Asia Minor. They were very warlike. The Byzantines forcibly relocated them to the northern frontiers of their empire, in what is now Bulgaria, rather than annihilating them, seeing them as a useful bulwark against barbarian tribes (Obolensky 1948). Over time, the Paulicians were conquered by the Bulgars, an Asian tribe, who adopted the Paulician religion as promulgated by a priest named Bogomil. The Bulgars sought a religion that would not be pagan, yet would define them against eastern *and* western Christianity (ibid.).

The dualistic beliefs of the *Bogomils,* as they came to be called, spread westward into Italy and France during the eleventh century at a time when Roman Catholicism was increasingly beset by contradictions. The Church had emerged from the tumult of the Dark Ages with great temporal wealth and power at a time when society was evolving from self-sufficient manors into a money economy. Feudal relations between lord and serf and between lord and vassal, forged during times of barbarian invasions, were weakening. Royal power, backed by royal armies, was growing—at the expense of the nobility. These new armies were paid in money, rather than in land, and money was increasingly needed to pay them. In short, European society had begun the transition from feudalism to capitalism.

Against this backdrop of social change, the Church clung to an essentially static view of society, governed by static social relations. Christendom was made up, according to this view, of a hierarchy of people, each assigned to his or her station in life, each required to obey his or her superiors, and each entitled to certain benificences from those superiors. In this system of mutual obligation, poverty was to be relieved by charity, not the creation of more wealth. The Church was to guide people to Heaven and protect them from falling into evil. The clergy was expected also to observe its vows of celibacy and poverty.

By the twelfth century, the contradictions between doctrine and practice had become more and more obvious, although nothing like what it would be two centuries later. The Church had not only accumulated wealth and temporal power, but it was ostentatious about it. The nobility had also accumulated great wealth. Artisans and merchants were creating wealth as more markets for goods were developed. In fact, everyone was doing better except the peasantry, which was paying extortionate taxes and increasing in numbers too quickly to be an economic power (Gottfried 1983).

In this environment of social contradiction, heresy found a ready ear. Particularly in the Langedoc region of southwestern France, economically advanced, yet oppressed by the growing power of the Capetian kings in the north, the Cathar doctrine of dualism gained in popularity. Cathars preached the tyranny of the body over the soul. Like Gnostics, Cathars believed in a good God, but that the world was the creation of an evil spirit (Rhodes 1954 20). Matter being evil, both material sacraments and the material Church were also evil. In fact, all human society was evil (ibid. 20). Chastity was the ideal of the *perfecti,* but if that were impossible, concubinage was considered preferable, since it was not permanent or considered productive (ibid. 20). The orthodox Church, on the other hand, was considered satanic, since it had surrendered to worldliness.

Because the Cathars believed the sacraments to be evil, they were able to worship secretly by reversing or changing the emphasis in Christian rites. Given that the Mass was in Latin, a language unknown to the congregation, and required a certain order of gestures, it was not difficult for a secretly Catharist priest to change some of the Mass in a way that would be apparent only to Cathar initiates and to perform a Cathar ceremony without the knowledge of orthodox Christians (ibid. 20).

Needless to say, both Church and state in France took a dim view of this subversion. The Cathars were suppressed by force in the thirteenth century in the Albigensian Crusade and the subsequent Inquisition. Repression, however, did not change people's minds about the nature of society or the underlying conditions that led them to a gnostic dualism. The repression of the Cathars merely confirmed many in the belief that Satan was lord of this world.

The calamities of the fourteenth century reinforced this belief. Prior to the fourteenth century, Europe had enjoyed abnormally warm weather. Crops flourished and the population grew. The "Little Ice Age," which is just now being recognized as one of the major events of European history, put an end to this. The climate turned abnormally cold and wet. Crops failed. People starved. Then came the Black Death.

The pestilence came in waves that began in 1348 and persisted until the beginning of the sixteenth century. The Black Death killed more than a third of the population of Europe (Gottfried 1983 100). Labor shortages caused by the pestilence made it possible for workers to demand higher wages (ibid.). Both Church and state responded with repression in an attempt to resurrect the preplague social system (ibid. 133). Central governments fixed the prices of goods and labor and curbed the independence of the new urban classes.

This attempt to legislate economics had the same effect on late medieval society that similar measures have had in the Soviet Union and Romania. Large families became an economic liability. The most effective means of contraception at that time, infanticide, became common in the fourteenth century and persisted into the nineteenth (Ben Yehuda 1985 20). Late marriages, another means of controlling family size, also became common. It also became more common for women to work outside the home (ibid. 22).

Women bore the brunt of the changes occurring in society. Merely to survive, women were forced to commit acts that the Church considered mortal sins, and capital crimes. Infanticide, "fornication," illegitimate birth were all common. A significant proportion of the population went through life in what they and the Church considered a state of damnation.

Parallel to this creation of a population that believed itself damned was the rise of a belief in magic. The fourteenth and fifteenth centuries were a time when magic piqued the interest of men and women more than ever before. The chaos engendered by the Black Death and the Little Ice Age drove people to grasp for explanations as well as any means of economic and social survival. People were dying faster than they could be born. Death was everywhere. Belief in a Kingdom of Heaven shriveled and died. The magical world view, that there are powers and principalities that could and should be manipulated, began to dominate. Eventually, the experimental mentality that magic fostered would lead to actual science and technology. But in the meantime, a culture conducive to a belief in the desirability of manipulating satanic power developed.

The Church also had its problems. Corruption in the Church was becoming more and more of an issue. The Church had built its reputation and legitimacy, not on any ethical system, but on the popular belief in the efficacy of the Mass. The idea that the priest could transform bread and wine into the body and blood of Christ was a kind of magic, and also the heart of medieval Christianity. During this period, masses were said for those who could pay for them. Thus, the institution of the mass priest, a sort of a spiritual mercenary saying masses for hire, developed (Rhodes 1954 74).

That the sale of masses and indulgences diminished the clergy in the eyes of the people of that period is well known. What the sale of indulgences also did was to make the priest into even more of a magician than he had been previously. For if a mass was efficacious only if said by a priest and if a priest had the power to absolve one of sins, (and the power not to if he chose), then salvation was a form of magic that operated in accordance with the operator's (in this case the priest's) will. As such, the sale of indulgences promoted not only cynicism, but also superstition.

What may have been going on among the clergy itself during this period remains a poorly researched area of medieval and early modern history.

Allegations of corruption and sexual perversion among Roman Catholic priests have been common from the fourteenth century right down to the present. Consider the controversy surrounding the alleged homosexual activities of Father Bruce Ritter, founder of Covenant House (Washington 1990 21). For the most part, such allegations were dismissed out of hand in the past. However, in light of what is known today about the behavior of pedophiles, the idea that some might have deliberately entered the Church seems plausible. Certainly as priests, such pedophiles might be above effective suspicion, able to meet their needs more safely in the Church than in society at large, given their protected position and the presumption of clerical celibacy.

Corrupt and/or sexually deviant priests if they existed (and some did) would have found themselves in a position of cognitive dissonance. It is the nature of people in a situation of cognitive dissonance that they act to relieve the dissonance, either by modifying their behavior or by modifying the beliefs that conflict with the behavior. Priests, who dealt with theology in the course of their daily lives had easy access to the raw materials they would need to change their beliefs. Priests who found the demands of celibacy intolerable had access through literacy to all manner of classical belief systems. They might well have modified their beliefs and determined that fair was foul and foul was fair, particularly in the environment of the fourteenth and fifteenth centuries. To the medieval mind a mass was a mass was a mass. Thus, the figure of a renegade priest celebrating a black mass does not seem at all impossible.

Taking into account what we know of the times, the witch craze of the fifteenth and sixteenth centuries begins to make a different kind of sense than has previously been assumed. Witchcraft may well have been a constellation of actual political and organized criminal movements. The idea that all who were accused of witchcraft were the victims of fanatical Dominican inquisitors using torture to extract confessions that would validate their preconceived notions appears to be a simplistic overreaction used to validate later rationalistic attacks on the Catholic Church. After all, the Inquisition at this time was also persecuting the "marranos," or secret Jews, who had converted to Christianity either voluntarily or by force, and yet retained their Jewish identity and some practices. The Spanish and Portuguese Inquisitions used torture to ferret out marranos, and no responsible scholar contends that marranos were a figment of the medieval imagination (Roth 1974).[1]

Although the contention of modern neopagans that witchcraft was a survival of prechristian European religion does not appear to be borne out by

---

[1]The study of marranism, while beyond the scope of this chapter, holds obvious relevance for the study of satanism or any other religion that must be practiced covertly. By studying marranism, it is possible to ascertain how religious beliefs are attenuated over time, due to the need to practice them secretly, what sort of practices are kept, what fall by the wayside, and how the need to dissemble about one's true beliefs alters those beliefs. This is an area of study that is on the frontier of religious studies.

current research,[2] "witches" appear to have been people engaged in meeting their needs and the needs of others that were not being met by licit social structures. Among these needs were the need for a belief system that would sanction rebellion against the established church and state and the need for relief from the double binds that church and state sometimes placed people in, particularly the dilemma of unwanted children.

Taken this way, the persecution of witchcraft fits a time when the Church was desperately attempting to maintain social discipline, both within its own ranks and in society as a whole, a time when the environment was forcing social change on Europe but a doctrine that allowed social change had not yet evolved. The Inquisition comes to be seen as a police force, perhaps no worse than the KGB, attempting to investigate and bring to justice criminals, some of whom were not only criminals under the laws of the medieval Church, but under the laws of any modern society. The problems that the Inquisition faced, of reliability of evidence, overzealousness, and political pressures, are also the problems of modern police forces and serious investigators of contemporary satanism.

During the sixteenth century, Christendom broke apart. The efficacy of the Mass was challenged successfully, and the result was the Reformation. Magic changed also as a result of this new skepticism. An interest in the Jewish Kabbalah developed among members of the magical traditions and gradually replaced the parodies and reversals of the Catholic Mass that had preceded them. Control rather than worship of Satan appears to have become more important. The sixteenth and seventeenth centuries are the time of Pico de Mirandola, Johannes Reuchlin, Giordano Bruno, and Heinrich Cornelius Agrippa, Renaissance men, who promoted not only magic, but mystical philosophy and theological speculation as well.

By providing religious alternatives and by forcing the Catholic Church to end some of its most flagrant abuses, the Reformation relieved much of the dissonance that had plagued medieval Europe. Unfortunately, however, while Protestantism provided a rationale that legitimated the accumulation of wealth, it did nothing to reconcile the lower classes with society. Calvinism in particular replaced the doctrine of absolvable mortal sin with one of predestina-

---

[2]The idea that pagan beliefs could survive in authentic, unchanged form in Britain appears to be a fallacy. Britain was christianized relatively early compared with other parts of Europe, and prior to its christianization during late antiquity was a center of Mithraism. Christianity won out in free competition with Mithraism in Britain, rather than being imposed upon Britain by force. The survival of authentic Celtic beliefs would be unlikely under these circumstances. Authentic pagan survivals would be far more likely in places such as Iceland or Sweden or Finland that were Christianized late and by force.

Michael Harrison, in his work *The Roots of Witchcraft* attempts to validate Margaret Murray's hypothesis of pagan survival, but through linguistic analysis, links the "witch cult" to the Basques, indicating that any possible pagan survival might have been an upper class import, probably during the High Middle Ages when England held Aquitaine and some of the Basque country.

tion. According to Calvin, God in His infinite wisdom had decided from the outset that some souls would be saved and some souls would be damned, and that there was nothing that people could do to alter that fact. One's behavior and fortunes on earth indicated whether one was saved or damned. Under Calvinism, whole classes of people were consigned to hellfire and damnation. For those on the bottom, or whose indiscretions were enough to convince them that they were hellbound, satanism may have offered an alternative.

Judith Spencer, in her landmark study *Suffer the Child*, gives us a case study of a woman subjected to incessant sexual abuse in a satanist cult in rural South Carolina among lower income people. Most of rural South Carolina is Scotch-Irish protestant by background, a particularly strict brand of Calvinism.

The satanist theology, at least in this cult, is as follows: "Evil ones cannot go to heaven. Those who are evil will abide in hell, a place of burning ruled by Satan. Those who serve Satan will go to hell, yet they will not burn" (Spencer 1989 17).

This logic is, from the point of view of those who believe it, a corollary of Calvinist predestination. If the goodness or evil of a person is a given, satanic worship is a reasonable choice for those who see themselves as predestined to damnation. I speculate that the same rationale may have been in force during the Reformation.

Thus, the Reformation did not substantially decrease the pressure or the need for satanic worship. Women still needed to be discreetly free of unwanted babies. People with paraphilias still needed a belief system that would justify their perversions. Although rationalism began to pervade Western intellectual circles in the latter half of the seventeenth century, satanism still persisted as a bonding mechanism for organized crime.

The La Voisin affair in France in the 1680s shows how satanic worship continued to operate. Catherine Deshayes, otherwise known as La Voisin, starting as a cosmetician, branched out into magic and astrology for her aristocratic clients (Rhodes 1954 113). She soon came to study black magic and satanism, which she practiced with the assistance of the Abbe Guibourg (ibid. 121). In the Guibourg Mass, children were sacrificed routinely to Astaroth and Asmodeus (ibid. 122).

The La Voisin organization appears to have started out as an abortion and infanticide racket (ibid. 120), but it soon branched out into the business of murder for hire by poison. Taking advantage of the fact that chemistry and pharmacology had long since outstripped the capability to detect death by poison, the La Voisin organization soon evolved into an early version of Murder Inc. (ibid. 114). It was this activity that ultimately led to her downfall. The poisoning of the Duke of Bouillon by his wife Anne-Marie Mancini led a nervous King Louis XIV to authorize an investigation into this growing practice under the leadership of his police commissioner La Reynie (ibid. 103). This is the first investigation of satanism using anything resembling modern police procedure. When the investigation led to the king's mistress, the Marchioness de

Montespan, and her mentor La Voisin, the king suppressed the evidence, banished Montespan from court, and permitted La Reynie and his *Chambre Ardente* (the "burning court") to send La Voisin to the stake as soon as it was politically safe to do so (ibid. 124).

The La Voisin affair is significant in that it establishes a pattern of criminal and commercial satanism that has persisted to the present day. The only substantive differences between the La Voisin affair and the 1989 Matamoros murders were that the Matamoros group was involved in drug smuggling rather than abortion and contract murder, and the fact that Adolfo Constanzo's satanism contained overtones of Aztec sacrificial ritual and afro-cuban Santeria and Palo Mayombe (Raschke 1990, 13-14). The use of magic as a source of spiritual protection of and ideological discipline for criminal enterprises is not and has not been uncommon (ibid. 9). When one's religious world view involves powers and principalities that must be appeased and controlled by magicians who have cultivated the ability to do so, the use of those abilities for financial gain does not detract from the credibility of the belief system nor the sincerity of the magician. Being an independent operator in a world of independently operating forces, a magician can freely and sincerely translate his or her spiritual powers into power over people through mind control, or the more tangible reward of financial wealth without losing his or her sincere belief in those spiritual powers. This is true even in the more accepted and prosaic "white" magic of psychics and mediums, who support themselves through their psychic readings. The idea that a religious practitioner is corrupted when he or she uses religious practice for financial gain is a bias of the Christian and more specifically the Protestant belief system, and is rejected by followers of Gnostic or magical paths. Students of magical and satanic belief systems often forget this.

The eighteenth century was the height of the Age of Reason, and satanism suffered in intellectual circles along with Christianity during this time. Satanism and black masses were ridiculed in educated circles in Great Britain by the rakish and dilettante circle of Sir Francis Dashwood and the Brotherhood of Medmenham (colloquially known as the "Hellfire Club") (Rhodes 1954 142). Skeptical of all religion, as most eighteen-century gentlemen were, the "devotees" of the "Hellfire Club" used the structure of satanic worship as a cover for every form of debauchery that the human imagination could devise. Freethinking writers and modern-day apologists for satanism who have treated this topic humorously—as a form of good clean fun—should consider the effect on the "nuns," most of whom probably had little choice about their participation. The degrading nature of the "fun" must have had devastating effects on these women. Nevertheless, this burlesque of satanism has continued to play a role in our understanding of it to the present day.

As the eighteenth century drew to a close, reaction to the cult of reason set in. The importance of *feeling,* of emotions, began to be emphasized. Romanticism was born, and Gnosticism was revived (Raschke 1980 50).

Romanticism developed "the idea of the self as a creative agent which transforms and actually reconstitutes ordinary reality with images and symbols" (ibid. 60). In place of an escape from a hostile reality as the Gnostics postulated, the Romantics yearned for escape from the mundane world of everyday experience. It was easy in this environment for magic to reenter the consciousness of educated Europe. As the nineteenth century passed, magic became more and more interesting and credible. Alphonse Louis Constance, a defrocked priest, changed his name to Eliphas Levi, and taught a form of kabbalistic magic that became a textbook for later magicians and satanists such as Aleister Crowley and sparked an occult revival in the Paris of the Second Empire.

Satanism received a great deal of support from the currents of middle and late nineteenth-century thought. Herbert Spencer promulgated the idea of "survival of the fittest" in his work *Social Statics*. Friedrich Wilhelm Nietzsche created the idea of the "will to power," which distinguished the overman (Übermensch) from common humanity. The overman, by cultivating and expressing his will to power, overcomes others *and* himself, according to Nietzsche, and attains new levels of self-transcendence (ibid. 95).

Other currents of occultism were coming out of the United States. As early as the 1830s, a synthesis of occult ideas was beginning to form in the United States in reaction to eighteenth-century Deism and Puritanism. Swedenborgianism, American Indian beliefs, and Unitarianism created the intellectual environment in which transcendentalism and mesmerism could thrive (Raschke 1980 177; Fuller 1986 55). Allegations of satanic rites being conducted as part of freemasonry in Charleston, South Carolina, also surfaced at this time. (Vaughan 1990 18). Out of this environment came Spiritualism, which emphasized communication with the dead, and Spiritualism begat Theosophy.

Founded by an immigrant from Russia, Helena Blavatsky, Theosophy borrowed Hindu terminology and tacked it on to western gnostic concepts. The archons became the "Lords of Karma." Lucifer was construed to be a benign earth planetary logos. Theosophy in particular acquired a great international cachet and quickly spread through Europe as well as the United States, adding its own definitions to the occult tradition. Particularly as it evolved under Anne Besant and Alice A. Bailey, it made occultisim more acceptable by creating a normative structure for it. Under Theosophy, magic was no longer a matter of doing whatever one could get away with. There were Lords of Karma to answer to regarding one's actions and motives and a definite path of evolution to follow. Under the aegis of Theosophy, definitions of "white" occultism were established that are followed by most Wiccans and New Agers today.

By the 1890s, it had become apparent to those who were willing to look that satanism had not vanished from Europe. The French writer J. K. Huysmans mentions attending a black mass in his thinly fictionalized novel *La Bas*, which was based on gossip that Huysmans had heard about Father Louis Van Haecke, or Bruges, Belgium (Langone and Blood 1990 15; Cavendish 1967 367; Irwin 1963 ix). The abbé Boullan, portrayed sympathetically by Huysmans, was also alleged to have performed black masses (Langone and Blood 1990 16; Cavendish 1967 367).

Other, more plausible accounts of satanism surfaced at this time. A French reporter for *Le Matin* alleged in 1889 that he had been invited to attend and was taken blindfolded to a satanic mass (Cavendish 1967 368). And in 1895, a satanic chapel was discovered in the Palzzzo Borghese in Rome (ibid.).

This, then was the environment that Aleister Crowley lived in at the beginning of the twentieth century.

Aleister Crowley related the body of occult knowledge that had previously accumulated and had been published both to eastern traditions, which were being popularized at this time, and to nineteenth- and early twentieth-century philosophy and most particularly psychology. An example of this follows:

> Now in order to invoke any being, it is said by Hermes Trismegistus that the magi employ three methods. The first, for the vulgar, is that of supplication. In this the crude objective theory is assumed as true. There is a god named A whom you, B, proceed to petition, in exactly the same sense as a boy might ask his father for pocket money.
>
> The second method involves a little more subtlety, inasmuch as the magician endeavours to harmonize himself with the nature of the god, and to a certain extent exalts himself, in the course of the ceremony: but the third method is the only one worthy of our consideration.
>
> This consists of a **real identification of the magician and the god** [emphasis Crowley's]. Note that **to do this in perfection involves the attainment of a species of Samadhi; and this fact alone suffices to link irrefragably magick with mysticism.**
>
> Let us describe the magical method of identification. The symbolic form of the god is first studied with as much care as an artist would bestow upon his model, so that a perfectly clear and unshakeable mental picture of the god is present to the mind. Similarly, the attributes of the god are enshrined in speech, and such speeches are commited perfectly to memory. The invocation will then begin with a prayer to the god, commemorating his physical attributes, always with a profound understanding of their real meaning. In the second part of the invocation, the voice of the god is heard and His characteristic utterance is recited.
>
> In the third part of the invocation the magician asserts the identity of himself with the god. In the fourth portion the god is again invoked, but as if by Himself, as if it were the will of the god that He should manifest in the magician. At the conclusion of this, the original object of the invocation is stated. (Crowley 1924 17–18)

It is easy to see from just this brief passage much of Crowley's accomplishment and his lasting appeal. Crowley created texts for the understanding of traditional magical grimores. He told his readers how magic should feel, giving a "blow by blow" description of the psychological processes involved in magic.

Crowley created a blueprint that enabled any initiate or dabbler with some aptitude for dissociation to experiment with magic and occultism and achieve at least psychological results. Prior to Crowley, dabblers might be deterred by a total lack of results and go on to dabble in something else. For those who lacked this aptitude, Crowley endorsed the use of drugs for the initial expansion of consciousness, including hashish, mescaline, ether, and cocaine (King 1977 154–56).

Not surprisingly, occultists of many persuasions, Wiccan (Adler 1986 63; Leek 1968 31) as well as satanist, respect Crowley and use his definitions. Gerald B. Gardner, a third-degree initiate of Crowley's order *Templi Orientis,* went on to found what has come to be known as "white witchcraft" or Wicca. Francis S. King alleges that Crowley himself wrote most of the rituals that Gardner promulgated (King 1977 175–177).

Crowley went on from his association with the Order of the Golden Dawn to involve himself in satanic rites at what he called the Abbey of Thelema at Cefalu, Sicily, in the 1920s and, in his later years, to write his primers on magic, dying in 1947. His legacy, which included the identification of magic with the expansion of consciousness, led to an explosion of interest in Crowley during the 1960s. Crowley's picture was published in the crowd of "people we like" by the Beatles on the cover of *Sergeant Pepper's Lonely Hearts Club Band* (King 1977 189). Crowley's emphasis on magic as consciousness expansion put him in the same category as such luminaries of the 1960s as Aldous Huxley, Timothy Leary, and Stanislav Grof. Crowley's relevance and moral ambiguity (was he a black magician, a white magician, or some shade of gray?) as well as his techniques, which if seriously practiced would yield psychological results if nothing else, lent credence and legitimacy to magic and, by extension, satanism.

One of Crowley's disciples was a rocket scientist named Jack Parsons, who among other things developed Jet Assisted Take Off in the late 1940s. One of Parsons' students, allegedly, was a science fiction writer named L. Ron Hubbard (ibid. 218). After failing in an attempt with Parsons to create a "moonchild," a demon child with magical powers, Hubbard went on to found the Church of Scientology, a self-improvement cult operating on Crowleyan and gnostic principles that has several million members. There is much controversy about the alleged psychological damage that its techniques may be causing its members.

The 1960s were a turbulent era in the United States and in the West at large. Social mores came to be questioned in what was an unprecedented manner. The assault on the American racial caste system, the popularization of the idea of consciousness expansion, and the war in Vietnam turned American morality upside down. The 1960s were an era of social disorganization, but they were also an era that can be described by a Russian cliché of today—*glasnost.*

Two trends ran counter to each other in the 1960s and the 1970s that made possible the revelations about satanism in the 1980s and 1990s. Magic became popular and accepted in the 1960s. In 1964, Sybil Leek made a tour of the

United States and published her book *Diary of a Witch,* which popularized the concept of witchcraft as a goddess-worshiping religion and built upon the already existing theosophical tradition in the United States. The idea that magic could be practiced in accordance with theosophical ethics of karma was one that Americans could accept. It harmonized with the ideal of consciousness expansion then being promulgated by Timothy Leary and Richard Alpert.

At the same time, vast changes were occuring in sexual ethics. The first birth control pills were developed about this time. The idea that women might have not only the right but the power to control their reproductive destinies began to spread, with Griswold vs. Connecticut (1964), the decision that allowed the dissemination of birth-control information. This notion of women's rights was subversive to traditional Christian morality, and it seems to have been equally subversive to satanism, which depends on social strictures against sex to enforce its code of silence. The identification of the *battered-child syndrome* by Dr. C. Henry Kempe also broke down some of the protection of the satanist subculture by causing society to question the prerogative of parents to "discipline" their children as they wished. Later, in the 1970s and 1980s, clinicians such as Cornelia Wilbur, Eugene Bliss, Richard Kluft, and Benett Braun would prove the relationship between child abuse and multiple personality, demystifying multiple personality, and making it possible for the first time for survivors of ritual abuse to adequately explain their experiences and be believed.

During the early 1970s, these trends accelerated. Feminism became a force in American society that launched a questioning and rethinking of traditional sex roles. It was soon joined by the gay rights movement, which broke down one of the last taboos that restrained victims to silence, that of homosexuality. For the first time, it became possible to discuss sexual matters openly.

Witchcraft, as the new religion of Wicca, became a spiritual force within the women's movement. According to allegations by some survivors, this seems to have had the effect of creating an accepting alternative to continued involvement in satanic activities for some women survivors. Women such as Z. Budapest and Starhawk, who combine Wicca with feminist consciousness raising, seem to have had a subversive effect on the more exploitative, hierarchical, male-centered satanic covens.[3]

As a result of the sea change in attitudes in the late 1960s and early 1970s, even the fundamentalist Christians who reacted to the climate of the times, and railed against it, seem to have been affected by it. Unlike the revivals of the 1920s, the Jesus Movement of the 1970s marked by a greater willingness to

---

[3]According to Spencer (1989 132), Sandy, the occult personality of Jenny Walters, became a solitary student of the occult, and for a while, entertained notions of going to the School of Wicca in North Carolina during the 1970s. This intent is indicative of how Wicca may have held and continued to hold itself out as an alternative to continued involvement in satanism. Certainly, because it obviously does not require the survivor-devotee to give up magic or belief in magic, it is less of an intellectual leap than becoming a Christian.

accept and forgive what the person may have been before. Moreover, it too seems to have made certain accommodations with the new morality. Fundamentalist Christians may emphasize chastity, but there appears to be an acceptance of the enjoyment of sex within marriage that previous generations did not allow, as evidenced by the sex manual for married couples written by Beverly La Haye (wife of Moral Majority founder Tim La Haye). Sterilization for birth control appears to be generally accepted among fundamentalist Christians as well. In such an environment, it is easier for survivors to tell their stories and be believed and forgiven than previous generations found possible.

Running counter to these trends, however, are trends that strengthened satanism during the 1960s. A counterpoint to the Summer of Love was the Manson murders. A counterpoint to Woodstock was Altamont, in which a rowdy fan was murdered by the Hell's Angels security force while the Rolling Stones played "Sympathy for the Devil."

An undercurrent of the glasnost and the release of inhibitions of the 1960s was an amoral antinomianism. Obviously, most "hippies" who experimented with LSD or amphetamines did not become satanists. But inasmuch as the new romantics of the 1960s experimented with breaking *all* the rules and with experiencing *all* the emotions, some could and did become fixated on the emotion of fear and as Carl Raschke puts it, the "aesthetics of terror" (Raschke 1990 103). Just as the 1960s produced experimentation with Eastern spiritual disciplines that in many cases degenerated into authoritarian if not totalitarian religious cults, so it produced experimentation with magical ideas that led into a fascination with magic and satanism. One can see the progression in the music of the time, as the late 1960s went from the acid-rock impressionism of the psychedelic bands like the Jefferson Airplane, to the fascination with the dark (evidenced in the work of the Rolling Stones and the Doors in 1969 and 1970), to the shock rock of Alice Cooper, and finally to the fascination with Satan of much of heavy metal and punk rock of the 1980s. The bounds of acceptable pornography also shifted during this period, from the artistry of the Vargas girls to bondage, kiddie porn, and snuff. The white magic of love-ins, antiwar demonstrations, and electioneering appeared to fail in 1968, to be replaced for some by the terrorism of the Weather Underground in the 1970s. Amphetamines with their attendant paranoia replaced LSD as the drug of choice among segments of the counterculture, and a fascination with the dark side of the magic developed in many parts of the counterculture, including in the arts. The emphasis on power in satanism appeared to reflect reality at a time when the war machine wouldn't stop and President Nixon, it seemed, could cover up burglaries with impunity.

It is not surprising, therefore, that within this climate in the 1960s, Anton LaVey founded the Church of Satan and wrote *The Satanic Bible*. Belittled as a huckster and a charlatan who cultivated relationships with movie stars such as Jayne Mansfield and Marilyn Monroe (Raschke 1990 123), LaVey may have had an impact far greater than observers would guess. According to Raschke,

LaVey took the idea of a conscious choice to live in a world without God found in Epicureanism, materialism, and Nietzscheism (and the author would add, Ayn Randian objectivism), and peddled it to the masses (ibid. 123).

As LaVey says,

> Each person must decide for himself what his obligations are to his respective friends, family, and community. . . . It is extremely difficult for a person to learn to say "no," when all his life he has said "yes." But unless he wants to be constantly taken advantage of, he **must** learn to say "no" when circumstances justify doing so. If you allow them, psychic vampires will gradually infiltrate your everyday life until you have no privacy left—and your constant feeling of concern for them will deplete you of all ambition." (LaVey 1969 77)

LaVey goes on to say, "Satanists are encouraged to indulge in the seven deadly sins as they need hurt no one; they were only invented by the Christian Church to insure guilt on the part of its followers. Their Christian Church knows that it is impossible for anyone to avoid committing these sins, as they are things which we, being human, most naturally do" (ibid. 85).

It is easy to trace an intellectual connection between LaVey, who popularized satanism as a sort of gestalt spiritual assertiveness training and some of the ideas of the human potential movement. The idea, popularized by Esalen founder Will Schutz and later by Werner Erhard, that there were no victims, that all people place themselves in whatever position that they find themselves, and therefore are ultimately responsible for whatever happens to them, including victimization by others, was an outgrowth of the Human Potential Movement. As Social Darwinism provided the intellectual support for the robber barons of the 1900s, so this notion provided the intellectual support for the yuppies of the late 1970s and early 1980s.

By the late 1970s, a climate of opinion and culture had developed in which satanism could become an issue. The post–baby boom generation, facing a very uncertain job market, and general uncertainty about the future, found Satan to be fascinating in many ways. Heavy metal music, and later punk and new wave music, began to emphasize the demonic explicitly. And the records sold!

At this time Michael Aquino, a lieutenant colonel in the U.S. Army psychological warfare division, was developing an offshoot of the Church of Satan known as the Temple of Set. Aquino considered LaVey's satanism to be "atheism with psychodrama (Raschke 1990). Aquino's teachings encourage the alleged occultism of the Third Reich as an ideal to which one should aspire. Aquino's teachings encourage the cultivation of the latent powers of personality locked in the minds of a few potential supermen that can be released through music resonating at three to seven cycles per second (Raschke 1990 150). This notion, born of Aquino's work with army psychological warfare and psychotronics, is well within the context of the contemporary Human Potential Movement at a time when "The Brain Machine" is being mass marketed as a tool for achieving hypnotic and other altered states of consciousness through pulsed light and sound stimulation.

Aquino's revival of Nazi occultism came on the heels of a fascination with Nazi occultism that developed in the 1970s and 1980s. Books with titles such as *The Spear of Destiny, The Occult Reich,* and *Hitler: The Occult Messiah* became commercial successes. This fascination with Naziism extended to teenage dabblers in the occult. By 1988, a synthesis of heavy-metal satanism with Nazi aryanism was very much in evidence. Rock bands such as Radio Werewolf promoted groups such as the Abraxas Foundation of Evil, the Aryan Youth Movement, and the Temple of Psychick Youth, which fused the ideologies of satanism with nazism and emphasized violence (Raschke 1990, 234–39). This is the situation in the youth satanic subculture that exists today.

Perhaps the first of the contemporary exposés of the workings of a self-styled satanic cult was that of the Manson Family. Unfortunately, in 1968, no one knew what to look for. Prosecutor Vincent Bugliosi had his hands full convicting Charles Manson and proving the admittedly satanic motive of "Helter-Skelter," the attempt to start a race war through acts of terrorism in a trial in which Manson's female codefendants made every effort to take the rap for him. He did not have a context to put the Tate–La Bianca murders in, other than society's vague fears of the youth revolt and the counterculture. Nor did he have any understanding of thought reform and brainwashing that might have enabled him to develop a more sophisticated understanding of what was going on. Only Ed Sanders, formerly of the rock group The Fugs, was able to take a somewhat dispassionate view of the Manson Family and relate it to an existing satanic underworld in Southern California. This he did in his book *The Family*.

The next book that came out about the subject, indeed the book that made the subject of satanism a live issue, was *Michelle Remembers*. Published in 1980, it details the childhood experiences of Michelle Smith (now Michelle Pazder), as told to the psychiatrist, Lawrence Pazder, whom she later married. Michelle claims that she was designated by a satanic coven operating in Victoria, British Columbia, to be a Bride of Satan, and to be presented to Satan at the Feast of the Beast, a ceremony occuring every twenty-eight years. The book details the extensive preparations made to turn Michelle into a fit bride for Satan, and how she resisted all the way. The most controversial part of the book is the ending, in which Satan attempts to claim her, and is defeated by Michelle, with the help of the Virgin Mary.

Michelle Remembers illustrates some of the major problems in researching this area. Many of the published accounts of satanic survivors have a definite sectarian point of view. In the case of *Michelle Remembers,* there is a sustained Roman Catholic perspective. The book received the imprimatur of the Bishop of Victoria, and offers an account of how Michelle Smith and Dr. Pazder went to the Vatican with their account, and how it was accepted.

For the serious researcher or therapist, the facts must be separated from the theological beliefs of the writer. It is extremely easy for people of a skeptical or scientific frame of mind to dismiss *Michelle Remembers* as a hoax, designed to make its readers devout Catholics. Other books such as *The Satan Seller* by Michael Warnke (1978), and more recently *Satan's Underground* by Lauren Stratford (1988), come out of the Protestant community and offer fundamentalist prescriptions for the problem. For the researcher, each of these books offers potential information, but the facts must be considered individually, as data that must be independently corroborated.

On a slightly higher level is Maury Terry's work, *The Ultimate Evil* (1986). Terry details the course of his independent investigation into the Son of Sam murders in New York in the late 1970s. He found evidence of a satanic cult called the Twenty-Two Disciples of Hell, which carried out the murders on auspicious days, some of which were random slayings designed to disguise their plan. The frustrations that Terry went through in getting the investigation reopened after Berkowitz confessed to all of the murders is a textbook example of the types of problems that emerge in this field. Unfortunately, in Terry's reach for the outré, he attempted to tie the Manson Family in to this group. Both Manson and Sam Carr were involved in the ideology of the Process Church of Final Judgement, a Scientology offshoot, but to postulate an underlying conspiracy linking the two seems to go beyond the evidence. Even more problematic, is that Terry leaves the reader with the impression that *all* satanism in the United States is related to the Process Church.

Conspiracy thinking is a major problem in the study of satanism. Conspiracy, except to police and prosecutors who attempt to prove legal definition of conspiracy, is a thought-terminating cliché. To postulate a conspiracy is to close the door to further intellectual inquiry into whatever might really be going on. To postulate one overarching conspiracy, is to betray one's own fears and mental state.

It is important to note that all historians do not concur with the view that satanism and the "Black Mass" have been practiced for centuries. Some writers argue that there is little evidence for such activity beyond accusations utilized to persecute oppressed groups or confessions resulting from torture during witch-hunts and inquisitions. For example, Richard Noll (1989) states that "it is the power of the *idea* of cannabalistic and organistic cults (who later were imbued with the traditional trappings of satanism in the Middle Ages) that has carried through the centuries *not* their reality" (1989 252). Thus, even among contemporary historians satanism remains something of a mystery, and the meaning of relevant historical phenomena continues to be debated.

It is easy to wax apocalyptic about satanism. The dominant religious culture in the West encourages it. But it does not help us to understand it. Conspiracy thinking encourages us to see people like satanists as one dimensional caricatures. The truth, as sketchy as it is right now, is obviously far more complex.

It is my belief that satanism is a subculture of Western civilization. It appears to be a product of our hitherto unyielding norms and caste system that consigned lower-class people and those guilty (or allegedly guilty) of sexual indiscretions to the ranks of the damned. Its exposure appears to be the product of the more open attitude toward sexuality that the West has exhibited since the 1960s, which has enabled victims and survivors to talk honestly about their experiences. Paradoxically, the current revival of satanism also appears to be a result of the same relaxation of norms. It remains to be seen whether the healthy or the unhealthy trend shall prevail.

References

Adler, Margot. 1986. *Drawing Down the Moon: Witches, Druids, Goddess Worshipers, and Other Pagans in America Today.* Boston: Beacon Press.

Ben Yehuda, Nachman. 1985. *Deviance and Moral Boundaries: Witchcraft, the Occult, Science Fiction, Deviant Science, and Scientists.* Chicago: University of Chicago Press.

Cavendish, Richard. 1967. *The Black Arts.* New York: G. P. Putnam and Sons.

Crowley, Aleister. 1924. *Magick in Theory and Practice.* Reprint. New York: Dover, 1976.

Fuller, Robert C. 1982. *Mesmerism and the American Cure of Souls.* Philadelphia: University of Pennsylvania Press.

Gottfried, Robert S. 1983. *The Black Death: Natural and Human Disaster in Medieval Europe.* New York: The Free Press.

Green, Henry A. 1985. *The Economic and Social Origins of Gnosticism.* Atlanta, Ga.: Scholar's Press.

Hill, Sally, and Goodwin, Jean. 1989. "Satanism: Similarities between Patient Accounts and Pre-Inquisition Historical Sources." *Dissociation,* 2 (1), 39–43.

Irwin, Constance. 1963. *Fair Gods and Stone Faces.* New York: St. Martin's Press.

Johnson, Jerry. 1989. *The Edge of Evil: The Rise of Satanism in North America.* Dallas, TX.: Word Publishing.

King, Francis. 1971. *Sexuality, Magic, and Perversion.* Secaucus, N.J.: Citadel Press.

———. 1977. The Magical World of Aleister Crawley. Great Britain: Neidenfeld and Nicolson.

Langone, Michael D., and Linda O. Blood. 1990. *Satanism and Occult Related Violence: What You Should Know.* Weston, Mass.: American Family Foundation.

LaVey, Anton. 1969. *The Satanic Bible.* New York: Avon Books.

Leek, Sybil. 1968. *Diary of a Witch.* New York: The New American Library/Signet.

Noll, Richard. 1989. "Satanism, UFO Abductions, Historians and Clinicians: Those Who do not Remember the Past. . . ." *Dissociation,* 2, 251–253.

Obolensky, Dmitri. 1948. *The Bogomils: A Study in Balkan NeoManicheanism.* New York: AMS Press.

Raschke, Carl. 1980. *The Interruption of Eternity.* Chicago, Ill.: Nelson-Hall Publishers.

———. 1990. *Painted Black: Satanic Crime in America.* San Francisco, Ca.: Harper and Row.

Rhodes, Henry T. F. 1954. *The Satanic Mass.* Secaucus, N.J.: Citadel Press.

Roth, Cecil. 1974. *A History of the Marranos.* New York: Schocken Books.

Smith, Michelle, and Lawrence Pazder. 1980. *Michelle Remembers*. New York: Congdon and Lattes.

Spencer, Judith. 1989. *Suffer the Child*. New York: Pocket Books.

Stratford, Lauren. 1987. *Satan's Underground*. Eugene, Ore.: Harvest House.

Terry, Maury. 1986. *The Ultimate Evil*. New York: Doubleday.

Vaughan, Diana. 1990. *Memoirs of an Ex-Palladist*. Chicago, Ill.: Voices In Action, Inc.

Warnke, Michael. 1972. *The Satan Seller*. Plainfield, N.J.: Logos International.

Washington, Frank. 1990. "Sex, Cash, and Family Favors: New Allegations Rock Covenant House." *Newsweek*, 21, 115.

2
Satanic Beliefs and Practices

Martin H. Katchen, M.A.
David K. Sakheim, Ph.D.

I n order to assist individuals who have experienced abuse and victimization within satanic cults it is essential for the therapist to understand cult beliefs and practices. The atrocities that survivors report are often difficult to imagine or comprehend. However, in order to intervene appropriately and effectively one must know something about the beliefs on which satanic cults are usually based. Although therapists may find such value systems to be morally repugnant, they must be familiar with the internal logic of such groups. Virtually all social groups have ways of enculturating and indoctrinating new members, as well as maintaining membership once someone has been initiated. Satanic cults are no exception. They appear to differ only in the extremes to which they are willing to go in order to control their membership. To the extent that therapists can understand cult activities as having elements similar to those of other groups (albeit far more extreme and cruel), they will be better able to help patients to make sense of their experiences.

The study of satanism is truly in its infancy. Basic demographic and ethnological data are yet to be compiled, and it is clear that not all groups that call themselves satanic practice the same things. Thus, any description of "beliefs and practices" is tentative at best. We are far from knowing all of the rituals or their various parameters. In fact, it would appear that these are limited only by the magician's or group's imagination. Most published *grimoires* or spellbooks are deliberately altered or left incomplete; the magician supplies what is needed from his own expertise. In addition, since black magicians are reported to be great experimenters, there are probably an unlimited variety of rituals.

Since many satanic groups originated from varying aboriginal, pagan, and other traditions, it is clearly not possible to describe one set of beliefs, symbols, practices, holidays, or rituals. However, there do appear to be some commonalities. The most widely documented satanic traditions in the United States trace their historical roots to a Scottish or Irish (Druid) tradition. However, in the southeastern United States, for example, occult practices have been influenced by another major tradition that appears to have originated in Spain, but which was profoundly altered in the New World. This tradition absorbed Aztec and

21

Mayan beliefs, as well as parts of Lecumi religion, brought to South America by Yoruba slaves, and gave rise to the religions now known as Santeria and Palo Mayombe. Factions that focus on the occult and the worship of "evil" have also emerged from and been influenced by these converging traditions (Raschke 1990; Tierney 1989).

It appears that interactions among all of the different occult groups have resulted in a high degree of cultural heterogeneity. Thus, while not all satanic groups practice in the same fashion, there is a magical world view that does pervade most of these occult belief systems, and survivors typically describe practices that adhere to such beliefs.

According to the magical world view, all living things contain power or energy. The Hindus call it *prana,* the Polynesians call it *mana,* the Chinese call it *qi,* and the Jews call it *ruach chaya,* or "animal spirit." According to the magical world view this power can be absorbed by eating the organism. It is believed to be most available when higher organisms are consumed or when organisms are consumed alive. As Aleister Crowley put it,

> It would be unwise to condemn as irrational the practice of those savages who tear the heart and liver from an adversary and devour them while yet warm. In any case it was the theory of the ancient Magicians, that any living being is a storehouse of energy varying in quantity according to the size and health of the animal, and in quality according to its mental and moral character. At the death of the animal this energy is liberated suddenly. (Crowley 1924 94–95)

The magical world view provides not only for the existence of power, but also the need for power and the desirability of acquiring it. Similar to the Gnostic world view, the magical world view states that while God may have created the world, He has either abandoned it, is not involved with it, or is even malevolently disposed against it. Thus, one must develop one's own power. According to most versions of the magical world view, the universe is made up of many intelligences that must act according to their nature or programming. These are called angels or demons. Unlike these intelligences, man is believed to be self-willed, and to have the potential to control these entities. The control of these forces is called magic (or "magick," according to the occult community). Individuals who have mastered the control of these entities are called magicians.

The idea that a subculture can exist in society while practicing an antiethical analog of that society's dominant religion often meets a great deal of resistance. However, this has occurred in many different contexts. Antinomian cultic offshoots are not uncommon in human society. For example, although Hinduism stresses enlightenment through asceticism and renunciation of the material world, there are people who practice the exact opposite. Their belief, known as "left-handed tantra," is that renunciation (*moksha*) is best achieved through satiation. In this view, the norms of Hindu religion are reversed. The violation of Hindu taboos, including drinking alcohol, performing ritual sex, and eating meat, are all practiced as a spiritual discipline. These "violations" are often associated with the worship of the goddess Kali, especially in her manifestation as Durga, the goddess of power. There have been reports that these groups have made human sacrifices to this goddess (Tierney 1989).

Another report of such an antinomian group appears in Wade Davis's landmark work *The Serpent and The Rainbow*. He not only documents the existence of such a group, but goes on to show how it actually performs certain social functions for the dominant society. Davis describes secret societies in Haiti, particularly the Bizango, who engage in the practice of slave trade with plantation owners. He reports that these groups take individuals who have transgressed certain norms of Haitian society, convince them that they have been turned into zombies, and then sell them into slavery. The transgressor is given a drug containing *tetrodotoxin*, which induces an almost deathlike state. The sorcerer (*bocor*) and his assistants first bury the victim in the ground and then dig him up and sell him into slavery as a zombie. These groups (the Bizango, Caho, Mandingue, and Macandal) worship a deity known as Samedi, who is considered evil in traditional vodun (Davis 1985). Part of what makes this so fascinating is that this is a living example of an ostensibly "evil" cultic society serving a social-regulatory function, while remaining antinomian. Rather than being punished openly, the transgressor of certain village norms can be "sold" to the forces of evil. Davis points out that these secret societies made up a strong base of support for the Duvalier regieme, thus, giving an ostensibly antinomian group a political role as well (ibid.).

Organized crime in various countries is another example of this phenomenon. The *Yakuza* in Japan reportedly control gambling, prostitution, drug trafficking, and other vices. They also are said to maintain a working relationship with the police through bribes and mutual obligations. Disorganized crime, on the other hand, is rare in Japan as the Yakuza harshly and efficiently suppress it.

Thus, antinomian groups may, in an undercover manner, actually fill certain social niches. They can organize crime and suppress disorganized crime. They can performing certain social functions that society finds must be forbidden and disapproved, yet finds necessary and useful. They can spread terror in the segments of the population that the society wishes to suppress, and perform activities that the official morality does not allow, which people nevertheless demand (such as gambling, drug sales, pornography, abortion, and prostitution).

Many people in society end up transgressing certain moral codes. This can be by choice or can occur by force of circumstance. Society rarely notices the distinction. Whether a transgression was willing or forced, society usually rejects the transgressor. For some who find themselves on the wrong side of such moral law, satanism and its concomitant magical belief system can offer a transcendent explanation for their situation. Satanism does not expect nor require individuals to pursue acts of contrition, an exercise rarely accepted by the dominant society anyway. Such a belief system explains the social contradictions in which the individual has been caught, and offers the opportunity to live according to "real" rules, instead of society's professed ones. It can be a comfortable home for people whose experiences have led them to see the world in terms of power, yet who do not believe that morality can protect them. In such a world view it is better to be the predator than the prey, especially if these are the only choices.

One can see how such influences have occurred even in mainstream American society. Our puritan Calvinist legacy, which includes the doctrine of predestination, suggests that some people are destined for salvation and some people are destined for damnation. Even in the last century, as the political influence of religious Calvinism declined in the United States, the doctrine of predestination was grafted onto the half-understood science of genetics, often in a form known as "Social Darwinism." Thus, instead of being hellbound, people with economic, emotional, or physical problems were considered the products of "bad genes," and thus equally irredeemable. This was carried to its extreme in Nazi Germany. It is not difficult to see why an adult whom society views as damned (or who views him or herself in that way) might turn to an alternative or antinomian belief system. For someone in that predicament, the idea of the world as a just and integrated whole under the rulership of one good god can be difficult to accept. The magical world view offers some people an explanation for the world as they have known it, as well as some hope of gaining the power to overcome their helplessness. Anyone who perceives the world in terms of power, and sees themselves as lacking in it, can be drawn to such a belief system. Such an individual may be led to see becoming a magician as a way to realize his or her potential. Satanism provides a justification for identification with the oppressor. It provides a theology that explains how *and why* the professed norms of society differ from the actual ones.

Looked at in this way, some aspects of satanism are similar to various types of psychotherapy. In fact, sociological studies such as those done by Gini Graham Scott (Scott 1983), (although often verging on apologetics for the more sanitized and socially acceptable religious satanic groups such as Anton LaVey's Church of Satan and Michael Aquino's Temple of Set), consistently report an increase in new members' self-confidence as they try out rituals and learn how to perform them correctly. Thus, were it not for its antisocial practices, satanism would probably be considered a harmless or even helpful form of New Age belief system such as psychosynthesis, est, or Lifespring.

Unfortunately, if the more antisocial forms of satanism also benefit their members, it is largely at the expense of innocent others. The psychological growth that comes with feeling more powerful occurs by preying on others. Such a social situation is similar to the interpersonal relationships among inmates in many prisons. Although the prisoner or the cult member may mature, feel more of a sense of power and self-esteem, gain an ability to bond and even to display loyalty to other group members, there are clearly major costs as well.

In the United States satanism usually manifests as an antinomian reversal of Christianity. Reversals of Judaism such as the Donmeh and the Frankists have also been reported (Scholem 1971). Although there may also be groups that reverse other dominant religions, there have yet to be documented reports of an Islamic antinomian group, or reversals of other major religions. As a reaction to Christianity, American satanic traditions take many of their cues from the Bible. For example, Leviticus 18 defines and proscribes incestuous relationships. The same chapter proscribes idolatry, magic, the sacrifice and/or consecration of children to Moloch, and the eating of blood. Many satanists believe therefore that a relationship exists between incest, magic, idolatry, sacrifice, and the consumption of blood since they are mentioned in the same context. It is thereby assumed that forbidden incestuous relationships, the consumption of blood, the human sacrifice all provide the power to do magic. Other reversals of Christianity include such things as the use of inverted crosses, backward prayers, reversed writing ("Nema" instead of "Amen"), and so forth. In this way they mock what they perceive to be hypocrisy, *and* seek magical power. The best known reversal of Christianity is the "Black Mass." The purpose of such a mass is to blaspheme the most important sacrament. Doreen Valiente (1973) points out that this practice may have come about as a response to oppression. In the Middle Ages the populace was told by the Church that freedom, enjoyment, sexuality, music, dance, etc. all belonged to the devil. Thus, a reversal of the Christian mass was utilized to celebrate life, not really to invoke "evil." However, Valiente also points out that much of the notoriety of the Black Mass with its sensational properties, such as the use of a nude woman for an altar, probably stems from fictional accounts. Some of these may have been based on the actual activities of such figures as Madame de Montespan in France, but other accounts are obviously inventions, some of which come from the writings of the Marquis de Sade (ibid.).

Other than reversals of Christian practices there also exist more specific rationales for various rituals. For example Richard Cavendish explains the reason for the use of sacrifices:

> In occult theory, a living creature is a storehouse of energy, and when it is killed most of this energy is suddenly liberated. The killing is done inside the circle to keep the animal's energy in and concentrate it. The animal should be young, healthy and virgin so that its supply of force has been dissipated as little as possible. The amount of energy let loose when the victim is killed is very great, all out of proportion to the animal's size or strength, and the magician must not allow it to get out of hand. If he is unsure of himself or lets his concentration slacken, he may be overwhelmed by the force he has unleashed. (Cavendish 1967 272).

Cavendish goes on to say that according to ancient magical principles, the blood is the vehicle of the animal's life energy, and through the blood, the spirit can be grasped. He also states that the most important reason for the sacrifice is the psychological charge that the magician obtains from it. The act of slaughter enhances the frenzy and concentration that the magician needs to do his magic (ibid.). Other ways to enhance the physiological arousal are also utilized. Judith Spencer (1989) describes the use of ritual sex as a prelude to sacrifice. According to interviews with survivors, the use of torture appears to be a common way to leave the victim in the maximum state of emotional arousal and thereby extract the maximum amount of life force from the victim at the moment of death. Some theoretical support is lent to such reports by writings such as those of a Gardnerian "white" witch coven that practices rituals such as flogging for similar reasons. It is explained that overloading the nervous system with sensations helps lead to a transcending of normal consciousness which the high priestess calls "the ecstasy of magic" (King 1971 8, 163).

The consumption of bodily fluids and wastes (feces, urine, and blood) is commonly reported by multigenerational satanic cult survivors, as is the use of aborted fetuses in various rituals. Again, it is reported that the groups believe that power and magic are enhanced in this fashion.

Most modern satanists appear to respect the works of Eliphas Levi and Aleister Crowley, who standardized the western occult tradition. Many non-satanic occult groups share aspects of this tradition, although some, like the Wiccans, believe that moral values must be included. Unlike the satanists, the Wiccans take morality from Theosophy and not just from the magician's will at the moment. Valiente (1973) points out that Aleister Crowley's famous "Law for the new Aeon," "Do what thou wilt shall be the whole of the law. Love is the law, love under will" is often taken out of context by certain groups. Satanists will often quote the first half of it, while Wiccans and others utilize the whole statement.

The shared aspects of the occult tradition make it possible to draw some parallels between Wicca and satanism in understanding some aspects of rituals and other practices. Clearly, it is very important to keep the distinctions clear between such groups and not to assume that all occult groups are satanic, nor that their goals or practices are all equivalent.

Wiccans and most satanists appear to share the same calendar (see Appendix A). This calendar is based on the Celtic belief that the year is broken into light and dark halves. The new year begins on Halloween, and this dark half of the year goes until May Day. The calendar includes the four cardinal quarterly sabbats of Samhain (October 31), Candlemas (February 2), Beltane (May 1), and Lammas (August 2). In addition, the vernal and autumnal equinoxes (March 21 and September 21) are celebrated, as are the summer and winter solstices (June 21 and December 21–25). The above dates are approximate as the exact dates of the equinoxes and solstices depend on the sun's entry into the corresponding zodiacal signs of Libra (fall equinox), Capricorn (winter solstice), Aries (spring solstice), and Cancer (summer solstice) (Valiente 1973).

Covens are also frequently reported to celebrate members' birthdays with rituals, as well as particular saints' days. Most of the ritual practices occur at night since the Celtic day begins at midnight and time is reckoned by nights rather than days (Conway 1990). The holiday can also be dependent on the occurrence of a full moon. What occurs at these festivals is very different for Wiccans and satanists. The Wiccans, particularly Gardnerians, celebrate life and nature. They consecrate these sabbats to the god or goddess (in Celtic, Cernunnos and Cerridwen). Satanists, on the other hand, use the power of these festivals for conjuring and controlling demons, and consecrating them to Satan and demonic forces. John Fratterola (1986) has attempted to provide more specific details about the types of rituals performed by satanists on each of the major holidays.

Rituals are not limited to these times, however. In Wicca, the waxing of the moon is associated with positive rituals intended to help people, while the waning of the moon appears to be associated with negative rituals designed to blast or curse people (Holtzer 1970). When the group or some of its members wish to perform a ritual directed toward a goal, it is not uncommon for members to build up to that goal by holding a ritual every night during the appropriate cycle of the moon. Many satanists appear to operate according to the same rules, and for that reason perform rituals not only on certain dates but throughout the year. Appendix A lists the most commonly reported holidays celebrated by various satanic groups. However, this is by no means definitive, since each group can be different. These particular dates are included only because they are so often mentioned by survivors.

Magic employs the use of symbols to represent forces. Some of the more commonly reported symbols are included in Appendix B. Of course, this is not an exhaustive list of symbols nor their possible meanings. The symbols that are reproduced are the ones that are most frequently reported by survivors in treatment. It is not uncommon for many of these symbols to be cut on parts of the body in episodes of self-mutilation.

In addition to the inverted Christian symbols, many satanists attribute power to certain geometric shapes. The circle is one of the most basic of these. In Wicca, the circle is believed to hold the force that the coven builds up in a ritual. In ceremonial magic and satanism the magician and the coven members use the magic circle as a protection against the demons that are being invoked and, therefore, stand inside the circle. The demon or spirit may be forced into a triangle preparatory to being commanded. It is believed that this will contain the spirit and thereby protect the group (Gardner 1949).

Pentagrams and hexagrams are some of the most difficult symbols to interpret. Their use depends entirely on the ritual in question and which angel or demon the magician is attempting to control. It is interesting to note, however, that the five-pointed star of the pentagram is often seen as the human form (head, arms, and legs), or as a classic representation of life. Thus, the inverted pentagram (*baphomet*) is a way to symbolize the inversion of usual culture and beliefs. The baphomet is also described as the head of the Goat (Satan) and a goat's head may be superimposed on it. Valiente (1973) notes that certain thirteenth-century pagan art collected by the renowned Knights Templar contained androgynous figures (eg., bearded but with female breasts) that displayed the sign of the pentagram. These appear to be the first objects called "baphomet". One of the most famous renditions of the baphomet was reproduced by the nineteenth century occultist Eliphas Levi. The androgenous figure's head combines the characteristics of a dog, a bull, and a goat. Michael Howard (1989) points out that these were the three components to the pagan mystery tradition. The jackal represents Anubis who was the guide to the underworld and who is related to the Greek god Hermes. The Indian sacred bull is tied to Mithras, and the scapegoat is associated with Judea and was sacrificed to cleanse the sins of the tribe (Howard, 1989). In some cases survivors report that the pentagram can be broken up into its constituent pentagon and triangles in a ritual, with the altar being placed in the pentagon and the coven members standing in the triangles.

Sigils or signs for individual spirits are also difficult to interpret. To do so requires an encyclopedic knowledge of occultism. These symbols are not likely to be known by the average survivor, and such information from a client probably indicates a high degree of magical knowledge and participation. In fact, one way to gauge the seriousness of a client's involvement in the occult and/or satanism may be by the degree of respect the client shows these symbols.

Colors are also used as part of magical symbolism. Black is used to represent death, darkness, and evil, and reportedly is used when human sacrifice is performed. Red usually represents blood, the life energy, or sexual potency and seems to be used in sexual rites. White is derided as a symbol of purity or truth, and is often worn by postulants. Purple is reportedly worn in some covens by the beneficiary of the sacrifice when receiving power (Spencer 1989, 54). In other covens, men will wear black while women wear purple. However, there are no hard and fast rules, as some survivors report robes of other colors (such as brown), and various sources describe different meanings for colors (Conway 1990).

In general, records of magical spells are kept in a *grimoire* or "book of shadows." This is common to Wiccans, ceremonial magicians, and satanists. These grimoires are often written in a secret alphabet. Some of these alphabets are reproduced in Appendix C. They include "runic" alphabets (Thorsson 1989) (popular among groups emphasizing an Odinist or neo-Nazi belief system), Theban (popular among Wiccans), and Enochian (which appears to be the alphabet of choice among many satanists). Enochian is a highly mathematical system of magic emphasizing the use of magical squares to control spirits. According to occult beliefs, it was the language spoken on the lost continent of Atlantis (Howard 1989). Enochian appears to dovetail best with Aleister

Crowley's magical system. Recognition of it by a client would likely imply that they are not merely a dabbler with occultism (see Appendix D for an example of Enochian writing done by one survivor). Dale Griffis (1990) has published a booklet that details these and many other alphabets as well.

A magician's grimoire is the experimental record of the magician's career. It functions as a journal, illustrating magical experimentation and its results (Crowley 1924). However, often key elements are deliberately left out so that only the magician can reproduce the effects.

An objective and detailed study of the western magical tradition remains to be written. It will require not only a study of the works of occultism that have appeared in print, but an exhaustive interview of many survivors. In the meantime, the therapist seeking more background information on occultism should examine the works of Aleister Crowley (1924), Eliphas Levi (1935), Samuel Liddell MacGregor Mathers (1975), Gerald Scheuler (1987), Margot Adler (1986), Janet and Stewart Farar (1984a, 1984b), Manly Hall (1961), Gerald Gardner (1952), and Doreen Valiente (1973).

Virtually every organized group or religion has practices that are geared toward indoctrinating initiates and maintaining membership. The kinds of practices that satanic cult survivors report are really only very extreme versions of such familiar activities. For example, most Americans accept circumcision as a moral practice despite little evidence of its health benefits. Few regard it as "sexual abuse" or think of it as "a mutilation of a child's genitalia." However, someone from another society certainly could. Similarly, Marine boot camp is described as a "character building" experience. The assumption is that the abuse and pain of the experience will make the recruit stronger. The process is often described as tearing down the civilian and then building him up in the new Marine way. These and many other examples of physical, emotional, and sexual "abuse" might be judged to be a very negative part of our society from the outside. However, the rationales of many groups allow emotional, physical, and even sexual abuses to be accepted (and viewed in a positive light) if they are not too extreme and if they can be justified by religious or some other reasons. Reports about the practices in some satanic groups take this to the very extreme. Character building through abuse is pursued as far as one could imagine. Like the Marine Corps, satanists believe that one's power is enhanced by undergoing various ordeals. Thus, it is not this premise that is so impossible to understand. The problems arise from the extent to which such practices are pursued. Keeping this concept in mind, it becomes a little easier to understand how the extreme victimization of satanism (or other ritual abuse) could have evolved and could be accepted and glorified by cult members.

Most survivors in psychotherapy describe very similar atrocities committed by satanic cults. Although most of these have yet to be proven, it is helpful to begin to examine them. There is not a great deal yet known about the religious significance of these alleged practices. In isolation, the abuses appear to be incidents of random violence. However, taken as a whole, they begin to form a picture not unlike the "brainwashing" or "thought reform" approaches that have been presented by scholars of other totalist groups. Dr. Robert J. Lifton has written about such practices, as in his seminal work on the thought reform methods used by the Chinese Communists (Lifton 1961). Although the religious development and rationales for most of the satanic rituals are not known, they can be viewed from a psychological perspective as forming part of an effective indoctrination protocol.

All "brainwashing" or "thought reform" appears to involve techniques that would result in the psychological destruction of the old self and the creation of a new indoctrinated self. It is very interesting to see how closely the descriptions of satanic cult indoctrination follow the same type of course. Using the material presented by survivors undergoing psychotherapy, one can see the described atrocities as part of a larger psychological purpose, namely, to indoctrinate the person into the group, to maintain membership, and to separate the member from outside connections. Although most groups have such practices, those utilized by satanic cults appear very similar to those utilized by other extreme totalist groups. Whether or not every report turns out to be accurate, it is helpful to understand how such experiences can be a part of a group's indoctrination.

As in the thought-reform methodology discussed by Lifton (1961), most of the reported satanic rituals are based around the theme of death and rebirth. There is the clear idea of killing off the old "good" self and finding or creating a new "evil" self. What typically seems to occur is that these attempts to destroy the old self end up creating what Lifton refers to as a "split personality." This is seen in the cult as possession by demons, but would be viewed from a psychological standpoint as the development of multiple personalities as a defense against the traumatic abuses. The cults will often deliberately encourage this dissociation, enabling cult members to keep the selves (and thereby the secret rituals) from being discovered. The "old self" functions in the normal world during the day while the "new" self is brought out for cult activities at night.

Lifton (1961) specifically describes eight characteristics of totalist thought reform. These are (1) milieu control, (2) mystical manipulation, (3) demand for purity, (4) the cult of confession, (5) a sacred science, (6) "loaded" language, (7) the primacy of doctrine over person, and (8) the dispensing of existence. Studied point by point, it is easy to see how reported cult rituals could fit into such an outline.

Many satanic cult survivors describe specific death and rebirth rituals. These are usually very literal in nature. For example, survivors report being buried in the ground (sometimes in a coffin with a dead animal or person) after being severely abused. The reported abuse usually involves some type of mutilation that would result in severe hemorrhaging. After these injuries are inflicted, the survivor is then told that he or she (the old self) is going to die and be buried. Rebirthing rituals also occur where the survivor's new self is "born into the cult." A number of survivors have described being placed inside a dead animal that had been cut open, and told that they were being "born unto satan" as they were pulled out. The message to the child involved is that a new "evil" person is being developed (or found within) who will be able to be a part of the cult. The cults have ways of making the membership very concrete. Once a member, the child will often be branded, scarred, or tattooed with a symbol of the cult to permanently indicate the cult's "ownership" of that new person. Many survivors also describe rituals that parallel Christian rites such as baptism. In the satanic version, the Christian symbolism is inverted. For example, instead of using "holy water," water is used that has been contaminated (e.g., by putting leeches in it). One survivor also reported having leeches put on her leg during such a ritual to represent "Satan's mark," as well as to transform her blood into "evil blood." Leeches and other such creatures (e.g., spiders, locusts, snakes) are used in these rituals because it is believed that they originate from the devil.

Survivors often describe what Lifton refers to among the thought-reform methods as a "fluctuation of assault and leniency," as well as "an assault on identity" (Lifton 1961 67–72). The child in a cult situation is reportedly told that he or she is evil. There are many rituals and situations created to enforce this notion. For example, one patient described having "holy water" (likely some type of acid) thrown on her that burned her skin. This was done to "prove" to her that she was really evil. Victims are also deliberately shown that they can no longer trust their senses or previous notions of how the world works. This is accomplished in many ways; some of these involve the use of drugs; electric shock; hypnosis; torture; rape; humiliation; illusion; long periods of isolation (e.g., locked in a box or a closet); sleep, water and food deprivation; or being partially drowned or hanged by the hands or feet. This fostering of an alternative consciousness and confusion make it easier to put the child into a more suggestible state—what Lifton describes as "more readily influenced and are more susceptible to destructive and aggressive impulses arising from within" (ibid. 68).

As in other thought-reform approaches, one of the most important components is the establishment of guilt in the victim. Most cult survivors report having been forced to commit atrocities by the adults in the group who would then point out how evil the child must have been to have done these things. For example, the child is forced to hold a knife and stab something living. The adult then lets go of the child's hand, stands back and says "Look at what you just did." In addition to various forms of physical violence, these activities can include forced sex with animals, or other children or adults or participation in pornography. Being forced to participate in rituals where other children are injured also undermines the child's sense of being a moral person. In addition, the child is often told that because he or she resisted a cult request, someone else close to the child will be punished. Thus, even when the child resists what feels immoral or wrong, he or she is made to feel that another person is suffering because of his or her actions. This makes it feel like terrible consequences will occur whenever cult edicts are violated, despite internal feelings to the contrary. Thus, the only path to morality (and safety) is to follow cult orders and teachings. Most survivors describe ultimately feeling as did one of the former prisoners whom Dr. Lifton interviewed, that there was a "Kafka-like maze of vague and yet damning accusations: he could neither understand exactly what he was guilty of . . . nor could he in any way establish his innocence. Overwhelmed by fatigue, confusion, and helplessness, he ceased all resistance" (ibid. 70).

Another essential ingredient in thought reform appears to be self-betrayal (Lifton 1961). The betrayal of the self occurs on many levels for cult members. Despite learning about religion in the outside world, the child is often forced to denounce and desecrate symbols of the church. This usually involves denouncing many of his or her own beliefs about morality as well as specific church teachings. Often survivors report being forced to engage in activities that are directly self-debasing such as "voluntarily" eating feces and human flesh, drinking blood, and so on. They also report being betrayed by significant people in their lives, which leaves them with a sense of worthlessness. Parents and siblings are often reported to have been passive witnesses to tortures, leaving the child feeling that he or she must have deserved these since nobody stopped them.

Some survivors report having been stimulated sexually while forced to watch or participate in atrocities. This creates an additional sense that the body's reactions can not be trusted. The confusion and shame inherent in feeling sexually excited during horrible events leads to further alienation from one's body. The child frequently blames him or herself for what occurs in order to hang on to some sense of perceived control amid overwhelming feelings of helplessness. Thus, the end result is a tormented individual who views him- or herself as evil, culpable, and dangerously out of control.

Dr. Lifton describes an event that he consistently saw in his observations of thought reform. He called it "the breaking point: total conflict and basic fear" (Lifton 1961 69–72). Most cult survivors describe a similar experience. Usually "the breaking point" is deliberately induced by torture. Cult members beat their victims, fracture their limbs, and/or rape them repeatedly until they "break." The most common "breaking" is psychological, through dissociation. Most survivors report psychotic episodes, feeling suicidal or experiencing delusions and hallucinations (some induced by involuntary drug use). Virtually every patient reports deliberately induced fear of annihilation.

Leniency and nurturance can be used as powerful compliance-inducing techniques. Many cult survivors report a sort of "good cop–bad cop" approach, in which one member of the cult acts as a nurturer after the tortures have occurred. This person appears to have the power to stop the abuse and to give back life. One patient reported that this "nurturant" person ended up with amazing power over her. She felt that she could not resist any of his requests, for he was the only one who could take away her terror.

In thought-reform methodology there is the creation of "a compulsion to confess." In the cults, this corresponds to the appearance of "a compulsion to accept the new teachings." There is no push in the cults to "confess," but rather to "freely" become a part of the group. The similarity lies in the spurious freedom of this commitment. One patient described a ritual in which she had to "voluntarily" sign "the book of names" for the cult. She was beaten and tortured until she was willing to do so. However, if there was any sense that she was only doing so to avoid further beating, that was not acceptable. The signing had to be because she "wanted to."

"The channeling of guilt" is another technique mentioned in the literature on thought reform (Lifton 1961). The cult reverses "good" and "evil," but the process involved is essentially the same. Since the cult sees "evil" as a redeeming trait and "goodness" as a liability, the child typically begins to accept this way of thinking. He or she starts to believe that evil is powerful, that through evil one can accomplish whatever is desired. Thus, "good" begins to be condemned internally. The cults' standards of action become more and more accepted internally and become ego-syntonic. It is only safe to act and feel in ways the cult allows. Specific indoctrination to teach the child these reversals is reported very frequently. Physical abuse is presented as "a reward" and something that will give the child special powers. The child is told that the more he or she can endure, the stronger person he or she will be. Specific language reversals are also taught, such as that "hate" means "love" or "evil" means "good" and vice versa. Usually, personalities develop that internalize the aggressive, tyrannical parts of the cult, as well as specialized language and symbols needed to make the internal corrections necessary to avoid the wrath that inevitably occurs if the cults' standards are violated. Thus, as did the POWs, the child in the cult environment develops an identification with the aggressors.

The cults also have specific rituals that reinforce, internalize, and concretize this sense of guilt. Some patients actually report being forced to eat an eye and then being told that it will always watch them and will tell the cult if they violate the rules. Other patients discuss what has been termed "magical surgery" in which the child is rendered unconscious and upon awakening is convinced that he or she has undergone a surgical procedure in which a bomb, a monster, a snake, or Satan himself has been placed inside of him or her. The child is told that the intruder will squeeze internal organs or that the bomb wil explode if the cult is ever betrayed. The child is also told that even thinking of telling someone about it, will start the process. Of course, this capitalizes on the child's own physiological reactions to the fear of telling. An increase in heart rate or tension in the stomach will be interpreted as a sign that the snake or the bomb is working. Thus, even the child's physiology is turned against him or her. This is a very literal version of what Lifton described among former prisoners as "penetration by the psychological forces of the environment into the inner experience of the individual person" (Lifton 1961). Many patients also report that the cult has told them that it has spies everywhere. There is a strong sense that no one can be trusted and that anyone could be a cult member who could trick them into betraying the cult and then turn them in.

The former prisoners whom Dr. Lifton interviewed described a component to thought reform that is referred to as "re-education and logical dishonoring" (ibid. 76). Part of the reeducation involves "loading the language." Steven Hassan (1988) points out that in such situations words and images take on tremendous significance. This is obviously true in magic where symbols and words become charged with power. In satanism, because of the paradoxical nature of its reality, language can often be loaded with a reversal of the usual meanings. For example, "God" will mean an object of derision or an enemy. "Good" and "Evil" will have multiple meanings. Often special names will be given to the member that are only for use in cult activities. Thus, participants must either learn a high degree of dissimulation or a high degree of dissociation in order to respond correctly to outsiders in social situations when words with loaded meanings are used. This clearly serves to further split cult members from outsiders by making communication that much more difficult. The Black Magician and the High Priest (or High Priestess) determine what is correct. All of the major published grimoires such as *The Sacred Magic of Abramelin the Mage* (Mathers 1975), *Goetla vel Salomonis Regis* (Crowley 1904), and *The Necronomicon* (1977), or books by Eliphas Levi (1969, 1970) constitute part of this "sacred science." In addition, as noted above, each cult or coven maintains its own "book of shadows" or grimoire, in which it codifies its rituals, often in secret languages or alphabets such as Theban or Enochian. Part of the reeducation involves teachings about the outside world. For example, the cults try to point out the inconsistencies of church teachings, much as the communists pointed out logical inconsistencies in the prisoners' views about religion and morality. The cult will portray the forces of "good" being at war with the forces of "evil," and that both sides are equally dangerous to the other. However, they claim that the forces of evil will win because they are not held back by rules of morality. Many patients report having heard numerous stories about brutality committed in the name of religion. The clear message is that everyone is violent despite what they preach. Thus, the important thing is to be on the side with the power, the side that will win. It is not difficult to confuse a child. The child's previous notions of what is good become unclear. The child begins to feel a part of an inevitable process whereby "evil will come again to rule the earth." The choice is to be part of it or to be left behind and be killed.

The cults do not only try to convince members to show loyalty to the group by appealing to notions of logic or correct action (as in the case of the communists in China). They also utilize very direct forms of blackmail. They may threaten members who have been previously forced to participate in pornography, murder, or other crimes. Members are reminded that they are equally in danger of society's wrath if the actions are revealed. There can also be threats toward family members or threats to reveal evidence of compromising activities (such as a film showing the member having sex with an animal). Physical threats are commonplace. For example, one patient reported being forced to witness the tongue being cut out of a live cow. She was then forced to wear it around her neck and was told that if she ever talked about the group, the same would happen to her tongue. Many patients report being personally threatened or being forced to witness a childhood pet being killed as an example of what could happen to them if they ever betray the group. Thus, patients usually continue to demonstrate a tremendous sense of fear that the cult has the power to retaliate toward them and will do so. This is especially the case early in treatment when they begin to discuss what has occurred, since talking about cult activities is a major violation of the cult's rules.

Similar to the experience of the prisoners in the Chinese camps, as the new cult member develops and passes through the various rituals he or she acquires a place of increasing status in the cult. Some cults have positions determined from birth, but even in these, the novitiate gains more and more privileges and suffers less and less abuse by moving through the various entry rituals. As the new member becomes more involved, he or she begins to reap the benefits of membership financially, interpersonally, and in terms of feeling power over others. Clearly, feeling harmony with the group contrasts starkly to the earlier terror and confusion. The person is also continually reminded that he or she will never fit into the outside world after having had such experiences. The clear message is that the cult is the only place where he or she belongs.

Just as the program of thought reform had specific stages, the satanic cults appear to have a series of rites of passage. The exact ages and corresponding rituals are not yet clear and may well differ across groups. However, it is clear that certain ages based on numerology appear to be selected for each of the types of initiation rituals. The prisoners in Lifton's study described a "final confession" experience. Similarly, various female patients have described an important ritual either at ages five to six or twelve to thirteen where they must give themselves to the cult. This is often described as a "marriage to the beast satan" in which the young woman is raped by the men of the group and tortured. She is told that this insures her place in the group and guarantees her return to it as an adult. The ceremony typically involves the use of sacrifices and/or other activities far outside the realm of usual life. Another "bonding" ritual described by numerous survivors is the "satanic abortion" in which they are first impregnated by a member of the group and later forced to abort the fetus, which is subsequently killed and consumed by the group's members as part of a ceremony. Such extreme actions of course further split the person from the outside world and bind her to the cult, for she feels that no one else could accept or believe her afterward.

Just as the prisoners of the Chinese were eventually integrated into the new system, the cult initiate is eventually given an important role in its functioning. Each member is reportedly groomed for a specific role, but as the process unfolds, the responsibilities and benefits increase for all. There is ultimately a sense of belonging and identification that can become so strong that the member will bring his or her own children to the cult to begin the process anew.

Lifton described the process of "release: transition and limbo" that occurred once the POWs were freed (1961 84). It is fascinating how similar this is to the presentation of patients who enter psychotherapy in order to psychologically (and sometimes physically) separate from the cult. In both cases the outside world does not understand what they have been through. There is shame and fear of discussing anything, as well as disbelief from others. A tremendous loneliness is often present, as are difficulties with trust and feelings of fragmentation. The patient often begins to become aware of just how split he or she has become. A major identity crisis usually occurs because most of the defenses developed to deal with the cult's brutality are not needed (and only cause problems) in the outside world. The senses had been honed and developed to anticipate danger, but now these abilities are only limiting and upsetting in usual circumstances. The patient may long for the simplicity of the cult (or prison in the case of the POWs) where moral choices and ambivalence were absent. The change from cult values entails a great deal of pain of its own. Changing constructs is an ordeal no matter what its direction or benefits.

Although the above examples of cult "thought reform" techniques are widely reported by survivors, most have yet to be fully detailed, documented, or verified. However, the similarities to the thought-reform techniques used by other totalist groups is apparent. In our efforts to develop helpful therapies we came to understand that many of the incidents of seemingly random violence that cult survivors describe can be understood as part of a broader picture. Even if every allegation does not prove accurate, it is clear that the impact of severe brutality in the service of a rigid belief system can create a picture much like what Lifton observed among the POWs. The cult's abuses may have developed to foster an effective coercive indoctrination process that sadly appears to have been discovered by many other totalist groups as well. Clearly, a lot can be learned from the study of such practices and how one can recover after being subjected to such extreme and overwhelming abuse. Toward this goal it will clearly be important for more specific details of satanic cult rituals to be published so that they can be better understood, verified, and compared across groups. Unfortunately, but not surprisingly, it would appear that many of the coercive ways that people find to influence each other utilize certain constant and recurring principles. We hope that it is also likely that the healing process will be similar across various groups that have been so victimized and that by better understanding the ways that people are injured in this process we will begin to learn more about the ways that people can recover as well.

Appendix A: Commonly Reported Satanic Holidays

Date	Holidays
1/1	New Year's Day (A Druid Feast Day)
1/17	Satanic Revels
2/1 (or the 1st full moon of Aquarius)	Imbolc
2/2	Candlemas
3/20–3/21 (sun's entry in Aries)	Feast Day Spring Equinox (called Alban Eiler by Druids)
4/19–26	Preparation for the sacrifice
4/30	Walpurgis Night (May Eve)
5/1 (or the 1st full moon of Taurus)	Beltane
6/21–6/22 (sun's entry in Cancer)	Feast Day Summer Solstice (called *Alban Heruin* by Druids)
7/1	Demon Revels
8/2 (or the 1st full moon of Leo)	Lammas (also called *Lughnassadh, Lunasa*)
8/3	Satanic Revels
9/7	Marriage to the Beast Satan
9/20–9/21 (sun's entry in Libra)	Midnight Host Fall Equinox (called *Alban Elved* by Druids)
10/29	All Hallows Eve
10/31 (or first full moon of Scorpio)	Samhain (Halloween) (Start of the Celtic new year)
12/22 (sun's entry in Capricorn)	Winter Solstice (called *Arthuan* by Druids, also called *Yule*)
12/24	Demon Revels

This is not an exhaustive listing of holidays for the various satanic groups. Survivors report ideosyncratic variations and cult-specific dates (such as members' birthdays). The reported practices for each date can be seen in Fratterola (1986). The above information is from Gallant (1985), Griffis (1989), Fratterola (1986), Voices in Action (1990), Conway (1990), Valiente (1973), and survivor reports.

Appendix B: Commonly Reported Satanic Symbols

Symbols

Key

1. Anarchy.
2. "Anti-Justice." Since the double-bladed axe was a Roman symbol for justice, this inversion of that symbol means the opposite.
3. Black Mass.
4. Black Mass.
5. Symbol for a blood ritual.
6. Eternity and completion. The circle is believed to be able to contain powerful forces when used in rituals. Specific circles are reported to be important (e.g., nine feet in diameter) for many rituals.
7. "Cross of confusion." This symbol from the Romans was used to indicate a questioning of Christianity.
8. The inverted cross is used to ridicule Christianity.
9. The "inverted cross of satanic justice" is a symbol used for someone who has betrayed the coven. It is ritually used when someone is cursed.
10. The inverted pentagram or "baphomet" is a satanic symbol of the goat's head (satan's head). It can also be interpreted as the inversion of the human form.

11. The pentagram is an occult symbol. The top point is usually interpreted to represent the spirit while the other points represent the elements (earth, wind, fire, and water). It can also be seen to represent the human form (head, arms, and legs).

12. This symbol is used to indicate where sexual magick is to occur.

13. This is the "sign of the beast" from Revelations 13. Aleister Crowely used this to identify himself.

14. This is another common way of writing 666 since F is the sixth letter of the alphabet.

15. The Swastika is an ancient symbol used to represent the four seasons and four directions (winds). As an occult symbol it was inverted so that instead of appearing to turn in a clockwise direction (in harmony with nature), it would instead show a lack of harmony with the natural order of things. It was chosen as the symbol of the Nazi Party.

16. The triangle is often drawn on the ground in a ritual since it is believed to be able to contain a demon.

Information from Griffis (1990), Kahaner (1988) and survivor reports. This is not an exhaustive list of symbols. They can mean different things in different groups.

Appendix C: Alphabets Used by Satanic Groups

Runic Alphabet

The Enochian Alphabet

Theban or Witch's Alphabet

This is not an exhaustive list of alphabets. See Thorsson (1989) and Griffis (1990) for a more complete listing of runes, glyphs, and alphabets. Dr. Griffis generously has provided the information.

Appendix D: Enochian Writing by a Survivor

MY LORD SATAN AND MASTER LUCIFER
I ACKNOWLEDGE YOU AS MY GOD AND PRAISE
AND PROMISE TO SERVE AND OBEY YOU WHILE
I LIVE I RENOUNCE THE OTHER GOD AND JESUS
CHRIST THE SAINTS AND THE CHURCH OF ROME
WITH ALL OF ITS SACRAMENTS AND ALL THE
PRAYERS THAT THE FAITHFUL MAY OFFER ME
I PROMISE TO DO AS MUCH EVIL AS I CAN AND
DRAW ALL OTHERS TO EVIL I RENOUNCE BAPTISM
AND ALL THE MERITS OF JESUS CHRIST AND
HIS SAINTS IF I FAIL TO SERVE YOU AND ADORE
YOU I GIVE MY LIFE AND I SHALL BURN
IN HELL

Note: The above was written inside of a big black book that the patient was forced to sign. It is written in Enochian.

References

Adler, Margot. 1986. *Drawing Down the Moon: Witches, Druids, Goddess Worshipers, and Other Pagans in American Today.* Boston: Beacon Press.

Cavendish, Richard. 1967. *The Black Arts.* New York: G. P. Putnam and Sons.

Conway, D. J. 1990. *Celtic Magic.* St. Paul, Minn.: Llewellyn Publications.

Crowley, Aleister. 1924. *Magick in Theory and Practice.* Reprint. New York: Dover, 1976.

———. *Goetia vel Salomonis Regis.* 1898. Translated by Samuel L. M. Mathers. Republished by Aleister Crowley, Society for Propegation of Religious Truth, 1904.

Davis, Wade. 1985. *The Serpent and the Rainbow.* New York: Simon and Schuster.

Farar, Janet, and Stewart Farar. 1984a. *A Witch's Bible Compleat.* New York: Magickal Childe Press.

———. 1984b. *The Witches Way.* Custer, Wash.: Phoenix Publishing.

Frattarola, John. 1986. "America's Best Kept Secret," *Passport Magazine,* edited by D.C. Skinner, Calvary Chapel, October, 1986.

Gallant, Sandi. 1985. "Sabbats, Festivals, Paganism, Witchcraft, and Satanism." Information furnished by Officer Gallant, San Francisco Police Department Intelligence Division.

Gardner, Gerald. 1949. *High Magic's Aid.* London: Michael Houghton.

Gardner, Gerald. 1952. *Witchcraft Today.* London: Rider & Co.

Griffis, Dale W. 1989, April. "Sabats or Celebrations." Information furnished by D. W. Griffis at the Massachusetts Juvenile Police Association Annual Training Conference. Waltham, Massachusetts.

———. 1990. *Rhunes, Glyphs, and Alphabets.* Tiffin, Oh.: Dale W. Griffis.

Hall, Manly P. 1961. *The Secret Teachings of All Ages.* Los Angeles: Philosophic Research Society.

Hassan, Steve. 1988. *Combatting Cult Mind Control.* Rochester, Vt.: Park Street Press.

Holtzer, Hans. 1970. *The Truth About Witchcraft.* London: Acorn Books.

Howard, Michael. 1989. *The Occult Conspiracy.* Rochester, Vt.: Destiny Books.

Kahaner, Larry. 1988. *Cults That Kill: Probing the Underworld of Occult Crime.* New York: Warner Books.

King, Francis. 1971. *Sexuality, Magic, and Perversion.* Secaucus, N.J.: Citadel Press.

Levi, Eliphas. 1969. *The History of Magick Including an Actual and Precise Exposition of Procedure, Rites, and Mystery.* London: Ryder Books.

———. 1910. *Transcendental Magick.* Reprint. New York: Samuel Weiser, 1970.

Lifton, Robert J. 1961. *Thought Reform and the Psychology of Totalism.* New York: W. W. Norton.

Mathers, Sameul Liddel MacGregor. 1975. *The Book of the Sacred Magick of Abremelin the Mage.* London: Dover Books.

Raschke, Carl. 1990. *Painted Black: Satanic Crime in America.* San Francisco, Ca.: Harper and Row.

Schueler, Gerald. 1987. *An Advanced Guide to Enochian Magick.* St. Paul, Minn.: Llewellyn Publications.

Schlangecraft, Inc., 1977. *Necronomicon.* Edited by Simon. Reprint. New York: Avon Books, 1979.

Scholem, Gershom Gerhard 1971. *The Messianic Idea in Judaism.* New York: Schocken Books.

Scott, Gini Graham. 1983. *The Magicians: A Study in the Use of Power in a Black Magic Group*. New York: Irvington Publishers.

Spencer, Judith. 1989. *Suffer the Child*. New York: Pocket Books.

Thorsson, Edred. 1989. *Rune Might: Secret Practices of the German Rune Magicians*. St. Paul, Minn.: Llewellyn Publications.

Tierney, Patrick. 1989. *The Highest Altar: The Story of Human Sacrifice*. New York: Viking Press.

Valiente, Doreen. 1973. *An ABC of Witchcraft Past and Present*. Custer, Wa.: Phoenix Publishing.

Voices in Action, Inc. 1990. *Sabats, Festivals, Paganism, Witchcraft, and Satanism*. Chicago, Ill.

3

Alternative Hypotheses Regarding Claims of Satanic Cult Activity: A Critical Analysis

George B. Greaves, Ph.D.

Beginning about 1984, a phenomenon occurred that was previously unknown to psychiatry. Literally hundreds of children, adolescents, and adults all over North America began to pour out stories to psychotherapists, clergy, law-enforcement officers, parents, and others about either current, recent, or past involvement in satanic cults. The accounts were almost unbelievably grisly, yet at the same time remarkably similar in their sometimes copious detail.

Now it was true that in 1980 a strange book had appeared in the trade press called *Michelle Remembers* (Smith and Pazder 1980), in which a young woman reported alleged satanic cult experiences to her Vancouver psychiatrist. Her subsequent treatment was undertaken at great expense to the Canadian government's health insurance plan. Her story was met with equally great interest by the Roman Catholic church.

Even earlier, a similar book was published in the Christian press called *The Satan Seller* (Warnke 1972), in which an alleged satanic high priest, now an influential Christian minister, published his memoirs of his former satanic priesthood.

But to conclude purely on the basis of chronology that these and similar books are the cause of the tidal wave that hit the psychiatric world *circa* 1984 is to argue nothing more than the *post hoc, propter hoc* fallacy (the erroneous assumption that that which appears earlier *causes* that which occurs later).

My opinion is somewhat more complex than simple acceptance or denial. My central theses are as follows:

1. Almost all hypotheses regarding the objective reality of the reports of alleged satanic cult survivors (SCSs) are *a priori* in nature (based on assumption and imagination, not facts).

2. Almost all writers and presenters on the subject, whether they believe in these reports or not, confuse hypotheses with fact, and assume their hypotheses to be fact.

45

3. Almost no one has systematically analyzed the empirical validity of the many competing hypotheses that have been generated in the field, examined the methodology of data gathering, looked carefully at the assumptions being made by various authors and presenters, or looked at the reports themselves for a validity perspective.

4. Researchers in the field, whatever their background, are working from very different data bases, resulting in failures to make key discriminations between issues. This has resulted in varying focuses and wide-ranging methods of collecting data. Attempting to do serious SCS research in the current climate is like attempting to construct the Tower of Babel. A common metalanguage is urgently needed.

As the SCS debate has escalated, I think one can rather clearly identify four groups of psychiatric clinicians, law enforcement officers, and authors working in the SCS field: (1) *nihilists,* (2) *apologists,* (3) *heuristics,* and (4) *methodologists.*

Nihilists seem to see their function as explaining how the presentations made by SCSs *cannot* be true. They believe that because they can concoct alternative explanations of the data, the data *are not* true. They hold themselves to no empirical criterion of truth, but they, nevertheless, rigorously demand such of others. Many of them fly the flag of scientific skepticism, but their skepticism—and their data gathering—are often unscientific in method. Rather than proving their hypotheses scientifically, they strike the pose of claiming that their hypotheses are factually correct until someone empirically proves them wrong. Among the nihilists I would include George Ganaway (1989, 1990), Richard Noll (1990), Arthur Lyons (1988), Robert Hicks (1990a, 1990b), and Kenneth Lanning (1989). Ganaway and Noll hold that SCS reports are the results of various kinds of psychodynamic distortions and/or artifacts induced in SCS subjects by clumsy or unwitting interviewers. Lyons, Hicks, and Lanning argue the *reductio ad absurdum* fallacy that if the reports were true, there would be physical evidence to back them up, which, they claim, there is not.

Apologists seem to conceive their task as explaining why SCS productions *must* be true. Arguing on the basis of the astonishing similarities among the data productions of their SCS subjects, pointing to the principle of independent observation as a very strong criterion of validity, they state with much conviction that it is logically inconceivable that the many points of correspondence among independently derived SCS reports cannot be the result of anything else but the reflection of an underground network of people practicing a secret satanic religion. "Softer" apologists—among whom I would count myself (Greaves 1989b), Jean Goodwin (1990), Sally Hill and Jean Goodwin (1989), Roland Summit (1989), and Catherine Gould (1989)—argue that many of the SCS reports *could* be true: that there is nothing in the history of man's inhumanity to man or in terms of known psychological principles which contradict the reports. Among the "harder" apologists I would count Bennett Braun (1989), Jerry Simandl (in Kahaner 1988, under pseudonym), Sandi Gallant (in Kahaner (1988), Dale Griffis (in Kahaner 1988), Maury Terry (1987), and Larry Kahaner (1988).

Heuristics consist mainly of a large group of clinicians who are uncommitted to any objective conclusions about the whole matter, but who have found that treating their SCS patients' reports in a confirming manner has resulted in favorable outcomes in treatment. Most of the clinical authors in this book follow the heuristic approach. I specifically have in mind the dozens of clinicians I know of who, while they really haven't grappled with the issues of the ultimate validity of these reports to the point of publishing their conclusions, nevertheless do good clinical work with these subjects. While I will articulate the heuristic position in detail later, I can capture its essence in a brief anecdote.

For a period of nine months I had been treating an SCS outpatient in co-therapy with a psychiatric colleague of mine, with apparently good result. When we got into some particularly heinous material with the patient I grew nervous, because I knew my colleague shared office space with a renowned skeptic of SCS productions. Seeking to avert a crisis, or at least to prepare for one, I told him I needed to know, as primary therapist, exactly where he stood with the material. He sensed my concern and paused thoughtfully to consider it. His reply was as follows: *"I think to treat this material as anything but real would be to undermine the patient."*

The *Methodologists* have the least developed perspective in the SCS field, since in any scientific investigation observation always precedes method. Something, after all, must catch the eye of the scientist, investigative reporter, or detective before there is any subject or object of methodical investigation. From a psychiatric perspective, after seven years of observing these phenomena we are only at the threshold of systematic investigation. We do not even agree yet on what should be observed. There have been two major breakthroughs to date. One is that of anthropologist Sherrill Mulhern's (1990) excellent study of how professionals in the field are resorting to group indoctrination techniques to convince others of the truth of SCS reports, thus biasing, or attempting to bias, attitudes regarding SCS reports. The second major contribution is that of Walter Young (1991) who, with his co-researchers, is the first clinician to look at collective SCS reports as *clinical data.*

At least thirty other clinicians come immediately to mind who have been working with SCS patients over long periods of time. If I have failed to mention them, it is either because they have no citable work on the subject, or because I am unclear where they stand. If those mentioned above take exception to my general classification of their views, I apologize.

The goals of this chapter are threefold. First, I want to bring to what is rapidly becoming a highly controversial area with little empirical discipline an analytically informed, empiricist perspective. Second, I wish to critically examine and begin to organize a maelstrom of diverse opinion, by drawing a number of distinctions and by examining the major competing hypotheses. Third, I wish to examine and expand upon George Ganaway's (1989, 1990) important contributions to the field of debate.

Conceptual Confusion in SCS Reports

One problem in the SCS field is that many writers employ equivocal language without realizing it. By way of example, what is a "satanic" cult or "cultist"? These terms are indiscriminately applied to five very diverse groups:

1. Allegedly, there are *transgenerational satanic cults,* which are said to date back several generations. Members of these cults are said to born into a secret religion that worships Lucifer/Satan as the Lord of the earth within the extremely restrictive rules of a pagan, occult theosophy, which includes human and animal sacrifice, and which strives to "resolve" all opposites: pleasure-pain, food-poison, love-hate, man-woman, joy-sorrow, Heaven-Earth, God-Satan.

2. There are *neo-satanic cults,* typified by the Church of Satan in San Francisco and the Temple of Set in St. Louis (Aquino, in Kahaner 1988; LaVey 1969, 1972, 1989). While these cults adamantly deny involvement in human, animal, or blood ritual, their leaders make clear in their writings that they and their followers should worship Satan and turn from godly teachings.

3. There are *self-styled satanic cult leaders.* Some of these leaders are dropouts from other satanic cults; others represent solitary ventures.

4. There are *"teen dabblers"* in satanism. These are disaffected adolescents attracted to satanic—in this case life-destructive—values. These allegedly read LaVey, Crowley, and listen to certain heavy metal rock groups. They have no known general theosophy, but engage in sexual experiments and murderous ventures.

5. There are *solitary satanists.* These are individuals who seem as called to the will of Satan as others proclaim they have been called to that of the Holy Ghost. Their notoriety arises out of their bizarre murders and/or suicides, such as the murder spree of Richard Ramirez, the Night Stalker.

It is not difficult to imagine that transgenerational satanic cults exist. The problem is that 98 percent of all writing on the subject of the alleged criminal activities of satanists has to do with the last four categories, especially the last three. The continuation of such confusion in categories of data allows authors to engage each other in endless "straw man" arguments.

Great confusion also exists in the field between the goals and objectives of *forensic psychiatry* and *clinical psychiatry*. Among the major goals of criminal forensic psychiatry are the identification, apprehension, and the conviction (or defense) of suspected criminals. Among the major goals of clinical psychiatry are the identification, control, arrestation and/or amelioration of psychiatric illnesses. To the criminal forensic psychiatrist it is crucial to know if SCS reports can be *proven* in a court of law. To the clinical psychiatrist it is crucial to discern what SCS productions *mean*. These are very different focuses with very different goals and methodologies.

When these two ways of thinking are combined inappropriately, it leads to the kind of confusion that Roland Summit speaks of eloquently:

> Ever since these cases [of alleged satanic ritual child abuse] exploded into awareness in 1984, there's been a great effort to understand how they didn't happen and why it couldn't be true. And the best answer people seem to come up with is the notion that therapists or police investigators are brainwashing the children into telling crazy stories. Why these people would want children to tell unbelievable stories that make them look stupid, make the investigators look stupid, has never been explained in that theory. But, there is a great willingness to believe that children will say anything in order to please adults, including come up with horror stories out of their nightmares and fairy tales. I think if we look at the coalition of data as it comes together, there's no way children have made these things up. There's no way therapists knew these stories before they heard them. There's no way the parents knew these stories before they came out in nightmares. And yet, the greatest interest I hear from journalists and from other professionals is how come people are questioning children in such a leading way that they're talking them into telling crazy stories. (Summit 1989).

Another point that those who insist on forensic levels of proof for SCS reports do not seem to realize is that clinical psychiatry is rarely aided directly in applying a generic body of facts to a particular case. For instance, we know that violent rape occurs and can be medically proven. But what about Sally who shows up in a psychotherapist's office five years after an alleged rape, having never made a police report or requested medical assistance at the time? How is such a production to be evaluated? There is certainly no smoking gun.

SCS Productions as Clinical Data

My own research during the past several years has led me to apply naturally occurring clinical research methods in an attempt to understand the meaning of SCS reports. I have seen as well the hypotheses and methodology others have applied in their own researchers.

As Walter Young summarized the SCS issue: "If absolutely everything these patients tell us is false, we have stumbled onto a clinical phenomenon most worthy of study and we are honored to study it; if anything these patients tell us is true, we have stumbled onto a phenomenon most horrible and are obliged to study it" (1990, 10). Much of what follows in this chapter is a summary of my findings.

Psychotherapists Provoke Data Both Normal and Skewed

In my observation clinicians react to and manage reports of extreme trauma in three basic ways. In the first, clinicians either overtly signal or frankly tell their patients they either do not want to hear their productions, or in their excessive skepticism are perceived by patients as being just one more human being who does not believe or want to hear about them. In the second, the clinician is so fascinated by the patients' reports that he or she signals or explicitly expresses an earnest desire to hear more and rewards the most bizarre accounts with the greatest level of attention and rapt interest. The third group of clinicians are very sophisticated in how signaling and verbally rewarding patients can produce artifacts in any number of directions. When confronted with any kind of new material, they scrupulously and meticulously draw it out as it appears, whether that is in free association, dreams flashbacks, intrusive thoughts, or the other typical ways in which productions are manifested for examination, exploration, and analysis.

Out of these varying perceptual and response sets arise three kinds of data. To use a metaphor from statistics they can be (1) skewed "left" (suppression of conscious and preconscious material with confabulation of utterances designed to please the therapist), (2) skewed "right" (sensitization to conscious and preconscious material with confabulation of material designed to please the therapist, or (3) a hypothetically "normal" distribution of uttered conscious and preconscious material more closely related to the patient's experience. In other words, anxious subjects will skew their remarks to an overtly skeptical observer in one direction by suppression of productions, partial productions, denial, or misdirection. A second group of subjects will skew their remarks to an eager observer by exaggeration or confabulation. Those subjects in the presence of a neutral, supportively empathic, or reflective observer will report in a more relaxed, less anxious, and therefore less distorted way.

The "skewing left" experience is described by one patient:

When you learn from a therapist that you must say the right things about your satanic cult experience—that it is all "screen memory," that it can't possibly be true, that you must tell the proper version of the story—you're right back in the cult. You start searching for what you're supposed to say. You start suspecting that the therapist is a cult member because what you are being taught all over again is that what you know happened to you in the past is not true, and what is happening now is not happening the way your senses and perceptions tell you it is. This approach destroys trust and invites every kind of confabulation your imagination can provide in the moment just to avoid the kind of punishment you know is coming because you did not say things precisely right.

The price to the patient is that therapy becomes reduced to telling a series of lies in order to be safe or finding "safe" material to talk about in sessions even though it has nothing to do with what is really bothering you. The cost of doing this is more and more anxiety, more and more pressure, more and more need to use dissociation as a way of coping with what you're not allowed to talk about.

Mrs. X, a second patient, told Dr. Y, amid great distress, that she had encountered a "memory" of seeing an infant tortured, murdered, and dismembered at a satanic ceremony. She stated that the infant was hers, that she had been impregnated by the cult leader during an earlier fertility ceremony for the purpose of delivering an infant for sacrifice on a certain date, and when the baby was not born on that date her labor was induced by pitocin. She went into much detail about the baby having been born during the course of a long ritual in which many people witnessed the birth. The baby's heart was cut out and eaten after its death, it was cooked, its entire flesh eaten by the assembled group, and its bones burned in the fire. [Considerable detail is omitted.]

Such a remarkable production, particularly when it meets the congruency criterion of validity, which I will attend to in detail below, ought surely to be "drawn out" through open-ended, nonsuggestive, nonprovoking questions and explored. Such material is certainly laden with possibilities ranging from unresolved oedipal fantasies to primary process, secondary process, derivatives, a germ of the truth, and/or an actual event. When faced with such a strange account, a therapist cannot possibly attach any interpretable significance to it until the production has been extensively explored with the patient.

Instead, the therapist reacted with an angry lecture. She told the patient to give up her fantasies and get out of the hospital. She said she believed the patient was making up such dreadful stories to cover for her malingering. She told the patient that such an event could not have happened because when babies are born they were given birth certificates and when they die they are given death certificates. And if they had been murdered someone would have known about it and reported it to the police and the body would have been found and subjected to autopsy and there would have been witnesses and the perpetrators of the crime would have been seized by the police, tried by a jury, and sent to prison.

While one way to skew SCS productions to the right is to show an exceptional interest in ritual abuse productions, there is an even more risky artifact: that of suggestion through question. The following hypothetical interview, while contrived, is not unknown to those researching in the field.

Therapist: Were there many people there?
Patient: Yes.
Therapist: Were there exactly thirteen?
Patient: Yes.
Therapist: Was there an altar?
Patient: Yes.
Therapist: Was there a circle?
Patient: Yes.
Therapist: Was the circle exactly nine feet in diameter?
Patient: Yes.
Therapist: How do you know?
Patient: Because that's how big it was supposed to be.
Therapist: Were the candles red during this ceremony?
Patient: Yes.
Therapist: Was a baby sacrificed?
Patient: Yes.
Therapist: Were you required to drink urine during this ceremony?
Patient: Yes.

While this example seems ludicrous to a psychiatric clinician, and the specific exchanges contrived, this approach to interviewing is rampant. I expected to encounter such interrogation methods by lay vigilantes in the field, from reporters, from attorneys, and from certain policemen and clergymen, and I did. When I heard this form of interviewing on an audiotape prepared by a very well respected psychiatrist while I was preparing for a court case, and when a second psychiatrist famous in the field of dissociative disorders, told me he asked direct questions as a means of obtaining corroborative information, I was appalled.

Against this background of blurred distinctions and methodological confusion, I turn now to the principle areas of hypothetical venturing in the SCS field, beginning with the heuristics, the largest clinical group.

The Principle Heuristic Hypotheses

The basic heuristic position is quite straightforward: although psychotherapists confront on a daily basis patients whose productions cannot be corroborated, they have objective, clinical methods for evaluating the truth of these utterances. This can be clarified by citing three cases that show the difficulties clinicians and others in the helping professions have had responding to SCS productions. These are "Sybil," "The Woman Who was Buried Alive," and "The Mother Who Smothered Her Children."

"Sybil" was treated over the course of sixteen years by Cornelia Wilbur (Schreiber 1973). When Dr. Wilbur sought to publish in psychiatric journals, she was turned down flatly (Wilbur 1989). When she finally published in the trade press, she was severely admonished by her peers (ibid.). In the long history of multiple personality disorder, however, "Sybil" is a landmark case. It is not only the first adequately documented instance of a multiple personality disorder with a successful resolution, it broke new ground in the field of the sequelae of severe child abuse. As events unfolded, Dr. Wilbur not only chose to believe Sybil's accounts of abuse, but she was also able to obtain corroboration of them in medical records of reported injuries and confirmation of the existence of the physical sites where the alleged abuse took place. This raises two questions: (1) was Sybil any the less abused in fact if Dr. Wilbur had not been able to verify her accounts? and (2) would Sybil have recovered if Dr. Wilbur had maintained a skeptical ("I doubt it"), neutral ("I have no way of knowing if what you are saying is true"), or critical ("It could or might have happened but convince me") therapeutic stance with her? The answer to the first question is obviously no. The reply to the second will be deferred, as it is an important epistemological question in the conduct of psychotherapy and requires considerable elaboration and exploration.

In a recent paper (Greaves 1989a), I cited the clinical example of a woman who was kidnapped from her college campus by two abductors, raped repeatedly, and twice buried alive. Her ordeal lasted approximately two weeks, at which time she escaped. Police authorities believed her story; psychiastrists did not. Because of her ordeal she required numerous hospitalizations for what we now know as post-traumatic stress disorder (PTSD) and was diagnosed as suffering, variously, from paranoid schizophrenia, psychotic depression, and hysterical neurosis. Only much later, after her assailants were captured, tried, and sentenced, and when the woman became wise enough to bring newspaper transcripts from the trial (containing pictures of the burial sites and the hideouts of her abductors) to her hospitalizations, did anyone realize that she was suffering from a traumatic illness. In this instance the patient was clearly misdiagnosed and mistreated by the psychiatric profession over a long period of time because her account was construed as delusional, fabricated, or exaggerated, and this even though she displayed no clinical signs or symptoms of any of the psychiatrically diagnosed disorders, *except for the content of her productions.*

As this is being written a woman is being tried in a metropolitan Atlanta superior court for allegedly smothering four of her children to death over the course of several years. These deaths have been attributed by investigating authorities as sudden infant death syndrome (SIDS). The pattern was discovered by an investigative reporter, writing for the *Atlanta Journal and Constitution,* as part of that newspaper's investigation of Georgia's inexplicably high child (not infant) mortality rate. It was only after the reporter's conjectures were published that the officers of the several police jurisdications and social services jurisdications compared records and arrested the mother as the probable cause of her children's deaths. As the case was unfolded in the court, several witnesses suspected that the children had been murdered and called authorities. A social worker from Georgia's protective services department, presenting such evidence as existed to a Clayton County Juvenile Judge, petitioned that the oldest child be removed from the mother. The judge refused. At age eleven this child became the fourth child of this mother to die of asphyxiation. She was clearly not a SIDS victim.

Such dilemmas—having to make strategic decisions about information one often cannot possibly verify independently at the moment—are daily fare for those in the helping professions.

Dr. Wilbur chose to believe Sybil's reports of child abuse years before she was able to validate it. Indeed, had she not believed Sybil, she would not have sought validation.

In the case of the "Woman Who was Buried Alive," truthful reports that held the key both to her recurring illness and to her recovery were explained away by skeptical psychiatrists who made spurious diagnoses based on their own preconceptions, with disastrous results.

Concerning the "Woman Who Smothered Her Children," a social worker trusted the suspicions of the male lover of the woman's estranged husband—that the woman was murdering her children—but could not meet the judge's stringent test of probable cause, whereupon the woman allegedly murdered her fourth child.

The Notion of "Aggregate Clinical Validity"

Since psychotherapists are constantly confronted with ambiguous productions (incongruent verbal utterances, behavior, and emotional displays) by their patients, as well as their own incongruities in response to the patient, they have, in order to remain oriented to their own sense of what is real, learned to apply several simultaneous tests of validity. Those educated in psychotherapy have been trained to look at the validity of patient productions from at least three concurrent perspectives:

1. Process checks of validity
2. Internal checks of validity
3. External checks of validity

Each of these validity checks contains several subcategories, and the global assessment of these evaluations results in a determination of what kind and level of intervention or interpretation the therapist will make in response to the patient production under consideration.

Process Checks of Validity

In the *cognitive process* check on validity, the therapist weighs content against the patient's manifestations of clear, secondary-process thinking (logical, rational, well-organized, linear thinking) versus disorganized, primary-process thinking, (in which thought processes are digressive, tangential, and purely associative).

In the *affective process* check on validity, the therapist relies on his or her empathic understanding of the emotional life of the patient. Is this patient emotionally bland in the face of traumatic material? Overreactive to minor irritations? Prone to expansive emotional exaggeration? Does this patient's affect match the content of his or her reports?

In the *nonverbal-behavior process* check on validity, the therapist observes whether the patient's body posture, tone of voice, facial expressions, and gestures fit with what is being said.

In the *congruency process* check on validity, the therapist notes whether the cognitive, affective, and behavioral components *in combination* fit the content of the material.

In the *symptom complex* check on validity, the therapist evaluates whether the manifest content of reports related by the patient are cogent in explaining the (reasonably and empirically related) symptoms presented, especially in reports of trauma.

It is not my purpose to examine what judgments clinicians do or should make about the relevant importance of these individual and global observations —subjects thoroughly covered in psychotherapy texts and training—but only to remind the reader that well-trained psychotherapists have these tools available to them. Later I shall turn to two other levels of *process analysis* that bear on the issue of validity.

Internal Checks of Validity

At the level of process checks on validity, one is at one's peak of skills as a psychological *observer*. At the level of internal checks on validity, one is at one's peak of skills as a psychological *thinker*.

At the internal level of validity the therapist must ask himself or herself the following questions. Is the patient's story logically possible? Does the patient contradict him- or herself? Does the account grow in consistent detail with the repeated telling? Does the material and the process grow more congealed in the telling, or more and more disorganized? What and how is being distorted in the telling? What is the derivative information in the telling? What is the primary process and metacommunication in the telling? How is the telling related to the patient's defensive structure? Where and how do resistances and transferences and countertransferences and counterresistances fit into the telling? What has the patient discerned from the therapist that would be pleasing for the therapist to hear (direct and indirect positive countertransference signals and suggestions) and displeasing to hear (direct and indirect counterresistance signals and suggestions)? The answers to these questions go a long way toward ascertaining the truth of a patient's productions.

External Checks of Validity

At this level of checking the clinical validity of patient reports, a clinician is taxed as a *scholar*.

The only data available in the day-to-day treatment of psychotherapy patients is a combination of (1) what the patient reports, (2) what the psychotherapist knows about the intra-active dyad, and (3) what the therapist objectively knows about history, science, anthropology, sociology, and the general humanities. The whole issue of what is presumed to be valid by a therapist is based on a combination of the therapist's ability to establish sufficient rapport with a patient to ensure willing verbal communication, (2) the therapist's knowledge of complex psychodynamics, and (3) the therapist's belief and knowledge about the nature of the external world.

I defer my discussion of external validity until later, because it represents a special case of intersection between clinical and forensic psychiatry requiring substantial elaboration.

From a purely methodological perspective, I believe that those with skewed-left and skewed-right SCS data, arising out of counterresistances and countertransferences (Greaves 1990), are not in possession of a data base sufficiently robust to lead them to external sources of clinical validation.

Other Heuristic Assessments Using the "Process Validity" Paradigm

Before leaving the important area of "aggregate clinical validity," I put before the reader two more aspects of *process validity*.

A particularly interesting concept of process validity is described by Robert Langs (1982). In the model presented below, Langs examines the validity of the *therapeutic process itself*, which enables the therapist to stay on course.

As Langs puts it:

> Without a validating clinical methodology, psychotherapy is bound to be overrun by the prejudices and idiosyncratic thinking of the therapist. Errors will go undetected, since most therapists assume they are working in correct fashion with their patients except on rare occasion. The therapist's narcissistic investment in his or her own ideas is likely to blunt his or her capacity to detect interventions to which the patient has not responded favorably. Thus sound psychotherapy cannot exist without a validating process. (ibid. 187)

He continues:

> All too often, there is an attitude of undue certainty or an implicit assumption of the correctness of a hypothesis, especially once it has been offered to the patient. Frequently, no special effort at validation is undertaken. Alternatively, the search is for the slightest sign of agreement or elaboration, and disagreement is treated as a sign of the patient's defenses rather than a signal that the therapist might well have been in error. (ibid. 202)

To summarize a long and careful exposition, Langs maintains that when therapists are making correct interventions *vis à vis* patient productions, confirmation of this correctness will manifest itself in the process through derivative responses, utterances with unconscious meaning to the patient. Ultimately these derivative responses will confirm not only when the therapist is on the right track, but that the therapeutic alliance is strong. Langs goes on to note that while conscious agreement with a therapist's interpretation or intervention cannot be taken as validating confirmation (since such agreements could easily be nothing more than efforts to please the therapist), conscious disagreement (the risky position) can be taken as disconfirming. As Langs puts it, "In most instances a negation of the therapist's intervention is followed by the absence of derivative confirmation. Thus, surface disagreements should be taken as a sign that an intervention is likely to have been in error" (ibid. 212). He goes on to state that only on "rare occasions . . . this type of negation proves to be highly defensive" (ibid. 212).

This is an important point. I have repeatedly encountered psychotherapists who have boasted about how "strong" their interpretations were and "so right on" that their patients fled from therapy in panic, at moments of great insight. What they failed to grasp is that their patients' "great insight" was how potentially dangerous their therapist was to them in terms of recapitulating traumatic persons and events in their past.

The second additional process validation is that of *symptom reduction.* Earlier I talked about the cogency of patients' reports in terms of explaining a particular symptom complex as an indicator of validity. Suppose now that a therapist explores with a patient the alleged history of a traumatically induced symptom and during the course of the working-on and working-through process, the symptom reduces or completely disappears. This would certainly appear to be at least partial confirmation of the psychological accuracy of historical events.

For example:

> An adult patient is phobic about going near a bread toaster. She will not even enter the quadrant of a kitchen where a toaster is located. She discovers upon recollection a memory that her grandmother used to burn her fingers on the top of the toaster for "being bad." Realizing that her grandmother is no longer near

the toaster, that it is not her grandmother's toaster at all, that she is not in her grandmother's house, that her grandmother is in fact dead, the patient begins to make toast for her family for the first time in many years.

This brings us to the essence of the heuristic argument. If a psychotherapy patient's productions meet the tests of congruent validity, *and* if such productions are treated as true, *and* if such a patient enjoys substantial improvement in condition as a result of interacting with the therapist, the main line of their productions are considered to be true. Most SCS productions meet the criteria of aggregate clinical validity. One would suppose that such phenomena would be difficult to dismiss; however, therapists with a very different psychiatric perspective manage to do so.

The Nihilistic Hypotheses

Nihilists are those in the SCS field who believe and attempt to prove— sometimes, it seems, at any cost—that SCS reports are not true. The two principal assumptions of the SCS nihilists are: (1) the productions can be satisfactorily accounted for beyond their manifest content and (2) there is no "smoking gun." These assumptions form the basis for the several hypotheses nihilists invoke to explain (away) SCS reports.

The "Incorporation" Hypothesis

Incorporation refers to the unconscious internalization of information (knowledge, material) that one later falsely "remembers" as one's own. For instance, a songwriter or lyricist may compose a melody or a poem, believing it to be original, only to be embarrassed later to discover that he or she has "recomposed" another's work. A classical example of incorporation occurs in Chris Sizemore's *I'm Eve* (Sizemore and Pittillo 1977). She seems unconsciously to quote verses from Walter Benton's *This is My Beloved* (Benton 1943), a poem known by millions of people around the world.

Chris Sizemore ("Eve") has been seeing her psychiatrist, Corbett Thigpen, for some time. She has been through a divorce; she has met a new lover. To quote from the manuscript:

During this time she wrote many poems to him [Don], in one of which, *My Beloved*, she wrote,

> *Because cold negative death*
> *Creeps in my heart to hide,*
> *And only your love*
> *Can turn the tide.*

(Sizemore and Pitillo 1977 309)

Compare this now to line ten of the opening of Benton's famous poem:

Because slow negative death
Withers the world—
And only yes can turn the tide.

(Benton 1943 3)

Sizemore's poem is called *My Beloved;* Benton's poem is called *This Is My Beloved.* (This line was borrowed from Benton again for the title of the memorable song in the Broadway hit, *Kismet.*) It is highly unlikely that Mrs. Sizemore would have brought certain embarrassment on herself by claiming another's poem as her own in a high-profile autobiography.

Consider, now, the following example from a patient's journal:

Come forth under the stars, & take your fill of love!
I am above you and in you. My ecstasy is yours. My joy is to see your joy.

Compare this passage with Aleister Crowley's *Book of the Law* (1976).

12. Come forth, o children, under the stars, & take your fill of love!
13. I am above you and in you. My ecstasy is yours. My joy is to see your joy.

This journal entry is not an example of incorporation of the Crowley passage for two evident reasons.

First of all, note the formal properties of the patient's production in relation to the source material. *It is literal recall.* Incorporations, because they arise out of unconscious processes, always undergo distortion, as in Chris Sizemore's poem.

Second, this patient clearly reports having learned these passages by rote, from a scroll, during "training sessions," and knows the author as Frater Perdurabo, which was Aleister Crowley's ceremonial name. She credibly purports never to have heard of Crowley and was incredulous when I brought her a copy of *Liber Legis.*

Incorporation, as a clinical phenomenon, represents a form of *source amnesia,* a phenomenon well known in experimental hypnosis. A subject is hypnotized and given instructions to experience or say or do something after the trance. The subject carries out or "experiences" what has been instructed, yet authentically appears unable to discern why the experience or action has taken place or, alternatively, misattributes it in a seemingly believing way to an event or cause suggested by the hypnotist.

Since many SCSs seen clinically suffer from multiple personality disorder (MPD), and since it is widely believed and accepted that those suffering from MPD are highly prone to spontaneous, autohypnotic trance states (Bliss 1980,

1986; Putnam 1989; Ross 1989), it is a cogent hypothesis that the clinical content of SCS productions may be attributable to source amnesia. The question then becomes: "What is the source of the alleged 'source amnesia' in SCS reports?"

It is not *Michelle Remembers* (Smith and Pazder 1980), as is suggested by Ganaway (1989, 1990) and Lanning (1989); it is not the debunked *Satan's Underground* (Stratford 1988); it is not the *Necronomicon* (Schlangecraft 1977); it is not Crowley's *Magick In Theory and Practice* (Crowley 1924).

What is being reported by these patients is a variously integrated mix of kabbalistic teachings (an old Jewish secret tradition that the mystical properties of the world can be expressed in numbers), ceremonial magick, sex magick, "brainwashing" techniques, a peculiar brand of theosophy that emphasizes blood and death rites in the core rituals of its system of worship, and an organizational and secrecy structure patterned much along the lines of secret societies (e.g., Daraul 1961; Goodrick-Clarke 1985; Howe 1978; Spence 1960; Waite 1972, 1987; Zalewski 1988).

Those who attempt to explain the extraordinary commonalities between satanic cult survivors' reports by way of *incorporation* must be able to cite a specific source for the incorporation, as my example of Sizemore's incorporation of Benton. One cannot simply make references to works the contents of do nothing to solve the "eyewitness problem."

By the "eyewitness problem" I mean this:

1. SCS patients nearly all state (testify) they were taught what they know by their parents or close relatives.

2. They profess to have no knowledge about any book or author I or others mention in the course of therapy.

3. There is no single book or movie that contains the material of even a single patient.

4. An extensive reading and integration of many occult source documents over the course of considerable time is required in order to reconstruct the basic tenets and practices with which nearly every alleged SCS seems readily familiar. It seems inconceivable that every SCS familiar with the intricate and consistent theosophy of secret societies and black magic has learned what he or she knows solely on the basis, if ever on the basis, of unremembered scholarly pursuits.

The "Screen Memory" Hypothesis

Screen memories refer to real or fantasy memories that disguise a deeper conflict. Greenson describes a patient whose accurate memories of happy events in his childhood "screened" him from the truth of realizing he was not the favorite child (Greenson 1967). Ganaway reports that a patient was so disturbed that a beloved grandmother would read scary detective magazines to her that she would rather believe and report a screen fantasy that she herself, as a young child, had witnessed or passively participated in the slaying of twelve children from her Sunday school (Ganaway 1989 211; see also Noll 1990).

The problem is SCS patients produce no discernable pattern of screen memories. Life at home was hell. Life in the cult was hell. They did this in the cult; they did the same at home. What then is the function of the alleged screen? Indeed, where is the screen? This hypothesis does not fit the facts.

The "Urban Legend" Hypothesis

Urban legends are "small tales," often first told as a hoax or a joke, spread by gossip and retold as true by those wishing either mischievously to perpetuate the hoax or joke or by those who actually believe the story to be true. The honest, earnest, emotionally congruent telling of these tales by a naive believer gives them their ultimate persuasive power (Brunvand 1986).

An urban legend I have heard in various forms since childhood centers on New York children who take winter vacations to Florida with their parents. While there, their parents purchase cute little baby alligators. Having no real place to keep alligators in their New York apartments, or tiring of having to care for them, the children would, so the story goes, dispose of them by flushing them down the toilet, where they subsequently wound up in the city sewers. In this warm, damp environment, the alligators naturally flourished, and grew into enormous and dangerous creatures that leave the sewers at night, pushing up manhole covers, in search of pet dogs and cats and, yes, even young children to eat. Another urban legend, which began to circulate widely about the time the sale of home microwave ovens began to soar, is that of a certain woman (in the version I heard) of Charleston, West Virginia, who had blown her cat to bits in her microwave when she attempted to dry his fur following a bath. The account I heard was quite graphic about the aftermath of the cat's explosion, the original source of which was attributed to an appliance repairman. In most cases the originator of what comes to be an urban legend is never identified. In some, the originator admits to the hoax or private joke or embarrassing experience, astonished that what started out as a sort of personal humor between two people was taken so seriously.

Reports of "ritual abuse survivors" seem to me very different from "urban legends" in several particulars (Brunvand 1990, personal correspondence):

1. They are told either as first-person victim accounts or as first-person eye-witness accounts.
2. They are told not only as true, but with often terrifying emotion.

3. The reporters of these stories often provide some sort of proof of what they are saying, such as scars on their bodies.

4. They tell not one, but many such stories.

5. The stories they tell, though ghastly in nature, do not circulate in the general culture in the detail with which they are told.

6. The stories are not brief. A single story may take from one to many hours to tell.

7. Unlike "urban legends" there is no measure of fun or delight in them. There is no punch line, no "gotcha!" outcome. One never laughs at these stories or takes any form of delight in hearing them.

Contamination and Contagion

Contamination is a form of incorporation in which a person unconsciously forms images from the utterances of others, then assimilate them as his or her own. Persons with tenuous ego boundaries and a high propensity for identification with the emotional states of others, and subjects under hypnosis, are particularly prone to contaminated recall.

I have observed that in group therapy situations where ritual abuse material is being discussed, some individuals remain quite clear that the material does not belong to them, but others repeat the material, like parrots, as their own, quite unaware of their incorporations. A therapist working with several ritual abuse survivors living together (as in an inpatient setting), thus familiar with the history and productions of each, can rather easily identify and trace such incorporations. However, a therapist who has no such access to the group flow of information may spot incorporated contaminations only with much difficulty. These partially informed therapists may be prone to "overincorporating" information, confusing crucial similarities and differences in reports.

Contamination through hypnosis may occur when the hypnotist allows his or her thoughts into the subject's mind by way of subtle comments, suggestions, signs, signals, cues, or clues.

Contagion refers to verbal or behavioral acting-out that is (often unconsciously) reinforced by secondary gain. This phenomenon is well known on inpatient psychiatric units. A patient in a state of emotional crisis attracts the attention of several staff members. Another patient, unconsciously experiencing the loss of immediate staff attention, loses emotional control, thus attracting staff to him- or herself. Such situations escalate fairly quickly.

The "ESP" Hypothesis

The phenomenon of the production of detailed, cross-personal, interlocking ritual abuse reports in the presence of open-ended questions, and the failure of various incorporation hypotheses to adequately account for them, has led one respected colleague in the direction of a novel hypothesis.

In order to attempt to present this view, I offer a condensed vignette of several discussions we have had:

Colleague: What I think is happening is that patients are reading our minds.
Me: There's no scientific basis for that.
Colleague: There's a literature on ESP.
Me: Yes. And it's very scant and ambiguous. If test subjects cannot even read "Zener cards" with accuracy when the sender is trying his dead level best to "send" them to a supposedly "sensitive" subject, how could subjects "read" the enormous detail of a cult ceremony?
Colleague: I think they're "gifted."
Me: They [MPD patients] are certainly intuitional. But intuition is not ESP. Intuition is the reading of cues and clues and signals that others overlook.
Colleague: I think it goes beyond that in MPD.
Me: Allowing purely for the sake of argument that MPD patients might be able to read minds, what could there have been in the beginning to read? Before I had the slightest notion about this material?
Colleague: In that case I think they read our unconscious mind.
Me: But unconscious processes are not temporal or orderly.
Colleague: They are made temporal and orderly when they begin to enter the conscious mind.
Me: But I've never even had a dream about a satanic ritual, or in a daydream, or in a flashback, or in an intrusive thought. Such material has never come up in my own therapy. Were this material to exist somewhere in my unconscious mind, somewhere it should have made itself manifest in my experience. I don't see where there is anything to read.
Colleague: Some things are buried so deep in even a therapist's mind that it takes a detector to detect it.

This example is instructive, not only for its novelty, but for its all but complete disregard of logic and the "principle of parsimony," also known as "Occam's razor." William of Occam, a fourteenth-century Franciscan, formulated one of the most important principles in the long evolution of modern science: "What can be explained in fewer principles is explained needlessly by more" (Jones 1952).

The "Collective Unconscious" Hypothesis

A hypothesis that requires fewer assumptions than the ESP hypothesis is that persons identifying themselves as satanic cult survivors are reading not the mind of their therapists, but their own unconscious mind. What provokes this? And, why are the productions so precise? Neither Jung nor Plato ever intended that the *Eidos*, the *archetypes*, were ever expressed or expressible in more than general forms. Jung's term is *facultas praeformandi*, "a possibility of representation." Jung goes on to say, "The representations themselves are not inherited, only the forms." In short, this hypothesis does not account for the level of specific content found in SCS reports (Campbell 1971).

The "Chinese Menu" Hypothesis

The genius of Chinese cuisine is that there are only half a dozen methods of Chinese cooking and each, in turn, can be combined in any possible array of textures and flavors. Hence the meal can be cooked and delivered in moments. By analogy, it can be argued that any who have some notions of candles, wax, colors, seasons, and paraphilias can combine them into "menus," according to the season and to the perceived disposition of the therapist.

The problem with this hypothesis is that it does not explain how the therapist, without ordering off the menu, without even seeing the menu, keeps getting served the same entree, prepared the same way. The First Marriage to the Beast, for example, *always* contains the same ingredients. SCSs learned their recipes somewhere.

The "Personal Myth" Hypothesis

Stanley Krippner of the Saybrook Institute in San Francisco, offered yet another possible explanation of SCS productions during the course of our correspondence (1990). Krippner, a psychologist with strong anthropological interests, points to the strong defensive proclivities of human beings to develop "personal myths" about themselves as a way of coping with trauma. "Myths," according to Joseph Campbell, are not "lies" at all, but well-constructed allegories and poetical forms that express "underlying truths" in a way utterable and conceivable in no other way. Krippner suggests that individuals create powerful myths about their lives which they attempt to live out, and which form into psychological complexes and belief systems of such compelling force that they are subject to analysis.

What Dr. Krippner does not account for is the recurring cycle of reports of SCSs seem to be sharing not a personal, but a *group* myth. As myths vary from culture to culture, rituals reported by SCSs vary from coven to coven with enough of the same ingredients to give them a connection.

The "Propagation of Rumor" Hypothesis

Jeffrey Victor, a sociologist, does an excellent job of researching how a report that an alleged teen victim was going to be sacrificed by a "satanic cult" was circulated by the newspapers, word of mouth, and police departments across a several-county area in three northeastern states, about the public hysteria that ensued, and the composure of the local sheriff's department in containing these claims (Victor 1990). The locus of the panic was in Jamestown, New York, on Friday the thirteenth of May 1988. Victor likened what happened to a buffalo stampede (ibid. 287), and was surprised to find in the course of his research evidence of twenty-one earlier stampedes (ibid. 288).

A retired police investigator, who knew of these "stampedes," said to me: "Certainly were I to be a satanist planning to murder someone and my plot had been widely circulated in the press, I would change my tactics and misdirect any information I could. I certainly would not carry out my original plan in a goldfish bowl. So the predicted murders didn't occur, so what?"

The point again is that the sociological phenomenon of rumor propagation seems to have no bearing on the clinical productions of SCSs, unless it can be shown that SCS productions have the formal properties of rumor. They do not as far as I can tell, and I have examined this above in my discussion of "urban legends."

In the final analysis, labeling does not explain, and certainly does not *explain away*, phenomena. It only points to concepts, consensual definitions, or provides models to investigate for ascertaining if a process or phenomenon is similar to what is already known or understood. Labels or models must be validated both definitionally and empirically before they can be accepted as *complete explanations for phenomena*.

The Apologist Hypotheses

Like the heuristics, clinical apologists see many SCS productions as meeting at least seven of the eight clinical criteria of validity. They find SCS productions congruent in affect, cognition, behavior, symptom, process, and symptom reduction. On purely clinical grounds, apologists cannot conceive of how this could be possible unless SCSs are objectively reporting actual experiences, especially when these same patients display prominent post-traumatic stress disorder (PTSD) symptoms when dealing with this alleged memory material. In short, apologists point out that there are very good reasons to believe that transgeneration satanic cults may well exist.

My particular research interest in the field has been in trying to close the circle of clinical validity through the resolution of *external validity* issues. I have collected thousands of pages of writings on witchcraft, secret societies, occult history, sorcery, black magick, cults and cult-related crimes, ceremonial magick, kabbalism, sex magick, alleged satanic cult activities, possession states and attended police seminars and psychiatric seminars from coast to coast that focused on the subject of transgenerational satanic cults.

From an empirical standpoint, I find an enormous amount of inductive, circumstantial evidence that such cults, in some form, do indeed exist.

I proceed cautiously below to avoid contaminating or skewing the data. This poses a most difficult methodological dilemma. To answer nihilists I would have to present exhaustive empirical data. But to do so is to invite the "indoctrination" of objective information and contaminate the data base. If I were to elaborate on the highly idiosyncratic jargon that distinguishes SCS productions from all others, that jargon would soon be taught to patients by unwitting therapists, who had read this chapter. Patients suspecting themselves to be SCSs may use such language, using this chapter as a source, when, in fact, they never learned it elsewhere. My solution is to cite only phenomena that everyone in the field has encountered and withhold certain empirical evidence that would strengthen my case at the expense of SCS patients. This principle is clinically valid *even if satanic cults do not exist*. The cost of curiosity can be too high.

The Physical Evidence

Through police sources I obtained a copy of a segment of a motion picture film that seems to record a cult ceremony, a human sacrifice, the extraction and cannibalistic devouring of the victim's liver by several people, and a subsequent sexual blood orgy. Both my sources and I consider it authentic.

Also through police sources, I have witnessed with a colleague a video tape made by members of the Chicago police department investigating two alleged satanic ceremonial sites to which they were directed by SCSs. I saw the following on this video tape:

> The [ceremonial] site was located in an isolated wooded area, accessible only by a long walk down a railroad track to a certain spot, then by turning quite some distance into the trees. The point at which to turn was marked by a single blue ribbon, tied to a tree branch. At the site was a clearing, completely invisible from the railway. In the middle of the site was a pile of stones on which were wax drippings of several colors. In front of the mound of stones was a circle of rocks, and a shallow pit, where obviously a fire or fires had been set. The ground in the immediate area was worn bare, indicating that the site had been used many times before, and recently. Beside the altar were the skeletons of several small animals, laid side by side in a row. As the officers, heavily armed and dressed in military fatigues, fanned out to explore the area, they found a number of security precautions, including carefully concealed patches of barbed wire, trip wires, and sentry platforms in the trees, much like deer blinds used by bow and arrow hunters, though this was not deer-hunting country. It was impossible to reach any other conclusion, based on the physical evidence, than that this site was being used for nefarious and deadly purposes. The second site was even more remote and contained less elaborate security features.

As I viewed this material, the hair on my arms and on the nape of my neck stood on end. I had heard many descriptions of such ceremonial sites in the relative comfort of my office.

Arthur Lyons (1988) has done a very creditable job of keeping up with the "satanic cult newsfront," but in my opinion he treats some forensic physical evidence in very odd ways. For example, there was a famous invasion of an alleged satanic worship site in Lucas County, Ohio (Toledo area), in which the sheriff's department excavated the area on the day before the summer solstice (June 20, 1985), for the overt purpose of uncovering evidence and preventing further bloodshed at the site. Among the items found were animal bones, a headless doll with nails driven through its feet, a pile of sixty male children's left shoes, and a nine-foot cross with ligatures attached. In a house adjoining the property were found drawings of a goat's head, pentagrams, and an anatomy dissection book. While Lyons minimizes these discoveries, I find them quite remarkable.

I have puzzled as to how two researchers could look at the same data and draw such diverse conclusions. The difference, again, lies in the data base. Lyons is in search of the "smoking gun"; I have spent four thousand hours listening to patient reports while wondering if evidence to support them existed. Lyons is served up the evidence on sterling and is unable to evaluate its significance. (See particularly Kahaner [1988] for his expanded discussion of "The Lucas County Incident.")

The point to be made in terms of "forensic validity" standards of truth is that the claim that there is "no physical evidence" to support SCS reports is invalid.

The Language Base

SCSs consistently employ terminology that in twenty years of clinical practice and in twenty-three years of liberal and scientific education, I have never heard elsewhere. I have collected some eighty different words and phrases of this type. I have no reason to believe that every SCS knows them all, but when SCSs do employ these terms they use them consistently.

SCSs have a wide range of "holidays" or "ritual dates" or "ceremonial dates" and often call them by different names than do the Christian, Jewish, secular, or pagan calendars. For instance, Christmas Eve is not called by that name among SCSs, nor is Valentine's Day; SCSs have other names for these dates and know both.

SCSs have an elaborate and idiosyncratic language connected with alleged satanic ceremonies, a consistent description of the specific objects involved, the names of the specific objects, the symbolism and meaning of the ceremonies, and the conduct and setting of the ceremonies. Nearly all of these can be traced to written occult sources.

The Source Material

Dr. Ganaway (1989, 1990) and other nihilists search for the meaning of SCS productions in the psychodynamic distortions of ego defense mechanisms. I think they are wrong to construct such inelegant assumptions where the more parsimonious solution is to link SCS productions with objective data. For instance, concerning the purpose and symbolic meaning of animal and human sacrifice, one easily locates in Crowley:

Chapter XII: Of the Bloody Sacrifice and Matters Cognate

The blood is the life . . . any living thing is a storehouse of energy varying in quantity according to the size and health . . . at the death of the animal this energy is liberated suddenly. The animal should therefore be killed within the Circle, or the Triangle, as the case may be, so that its energy cannot escape. . . . For the highest spiritual working one must accordingly choose that victim which contains the greatest and purest force. A male child of perfect innocence and high intelligence is the most satisfactory and suitable victim. . . . Frater Perdurabo made this particular sacrifice [very many times between 1912 and 1928]. (Crowley 1924 92–95)

In another work Crowley (1973 478–80) talks openly about one of his experiences with debauchery: "Time: a fine evening in June, just one and twenty years ago. Place: Paris, just off the Place des Tertres." Crowley goes on to describe a scene in which a naked woman in her forties rubs roquefort cheese on her body and allows herself to be attacked by hungry rats. She bites the rats' necks and otherwise kills them for half an hour until she is the victor.

As Crowley describes it: "It was not so easy a victory as I have perhaps described it, once she slipped on the slime and came down with a thud; and at the end blood squirted from innumerable bites . . . Summary: a pleasant time was had by all" (ibid. 480). He adds: "Note for political economists: the woman took 10,000 franks . . . three weeks in hospital and three weeks' holiday between the shows" (ibid.). He cursorily identifies the woman as the mistress of a French Minister whose own contribution to the collective depravity is to see that the woman's daughters are raised in an exclusive convent.

Colin Wilson, a prominent scholar and historian of the occult, vividly describes Crowley's allowing his children to witness sexual rites, "believing it keep leave them free from repressions" (1987 132), and goes on to describe the sacrifice of a cat:

Loveday, as a high priest, had to kill the cat. Invocations went on for two hours. Then Raoul [Loveday's first name] took a . . . big Gurkha knife . . . and went towards . . . the altar. When he slashed the cat's throat, it escaped and ran around the room. It had to be anesthetized before Lovejoy could complete the sacrifice. Then Leah held a bowl under the throat to catch the blood. Crowley dipped his finger in the blood and traced the pentagram on Loveday's forehead, after which he handed Loveday a silver cup of the blood, which the high priest drained to the last drop. (ibid. 132–33)

In another of Wilson's researches of Crowley's self-recorded activities, he reports the following: "Oliver Wilkinson mentions that among Crowley's papers, there is a description of tying a negro to a tree, cutting a hole in his stomach, then inserting his penis" (ibid. 153).

Conclusion

The subject of satanic cult survivor's productions has become a matter of utmost interest and concern among those practicing in the field of dissociative disorders. One can emphasize by equivocal apostrophes many terms in dealing with these phenomena: "alleged" "SCSs," "iatrogenesis," "skewed data," "defensive distortions," and "urban legends," to name a few. Applying simple names to complex psychological, interpersonal, and social-psychological processes will not lead to clarifications about these productions. The purpose of this chapter has been to pursue and clarify the equivocations of terminology and empirical methodologies that have led to the general lack of clinically based external scholarship in the field.

The author of this chapter wishes to recognize the contributions of many readers over the course of its preparation: Colin Ross, M.D., Jeffrey Brandsma, Ph.D., Richard Maser, Christine Comstock, Helen Friedman, Ph.D., Mimi Dixon, Walter Young, M.D., and numerous satanic cult survivors.

References

Adler, Margot. 1986. *Drawing Down the Moon: Witches, Druids, Goddess Worshipers, and Other Pagans in America Today.* Boston: Beacon Press.

Benton, Walter. 1943. *This is My Beloved.* New York: Knopf.

Bliss, Eugene. 1980. "Multiple Personalities: A Report of 14 Cases with Implications for Schizophrenia and Hysteria." *Archives of General Psychiatry* 37: 1388–97.

———. 1986. *Multiple Personality, Allied Disorders, and Hypnosis.* New York: Oxford University Press.

Braun, Bennett. 1989. Comments. *Ritual child abuse: A professional overview.* Ukia, Ca.: Cavalcade Productions (videotape).

Brunvand, J. H. 1986. *The Choking Doberman and Other "New" Urban Legends.* New York: W.W. Norton.

———. 1990. Personal communication.

Campbell, Joseph, ed. 1971. *The Portable Jung.* New York: Vintage.

Crowley, Aleister 1924. *Magick In theory and practice.* Reprint. New York: Dover, 1976.

———. 1973. *777 and other qabalistic writings.* Reprint. York Beach, Maine: Samuel Weiser, 1988.

———. 1979. *The Confessions of Aleister Crowley,* ed. J. Symonds and Kenneth Grant. Reprint. London: Arkana, 1989.

———. 1980. *Book 4.* York Beach, Me: Samuel Weiser.

———. 1988. *The Law Is for All.* Las Vegas: Falcon Press.

Crowley, Aleister. 1909. *The Book of the Law.* Reprint. Kings Beach, Ca.: Thelema,. 1976.

———. 1989. *Magick without Tears.* Las Vegas: Golden Dawn.

Daraul, Arkon. 1961. *A History of Secret Societies.* Secaucus, N.J.: Citadel Press.

Ganaway, George 1989. "Historical Truth Versus Narrative Truth: Clarifying the Role of Exogenous Trauma in the Etiology of Multiple Personality and Its Variants." *Dissociation* 2, no. 4: 205–20.

———. 1990. "A Psychodynamic Look at Alternative Explanations for Satanic Ritual Abuse in MPD Patients." Paper delivered at Seventh International Conference on Multiple Personality/Dissociative States. Chicago, November.

Goodrick-Clarke, N. A. 1985. *The Occult Roots of Nazism.* Wellingborough, U.K.: Aquarian Press.

Goodwin, Jean. 1990. "Sadistic Sexual Abuse: Illustration from the Marquis de Sade." Paper delivered at Seventh International Conference on Multiple Personality/Dissociative States. Chicago, November.

Gould, Catherine. 1989. Comments. *Ritual Child Abuse: A Professional Overview.* Ukia, Ca.: Cavalcade Productions (videotape).

Greaves, George. 1989a. "Observations on the Claim of Iatrogenesis in the Promulgation of MPD: A Discussion." *Dissociation* 2, no. 2: 99–104.

———. 1989b. "A Cognitive-Behavioral Approach to the Treatment of MPD Ritually Abused Satanic Cult Survivors." Paper presented at Sixth International Conference on Multiple Personality/Dissociative States. Chicago, October.

———. 1990. "Counterresistance Phenomena in the Treatment of MPD." Paper delivered at the Seventh International Conference on Multiple Personality/Dissociative States. Chicago, November.

Greenson, R. R. 1967. *The Technique and Practice of Psychoanalysis.* Madison, Conn.: International Universities Press.

Hill, Sally, and Jean Goodwin. 1989. "Satanism: Similarities between Patient Accounts and Pre-Inquisition Historical Sources." *Dissociation* 2, no. 1: 39–44.

Hicks, Robert 1990a. "Police Pursuit of Satanic Crime: I." *Skeptical Inquirer* 14:(2)276–86.

———. 1990b. "Police Pursuit of Satanic Crime: II." *Skeptical Inquirer,* 14(2)378–89.

Howe, Ellie. 1978. *The Magicians of the Golden Dawn: A Documentary History of a Magical Order 1887–1923.* York Beach, Me: Samuel Weiser.

Kahaner, Larry. 1988. *Cults That Kill.* New York: Warner Books.

Jones, W. T. 1952. *A History of Western Philosophy.* Reprint. New York: Harcourt Brace, 1969.

Kraig, D. 1988. *Modern Magick: Eleven Lessons in the High Magickal Arts*. St. Paul, Minn.: Llewellyn Publications.

Krippner, Samuel. 1990. Personal communication.

Lanning, Kenneth 1989. "Satanic, Occult, Ritualistic Crime: A Law-Enforcement Perspective." *The Police Chief*, October. 88–107.

Langs, Robert 1982. *Psychotherapy: A Basic Text*. New York: Jason Aronson.

LaVey, Anton 1969. *The Satanic Bible*. New York: Avon.

———. 1972. *The Satanic Rituals*. New York: Avon.

———. 1989. *The Satanic Witch*. Los Angeles: Feral House.

Lyons, Arthur 1988. *Satan Wants You: The Cult of Devil Worship in America*. New York: Mysterious Press.

Mulhern, Sherrill 1990. "Training Courses and Seminars on Satanic Ritual Abuse: A Critical Review." Paper delivered at Seventh International Conference on Multiple Personality/Dissociative States. Chicago, November.

Noll, Richard 1990. *Bizarre Diseases of the Mind*. New York: Berkeley.

Putnam, Frank. 1989. *Diagnosis and Treatment of Multiple Personality Disorder*. New York: Guilford.

Regardie, Israel 1970. *The Eye of the Triangle: An Interpretation of Aleister Crowley*. Reprint. Las Vegas: Falcon Press, 1989.

———. 1980. *Ceremonial Magic: A Guide to the Mechanisms of Ritual*. Wellingborough, U.K.: Aquarian Press.

Ross, Colin. 1989. *Multiple Personality Disorder: Diagnosis, Clinical Features, and Treatment*. New York: John Wiley and Sons.

Schlangecraft, Inc. 1977. *Necronomicon*. Edited by Simon. Reprint: New York: Avon Books, 1979.

Schreiber, Flora Rheta. 1973. *Sybil*. Chicago: Regnery.

Schueler, G. (1985). *Enochian magick: A practical manual*. St. Paul, Minn.: Llewellyn Publications.

Sizemore, Chris, and Pittillo. Elen Sain. 1977. *I'm Eve*. New York: Doubleday.

Smith, Michelle, and Lawrence Pazder. 1980. *Michelle Remembers*. New York: Congdon and Lattes.

Spence, Lewis. 1960. *An Encyclopedia of Occultism*. Secaucus, N.J.: Citadel Press.

Stratford, Lauren. 1988. *Satan's Underground*. Eugene, Ore.: Harvest House.

Summit, Roland. 1989. Comments. *Ritual Child Abuse: A Professional Overview*. Ukia, Ca.: Cavalcade Productions (videotape).

Terry, Maury. 1987. *The Ultimate Evil: An Investigation of America's Most Dangerous Satanic Cult*. Garden City, N.Y.: Doubleday.

Victor, Jeffery S. 1990. "The Spread of Satanic-Cult Rumors." *Skeptical Inquirer* 14:287–291.

Waite, A. E. 1972. *The Book of Black Magic*. York Beach, Me: Samuel Weiser.

———. 1987. *Hermetic Papers of A. E. Waite: The Unknown Writings of a Modern Mystic*, ed. R. A. Gilbert. Wellingborough, U. K.: Aquarian Press.

Warnke, Michael 1972. *The Satan Seller*. Plainfield, N.J.: Logos International.

Wilbur, Cornelia. 1989. "The Making of Sybil." Address delivered at First Regional Conference on Multiple Personality/Dissociation. Alexandria, Va., June.

Wilson, Colin. 1987. *Aleister Crowley: The Nature of the Beast*. Wellingborough, U.K.: Aquarian Press.

Young, Walter. 1990. President's Report. International Society for the Study of Multiple Personality and Dissociation, Executive Council Meeting. Ottawa, Ontario, May.

Young, Walter, "Patients Reporting Ritual Abuse in Childhood: A Clinical Syndrome." *International Journal of Child Abuse and Neglect,* 2nd Quarter, 1991.

Zalewski, P. M. 1988. *Secret Inner Order Rituals of the Golden Dawn.* Phoenix, Az.: Golden Dawn Press.

4

Child Forensic Evaluation and Claims of Ritual Abuse or Satanic Cult Activity: A Critical Analysis

Robert Kinscherff, Ph.D.
Richard Barnum, M.D.

Introduction

Forensic mental health involvement in cases of alleged ritual child abuse is fundamentally the same as forensic evaluation in any other form of child abuse in which the abuser terrorizes the victim. Similarly, evaluation of an adolescent accused of a criminal or delinquent act associated with an occult or satanic belief system is guided by the same principles that guide forensic assessment of any youth whose functioning includes deviant behavior associated with an unusual belief system.

We understand "ritualized" maltreatment to be abuse inflicted upon a victim in a repetitive, systematic, stylized, and methodical fashion. The characteristics of the abuse, rather than a specific link to any metaphysical beliefs or religious practices, make it "ritualized." Therefore, maltreatment can be "ritualized" even when it is not associated with or motivated by a specifically metaphysical belief system. Ritual maltreatment may be related to highly idiosyncratic or even psychotic beliefs or delusions held by a single perpetrator. It may reflect the intimidation of child victims, the process required for sadistic or perverse sexual gratification, and/or the expression of a more organized belief system in which the ritual is also a means to secure other goals such as special powers.

Some ritualized maltreatment is structured by the metaphysical practices and beliefs of the perpetrators. In such cases the maltreatment serves a symbolic or metaphysical purpose, exclusively or perhaps in combination with other purposes. A "cult" is involved in the practices when the motivating metaphysical practices and beliefs are shared by a group of persons whose association is characterized by the features of totalist groups. These include polarized thinking, rigid enforcement of boundaries, organization around a hierarchical or charismatic leadership, and suppression of individual autonomy. It is the totalist group process, boundary and member monitoring and control, centrality of a metaphysical system, and often the domination of a charismatic leader that makes the group a "cult" rather than simply a criminal gang or conspiracy. Some cults also engage in criminal acts and conspiracy, and that conduct may or may not be specifically motivated by the metaphysical beliefs held by the group.

The content of the belief system alone does not make it a "cult"; the content of "cult" beliefs may be highly variable. Some cults may be satanic, but many cults in the United States that have engaged in dangerous conduct including torture and homicide are not satanic. The longevity and structural stability of cults may also vary widely, as can the degrees of secrecy maintained about their operations or even their existence. Many cults are also "occult" in the sense that they shroud beliefs and practices in secrecy, and the metaphysical rituals utilized are intended to yield various results through supernatural means. Again, however, not all "occult" groups are satanic or engage in conduct dangerous to others.

Statistics on ritualized maltreatment cases are not kept as a separate category so it is not clear how many of the approximately 1.5 million cases of child maltreatment recorded annually by the federal government involve this form of maltreatment (U.S. Dept. of Health and Human Services 1988). Definitional differences also complicate the accumulation of information about "ritualized" maltreatment, since the term is sometimes used virtually exclusively to refer to abuse inflicted in the context of cult or satanic practices. However, given the severe consequences for the victims of this form of extreme maltreatment, and the legal and clinical challenges it poses, consideration of the forensic evaluation of ritualized maltreatment is warranted even if these cases comprise only a very small percentage of total cases of maltreatment.

The core of any comprehensive forensic mental health evaluation is a detailed clinical evaluation that draws upon multiple sources of information, whether the child presents as a victim or as a perpetrator. Adequate evaluation includes as many of the following as are possible and relevant in a given case: (1) detailed diagnostic and functional assessment of the child, (2) review of family, medical, social, psychiatric, trauma, school, and substance-abuse history, (3) interview of principal caretakers, parents, caseworkers, therapists, or others who can provide information about the child, (4) analysis of the presenting circumstances and the history of the concerns or allegations, (5) any available information regarding the specific nature of the alleged victimization or delinquent activity, (6) information regarding any other particular individuals or groups allegedly involved in the maltreatment or delinquent activity, and (6) consideration of the relevant and likely legal issues that may be involved in the court process.

Forensic evaluation assesses the functioning and clinical mental health needs of children by seeking to understand their experiences, but also tries specifically to generate evidence that may be used in legal actions. The forensic evaluator must be aware of the legal issues currently or potentially at stake in the case. In cases of ritualized maltreatment, proper evaluation also includes consideration of information about the wide variation in the organization and practices of the many non-orthodox groups that exist in the United States, the many patterns and motives for ritualized maltreatment, and the clinical presentation of traumatized persons.

The variation in clinical presentation and legal issues involved in cases of suspected or known ritualized maltreatment prevent reliance upon a single protocol or "recipe" for forensic evaluation. This paper presents general considerations and strategies for evaluation in cases where children or adolescents present for forensic evaluation as victims or perpetrators of ritualized maltreatment.

There is disagreement about how common ritualized maltreatment of children may be, and what links may exist between this form of child abuse and organized criminal, religious, or satanic activities. The contours of this debate have been outlined elsewhere (State of California 1990), and other chapters in this book will discuss them in detail. To date, these disputes have often generated at least as much heat as light, and certainly more workshops and seminars than careful documentation, corroboration, discussion, or study. However, several points are clear.

First, children are subjected to "ritualized" maltreatment. The perpetrators may act from a variety of motivations that range from idiosyncratic psychotic delusions to the enactment of complex belief systems shared with others. Our experience has been that only a small percentage of reported child maltreatment cases involve ritualized maltreatment. Not all cases involving ritualized maltreatment involve non-mainstream religious groups, and not all cases involving non-mainstream religions involve satanism. In addition, not all groups that espouse satanism or other extremely unorthodox beliefs are involved with ritual maltreatment or homicide.

Adolescents and adults may engage in criminal or predatory actions under the influence of motivations derived from strongly held belief systems that are idiosyncratic, informally shared with others, or shared with others in small groups or "cults." However, the relationship between beliefs or practices and antisocial or predatory conduct is not simple. Victimizers can also commit criminal or predatory actions for more ordinary motives, and rely upon the beliefs or practices as obfuscations or justifications for their conduct. Sometimes the relationship between the criminal conduct and the beliefs and practices can be entirely spurious, no more linked together than the mainstream political beliefs of John Wayne Gacey and his predatory torture homicides of young men (Cahill 1986).

Second, suspected cases of ritualized maltreatment are likely to appear more frequently before civil and criminal courts as more therapists, law-enforcement officers, and others begin considering the possibility of cult involvement or ritualized harm to others. Law-enforcement officers and prosecutors will become more proficient at recognizing potential evidence of cultic or ritualized elements in child maltreatment or other crimes. As police and prosecutors become more familiar with these kinds of cases they will be less reluctant to use information regarding beliefs held by perpetrators as a way of establishing motive and intent. Increasing amounts of popular and professional literature (Blood 1989), although often focused still specifically on satanism, signal increased social and professional awareness of the possibility of ritualized maltreatment.

Third, there will continue to be conflict among the social systems and individual roles of persons who come into contact with these cases. For example, the roles of therapist, police officer, prosecutor, forensic evaluator, child protective worker, judge, and jury are not the same. There are important differences among these roles regarding ultimate goals, appropriate kinds of professional involvement, standards of credibility and proof, and perception and use of information. Responsibilities and means of control over the therapeutic, protective, and punitive mechanisms of society will differ and may sometimes operate at cross-purposes.

Finally, it is time for the development of this area to move beyond the polarized debate between "skeptics" who deny any possibility of ritualized maltreatment and "believers" who find cult activity and conspiracy everywhere. Extreme positions have served to define the debate in the initial phases of the development of this area of clinical knowledge. Now the goal must be to develop sound ways of understanding, researching, and documenting the various patterns and motives for ritualized maltreatment, sound methods of investigation, and effective means of intervention.

Ritualized Maltreatment and the Law

The First Amendment to the Constitution protects religious beliefs. Courts will not weigh the truth or falsity of a belief or doctrine (United States v. Ballard). "The freedom to hold religious beliefs and opinions is absolute" (Braunfeld v. Brown). However, the freedom to act pursuant to religious belief is not. "Conduct remains subject to regulation for the protection of society" (Cartwell v. Conn.). The kinds of exploitative, assaultive, or even homicidal conduct involved when a victim is ritually maltreated or killed in a murder motivated by a particular belief system are not protected. This conduct violates criminal and civil law, and could result in a variety of legal actions by the state and by individuals.[1]

While beliefs and practices may not be admitted when they are ruled to be irrelevant to the crime charged or more prejudicial than probative, courts permit

---

[1]For example, in October 1990, private parties in a civil action suit won a $12.5 million verdict against white supremacists Tom and John Metzger for the role that their organization, the White Aryan Resistance, played in an Oregon racial killing.

evidence regarding beliefs if they relate to the nature, circumstances, or the motivation of an alleged act. In the Massachusetts case of Commonwealth v. Drew a defendant's involvement in satanism was admitted to evidence because the victim of a ritualistic killing had intended to leave the cult and had already reported an earlier instance of human sacrifice to the police. In the 1986 murder case of State of Maine v. Scott Waterhouse evidence of the defendant's satanic beliefs was admitted as probative of both motive and intent. Similarly, a 1989 ruling of the Supreme Court of Nebraska in State of Nebraska v. Michael Ryan upheld the murder conviction and death sentence of a non-satanic cult leader whose trial for torture murder included evidence admitted pertaining to the beliefs, organization, and practices of the cult.

However, until an illegal act or major parenting failure has occurred there is no legal basis for law-enforcement or state child protective agency intervention. Police officials may pursue information or leads, but unless there is some indication that criminal conduct is involved they may not engage in surveillance, undercover operations, or wiretapping. State child protective agencies in many jurisdictions may respond to reports that a child is "at risk" of being maltreated. However, if some evidence of risk of abuse or neglect is not discovered during a brief initial investigation, there will be little grounds for pursuing the case. Unusual religious beliefs or practices alone may get some attention from authorities, but will rarely be enough to support sustained investigation or intervention.[2]

Impediments to effective official intervention arise even when criminal or abusive activities have been disclosed to the authorities. In the criminal context, the primary problem is that the contemporary criminal justice system is simply overwhelmed to the point of barely functioning. Most law-enforcement officials and prosecutors are simply not in a position to devote significant resources to investigate crimes reported to have occurred many years ago by adult survivors of ritualized maltreatment. Evidentiary problems often forestall prosecutions for contemporary child maltreatment, particularly when the victims are younger children.

These difficulties may reflect a sadly familiar social and professional denial and skepticism regarding the kinds of victimization that exist (Masson 1984; Miller 1986). They also stem from the lack of training available to many law-enforcement personnel in the identification of ritualized maltreatment or crime, whether motivated by delusions, sexual perversons, or the cult beliefs of small, unorthodox groups. However, there are also other realities that victims, their families, and their therapists must understand.

First, evidence for crimes committed years ago or against young children is difficult to collect or corroborate. Often, the police and forensic evalu-

---

[2] See, for example, In the Matter of Margery Karr, where parental involvement in a religious cult alone was insufficient to sustain a custody action.

ators genuinely believe the statements of the victim and understand that the available evidence is consistent with the statements. When parents are the perpetrators, courts may find the presentation of this evidence meets the "clear and convincing" standard of evidence required to transfer legal and permanent physical custody of the child to the state. However, the same evidence may be too inconclusive or too vulnerable to defense challenges to warrant proceeding to a costly and difficult criminal trial, where the evidence must be enough to persuade all twelve members of a jury "beyond a reasonable doubt."

Second, law-enforcement personnel may actually be investigating reports received, but are unable to communicate with victims about the details of the investigation. Police are often reluctant to discuss their activities with potential witnesses because it may provide ground for challenges by defense attorneys. We are aware of cases where families of victims were convinced that local police were implicated in cult conspiracies because "nothing was being done" when in fact the police were gathering evidence for prosecution.

Third, many survivors of ritualized maltreatment are vulnerable to challenges to their credibility by defense attorneys who will try to point to any history of psychiatric disturbance or treatment. Child and adult victims of severe and chronic maltreatment often have serious credibility problems even with medical and mental health professionals (Goodwin 1985).

Knowing the vulnerabilities of these persons in legal proceedings, police and prosecutors often seek independent corroborating evidence of the alleged crimes to avoid placing a vulnerable child or adult survivor as the sole linchpin of a difficult, expensive prosecution that must reach a very high standard of proof for conviction.

Overview of Forensic Mental Health

The practice of mental health professions consulting with the legal system is the subspecialty of forensic mental health. On the criminal side, forensic mental health clinicians may provide services to courts or attorneys in determining issues such as competency to stand trial, criminal responsibility, sentencing or other dispositions, and other areas related to prosecutions for criminal charges. On the civil side, forensic mental health clinicians provide services in such diverse areas as child protection, child custody, involuntary civil commitment of the mentally ill, legal competence and guardianship, and impact of tortious conduct in civil lawsuits.

Cases involving children and adolescents are typically heard in juvenile or family courts. While not considered strictly criminal proceedings, minors may be tried for criminal charges and found "delinquent" in juvenile court. Proceedings here can involve the range of criminal court issues such as competence to stand trial (Grisso, Miller, and Sales 1987) or criminal responsibility for the alleged conduct (the "insanity defense"). If found delinquent a juvenile may be "committed" to state supervision and custody.

All states now have some provision for juveniles to be tried as adults under some circumstances (Bureau of Justice Statistics 1988). In some states the criminal courts have original jurisdiction over juveniles accused of committing some kinds of crimes, with the option of transferring them to juvenile court. More frequently, however, there is a procedure (variously termed "transfer," "waiver," or "bind over" proceedings) that begins in juvenile session in which the court determines whether a juvenile is to be "transferred" to adult criminal court for trial and sentencing as an adult.

While state practices and statutory requirements vary, forensic mental health evaluations may be involved in "transfer" hearings in order to provide the juvenile court with information about the psychological functioning and "amenability to treatment" of these youths. The stakes can be very high. Adult trial and sentencing of adolescents who committed homicides linked with satanic or occult activities have been upheld in recent cases that resulted in imposition of the death penalty and life sentences without parole (S.R.S. v. Oklahoma; Green and Tamarkin 1988; Raschke 1990).

On the civil side, forensic evaluation may be sought when a state, private agency, or individual alleges that the parents are "unfit." State laws and practices vary, but these "dependency" or "care and protection" cases typically involve claims that parents have been abusive, neglectful, or unwilling or unable to provide adequate protection from deprivation, maltreatment, or exploitation. In order to protect the children another party seeks legal and/or physical custody of the child. On occasion, courts may also use forensic evaluators in cases involving the involuntary civil commitment to a psychiatric hospital of a child who is mentally ill and by virtue of the illness is posing an acute danger to itself or others. State agencies involved with child protection or juvenile delinquents may also request forensic evaluations when issues of continued custody or case management arise.

Allegations of maltreatment can also arise in divorce or custody disputes in which a parent rather than the state is seeking custody of a child. Divorce and custody proceedings may involve mental health evaluations of the children and parents, particularly if one parent is alleging maltreatment of the child by the other.

In virtually any legal proceeding involving child maltreatment the children are potential witnesses. Forensic evaluation may play a role in considerations of a child's competency as a witness (Melton 1981; Quinn 1986; Nurcombe and Langelier 1986; Terr 1986) and the need for special procedures during courtroom testimony intended to protect the witness from further harm. In the case of Maryland v. Craig the United States Supreme Court decided that the state has a compelling interest in protecting child witnesses from further traumatization, and that this "compelling interest" permits special protective procedures under certain circumstances.

The forensic assessment can assist in documenting any deleterious consequences for the child witness of testifying before the defendant in open court. The evaluation can also assist in considering what special interventions (Wolfe, Sas, and Wilson 1987) or protective procedures may be most effective, within the rules and statutes of the relevant jurisdiction, and yet maintain the constitutional balance with the rights of the defendant. This continues to be an active area of research and innovation (Lipovsky 1990; Runyan et al. 1988; Tedesco and Schnell 1987; Bauer 1983; Goodman et al. 1988) as more child victims come into contact with the legal system and there is greater appreciation of the ways in which court involvement may aggrevate or ameliorate the effects of maltreatment (Burgess and Holstrom 1978; Parker 1982; Berliner and Barbieri 1984; American Bar Association 1985).

Child Forensic Evaluation

Any mental-health or medical contact with a child can generate information that will ultimately lead to legal action on behalf of the child or against an alleged perpetrator. We are concerned that once legal action appears possible many clinicians unfamiliar with potential legal issues or specific relevant law in their jurisdictions fail to secure a forensic consultation. Similarly, it is our impression that district attorneys, children's attorneys or advocates, state child protective agencies, courts, and other key players often fail to secure consultations or evaluations.

Not all "ritualized" maltreatment involves occult or satanic belief systems, cults, or religiously motivated rituals. Forensic evaluators and other clinicians may err in presuming that indications of a ritualized form of maltreatment necessarily mean that the child was the victim of specifically occult or satanic practices. The discovery of indications of ritualized maltreatment should be followed promptly by careful inquiry into the concrete experience of the victim, the circumstances surrounding the presentation of the case, any ongoing protective concerns, the existence of any corroborating information, and sophisticated clinical evaluation. Preliminary indications of ritualized abuse should *not* result in hasty conclusions about the nature or the motivations of the maltreatment.

The clinical and legal implications that follow from understanding the experience and conduct of the victim or the perpetrator are important to appreciate. Children may receive forensic mental health evaluations for many reasons that will vary depending upon whether the child is a perpetrator, a victim, or a witness, and whether the legal issues involve civil or criminal proceedings. The most common legal issues are (1) the child's capacity as a witness and his or her need for support during trial; (2) the child's needs for long-term protection; (3) the child's needs for long-term care and treatment; (4) the capacity of perpetrating or non-perpetrating parents to respond to the clinical, developmental, and protective needs of the child; (5) the reporting duties of professionals; (6) the development of information from the child victim; (7) the competence, criminal responsibility, and amenability to treatment of an adolescent perpetrator.

Forensic evaluation in cases of ritualized maltreatment has several distinct dimensions that overlap with ongoing controversies. Considerable controversy already exists about the investigation of less extreme forms of child maltreatment. The introduction of alleged cases of ritualized, satanic, or other occult maltreatment promises to fuel an already intense and often emotional debate on the following issues.

Eliciting Information from Children

Concerns abound about the manner and frequency with which evaluators may distort, suggest, or elicit the reports of maltreatment from children by using leading questions, pressures and rewards for particular content, or situational cues. Critics have pointed to several different sources of potential error and contamination (Quinn, White, and Santilli 1989; Underwager and Wakefield 1989; Loftus 1979; Melton and Limber 1989). Sources of potential interview and investigatory contamination include several methods of contaminatory questioning (White and Quinn 1988), overt and covert coercion and reinforcement during inquiry (ibid.), use of therapeutic emotional and interpretive techniques that risk altering the child's perception, emotional valence, or memory of events as they are disclosed (Weithorn and Grisso 1987; Melton et al. 1987), a range of interviewer behaviors (Quinn, White, and Santilli 1989), and situations in which there are multiple sources of potential contamination and suggestion before, during, and after the forensic evaluation.

It is beyond the scope of this paper to review the considerable literature on the memory capacities of children. However, it is clear that even very young children can be reliable reporters, although their capacities will vary with age, developmental factors, the nature of the original experience, and the means by which their recollections are elicited. Research indicates that children four to five years old under standard testing conditions resist false suggestions of abuse, and that the suggestibility of very young children varies with the conditions of evaluation (Goodman 1990). At the heart of this debate is whether, and under what circumstances, reports of maltreatment are either false or overdiagnosed (Benedek and Schetky 1985; Berliner et al. 1989; Everson and Boat 1989; Terr 1989; Green 1988; Gardner 1987). Research and clinical experience in non-forensic evaluation not involving maltreatment show that distorting conditions exist. A forensic evaluator can wittingly or unwittingly create or contribute to this distortion. Nonetheless, a forensic evaluator can minimize these conditions if he or she is aware of distorting variables, proceeds with appropriate techniques, and does not apply a personal or professional agenda. It is also crucial to maintain investigatory independence in the evaluation of specific cases (White and Quinn 1989).

But there will always be an inherent tension between the methods utilized to secure clinical information for forensic purposes and the rules of evidence. For example, legal doctrine in some circumstances may find even simple "yes or no" questions suspect, particularly in the case of a young child who otherwise does not provide information spontaneously. Yet, it has been argued that children may not provide relevant information during forensic evaluation unless directly questioned about the alleged victimization (Myers, Goodman, and Saywitz 1990). Research exists suggesting that children can fail to spontaneously provide relevant information, including reports of direct genital contact (Saywitz et al., cited in Goodman 1990).

Forensic and mental health evaluators should be aware that courts have become increasingly wary of the potential for contaminated evidence in legal proceedings involving child maltreatment allegations. Appellate review of disputes about the admissibility of such evidence can be found in both civil (In re J.H.; In the Matter of X; Louisiana 1986) and criminal (Utah v. Hadfield) cases involving child maltreatment. The Country Walk day-care case in Miami demonstrates (Hollingsworth 1986) that the use of mental health professionals for the initial investigation and for expert testimony on the reliability of methods used to secure and document children's testimony, can constitute a major dimension in a case even at the trial level.

The Hadfield case decided by the Utah Supreme Court in February 1990 is of particular interest because the clinicians there developed information alleging organized "sex ring" exploitation of the children along with satanic rituals. The defendant appealed his conviction on charges of sodomy with a child on the grounds that testimony had been given that (1) a primary clinician in the case had used authority and punishment to modify the responses of the children, (2) false information deliberately "fed" to the clinician by law-enforcement investigators rapidly appeared in the statements elicited from the children, and (3) there was a striking similarity among the facts unearthed in at least four other maltreatment cases in which that clinician was involved.

The Utah court ruled that these challenges were insufficient to warrant a new trial as a matter of law, since this evidence was cumulative rather than new and the jury had sufficient opportunity to weigh the testimony. However, the Hadfield case is instructive. First, a trial jury did accept evidence of child maltreatment linked to cult practices for conviction in a felony criminal case. Secondly, Hadfield, the McMartin case in California, and other recent cases show that state trial attorneys and courts are becoming more sophisticated about the methods used to develop children's testimony in maltreatment cases, and challenges to methods used are likely to become more frequent.

Forensic evaluators and other clinicians whose treatment or assessment work may be used in legal proceedings should also familiarize themselves with the important 1990 United States Supreme Court decision of Idaho v. Wright (110 S. Ct.). In brief, this decision upheld the action of a state court striking the testimony of a physician who had testified to the statements of a child sexual abuse victim during an evaluation. The Idaho Supreme Court had found that the evaluation by the doctor had lacked sufficient procedural safeguards. The Idaho ruling specifically cited the doctor's "suggestive, inadequately reviewable interview technique" stemming from his failure to record the interview on videotape, the use of leading questions, and the questioning of the child with a preconceived idea of what she should be disclosing (Idaho v. Wright, 116 Idaho 1989).

The United States Supreme Court held that the out-of-court statements of the child were presumptively barred by the hearsay rule and the Sixth Amendment, and that prosecutors had failed to demonstrate the reliability of the child's statements. The Supreme Court declined to specify a particular procedure to guarantee adequate reliability, simply stating that courts would have to consider the "totality of circumstances" under which the child's statements regarding abuse were made. However, the Supreme Court did cite a number of factors to be considered in weighing the "total circumstances," and held that other corroborating evidence (such as medical findings or identification by other witnesses) may not be used to support a court's finding that the child's statements had the necessary "particularized guarantees" of reliability.

The information that children provide can undoubtedly be shaped by improper interview techniques, or by the influence of adults bringing to bear their own assumptions, anxieties, or agendas. And, just as in evaluations regarding alleged delinquent behavior or status offenses where maltreatment is not alleged, older children and adolescents may chose to provide, distort, or withhold information out of their own conceptions of their interests.

However, in our view, the recent emphasis in the literature upon the conditions under which children may be manipulated or may lie is potentially misleading. It can represent as rigid and extreme a position as a view that children's memories are never faulty nor are there any conditions under which information elicited from them may be inaccurate, incomplete, or fabricated. The more pressing and relevant inquiry should be about the conditions under which children can provide information about their experiences without impingement by potentially contaminating or deterring factors.

Specific Investigative Techniques

Various concerns exist about the reliability of specific investigative techniques such as the use of anatomically correct dolls (Yates and Terr 1988; White 1986; White and Santilli 1988). Although use of such dolls has become common in many settings (Boat and Everson 1988), this controversy has led to discussion of the role of courts in regulating investigatory use of the dolls for legal purposes (White 1988). Recent court decisions in some jurisdictions sharply curtail admission into evidence any data derived from anatomical doll observations (In re Amber B. and Teela B.).

Adequate forensic evaluation should develop multiple sources of information and clinical data. These sources should include interviews whenever possible with all relevant parties, careful history-taking, and review of available documents and records. For example, in child custody disputes it is very difficult to arrive at a confident clinical assessment of the family and the dynamics of any alleged maltreatment without interviewing all of the adult parties to the dispute. It is difficult to imagine an adequately investigated case in which the use of anatomical dolls would contribute the bulk of the clinical evidence of maltreatment. Rather, any anatomical doll data should comprise only one of many documented data points. Evaluators and courts should appreciate that empirical support for specific conclusions drawn from the technique is still uncertain.

The Role of the Forensic Evaluator

The role of the clinical or forensic evaluator in "validating" the allegations of maltreatment is controversial. State and private agencies, police, and courts often request clinicians to perform evaluations to determine whether or not the alleged maltreatment took place and has been accurately reported by the child. Acceptance of this duty is common in mental health professions, as reflected in standards promulgated by the American Academy of Child and Adolescent Psychiatry (Schetky et al. 1988) that recommend that mental health evaluators "decide . . . whether or not any sexual abuse occurred."

We have often received referrals for evaluation in which the referral question was simply, "Was this child abused?" or "Did this alleged perpetrator do it?" Many agencies and courts demand this "validation" from mental health clinicians. Many clinicians and evaluators apparently feel comfortable offering such "validations" for use in legal determinations of fact, or defend them as a necessary evil because it is demanded of them. We hold another position regarding "validation."

The first step in clinical assessment of alleged child maltreatment—whether or not "validation" is sought for legal purposes—is a sophisticated and rigorous clinical assessment and analysis of the information obtained (Krugman and Jones 1987; Sgroi, Porter, and Blick 1982; Berliner 1988). This may include forming opinions about the relative merits of competing explanations of events. However, to "validate" in circumstances of potential or actual legal action is to take a conceptual step beyond the process of collection and assessment of clinical data. This additional step—deciding whether abuse occurred and which account of the abuse is most meritorious—risks obscuring the difference between the legal and clinical determination of child maltreatment, and the difference between degrees of clinical confidence and legal burdens of proof. When the facts of past events are in dispute, it is the court's role to "find fact," to reach a legal determination of what happened. It is important to appreciate that this legal determination of "fact" is not the same as establishing the "truth" of an event.

Asking a clinical evaluator to "validate" evidence of the "truth" of a past event amounts to asking the clinician to testify as a witness to events that are in fact beyond his or her direct knowledge. Ethical concerns regarding testifying to the truth of events beyond direct knowledge point to an even more fundamental epistemological problem. "Validation" requires that the clinician make a dichotomous judgement about whether the events occurred or did not occur; but the truth of whether or how the events occurred is not something that can be "decided" by anyone, and can truly be known only by the direct participants in the event. "Validation" therefore creates ethical problems by asking a mental health professional to "find facts" beyond their direct experience, and philosophical problems by asking them to reach certainty about the experience of another person by "deciding" what "really" happened. Additional problems are created by "validation" by the way the procedure introduces a clinician role into the legal process. Allegations or evidence of ritualized maltreatment tend to exacerbate the tensions and ambiguities reflected in these problems.

First, at the very least, the professional might simply be wrong entirely or in part, thus potentially undermining the child who has been abused, or colluding in the distortions of reality or coercion by others of a child who has not. This can result in failures of protection or empathy for a child who fails to be officially "validated," or the unnecessary loss of important relationships, labeling as a "victim," and assignment to specialized psychotherapy in response to experiences that did not occur or have not yet been understood in crucial respects. In our experience, child victims of ritualized maltreatment may present in a disclosure process that is very complex clinically and may occur over an extended period of time. This makes it especially risky to "validate" or "not validate" for legal purposes a particular presentation at a single moment in the disclosure process.

Second, the responsibility of "validation" for legal purposes makes clinicians vulnerable to usurping or being burdened with the responsibility of the court as the finder of legal "fact." In our experience, the press for "validation" takes on a more critical role when the evidence is ambiguous, and the court is unwilling or unable to rely upon standard methods of presenting expert testimony.

Indeed, in cases where the child presents with patterned burns or esophogeal gonnorhea, or in which videotapes or photographs portray the perpetrator in sexual acts with the child, or in which there are other clear indications of ritualized maltreatment, it is not clear what purpose specialized "validation" would serve. Any court could draw its own conclusions from the evidence.

In more ambiguous circumstances, however, the clinician is pressed into service as a gatekeeper. The "validation" process is used beyond clinical purposes as an official sanction or disconfirmation of the child's report by courts, law-enforcement officials, and child protective and social service systems. Clinicians who "validate" child maltreatment allegations—and the courts who press them to perform this function—risk confusing differences between clinical, legal, and historical "facts." Each of these facts are established in different ways and for different purposes and should not be confused.

Courts risk substituting what actually amounts to a clinical "validation" for the legal fact finding that is the ultimate responsibility of the courts. Clinicians risk subtly shifting from the role of scientist-practitioner into that of legal, moral, and social gatekeeper. This confusion between different kinds of "facts" and between "facts" and "values" is a disservice to both victims and alleged perpetrators who may in fact be innocent. It also permits the circus of paraded "experts" reminiscent of insanity defense trials, with the same perceptions among the public and legal commmunities that mental health practices are fundamentally biased and unscientific.

Third, the process of "validation" makes abused children a special class of crime victims whose initial presentation is presumptively suspect. J.R. Conte (1990) has observed that "it is not clear why children who may have been sexually abused should be exposed to a process designed to determine what happened to them before they are regarded by law-enforcement, social service, and mental health professionals as 'real clients.'" In our view, clinicians risk colluding with a system that is often presumptively disconfirming of child victims.

The deep dilemmas and limitations of expert mental health testimony have been commented upon elsewhere (Stone 1984; Melton et al. 1987; Waithe et al. 1982). The point here is that clinicians in child maltreatment cases sometimes are asked to step beyond providing the court with properly obtained and documented information. However, upon entering the territory of "validating" maltreatment of children, speaking directly to the "best interests" of a child, or whether an alleged perpetrator "did it," mental health professionals and courts run the risk of making important errors of knowledge and role. These errors have their roots in the limitations of our scientific knowledge, the willingness of courts to abdicate their responsibilities in difficult or ambiguous cases, and the eagerness of many mental health professionals to step forward despite the major empirical and conceptual problems involved.

Allegations of ritualized maltreatment simply exacerbate these tensions, particularly given the still very limited understanding mental health professionals have of the clinical dimensions of this form of extreme maltreatment. Aside from the problems mentioned above, however, our limited knowledge base poses a major clinical problem. When a child has been extremely and ritually victimized, particularly if the victimization has been chronic, the process of disclosure may occur over months or even years, there may have been skillful manipulations of experience in order to make the child less credible, and the mental status of the extremely victimized child may variable and fragile. These factors can preclude highly confident forensic clinical assessment in short periods of time.

In some ways, this issue parallels the dispute in psychotherapeutic circles about the best way to understand the recollections of adult survivors who report cultic or ritualized maltreatment (Van Benschoten 1990; Ganaway 1989; Hill and Goodwin 1989). However, in an ongoing psychotherapeutic relationship the therapist has opportunities over a relatively extended period of time to gather information, piece together data, consider alternative hypotheses and formulations, and to test these insights through observing the effectiveness of interventions. Any particular patient may go through a complex process involving emergence and loss of recollections, recanting and reasserting, and denial and acceptance of their experiences. The clinician may respect as genuine the reports of the victim while also appreciating the complexity and variability of the process. Some clinicians may even feel ready to commit to a concrete account of historical detail at some point in the therapeutic process, but the process still remains essentially therapeutic in a way that is profoundly different from the processes of legal action.

Forensic evaluators do not typically have the luxury of extended time nor the primarily therapeutic boundaries and goals of the psychotherapeutic relationship. Forensic and clinical methods, obligations, and roles are distinct. This is true even though forensic mental health evaluation typically also addresses the therapeutic resources and needs of the subject of evaluation.

The goal of the forensic evaluator should be to gather information in a clinically sensitive and sophisiticated fashion, and to educate the court—as the ultimate fact finder—in the meaning and the limitations of the available information, and its potential relevance to legal issues in a case. More generally, forensic evaluators must attempt to educate the courts about the clinical presentation and evaluation of child maltreatment in order to demystify the process, and encourage courts to assume their proper role as ultimate fact finder for legal purposes.

We must stress that this view does *not* mean that we do not believe the child victim. Rather, it speaks to the differences between forensic work and other kinds of mental health evaluation or intervention, and the uses to which forensic clinical data is put beyond therapeutic purposes.

Use of Law-Enforcement Information

Law enforcement is divided over whether or not "occult" or "satanic" crime should be considered a distinct category of crime. Some law-enforcement officials assert that the focus of law enforcement should be upon the commission of crime rather than the particular belief systems of perpetrators, and discount reports that many crimes are primarily motivated by occult belief systems (Lanning 1989; Hicks 1989). Others argue that the signs or motivations of "occult crime" may not be recognized without specific attention to the belief systems of the perpetrators.[3]

Whatever their views on this question, many in law enforcement are increasingly aware of the importance of noting evidence of unusual group activities or belief systems. All of them advocate solid and informed police work as the basic foundation of any investigation of alleged ritualized maltreatment or occult crime. To assign criminal responsibility or to document evidence of abuse, the evaluator should seek to review any available police incident reports or crime scene investigations. These may yield information relevant to understanding the nature and circumstances of the delinquent behavior or the victimization of the child, as well as clinical functioning and mental status.

Police investigation or execution of a search warrant may yield information from which the belief system held by the perpetrator(s) and the nature of maltreatment or criminal activity may be deduced.[4] Of particular interest are collections of ritual objects, books or other written documents, drawings, weapons, diaries and journals, costumes and other clothing, flags and ornamentation, maps, and indications of special writing, codes, or other secretive means of communication. Police may have seized photographs, videotapes, various collections, and computer discs that yield relevant forensic information or other indications of the degree of immersion of the perpetrator. Police may also have had authorization to secure mail, records of phone calls, credit card receipts, and commercial billings. There may be evidence of drug use, pornography, objects used for restraining persons, sexual activities, or other evidence of other group or individual ritual or criminal activities.

Clinicians and investigators should seek information about the specific belief system involved (whether political, racist, religious, militarist, metaphysical, psychotherapeutic, or subcultural-ethnic in any benign and dangerous variations), as well as what is known about local variations in practices (Wetli and Martinez 1983a, 1983b; Simpson 1978). Detailed reports of the crime scene, physical evidence, and statements by witnesses or victims are also useful in understanding the nature and motivation of the crime.

---

[3]Dale Griffis and Jay Bowman, the latter of the Massachusetts State Police, are of this opinion (personal communications to the authors). Larry Jones, of the Boise, Idaho, Police Department and Director of the Cult Crime Impact Network, and R. Valdemar, of the Los Angeles Sheriff's Department also express this opinion (in interviews in State of California 1989 37). See also Kahaner (1988).

[4]We acknowledge as particularly helpful the work of Dr. Dale Griffis on how police investigations may produce information useful for forensic mental health evaluations in cases of ritualized maltreatment or cult criminal activity. We also thank Jerry Simandl of the Chicago Police Department and Jay Bowman of the Massachusetts State Police for their information on this topic.

Forensic Evaluation and Ritualized Maltreatment

It is beyond the scope of this paper to detail the many ways in which forensic or other mental health clinicians may become involved in legal processes in cases of ritualized maltreatment. It is our impression that many clinicians become involved as witnesses after disclosures have been made during specific sexual abuse evaluations, or after material emerges in psychotherapy. As with many other child abuse situations, the initial legal or forensic mental health involvement may develop unexpectedly as the result of ordinary mental health attention to a child showing some signs of emotional disturbance.

The focus of forensic mental health involvement in cases involving ritual child abuse, like that of forensic involvement in any other kind of child abuse, may vary widely depending upon whether the case involves criminal or civil proceedings, whether the victim or perpetrator has been referred for evaluation, or whether the purpose of the evaluation is primarily for legal or clinical purposes. The basic process of forensic evaluation will be essentially the same as in any case where the perpetrator terrorizes the child victim, or in which the perpetrator subscribes to an unorthodox belief system that may have motivated the conduct. While the basic process of evaluation is the same, however, there are potential diagnostic and forensic complexities. These complexities make it unwise for clinicians to accept these cases if they are novices, unaccustomed to performing forensic evaluations involving children, or unfamiliar with the literature on traumatic stress responses, dissociative disorders, totalist and cult group processes, sexual perversions and pedophilia, and the practices of various occult groups.

We find a multidimensional framework is extremely useful in understanding and in guiding the forensic evaluation of cases of alleged ritualized maltreatment, or juvenile delinquent behavior believed to be motivated by a deviant belief system. This framework assists in focusing and organizing the information gathered from a comprehensive forensic assessment developed from multiple sources and should not be understood as limiting the inquiry to the dimensions mentioned below.

Degree and Nature of Any Group Involvement

Perpetrators may operate on a continuum from individual activities to participation in highly organized "totalist" groups. Evaluators must be familiar with the general literature on the psychology of socially deviant small and totalist groups (Galanter 1982, 1989; Lifton 1961; Clark et al. 1981; Clark 1979; Griel and Rudy 1984; Robbins and Anthony 1980). At a minimum, information must be gathered regarding (1) whether the perpetrator acted individually or with others; (2) indications of possible motivations, including both those related to particular belief systems; (3) the details and import of any unorthodox belief system; (4) any links between group beliefs and practices and the concrete details of the maltreatment; (5) whether other persons might have been victimized; and (6) any indications that the subject or others remain at risk.

M. D. Langone and L. O. Blood (1990) have developed a summary typology that characterizes an individual's degree of involvement in satanic activities. Although the specific beliefs, practices, and instrumentalities will differ, this typology generally reflects the types and continuum of involvement in deviant subgroups:

1. "Dabblers," usually teenagers who become attracted to satanism on a relatively superficial level through easily available books, "heavy metal" music, fantasy role-playing games and the like.

2. "Self-styled" or "psychopathic" satanists, usually loners attracted to the more violent forms of satanism that are then grafted on to their preexisting pathology.

3. "Religious" satanists involved in well-organized, publically acknowledged groups.

4. "Satanic cults," the sophisticated, clandestine groups, which may be engaged in criminal activities.

Evaluators should carefully consider evidence of the degree of involvement and preoccupation with the belief systems. Police reports and investigators may be important sources of evidence for the degree of involvement. Where available, evaluators must also attend to other potential sources of information such as family members, the victim, or other community or professional sources.

As the MOVE, Jonestown, and Manson cases illustrate, groups that have successfully established psychological and/or physical isolation can have immense influence over their members. Evaluators should attend carefully to indicators of psychological investment in a group or belief system. In occult groups, this includes assessment of patterns of association with cult members and nonmembers, investment of money and time in securing the objects and learning the dogma and rituals of the group, and degree of subordination to group ideology and leadership. Evidence of the use of means or techniques of psychological intimidation, manipulation, or coercive persuasion should also be carefully assessed and documented.

Motivations for Ritualized Maltreatment

We have found Finkelhor, Williams, and Burns's (1988) description of (1) *psychopathological*, (2) *pseudoritual*, and (3) *true ritual* maltreatment extremely useful in guiding the gathering and analysis of data in forensic evaluations.

The "psychopathological" type involves maltreatment related to the mental illness of the perpetrator. For example, a parent with a psychotic delusion may believe that their child is being "contaminated" and in an effort to "save" the child inflicts harm through practices such as the ritualized administration of multiple enemas or a highly stylized physical punishment. In such a case it is highly unlikely that a district attorney will devote resources to a prosecution. A defense attorney would be quick to raise questions of competence and criminal responsibility if there were a prosecution. A sophisticated juvenile court considering the case would want information regarding the link between the mental illness and the maltreatment, the prognosis for compliance and outcome of any treatment of the parent, and the alternatives for protective custody or supervision.

The "pseudoritualized" type involves use of rituals to further non-metaphysical aims. In our view, this form includes various aims such as intimidation of child victims, and/or the gratification of sadistic and sexual perversions, and/or the use of rituals to enhance group cohesion and loyalty in sex rings. This type may appear in cases involving "cottage" or commercial child pornography and can include props, objects, and behavior that might be suggestive of true ritualized abuse. This category also covers cases in which a parent or other person has systematically beaten, tortured, and/or sexually violated a child for purposes of intimidation and/or sadistic sexual gratification, but without links to a metaphysical belief system. This kind of maltreatment is characteristic of most of the cases of which we are aware. These include cases of systematic and stylized physical and/or sexual maltreatment used (1) against adolescents attempting to leave an "occult" peer group also involved in criminal activities; (2) on children serving to gratify sadistic sexual perversions of parents or other perpetrators; (3) for group bonding and intimidation of children involved in organized extrafamilial sex rings; and (4) as a means of enforcing group cohesiveness and secrecy in incestuous families. Key variables in this form of maltreatment are the duration and intensity of the abuse, the number of perpetrators and whether the abuse was extrafamilial or intrafamilial, the degree and manner of any intimidation techniques utilized, and the age of the victim(s).

Prosecutions are more likely in these cases than in the "psychopathological" case. The younger or more emotionally fragile the child victims, however, the less the prosecutor will want to rely upon their testimony, the more corroborative evidence such as videotapes, pictures, or adult witnesses will be valued, and the more likely that charges will be reduced or plea bargains will be accepted. Forensic evaluators may become involved in documenting the psychiatric sequelae of the maltreatment, and making recommendations for legal and clinical management of the case.

The "true ritual" form of abuse is defined by Finkelhor, Williams, and Burns as follows: "abuse that occurs in a context linked to some symbols or group activity that have a religious, magical, or supernatural connotation, and where the invocation of these symbols or activities are repeated over time and used to frighten and intimidate children" (ibid. 15). "True ritual" maltreatment is not legally protected even if it is motivated by religious or magical beliefs. In some ways, these cases would be the least challenging to forensic evaluators unless the perpetrators raised an "insanity defense" or other legal defenses based upon claims of a perpetrator's mental illness, or parties were concerned about a child's competence or ability to testify. However, our experience has been that these closed groups are particularly resistant to law enforcement penetration and therefore the gathering of nonclinical corroborating evidence for prosecutions. This can leave the victims of the maltreatment the sole source of information about what happened to them. The victims of this form of maltreatment also appear to be among the most severely damaged by the experience, particularly if the maltreatment was chronic and occurred within the family.

Gould (1987, in Cozolino 1989), Kelley (1988, 1989), Edwards (1990), and the Ritual Abuse Task Force of Los Angeles County (1989) have developed ways to identify potential cases of occult, specifically satanic, abuse. There are many potential indicators, but clinicians should be especially alert to reports of animal sacrifices, extreme fear of supernatural creatures or spirits, evidence of ritual activities, familiarity with occult symbols, bizarre ideas or unusual fears about body products or foods, use of restraints and confinement, drug intoxication, and behaviors such as chanting or performing ritualized dances.

Intrafamilial or Extrafamilial Perpetrators

Intrafamilial maltreatment can be particularly damaging since it distorts the child's experiences of basic human relationships and leaves the child vulnerable to ongoing control and repeated abuse by the perpetrators. Putnam (1989) has noted that incest is the most commonly reported form of sexual abuse among his sample of persons with multiple personality disorder, a dissociative disorder believed to originate in severe traumatic experiences. Repeated predation by family members also creates the "long-standing or repeated exposure to extreme external events" that Terr (1991) cites as producing particularly damaging post-traumatic distortion of psychological development.

Intrafamilial maltreatment immediately raises the forensic question of the capacity of family members to protect the child, refrain from any further victimization, respond to clinical and legal interventions, and meet the ongoing needs of the victimized child. When the maltreatment has been ritualized, or motivated by pseudoritual or true ritual aims, our experience has been that the child continues to be at extremely high risk if left within the family. Even when the ritualized maltreatment is the product of a major mental illness, the effectiveness of treatment, the guarantees of treatment compliance by the perpetrator, and the capacity of other family members to prevent recurrence of the maltreatment remain major issues.

Extrafamilial maltreatment that has been ritualized also has a severe impact upon children and their families. Kelley's (1989, 1990) research of ritualized maltreatment in a day-care setting demonstrates that this form of abuse has more extreme and chronic impact upon child victims and their parents even when compared to other sexually abused children. Kelley also found that the ritual maltreatment victims also experienced significantly more specific types of sexual abuse, and more severe and bizarre kinds of maltreatment, including supernatural threats and extreme intimidation, involvement in ceremonies, consumption of human excrement, drug intoxication, pornographic production, and forced sexual activity with other children.

Forensic evaluation of the children in these cases could focus on (1) the capacity of the children to act as competent and credible informants during investigation and as witnesses in a trial; (2) indications of the variety of criminal activities involved in their victimization; (3) the capacity of the parents to respond to the needs of their victimized children, or the role of legal action in providing appropriate services and supports; (4) a determination of potential risks to the children from perpetrators still at large; and (5) the coordination of forensic evaluation and recommendations with other investigators, medical and mental health caretakers, or other service providers.

Sources of "Contagion" or External Agendas

Contagion is a common impediment to factual and clinical clarity in abuse situations, especially in cases involving ritualized abuse in institutional settings such as nursery schools and day-care centers. When one child in such a setting is identified as a possible abuse victim, one immediately wonders whether any other children have been maltreated. It is very difficult to raise this question with children or parents who have not independently raised concerns without generating stress and anxiety, suggesting areas for concern, and creating conditions for overattribution and misinterpretation of children's behavior. Whether or not other children have been maltreated can become seriously obscured for forensic purposes by questions about whether or to what extent the inquiry about maltreatment or its details may have suggested or elicited responses that reflect investigator's assumptions or need for answers rather than a young child's actual experience. Even in cases where the other clinical evidence is consistent with maltreatment, the problem of contagion may reduce confidence for legal purposes in the details provided by the child. We have also observed emotional contagion in the families of child victims of extrafamilial ritual abuse, and sometimes among their attorneys, therapists, and other adults providing services. As with other forms of abuse, the possibility of ritual abuse can become an extreme preoccupation with parents or other important family members. They can respond in various ways, including becoming intimately acquainted with the various signs of ritual involvement, and highly sensitized to the possible presence of these signs in their children. This preoccupation can color their own perceptions of their children and create in the children independent suggestions and expectations about what experiences they must have had and should report. We have observed children develop behaviors consistent with family expectations of specific pathology similar to those described in cases of false allegations of sexual abuse in custody disputes (Gardner 1987).

We have seen two cases in which the allegations by the parent of cult involvement and ritual maltreatment of a child may have involved a process very similar to Munchausen's Syndrome by Proxy (Rosenberg 1987; Meadow 1977). This syndrome classically has been described in cases where a parent becomes preoccupied with medical illness in a child, and may communicate with the child in a way that contributes to the child's development of somatic symptoms without physical pathology. In extreme cases, the syndrome involves parental fabrication or even inducement of potentially life-threatening symptoms in the child (Libow 1986). Munchausen Syndrome by Proxy dynamics have been described in recent years in cases of false allegations of child maltreatment (Rand 1989, 1990). Similarly, the allegations of ritualized child maltreatment in the cases we saw entangled the child in a variety of evaluations and interventions over prolonged periods, and the waxing and waning of the children's "symptoms" appeared to be a function of ongoing contact with the parent.

Whether the contagion involves an extreme reaction of a parent to possible ritualized maltreatment of the child, or the more malignant Munchausen Syndrome by Proxy, it is important that it not be permitted to develop into a form of maltreatment of the child. As in cases of medical Munchausen by Proxy (Zitelli, Seltman, and Shannon 1987), clinicians and protective service workers may unwittingly contribute to the victimization of the child by failing to recognize and intervene to interrupt these dynamics and produce a favorable outcome for the child. Professionals who themselves introduce assumptions and agendas, or who are influenced by the emotional contagion of the case, are in a poor position to halt the processes of contamination, determine what has actually happened to the child, and respond in ways that are either clinically or forensically effective in securing the welfare of the child.

Clinical Sequelae of Ritualized Maltreatment

There is an extensive literature on the impact of traumatic child maltreatment with which forensic mental health clinicians must become familiar, but that is beyond the scope of this chapter. At the core of ritualized maltreatment are experiences of extreme terror and loss of control, severe pain, shame and guilt, isolation and despair, betrayal of basic trust, and profound rage. Empirical studies on ritual maltreatment are scarce. However, the severity of the experience and the likelihood that there have been repeated incidents of victimization would predictably exacerbate the expectable disabling effects of childhood treatment. Predictable effects of repeated episodes of ritualized maltreatment include symptoms of post-traumatic stress disorder, distortion and impairment of cognitive capacities (Fish-Murray, Kobey, and van der Kolk 1987), heightened risk for development of some personality disorders (Herman and van der Kolk 1987), and in some cases the emergence of precursors for major dissociative disorders such as multiple personality disorder (Kluft 1985).

There is evidence that post-traumatic stress disorder (PTSD) in maltreated children is relatively common (McLeer et al. 1988; Famularo, Kinscherff, and Fenton 1989). Forensic evaluators of severely maltreated children must include consideration of PTSD as a differential diagnosis. Because the clinical symptoms may shift dramatically between the acute and chronic forms of the disorder (Famularo, Kinscherff, and Fenton 1990), and because the children remain vulnerable to retraumatization upon exposure to stimuli reminiscent of the tramatization, forensic evaluators must also consider what the child's probable clinical presentation and response to the courtroom process will be at the time that legal proceedings actually occur. The clinical variability of childhood PTSD makes it a "chameleon" for child and adolescent psychiatric diagnosis, and forensic evaluators should cautiously assess the presentation of maltreated children for PTSD, particularly if the child also presents with attentional deficits, visual or auditory anomalies that resemble hallucinations or illusions, or behavioral dyscontrol.

Terr (1991) has described the sequelae of single episode (Type I) and multiple episode (Type II) traumatization. Variations in the post-traumatic presentation of Types I and II suggest that different issues may be the focus of forensic evaluation. Type I victims tend to be able to "remember the event and to give impressively clear, detailed accounts of their experiences" although they may also experience "misidentifications, visual hallucinations, and peculiar time distortions" (ibid. 14–15). Forensic assessment in Type I cases would generally focus less upon the child's competence as a witness, and more on what support the child would need to actually testify. This would involve consideration of whether the legal process will retraumatize or benefit the child.

Type II victims tend to be able to identify the perpetrators reliably because of the repetitive nature of the maltreatment (unless the perpetrators were disguised), but their clinical presentation is marked by massive denial, spontaneous self-hypnosis and dissociation, and risks of behavioral dyscontrol including suicide. Since these difficulties bear directly on capacity to testify, forensic evaluation should focus more attention on the memory and other psychological capacities of the child, *and* on the supports necessary for maintaining functional stability and avoiding any retraumatization.

As suggested above, evaluation must also take into account the stressors on the family or other caretakers of the child. Of course, if the child was victimized by family members directly or by an unwillingness or persistent inability to protect the child, then forensic assessment must address the protective needs of the child directly.

In addition to the often dramatic clinical consequences of severe or ritualized maltreatment, children may show the effects of extreme intimidation and specific efforts to make them less credible through manipulations of experience. Forensic evaluators in cases of ritualized maltreatment must consider whether bizarre beliefs or behaviors, extreme reactions to common stimuli, or unusual fears actually reflect the intimidation techniques of perpetrators rather than formal psychiatric symptoms.

It may be difficult or impossible with child victims of ritualized maltreatment to establish the kind of safe and reliable relationship required to elicit full disclosures in the limited period of time often available for forensic evaluation. Disclosures may only occur over a period of months or years, and forensic evaluators must not retraumatize the child or goad the child into responding. There will be cases in which children are not yet able to provide legally useful accounts of their experiences, and the provision of safety and therapeutic intervention becomes more important than risking further harm to the child in attempts to elicit information.

Forensic Evaluation of Delinquency and Occult Involvement

Adolescents involved in the perpetration of ritualized maltreatment or other criminal activity may become defendants in either juvenile or criminal court, depending upon their ages, the nature of the offenses, the jurisdiction, and other case-specific factors. Their evaluation should also be guided by the dimensions discussed above.

Most of our contact has been with youth who would be classified as "dabblers" in the Langone and Blood (1990) typology. These are typically youths in late latency through adolescence who have become superficially involved with occult practices through their interests in heavy metal music, fantasy games, and media presentations. Similarly, there are youths superficially involved in racist organizations or street gangs who may become increasingly involved in occult practices over time. Wheeler, Wood, and Hatch's (1988) analysis of the needs met by satanic involvement shows that the common core of adolescent needs can be met by participation in such groups. The needs he discusses are peer group acceptance or leadership; experiences of power and control; opportunities for rebellion, antisocial conduct, and thrill-seeking behaviors; access to potential sexual partners; a sense of religious or personal value; a sense of distinction and status due to membership; and claims to special powers. Bourget, Gagnon, and Bradford (1988) also point to certain predisposing factors such as poor self-esteem, alienation, and developmental struggles with identity, that will lead to participation in satanic or occult groups, and factors such as a sense of identify formed by cohesiveness with the group and altered states of consciousness that maintain involvement in such groups.

We cannot overemphasize the need for forensic evaluators to take a detailed history developed from multiple sources of data as part of a comprehensive assessment. This view is reinforced by Tucker's (1989) observation of two major forms of adolescent satanic involvement. One form is reportedly very resistant to intervention and is characterized by longstanding adjustment, family, and socialization difficulties; these youths show histories consistent with other observations (Bourget, Gagnon, and Bradford 1988; Wheeler, Wood, and Hatch 1988; Olsson 1983) that many persons who become deeply involved in satanism or other cult groups have preexisting histories of significant psychopathology. The second describes adolescents whose pre-occult background involvement appears relatively undisturbed and whose cult involvement appears to be the product of a developmental crisis.

Because many delinquents have previously documented histories of victimization (Famularo et al. 1989), maltreatment histories must be taken in all cases. Histories of drug and alcohol use, other delinquent activities, sexual activities, school and community functioning, peer-group relations, family history, psychiatric symptoms, and medical contacts are all important elements in understanding the psychological functioning and conduct of the adolescent delinquent. History must also be supplemented by investigation of the specific nature and dynamics of any group involvement since it is likely that, just as with non-occult groups, initial experimentation may be reinforced and sustained by group psychological processes, recruitment methods, or activities. Even "dabblers" may become involved in illegal activities as part of the process of experimentation, indoctrination, acceptance and participation in such groups. Occult dabblers may become involved in rituals that include drug use, animal sacrifice, and self-mutilation, or illegal activities including drug possession and trafficking, vandalism, arson, and assault. As youths become deeply involved in and influenced by the beliefs and activities of the cult (or other deviant subgroup), the frequency of their deviant and criminal behavior is likely to increase over time.

Still other adolescents experiment or practice in a solitary fashion. These "loners" seem more likely to be attracted to violent variants of occult practices, and to elaborate them in a manner consistent with preexisting pathology (Tucker 1989; Griffis n.d.). In such cases, comprehensive forensic assessment should include evaluation of any long-term indicators of psychiatric disturbance, social dysfunction, and predatory behavior. Structured psychological testing may be useful in documenting personality disturbance, delusion or thought disorder, paranoia, preoccupations with violence or perversions, or other forms of psychotic or psychopathic process.

Evaluators must undertake a careful process of differential diagnosis especially when adolescent perpetrators present with indications of thought disorder, hallucinations, other indications of possible psychosis, or other oddities of affect and interpersonal presentation. Any indication of a history of significant maltreatment underscores the need to understand the clinical implications of an unusual presentation. While we do not wish to underestimate the impact of group socialization processes, we stress that consideration should be also be given to psychiatric diagnoses, including malingering, schizophrenia, schizoid and schizotypal personality disorders, dissociative disorders and dissociative hallucinosis, post-traumatic stress disorder, temporal lobe epilepsy (Schenk and Bear 1981; Kinscherff 1988), and intoxication with drugs including hallucinogens.

Just as with adults, criminal conduct committed merely due to association with deviant groups, or motivated by shared or idiosyncratic belief systems are not legally protected. Forensic evaluators must not rapidly conclude that any criminal conduct is linked to occult or other unorthodox belief systems even where there is evidence that the adolescent is involved. Some groups or individuals become involved in drug trafficking or other illegal conduct even before they adopt an occult belief system. Criminal intimidation of members or other persons aware of the illegal activities in such and similar instances may be motivated more by the need to keep the illegal activities secret than by the need or desire to conceal occult secrets or practices. Unorthodox group affiliations or belief systems are often used belatedly to explain, rationalize, or justify criminal activity when more common motivations are actually at the heart of the conduct.

The usual forensic mental health questions arising in all criminal proceedings may be raised in prosecuting these adolescents. However, in some jurisdictions it may not be legally relevant in juvenile proceedings to raise questions of competence to stand trial (capacity to understand the proceedings and assist in his own defense) and criminal responsibility (whether the defendant's mental state at the time of the crime was such that he can be considered morally responsible for the offense). Even where questions of competence and responsibility are legally allowed, there is often uncertainty whether these issues are relevant in juvenile cases (Weissman 1983; Grisso, Miller, and Sales 1987). They rarely come up in the prosecution of adolescent perpetrators. However, there are several specific issues that are likely to be raised in cases of juvenile occult involvement linked to criminal activity. In some situations involving adolescent perpetrators the juvenile may be acting as part of a group that includes adult perpetrators, or other juveniles that authorities are more interested in successfully prosecuting. In some cases it may appear that the adult perpetrators traumatized or otherwise coerced the adolescent to engage in the illegal conduct. In such situations the prosecution may offer the adolescent the opportunity to plead guilty to a reduced charge in exchange for testimony against the other perpetrators. Then the question is whether the traumatized adolescent has incurred any emotional or other psychiatric damage that may interfere with his ability to understand the legal implications of pleading guilty, and in agreeing to offer testimony. Forensic evaluation may assist in determining whether or not the adolescent is capable of appreciating the legal issues, or what special arrangements might be made to assist him to develop the necessary capacities.

The issue of "amenability to treatment" as a juvenile is the mainstay of forensic mental health evaluations of juveniles. The goal of the evaluation is to determine whether the juvenile suffers from any psychiatric or emotional impairment, what might be expected from any treatment for these impairments, and how the legal system might best respond to the offender in light of the clinical needs and prognosis.

When the juvenile is charged with crimes that appear ritualized, or to have stemmed from involvement in the activities of cult groups, gangs, skinheads, or other deviant subgroups, the multidimensional factors detailed above are also useful in assessing amenability to treatment. Fundamental elements of the evaluation are (1) the precise nature of the maltreatment or other crimes the juvenile is alleged to have committed; (2) whether or not the juvenile's conduct was committed in the context of a group; (3) the degree of involvement of the juvenile and the specific beliefs and practices of the group; (4) possible experiences of traumatic indoctrination, psychological manipulation, or ongoing coercion; and (5) any history of psychopathology that predates group involvement, or appears to exist independent of group practices.

There are important legal implications among cases depending upon whether the alleged conduct seems to stem from any specific psychopathology, coercion, peer support, indoctrination and embraced belief, or direct rewards from the criminal conduct itself. For example, a claim of direct coercion for the alleged conduct may constitute a legal defense in some cases, while evidence that the same conduct was committed for peer approval or rewards such as money will not have merit as a legal defense.

Maltreatment or other criminal conduct motivated by a belief system is not protected. However, a defendant may have legal defenses available if those beliefs and related conduct were the product of a mental illness, and possibly if it can be shown that the conduct stemmed from traumatization and extreme intimidation by others short of direct coercion. However, "brainwashing" defenses that rely upon claims that the defendant acted from beliefs inculcated by others using extreme methods of manipulation and intimidation are extremely rare even in adult court, and are not likely to be realistic defenses under current legal doctrine.

The relatively informal procedures in juvenile settings often encourage assessment early in the legal process, before there has been an adjudication of the facts. When the details of the youth's involvement are in dispute or otherwise remain unclear despite review of interview material, victim statements to police, police reports, or other sources of information, it may be wise to defer evaluation of amenability to treatment until after formal adjudication of the facts. Though legal adjudication does not guarantee that the whole truth of the matter will be clear, the fact that the case has been resolved may improve the validity of the evaluation data base. Validity may be improved after adjudication simply because there will be a wider variety of evidence available, that evidence itself will have been tested by the adversarial process, and the defendant being at less legal risk will be more open about sharing details of events.

If the question is whether the juvenile should be tried in juvenile or criminal court, then evaluation of amenability to treatment must be carried out prior to adjudication, and according to the legal requirements of the relevant jurisdiction (Breed v. Jones). This situation presents special challenges in terms of ethics and clinical validity that are beyond the scope of this chapter (Barnum 1987; Quinn 1988; Benedek 1985). However, it is very important for forensic examiners to be quite clear with the juvenile defendant and his attorney about the purpose and stakes of the evaluation. Specifically, the examiner should clarify with them whether or not the defendant will discuss the offenses in question during the evaluation, given that no adjudication has yet been made and any information given during the interviews will not be confidential (Barnum, Silverberg, and Nied 1987; Barnum 1990).

Conclusion

The area of ritualized maltreatment is still a controversial and developing area of inquiry, one that deserves a measured approach. For forensic mental health clinicians there can be no more personally and professionally challenging responsibility, operating as they do between two very different worlds and ways of thinking. We must adapt to the fact that clinicians can endure more uncertainty and extremes of human behavior than can the legal process and resign ourselves to accepting that we may never establish certainty about the experiences of victims of child maltreatment.

The first step to dealing with this frustration and uncertainty is to accept it, to avoid overinterpreting ambiguous data in order to confirm or refute details of maltreatment, and to avoid getting lost in unending attempts to determining the "facts." Clinicians must be able to attend to the pain and functional distur-bances of a child and family even if the details of its origins remain obscure.

A second step is to come to terms with the horror of the experiences of these children, and the seriousness and pervasiveness of their disturbances. It is important to avoid becoming preoccupied with the abuse, or with the fantasy that by somehow finding a direct route to addressing the emotional effects of their abusive experiences that we can rapidly make the child or family whole. Rather, it is important to begin focusing on the strengths of the survivors, and to intervene in comprehensive ways. These interventions will often include combinations of individual and family psychotherapy, psychopharmacy, and educational and peer socializing interventions. It may include supporting the child and family in developing a deep personal or spiritual understanding of the experience.

References

American Bar Association. 1985. "Guidelines for the Fair Treatment of Child Witnesses in Cases Where Child Abuse is Alleged." In *Sexual Abuse Allegations in Custody and Visitation Cases*, ed. E. B. Nicholson, 291–96. Washington, D.C.: American Bar Association.

Barnum, Richard. 1987. "Clinical Evaluation of Juvenile Delinquents Facing Transfer to Adult Court." *Journal of the American Academy of Child and Adolescent Psychiatry* 26:922–25.

———. 1990. "Self-Incrimination and Denial in the Juvenile Transfer Evaluation." *Bulletin of the American Academy of Psychiatry and the Law* 18:413–28.

———. Janet Silverberg, and David Nied. 1987. "Patient Warnings in Court-Ordered Evaluations of Children and Families." *Bulletin of the American Academy of Psychiatry and the Law* 15:283–300.

Bauer, H. 1983. "Preparation of the Sexually Abused Child for Court Testimony." *Bulletin of the American Academy of Psychiatry and Law* 11:287–89.

Benedek, E. P. 1985. "Waiver of Juveniles to Adult Court." In *Emerging Issues in Child Psychiatry and the Law*, ed E. P. Benedek and D. H. Schetky. New York: Brunner/Mazel.

———. , and D. H. Schetky. 1985. "Allegations of Sexual Abuse in Custody and Visitation Disputes." In *Emerging Issues in Child Psychiatry and the Law*, ed. E. P. Benedek and D. H. Schetky, (23–30.New York: Brunner/Mazel.

Berliner, Lucy. 1988. "Deciding Whether a Child Has Been Sexually Abused." In *Sexual Abuse Allegations in Custody and Visitation Cases*, ed. E. B. Nicholson, 48–69. Washington, D.C.: American Bar Association.

———. , and M. K. Barbieri. 1984. "The Testimony of the Child Victim of Sexual Assault." *Journal of Social Issues* 40:125–37.

———. , K. M. Quinn, M. Sauzier, and D. H. Schetky. 1989. "Resolved: Child Sexual Abuse is Overdiagnosed." *Journal of the American Academy of Child and Adolescent Psychiatry* 28:789–97.

Blood, L. O. 1989. *Satanism and Satanism-Related Crime: A Resource Guide*. Weston, Mass.: American Family Foundation.

Boat, Barbara, and M. D. Everson. 1988. "Use of Anatomical Dolls among Professionals in Sexual Abuse Evaluations." *Child Abuse and Neglect* 12, no. 2:171–79.

Bourget, Dominique, André Gagnon, and J. M. W. Bradford. 1988. "Satanism in a Psychiatric Adolescent Population." *Canadian Journal of Psychiatry* 33(3):197–202.

Bowman, Jerry, Massachusetts State Police. 1990. Personal Communication.

Braunfield v. Brown, 366 U.S. 599, 81 S.Ct. 1144, 6 L. Ed. 2d 563 (1961).

Breed v. Jones, 421 U.S. 519, 955 S.Ct. 1779, 44 L.Ed.2d 346.

Bureau of Justice Statistics, U.S. Department of Justice. 1988. *Report to the Nation on Crime and Justice.* 2d ed. Washington, D.C.: Document No. NJC-105506, March 1988.

Burgess, A. W., and L. L. Holstrom. 1978. "The Child and the Family during the Court Process." In *Sexual Assault of Children and Adolescents,* ed. A. W. Burgess, A. N. Groth, L. L. Holstrom, and S. M. Sgroi, 205–30. Lexington, Mass.: Lexington Books.

Cahill, Tim. 1986. *Buried Dreams: Inside the Mind of a Serial Killer.* New York: Bantam Books.

Cantwell v. Connecticut, 310 U.S. 296, 60 S.Ct. 900, 84 L. Ed. 1213 (1940).

Clark, J. G. 1979. "Cults.' *Journal of the American Medical Association* 242: 279–81.
———. M.D. Langone, R. E. Schechter, and R.C.B. Daley. 1981. *Destructive Cult Conversion: Theory, Research, and Treatment.* Weston, Mass.: American Family Foundation.

Commonwealth v. Drew, 397 Mass. 65, 78–80, 489 N.E.2d 1233 (1986).

Conte, J. R. 1990. "Validating Allegations of Child Sexual Abuse: Dilemmas for the Mental Health Professional. *Child, Youth, and Family Services Quarterly* (APA Division 37) 13, no. 3 (Summer):7, 18–19.

Cozolino, Louis. 1989. "The Ritual Abuse of Children: Implications for Clinical Research and Practice." *Journal of Sex Research* 26: 131–138.

Edwards, L. M. 1990. "Ritual Assault and Sexual Abuse." *Journal of Child and Youth Care* (Special Issue: *In the Shadow of Satan: The Ritual Abuse of Children*): 67–88.

Everson, M. D., and B. W. Boat. 1989. "False Allegations of Sexual Abuse by Children and Adolescents." *Journal of the American Academy of Child and Adolescent Psychiatry* 28(2):230–35.

Famularo, Richard, Robert Kinscherff, Terence Fenton, and S. M. Bolduc. 1989. "Child Maltreatment Histories among Runaway and Delinquent Children." (In press)

Famularo, Richard, Robert Kinscherff, and Terence Fenton. 1989. "Posttraumatic Stress Disorder among Maltreated Children Presenting to a Juvenile Court." *American Journal of Forensic Psychiatry* 10 no. (3):33–39.

Famularo, Richard, Robert Kinscherff, and Terence Fenton. 1990. "Differences in Acute and Chronic Presentation of Childhood Posttraumatic Stress Disorder." *Child Abuse and Neglect* 14: 439–44.

Famularo, Richard, Robert Kinscherff, and Terence Fenton. 1990. "Posttraumatic Stress Disorder among Children Clinically Diagnosed as Borderline Personality Disorder." *Journal of Nervous and Mental Disease* (in press).

Finkelhor, David, L. Williams, and N. Burns. 1988. *Sexual Abuse in Day Care: A National Study.* Durham, N.H.: Family Research Laboratory.

Fish-Murray, C. C., E. V. Kobey, and B. A. van der Kolk. 1987. "Evolving Ideas: The Effect of Abuse on Children's Thought." In *Psychological Trauma,* ed. B. A. van der Kolk, 89–110. Washington, D.C.: American Psychiatric Press.

Galanter, Mark. 1982. "Charismatic Religious Sects and Psychiatry: An Overview." *American Journal of Psychiatry* 139:1539–48.
———. 1989. *Cults.* New York: Oxford University Press.

Ganaway, G. K. 1989. "Historical Truth versus Narrative Truth: Clarifying the Role of

Exogenous Trauma in the Etiology of Multiple Personality Disorder and Its Variants." *Dissociation* 2 no. (4):205–20.

Gardner, R. A. 1987. *The Parental Alienation Syndrome and the Differentiation between Fabricated and Genuine Child Sex Abuse.* Cresskill, N.J.: Creative Therapeutics.

Goodman, G. S. 1990. "Child Sexual Abuse: The Search for Professional Agreement on 'Relevant' Research on Children's Reports." *Child, Youth, and Family Services Quarterly* (APA Division 37) 13, no. 3 (Summer):4.

———. E. A. Pyle, D. P. H. Jones, P. England, L. K. Port, L. Rudy, and L. Prado. 1988. "Emotional Effects of Criminal Court Testimony on Child Sexual Assault Victims." Final Report to the National Institute of Justice.

Goodwin, Jean. 1985. "Credibility Problems in Multiple Personality Disorder Patients and Abused Children." In *Childhood Antecedents of Multiple Personality,* ed. R. P. Kluft, 3–19. Washington, D.C.: American Psychiatric Press.

Gould, Catherine. 1987. "Satanic Ritual Abuse: Child Victims, Adult Survivors, System Response." *California Psychologist* 22, no. 3:76–92.

Green, A. 1988. "True and False Allegations of Sexual Abuse in Child Custody Disputes." *Journal of the American Academy of Child and Adolescent Psychiatry* 25:449–56.

Green, M. A., and C. L. Tamarkin. 1988. "A Boy's Love of Satan Ends in Murder, a Death Sentence—and Grisly Memories." *People Magazine,* December.

Griel, A. R., and D. R. Rudy. 1984. "Social Cocoons: Encapsulation and Identity Transformation Organizations." *Social Inquiry* 54: 260–78.

Griffis, Dale. 1990. Personal Communication.

———. (n.d.) *The Four Faces of Satan.* Unpublished manuscript.

Grisso, Thomas, M. O. Miller, and Bruce D. Sales. 1987. "Competence to Stand Trial in Juvenile Court." *International Journal of Law and Psychiatry* 10, no. 1: 1–20.

Herman, J. L., and B. A. van der Kolk. 1987. "Traumatic Antecedents of Borderline Personality Disorder." In *Psychological Trauma,* ed. B. A. van der Kolk, 111–26. Washington, D.C.: American Psychiatric Press.

Hicks, R. D. 1989. "The Devil and Dick Tracy: The Police Pursuit of Satanic Crime." Cited in *Occult Crime: A Law-Enforcement Primer,* State of California, Office of Criminal Justice Planning, 86.

Hill, Sally, and Jean Goodwin. 1989. "Satanism: Similarities between Patient Accounts and Pre-Inquisition Historical Sources." *Dissociation* 2:39–44.

Hollingsworth, Jan. 1986. *Unspeakable Acts.* New York: Contemporary Books.

Idaho v. Wright, 110 S.Ct. 3139.

Idaho v. Wright, 116 Idaho, at 388, 775 P.2d, at 1230 (1989).

In re Amber B. and Teela B., 191 Cal.App. 3rd, 682 (1987).

In re J. H., 505 N.E.2d (1987).

In the Matter of Margery Karr, 323 N.Y.S.2d 122 (1971).

In the Matter of X, a child under the age of 18 years, Idaho Department of Health and Welfare v. Syme, 110 Idaho 44, 714 P2d 13 (1986).

Jones, Larry, Boise, Idaho, Police Department and Director of Cult Crime Impact Network. As quoted in *Occult Crime: A Law-Enforcement Primer,* State of California, Office of Criminal Justice Planning, 37.

Kahaner, Larry. 1988. *Cults That Kill.* New York: Warner Books.

Kelley, S. J. 1988. "Ritualistic Abuse of Children: Dynamics and Impact." *Cultic Studies Journal* 5, no. 2:228–36.

———. 1989. "Stress Responses of Children to Sexual Abuse and Ritualistic Abuse in Day-Care Centers." *Journal of Interpersonal Violence* 4, no. 4: 501–13.

———. 1990. "Parental Stress Response to Sexual Abuse and Ritualistic Abuse of Children in Day-Care Centers." *Nursing Research* 39, no. 1: 25–29.

Kinscherff, Robert. 1988. "Dissociative States in Temporal Lobe Epilepsy and Multiple Personality Disorder." Ph.D. diss., City University of New York. (University Microfilms, University of Michigan, Ann Arbor.)

Kluft, R. P. 1985. "Childhood Multiple Personality Disorder: Predictors, Clinical Findings, and Treatment Results." In *Childhood Antecedents of Multiple Personality*, ed. R. P. Kluft, 167–96. Washington, D.C.: American Psychiatric Press.

Krugman, Richard, and D.P.H. Jones. 1987. "Incest and Other Forms of Sexual Abuse." In *The Battered Child*, ed. R. E. Hefler and R. S. Kempe, 4th ed., 286–300. Chicago: University of Chicago Press.

Langone, M. D., and L. O. Blood. 1990. *Satanism and Occult Related Violence: What You Should Know.* Weston, Mass.: American Family Foundation.

Lanning, Kenneth V. 1989. *Satanic, Occult, Ritualistic Crime: A Law-Enforcement Perspective.* Quantico, Va.: FBI Academy.

Libow, J. A. 1986. "Three Forms of Factitious Illness in Children: When Is It Munchausen Syndrome by Proxy?" *American Journal of Orthopsychiatry* 56, no. 4: 602–11.

Lifton, Robert. 1961. *Thought Reform and the Psychology of Totalism.* New York: W. W. Norton.

Lipovsky, J. A. 1990. "Innovative Practices for Sexually Abused Children in the Court System: Where Are They Needed?" *Child, Youth, and Family Services Quarterly* (APA Division 37) 13, no. 3:8–9.

Loftus, E. F. 1979. *Eyewitness Testimony.* Cambridge, Mass.: Harvard University Press.

Louisiana in the interests of the Minors R. W. and K. L. W. v. J. L. W., 491 So.2d 652 (1986).

Maryland v. Craig, 110 S.Ct. 3157 (1990).

Masson, Jeffery. 1984. *Assault on Truth.* Toronto, Ont.: Collins.

McLeer, S. V., Esther Deblinger, M. S. Atkins, E. B. Foa, and D. L. Ralphe. 1988. "Post-traumatic Stress Disorder in Sexually Abused Children." *Journal of the American Academy of Child and Adolescent Psychiatry* 27, no. 5: 650–54.

Meadow, Ray. 1977. "Munchausen Syndrome by Proxy: The Hinterland of Child Abuse." *Lancet* 2: 343–45.

Melton, G. B. 1981. "Children's Competency to Testify." *Law and Human Behavior* 5: 73–85.

———. John Petrila, N. G. Poythress, and C. Slobogin. 1987. *Psychological Evaluations for the Courts: A Handbook for Mental Health Professionals and Lawyers.* New York: Guilford Press.

———. and So. Limber. 1989. "Psychologists' Involvement in Cases of Maltreatment: Limits of Role Expertise." *American Psychologist* 44:1225–33.

Miller, Alice. 1986. *Thou Shalt Not Be Aware.* New York: Meridian.

Myers, J. B., G. S. Goodman, and KD. Saywitz. 1990. Amicus brief to the United States Supreme Court in Wright v. Idaho.

Nurcombe, B, and P Langelier. 1986. "The Child as Witness: Competency and Credibility." *Journal of the American Academy of Adolescent and Child Psychiatry* 25, no. 2: 462–73.

Olsson, P. A. 1983. "Adolescent Involvement with the Supernatural and Cults." In *Psychodynamic Perspectives on Religion, Sect, and Cult,* ed. D. A. Halperin. Boston: John Wright.

Parker, J. 1982. "The Rights of Child Witnesses: Is the Court a Protector or Perpetrator?" *New England Law Review* 17:643–717.

Putnam, F. W. 1989. *Diagnosis and Treatment of Multiple Personality Disorder.* New York: Guilford Press.

Quinn, K. M. 1986. "Competency to Be a Witness: A Major Child Forensic Issue." *Bulletin of the American Academy of Psychiatry and the Law* 14, no. 4: 311–21.

———. 1988. "Waiver of Juveniles to Adult Court and the Prediction of Dangerousness." *American Academy of Psychiatry and the Law Newsletter* 13:33–34.

———. Sue White, and Gail Santilli. 1989. "Influences of an Interviewer's Behaviors in Child Sexual Abuse Investigations." *Bulletin of the American Academy of Psychiatry and the Law* 17:45–52.

Rand, D. C. 1989. "Munchausen Syndrome by Proxy as a Possible Factor When Abuse is Falsely Alleged." *Issues in Child Abuse Accusations* 1, no. 4: 32–34.

———. 1990. "Munchausen Syndrome by Proxy: Integration of Classic and Contemporary Types." *Issues in Child Abuse Accusations* 2, no. 2: 83–89.

Raschke, Carl. 1990. *Painted Black.* San Francisco: Harper & Row.

Ritual Abuse Task Force, Los Angeles County Commission for Women. September 15, 1989. *Ritual Abuse: Definitions, Glossary, The Use of Mind Control.*

Robbins, TR., and DA. Anthony. 1980. "The Limits of 'Coercive Persuasion' As an Explanation for Conversion to Authoritarian Sects." *Political Psychology* 2, no. 2:22–37.

Rosenberg, D. A. 1987. "Web of Deceit: A Literature Review of Munchausen Syndrome by Proxy." *Child Abuse and Neglect* 2:547–63.

Runyan, B. K., M. D. Everson, G. A. Edelshon, W. M. Hunter, and M. L. Coulter. 1988. "Impact of Legal Intervention on Sexually Abused Children." *Journal of Pediatrics* 113:647–53.

Schenk, L., and D. Bear. 1981. "Multiple Personality and Related Dissociative Phenomena in Patients with Temporal Lobe Epilepsy." *American Journal of Psychiatry* 138:1311–15.

Schetky, D. H., 1988. *Standards for the Evaluation of Sexually Abused Children.* Washington, D.C.: American Academy of Child and Adolescent Psychiatry.

Sgroi, S. M., F. S. Porter, and L. C. Blick. 1982. "Validation of Child Sexual Abuse." In *Handbook of Clinical Intervention in Child Sexual Abuse,* ed. S. M. Sgroi, 140–156. Lexington, Mass.: Lexington Books.

Simpson, G. E. 1978. *Black Religions in the New World.* New York: Columbia University Press.

S.R.S. v. Oklahoma, 728 P.2d 515.

State of California, Office of Criminal Justice Planning. 1990. *Occult Crime: A Law-Enforcement Primer.* Sacramento, Ca.

State of Maine v. Waterhouse, Decision No. 4216, Law Docket No. Lin-85-23.

State of Nebraska v. Michael Ryan, 444 N.W.2d 610, 233 Neb. 74 (1989).

Stone, A. A. 1984. "The Ethics of Forensic Psychiatry: A View from the Ivory Tower." In *Law, Psychiatry, and Morality,* 57–75.

Tedesco, J. F., and S. V. Schnell. 1987. "Children's Reactions to Sex Abuse Investigation and Litigation." *Child Abuse and Neglect* 11:267–72.

Terr, L. C. 1986. "The Child Psychiatrist and the Child Witness." *Journal of the American Academy of Child and Adolescent Psychiatry* 25, no. 2: 473–81.

———. 1989. "Child Sexual Abuse: Why the Controversy?" *Journal of the American Academy of Child and Adolescent Psychiatry* 28: 788–795.

———. 1991. "Childhood Traumas: An Outline and an Overview." *American Journal of Psychiatry* 148, no. 1: 10–20.

Tucker, Roy. 1989. "Teen Satanism." Paper presented at the "Ritual Abuse: Fact or Fiction?" Conference. Institute for the Prevention of Child Abuse. Alymer, Ontario, May 29–30. As cited in *Satanism and Occult Related Violence: What You Should Know,* by M. D. Langone and L. O. Blood, 77–81. Weston, Mass.: American Family Foundation.

Underwager, Ralph, and Hollida Wakefield. 1989. *The Real World of Child Interrogations.* Springfield, Ill.: C. C. Thomas.

United States Department of Health and Human Services. 1988. *Study Findings: Study of National Incidence and Prevalence of Child Abuse and Neglect.*

United States v. Ballard, 322 U.S. 78, 64 S.Ct. 882, 88 L. Ed.2d 1148 (1944).

Utah v. Hadfield, 788 P.2d 500 (1990).

Van Benschoten, S. C. 1990. "Multiple Personality Disorder and Satanic Ritual Abuse: The Issue of Credibility." *Dissociation* 3, no. 1:22–30.

Waithe, M. E., J. R. Rappaport, H. C. Weinstein, and B. R, Baumrim. 1982. "Ethical Issues in the Practice of Forensic Psychiatry." *Journal of Psychiatry and Law* 10, no. 1:7–43.

Weissman, J. 1983. "Toward an Integrated Theory of Responsibility in Juvenile Justice." *Denver Law Journal* 60:3.

Weithorn, L. A., and T. Grisso. 1987. "Psychological Evaluations in Divorce Custody: Problems, Principles, Procedures." In *Psychology and Child Custody Determinations: Knowledge, Roles, and Expertise,* ed. L. A. Weithorn, 157–81. Lincoln: University of Nebraska Press.

Wetli, C., and R. Martinez. 1983a. "Forensic Sciences Aspects of Santeria, A Religious Cult of African Origin." *Journal of the Forensic Sciences* (July).

Wetli, C., and R. Martinez. 1983b. "Brujeria: Manifestations of Palo Mayombe in South Florida." *Journal of the Florida Medical Association* (August)

Wheeler, Barbara R., Spence Wood, and J. R. Hatch. 1988. "Assessment and Intervention with Adolescents Involved in Satanism." *Social Work* (November–December) 33(6): 547–550.

White, S R. 1986. "Uses and Abuses of the Sexually Anatomically Correct Dolls." *Division of Child, Youth, and Family Services Newsletter* (APA Division 37) 9, no. 1: 3–6.

———. 1988. "Should Investigatory Use of Anatomical Dolls Be Defined by the Courts?" *Journal of Interpersonal Violence* 3:471–75.

———. and K. M. Quinn. 1988. "Investigatory Independence in Child Sexual Abuse Evaluations: Conceptual Considerations." *Bulletin of the American Academy of Psychiatry and the Law* 16:269–73.

————. and G. Santilli. 1988. "A Review of Clinical Practices and Research Data on Anatomical Dolls." *Journal of Interpersonal Violence* 3: 422–30.

————. and K. M. Quinn. 1989. "Investigatory Independence in Child Sexual Abuse Evaluations: Conceptual Considerations." *Bulletin of the American Academy of Psychiatry and the Law* 17:269–78.

Wolfe, Vicky V., Louise Sas, and Susan K. Wilson. 1987. "Some Issues in Preparing Sexually Abused Children for Courtroom Testimony." *The Behavior Therapist* 10(5):107–13.

Yates, Alayne, and Lenore C. Terr. 1988.(Mar)"Anatomically Correct Dolls—Should They Be Used as the Basis for Expert Testimony?" Academy of *Child and Adolescent Psychiatry* 27, no. 2: 254–57.

Zitelli, B.J., M. F. Seltman, and R. M. Shannon. 1987. "Munchausen Syndrome by Proxy and Its Professional Participants." *American Journal of the Diseases of Children* 141: 1099–1102.

5

A Law-Enforcement Perspective on Allegations of Ritual Abuse

Kenneth V. Lanning, Supervisory Special Agent

Since 1981, I have been assigned to the Behavioral Science Unit at the FBI Academy in Quantico, Virginia, and have specialized in studying all aspects of the sexual victimization of children. The FBI Behavioral Science Unit assists law-enforcement agencies and prosecutors in the United States and foreign countries. It attempts to develop practical applications of the behavioral sciences to the criminal justice system. As a result of training and research conducted by the unit and its successes in analyzing violent crime, many professionals contact the Behavioral Science Unit for assistance and guidance in dealing with violent crime, especially those cases considered different, unusual, or bizarre. This service is provided at no cost and is not limited to crimes under the investigative jurisdiction of the FBI.

In 1983 and 1984, when I first began to hear stories of bizarre cults and human sacrifice in connection with allegations of sexual victimization of children, I tended to believe them. I had been dealing with bizarre, deviant behavior for many years and had long since realized that almost anything is possible. Just when you think that you have heard it all, along comes another strange case. The idea that there are a few cunning, secretive individuals in positions of power somewhere in this country regularly killing a few people as part of some ritual or ceremony and getting away with it is certainly within the realm of possibility. But the number of alleged cases began to grow. We now have hundreds of victims alleging that thousands of offenders are murdering tens of thousands of people, and there is little or no corroborative evidence. The very reason many experts cite for believing these allegations (i.e., many victims, who never met each other, reporting the same events) is the primary reason I began to question some aspects of these allegations.

I have devoted more than seven years part time, and ten years full time, of my professional life to researching, training, and consulting in the area of child sexual abuse and exploitation. The issues of child sexual abuse and exploitation are a big part of my professional life's work. I have no reason to deny their existence or nature. In fact, I have done everything I can to make people more aware of the problem. I can accept no outside income and am paid the same salary by the FBI whether or not children are abused and exploited—and

109

whether the number is one or one million. As someone deeply concerned about and professionally committed to the issue, I do not lightly question the allegations of thousands of victims of child sexual abuse and exploitation.

In response to the accusations that I am a "satanist" who has infiltrated the FBI to facilitate a cover-up, how does anyone (or should anyone have to) disprove such allegations? Although reluctant to dignify such absurd accusations with a reply, all I can say to those who have made such allegations is that they are wrong, and to those who have heard such allegations to carefully consider the source.

The reason I have taken the position I have is not because I support or believe in "satanism," but because I sincerely believe that my approach is the proper and most effective investigative strategy. It would have been easy to sit back, as many have, and say nothing publicly on this controversy. I have spoken out and published on this issue because I am concerned about the credibility of the child sexual abuse issue and outraged that, in some cases, individuals are getting away with molesting children because we cannot prove they are satanic devil worshipers who engage in brainwashing, human sacrifice, and cannibalism as part of a large conspiracy.

There are many valid perspectives from which to assess and evaluate allegations of child sexual abuse. Parents may choose to believe simply because their children make the claims. The level of proof necessary may be minimal because the consequences of believing are within the family.

A therapist may choose to believe simply because his or her professional assessment is that the patient believes the victimization and describes it so vividly. The level of proof necessary may be no more than therapeutic evaluation because the consequences are between the therapist and patient. No independent corroboration may be required.

A social worker must have more real, tangible evidence of abuse in order to take protective action and initiate legal proceedings. The level of proof necessary must be higher because the consequences (denial of visitation, foster care) are greater.

The law-enforcement officer deals with the criminal justice system. The levels of proof necessary are reasonable suspicion, probable cause, and beyond a reasonable doubt, because the consequences (criminal investigation, search and seizure, arrest, incarceration) are so great. The level of proof for taking action on allegations of criminal acts must be more than simply that someone alleged it and it is possible. This in no way denies the validity and importance of the parental, therapeutic, social welfare, or any other perspective of these allegations.

When, however, therapists and other professionals begin to conduct training, publish articles, and communicate through the media the consequences become greater, and therefore the level of proof must be greater. The amount of corroboration necessary to act upon allegations of abuse is dependent upon consequences of such action. We need to be concerned about the dissemination and publication of unsubstantiated allegations of bizarre sexual abuse. Information needs to be disseminated to encourage communication and research about the phenomena. The risks, however, of intervenor and victim "contagion" and public hysteria are potential negative aspects of such dissemination.

Because of the highly emotional and religious nature of this topic, there is a greater possibility that dissemination of information will result in a kind of self-fulfilling prophesy. If such extreme allegations are going to be disseminated to the general public, they must be presented in the context of being assessed and evaluated from a professional perspective. Since most therapists do not have a staff of investigators, the assessment and evaluation of such allegations are areas where law enforcement and other professionals (anthropologists, folklorists, sociologists, etc.) may be of some assistance to each other in validating these cases individually and in general.

The belief that there is a connection between satanism and crime is certainly not new. In fact, one of the oldest theories concerning the causes of crime is demonology. Fear of satanic or occult activity has peaked from time to time throughout history. Concern in the late 1970s focused primarily on "unexplained" deaths and mutilations of animals, and in recent years has focused on child sexual abuse and the human sacrifice of missing children. In 1999 it will probably focus on the impending "end of the world."

Today, "satanism" and a wide variety of other terms are used interchangeably in reference to certain crimes. This discussion will analyze the nature of "satanic, occult, ritualistic" crime and focus on appropriate law-enforcement responses to it.

Recently a flood of law-enforcement seminars and conferences have dealt with satanic and ritualistic crime. These training conferences have various titles, such as "Occult in Crime," "Satanic Cults," "Ritualistic Crime Seminar," "Satanic Influences in Homicide," "Occult Crimes, Satanism, and Teen Suicide," and "Ritualistic Abuse of Children."

The typical conference runs from one to three days, and many of them include the same presenters and instructors. A wide variety of topics are usually discussed during this training as individual presentations by different instructors or grouped together by one of more instructors. Typical topics covered include the following:

1. Historical overview of satanism, witchcraft, and paganism from ancient to modern times

2. Nature and influence of fantasy role-playing games, such as *Dungeons and Dragons*

3. Lyrics, symbolism, and influence of rock and roll, Heavy Metal, and Black Metal music

4. Teenage "stoner" gangs, their symbols, and their vandalism

5. Teenage suicide by adolescents dabbling in the occult

6. Crimes committed by self-styled satanic practitioners, including grave and church desecrations and robberies, animal mutilations, and even murders

7. Ritualistic abuse of children as part of bizarre ceremonies and human sacrifices

8. Organized, traditional, or multigenerational satanic groups involved in organized conspiracies, such as taking over day-care centers, infiltrating police departments, and trafficking in human sacrifice victims

9. The "Big Conspiracy" theory, which implies that satanists are responsible for such things as Adolf Hitler, World War II, abortion, pornography, Watergate, Irangate, and the infiltration of the Department of Justice, the Pentagon, and the White House

During the conferences, these nine areas are linked together through the liberal use of the word "satanism" and some common symbolism (pentagrams, 666, demons, etc.). The implication often is that all are part of a continuum of behavior, a single problem, or some common conspiracy. The information presented is a mixture of fact, theory, opinion, fantasy, and paranoia, and because some of it can be proven or corroborated (desecration of cemeteries, vandalism, etc.), the implication is that it is all true and documented. The distinctions among the different areas are blurred. All this is further complicated by the fact that almost any discussion of satanism and witchcraft is interpreted in the light of the religious beliefs of those in the audience. Faith, not logic and reason, controls the religious beliefs of most people. As a result, some normally skeptical law-enforcement officers accept the information disseminated at these conferences without critically evaluating it or questioning the sources. Nothing said at such conferences will change the religious beliefs of the attendees. Such conferences illustrate the ambiguity and wide variety of terms involved in this issue.

Definitions

The words *satanic, occult,* and *ritualistic* are often used interchangeably. It is difficult to define satanism precisely. No attempt will be made to do so here. However, it is important to realize that, for some people, any religious belief system other than their own is satanic. The Ayatollah Khomeni and Saddam Hussein referred to the United States as the "Great Satan." In the British Parliament, a Protestant leader called the Pope the anti-Christ. In a book titled *Prepare for War,* the author, Rebecca Brown, M.D. (1987), has a chapter entitled "Is Roman Catholicism Witchcraft?" Dr. Brown (1987) also lists among the "doorways" to satanic power and/or demon infestation the following: fortune tellers, horoscopes, fraternity oaths, vegetarianism, yoga, self-hypnosis, relaxation tapes, acupuncture, biofeedback, fantasy role-playing games, adultery, homosexuality, pornography, judo, karate, and rock music. Dr. Brown states that rock music "was a carefully masterminded plan by none other than Satan himself" (ibid. 84). The ideas expressed in this book may seem extreme and even humorous. This book, however, has been recommended as a serious reference in law-enforcement training material on this topic.

In books, lectures, handout material, and conversations, the author has heard all of the following referred to as satanism:

Church of Satan	Scientology
Ordo Templi Orientis	Unification Church
Temple of Set	The Way
Demonology	Hare Krishna
Witchcraft	Rajneesh
Occult	Religious Cults
Paganism	New Age
Santeria	Astrology
Voodoo	Channeling
Rosicrucians	Transcendental Meditation
Freemasonry	Holistic Medicine
Knights Templar	Buddhism
Stoner Gangs	Hinduism
Heavy Metal Music	Mormonism
Rock Music	Islam
Ku Klux Klan	Orthodox Church
Nazis	Roman Catholicism

At law-enforcement training conferences, witchcraft, Santeria, paganism, and the occult are most frequently referred to as forms of satanism. It may be a matter of definition, but these things are not necessarily the same as traditional satanism. The worship of lunar goddesses and nature and the practice of fertility rituals are not satanism. Santeria is a combination of seventeenth-century Roman Catholicism and African paganism.

Occult means simply "hidden." All unreported or unsolved crimes might be regarded as occult, but in this context the term refers to the action or influence of supernatural powers, some secret knowledge of them, or an interest in paranormal phenomena, and does not imply satanism, evil, wrongdoing, or crime. Indeed, historically, the principle crimes deserving consideration as "occult crimes" are the frauds perpetrated by fortune tellers and "psychics" who for a fee arrange visitations with dead loved ones and commit other financial crimes against the gullible.

Many individuals define satanism from a totally Christian perspective, using this word to describe the power of evil in the world. With this definition, any crime, especially those which are particularly bizarre, repulsive, or cruel, can be viewed as satanic in nature. Yet, it is just as difficult to define satanism as it is to define Christianity or any complex spiritual belief system.

What Is Ritualistic Crime?

The biggest confusion, however, is over the word "ritualistic." During law-enforcement training conferences on this topic, "ritualistic" almost always comes to mean satanic or at least spiritual. Ritual can refer to a prescribed religious ceremony, but in its broader meaning refers to any customarily repeated act or series of acts. The need to repeat these acts can be cultural, sexual, or psychological as well as spiritual.

Cultural rituals could include such things as what a family eats on Thanksgiving Day or when and how presents are opened at Christmas. The initiation ceremonies of fraternities, sororities, gangs, and other social clubs are other examples of cultural rituals.

Since 1972, the author has lectured about sexual ritualism, which is nothing more than repeatedly engaging in an act or series of acts in a certain manner because of a sexual need. In order to become aroused and/or gratified, a person must engage in the act in a certain way. This sexual ritualism can include such things as the physical characteristics, age, or gender of the victim, the particular sequence of acts, the bringing or taking of specific objects, and the use of certain words or phrases. This is more than the concept of M.O. (method of operation) known to most police officers. M.O. is something done by an offender because it works. Sexual ritual is something done by an offender because of a need. Deviant acts, such as urinating on, defecating on, or even eviscerating a victim, are far more likely to be the result of sexual ritualism than religious or "satanic" ritualism.

From a criminal investigative perspective, two other forms of ritualism must be recognized. The *Diagnostic and Statistical Manual of Mental Disorders* (DSM-III-R) defines Obsessive-Compulsive Disorder as "repetitive, purposeful, and intentional behaviors that are performed in response to an obsession, or according to certain rules or in a stereotyped fashion" (1987 247). Such compulsive behavior frequently involves rituals. Compulsive ritualism (e.g. excessive cleanliness or fear of disease) can be introduced into sexual behavior. Even many "normal" people have a need for order and predictability and therefore may engage in family or work rituals. Under stress or in times of change, this need for order and ritual may increase. Although such behavior is usually noncriminal such as excessive hand washing or checking that doors are locked, occasionally compulsive ritualism can be part of criminal activity. Certain gamblers or firesetters, for example, are thought by some authorities to be motivated in part through such compulsions. Ritual can also stem from psychotic hallucinations and delusions. A crime can be committed in a precise manner because a voice told the offender to do it that way or because a divine mission required it.

Some psychotics are preoccupied with religious delusions and hear the voice of God or Satan telling them to do things of a religious nature. Offenders who feel little, if any, guilt over their crimes may need little justification for their antisocial behavior. As human beings, however, they fear getting caught and punished for their criminal acts. It is difficult to pray to God for success in doing things that are against His Commandments. A negative spiritual belief system may fulfill their human need for assistance from and belief in a greater power or to deal with superstitions.

Ritualistic crime may fulfill the cultural, spiritual, sexual, and psychological needs of an offender. Crimes may be ritualistically motivated or may have ritualistic elements. The ritual behavior may also fulfill basic criminal needs to manipulate victims, get rid of rivals, send a message to enemies, and intimidate co-conspirators. The leaders of a group may want to play upon the beliefs and superstitions of those around them and try to convince accomplices and enemies that they, the leaders, have special or "supernatural" powers.

The important point for the criminal investigator is to realize that most ritualistic criminal behavior is not motivated simply by satanic or religious ceremonies.

What Is Ritualistic Abuse of Children?

It is not an easy question to answer. Most people today use the term to refer to abuse of children that is part of some evil spiritual belief system, which almost by definition must be satanic.

Dr. Lawrence Pazder, coauthor of *Michelle Remembers* (1980), defines ritualized abuse of children as "repeated physical, emotional, mental, and spiritual assaults combined with a systematic use of symbols and secret ceremonies designed to turn a child against itself, family, society, and God" (Presentation, May 7, 1987, Richmond, Virginia). He also states that "the sexual assault has ritualistic meaning and is not for sexual gratification" (ibid.).

This definition may have value for academics, sociologists, and therapists, but it creates potential problems for law enforcement. Certain acts engaged in with children (kissing, touching, appearing naked, etc.) may be criminal if performed for sexual gratification. If the ritualistic acts were in fact performed for spiritual indoctrination, potential prosecution can be jeopardized, particularly if the acts can be defended as constitutionally protected religious expression. The mutilation of a baby's genitals for sadistic sexual pleasure is a crime. The circumcision of a baby's genitals for religious reasons is most likely *not* a crime. The intent of the acts is important for criminal prosecution.

I cannot define ritualistic abuse precisely and prefer not to use the term. It is confusing, misleading, and counterproductive. The newer term *satanic ritual abuse* (SRA) is even worse. Certain observations, however, are important for investigative understanding.

Not all spiritually motivated ritualistic activity is satanic. Santeria, witchcraft, voodoo, and most religious cults are not satanism. In fact, most spiritually or religiously based abuse of children has nothing to do with satanism. Most child abuse that could be termed ritualistic by various definitions is more likely to be physical and psychological rather than sexual in nature. If a distinction needs to be made between satanic and nonsatanic child abuse, the indicators for that distinction must be related to specific satanic symbols, artifacts, or doctrine rather than the mere presence of any ritualistic element.

Not all such ritualistic activity with a child is a crime. Almost all parents with religious beliefs indoctrinate their children into that belief system. Is circumcision for religious reasons child abuse? Does having a child kneel on a hard floor reciting the rosary constitute child abuse? Does having a child chant a satanic prayer or attend a black mass constitute child abuse? Does a religious belief in corporal punishment constitute child abuse? Does group care of children in a commune or cult constitute child abuse? Does the fact that any acts in question were performed with parental permission affect the nature of the crime? Many ritualistic acts, whether satanic or not, are simply not crimes. To open the Pandora's box of labeling child abuse as "ritualistic" means to apply the definition to all acts by all spiritual belief systems.

When a victim describes and investigation corroborates what sounds like ritualistic activity, several possibilities must be considered. The ritualistic activity may be part of the excessive religiosity of mentally disturbed, even psychotic offenders. It may be a misunderstood part of sexual ritualism. The ritualistic activity may be incidental to any real abuse. The offender may be involved in ritualistic activity with a child and also may be abusing a child, but one may have little or nothing to do with the other.

The offender may be deliberately engaging in ritualistic activity with a child as part of child abuse. The motivation, however, may be not to indoctrinate the child into a belief system, but to lower the inhibitions of, to control and manipulate, and/or to confuse the child. In all the turmoil over this issue, it would be a very effective strategy for any child molester to deliberately introduce ritualistic elements to his crime to confuse the child and therefore the criminal justice system.

The ritualistic activity and the child abuse may be integral parts of some spiritual belief system. In that case, the greatest risk is to the children of the practitioners. But this is true of all cults, not just satanic cults. A high potential of abuse exists for any children raised in a group isolated from the mainstream of society, especially if the group has a charismatic leader whose orders are blindly obeyed by the members. Sex, money, and power are most often the main motivations of the leaders of such cults.

What Makes a Crime Satanic, Occult, or Ritualistic?

Some would answer that it is the offender's spiritual beliefs or membership in a cult or "church." If that is the criteria, why not label the crimes committed by Protestants, Catholics, and Jews in the same way? Were Jim Jones's atrocities in Guyana "Christian" crimes?

Some would answer that it is the presence of certain symbols in the possession or home of the perpetrator. What does it mean then to find a crucifix, Bible, or rosary in the possession or home of a bank robber, embezzler, child molester, or murderer? If different criminals possess the same symbols, are they necessarily part of one big conspiracy?

Others would answer that it is the presence of certain symbols such as pentagrams or inverted crosses at the crime scene. What does it mean then to find a cross spray-painted on a wall or carved into the body of a victim? What does it mean for a perpetrator to leave a Bible tied to his murder victim? What about the possibility that an offender deliberately left such symbols to make it look like a "satanic" crime?

Some would argue that it is the bizarreness or cruelness of the crime perhaps involving body mutilation, amputation, drinking of blood, eating of flesh, or use of urine or feces. Does this mean that all individuals involved in lust, murder, sadism, vampirism, cannibalism, urophilia, and coprophilia are satanists or occult practitioners? What does this say about the bizarre crimes of psychotic killers such as Ed Gein or Richard Trenton Chase, both of whom mutilated their victims as part of their psychotic delusions?

A few might even answer that it is the fact that the crime was committed on a date with satanic or occult significance (Halloween, May Eve, etc.) or the fact that the perpetrator claims that Satan told him to commit the crime. What does this mean for crimes committed on Thanksgiving or Christmas? What does this say about crimes committed by perpetrators who claim that God or Jesus told them to do it? One note of interest is the fact that in handout and reference material I collected, the number of dates with satanic or occult significance ranges from 8 to 110. This is compounded by the fact that it is sometimes stated that satanists can celebrate these holidays on several days on either side of the official date or that the birthdays of practitioners can also be holidays. Thus, according to these handouts, any day could be such a holiday. The exact names and exact dates of the holidays and the meaning of symbols listed may also vary depending on who prepared the material. In addition, the handout material is typically distributed without identifying the author or documenting the original source of the information. It is then frequently photocopied by attendees and passed on to other police officers with no one really knowing its validity or origin.

Most, however, would probably answer that what makes a crime satanic, occult, or ritualistic is the motivation for the crime. It is a crime that is spiritually motivated by a religious belief system. How then do we label the following crimes?

- Parents defy a court order and send their children to an unlicensed Christian school.

- Parents refuse to send their children to any school because they are waiting for the Second Coming of Christ.

- Parents beat their child to death because he or she will not follow their Christian beliefs.

- Parents violate child labor laws because they believe the Bible requires such work.

- Individuals bomb an abortion clinic or kidnap the doctor because their religious belief system says abortion is murder.

- A child molester reads the Bible to his victims in order to justify his sex acts with them.

- Parents refuse lifesaving medical treatment for a child because of their religious beliefs.

- Parents starve and beat their child to death because their minister said the child was possessed by demonic spirits.

Some people would argue that the Christians who committed these crimes misunderstood and distorted their religion while satanists who commit crimes are following theirs. But who decides what constitutes a misinterpretation of a religious belief system? The individuals who committed the crimes described above, however misguided, believed that they were following their religion as they understood it. Religion was and is used to justify such social behavior as the Crusades, the Inquisition, Apartheid, segregation, and recent violence in Northern Ireland, India, Lebanon and Nigeria.

Who decides exactly what "satanists" believe? In this country, we cannot even agree on what Christians believe. At many law-enforcement conferences *The Satanic Bible* (1969) is used to answer this question, and it is often contrasted or compared with the Christian Bible. *The Satanic Bible* is, in essence, a short paperback book written by one man in 1969. To compare it to a book written by over thirty authors over a period of thousands of years is ridiculous, even ignoring the possibility of Divine revelation in the Judeo-Christian Bible. What satanists believe certainly isn't limited to other peoples' interpretation of a few books. More importantly, it is subject to some degree of interpretation by individual believers just as Christianity is. The criminal behavior of one person claiming belief in a religion does not necessarily imply guilt or blame to others claiming belief. In addition, simply claiming membership in a religion does not necessarily make it so.

The fact is that far more crime and child abuse have been committed by zealots in the name of God, Jesus, Mohammed and other mainstream religion than has ever been committed in the name of Satan. Many people, including myself, don't like that statement, but few can argue with it.

Although defining a crime as satanic, occult, or ritualistic would probably involve a combination of the criteria set forth above, the author has been unable to clearly define such a crime. Each potential definition presents a different set of problems when measured against an objective, rational, and constitutional perspective. Each offender in a group may have a different motivation for the crime. I have discovered that the facts of so-called satanic crimes are often significantly different from what is described at law-enforcement training conferences or in the media. The actual involvement of satanism or the occult in these cases usually turns out to be secondary, insignificant, or nonexistent.

Historical Overview

In order to deal with the problem of child sex rings, it is important to have an historical perspective of society's attitudes about child sexual abuse. I can provide a brief synopsis of recent attitudes in the United States here, but those desiring more detailed information about such societal attitudes, particularly in other cultures and in the more distant past, should refer to Florence Rush's book, *The Best Kept Secret: Sexual Abuse of Children* (1980) and Sander J. Breiner's book, *Slaughter of the Innocents* (1990).

Society's attitude about child sexual abuse and exploitation can be summed up in one word: denial. Most people do not want to hear about and would prefer to pretend that child sexual victimization just does not occur. Today, however, it is difficult to pretend that it does not happen. Stories and reports about child sexual victimization are a daily occurrence.

It is important for professionals dealing with child sexual abuse to recognize and learn to manage this denial of a serious problem. Professionals must overcome the denial and encourage society to deal with, report, and prevent child sexual abuse.

Some professionals, however, in their zeal to make American society aware of the sexual victimization of children, may exaggerate the problem. Presentations and literature with poorly documented or misleading claims that one child in three is being sexually molested, about a $5 billion kiddie-porn industry, about child slavery rings, and about 50,000 stranger-abducted children are not uncommon. The problem is bad enough without this kind of hysteria. Professionals should cite reputable and scientific studies and note the sources of information. If they do not, when the exaggerations and distortions are discovered, their credibility and the credibility of the issue are lost.

Stranger Danger

During the 1950s and early 1960s, the primary focus in the literature on sexual abuse of children was on "stranger danger"—the dirty old man in the wrinkled raincoat. If one could not deny the existence of child sexual abuse, one described victimization in simplistic terms of good and evil. The "stranger danger" approach to preventing child sexual abuse is clear-cut. We immediately know who and what the good guys and bad guys are.

The FBI distributed a poster that epitomized this attitude. It showed a man, with his hat pulled down, hiding behind a tree with a bag of candy in his hands. He was waiting for a sweet little girl walking home from school alone. At the top it read, "Boys and girls, color the page, memorize the rules." At the bottom it read, "For your protection, remember to turn down gifts from strangers, and refuse rides offered by strangers." The poster clearly contrasts the evil of the offender with the goodness of the child victim.

The myth of the child molester as the dirty old man in the wrinkled raincoat is now being reevaluated based on what we now know about the kinds of people who victimize children. In fact, the child molester can look like anyone else and even be someone we know and like.

There is another myth that is still with us and is far less likely to be discussed. This is the myth of the victim as a completely innocent little girl walking down the street minding her own business. It may be more important to dispel this myth than the myth of stranger danger, especially when talking about the sexual exploitation of children and child sex rings. Society seems to have a problem dealing with any sexual abuse case in which the offender is not completely "bad" or the victim is not completely "good." Society seems to find it difficult to deal with child victims who simply behave like human beings and respond to the attention and affection of offenders by voluntarily and repeatedly returning to the offender's home. It confuses us to see the victims in child pornography giggling or laughing. At professional conferences on child sexual abuse, child prostitution is almost never discussed. It is the form of sexual victimization of children most unlike the stereotype of the innocent girl victim. Child prostitutes, by definition, participate in and often initiate their victimization. Furthermore, child prostitutes and the participants in child sex rings are frequently boys. One therapist recently told the author that a researcher's data on child molestation were misleading because many of the child victims in question were child prostitutes. This implies that child prostitutes are not "real" victims. In a survey by the *Los Angeles Times,* only 37 percent of those responding thought that child prostitution constituted child sexual abuse (Timnik 1985). Whether or not it seems fair, when adults and children have sex, the child is always the victim.

Intrafamilial Child Sexual Abuse

During the 1970s, primarily as a result of the women's movement, society began to learn more about the sexual victimization of children. We began to realize that most children are sexually molested by someone they know, usually a relative—a father, stepfather, uncle, grandfather, or older brother. Some mitigate the difficulty in accepting this by expressing the belief that only members of socioeconomic groups other than theirs engage in this behavior. It quickly became apparent that warnings about not taking gifts from strangers were not enough to prevent child sexual abuse. Consequently, we began to develop prevention programs based on more complex concepts, such as good touching and bad touching, the "yucky" feeling, and the child's right to say no. These are not the kinds of things you can easily and effectively communicate in forty-five minutes to hundreds of kids packed into an auditorium. These are very difficult issues, and they must be carefully developed and evaluated.

In the late 1970s child sexual abuse became almost synonymous with incest, and incest meant father-daughter sexual relations. Therefore, the focus of child sexual abuse intervention became father-daughter incest. Even today, the vast majority of training materials, articles, and books on this topic refer to child sexual abuse only in terms of father-daughter incest.

Incest is, in fact, sexual relations between individuals of any age too closely related to marry. It need not necessarily involve an adult and a child, and it goes beyond child sexual abuse. But more important, child sexual abuse goes beyond father-daughter incest. Intrafamilial incest between an adult and child may be the most common form of child sexual abuse, but it is not the only form.

The progress of the 1970s in recognizing that child sexual abuse was not simply a result of "stranger danger" was an important breakthrough in dealing with society's denial. The battle, however, is not over. The persistent voice of society luring us back to the more simple concept of "stranger danger" may never go away. It is the voice of denial.

Return to "Stranger Danger"

In the early 1980s the issue of missing children became prominent and was focused primarily on the stranger abduction of little children. Runaways, throwaways, noncustodial abductions, non-family abductions of teenagers—all major problems within the missing-children issue—were almost forgotten. People no longer wanted to hear about good touching and bad touching and the child's right to say no. They wanted to be told, in thirty minutes or less, how they could protect their children from abduction by strangers. We were back to the horrible but simple and clear-cut concept of "stranger danger."

In the emotional zeal over the problem of missing children, isolated horror stories and distorted numbers were sometimes used. The American public was led to believe that most of the missing children had been kidnapped by pedophiles—a new term for child molesters. The media, profiteers, and well-intentioned zealots all played big roles in this hype and hysteria over missing children.

The Acquaintance Molester

Only recently has society begun to deal openly with a critical piece of the puzzle of child sexual abuse—acquaintance molestation. This seems to be the most difficult aspect of the problem for us to face. People seem more willing to accept a father or stepfather as a child molester than a parish priest, a next-door neighbor, a police officer, a pediatrician, an FBI agent, or a scout leader. These kinds of molesters have always existed, but our society has not been willing to accept that fact.

Sadly, one of the main reasons that the criminal justice system and the public were forced to confront the problem of acquaintance molestation was the preponderance of lawsuits arising from the negligence of many institutions.

One of the unfortunate outcomes of society's preference for the "stranger danger" concept is what I call "say no, yell, and tell" guilt. This is the result of prevention programs that tell potential child victims to avoid sexual abuse by saying no, yelling, and telling. This might work with the stranger hiding behind a tree. Adolescent boys seduced by a scout leader or parish priest often feel guilty and blame themselves because they did not do what they were supposed to do.

While American society has become increasingly aware of the problem of the acquaintance molester and related problems such as child pornography, the voice calling us back to "stranger danger" still persists.

Satanism: A New Form of "Stranger Danger"

In today's version of "stranger danger," it is the satanic devil worshipers who are snatching the children. Many who warned us in the early 1980s about pedophiles snatching fifty thousand kids a year now contend they were wrong only about who was doing the kidnapping, not about the number abducted. This is again the desire for the simple and clear-cut explanation.

For those who know anything about criminology, the oldest theory of crime is demonology: The devil makes you do it. This makes it even easier to deal with the child molester who is the "pillar of the community." It is not his fault, he is really a good guy, the devil made him do it. This explanation has tremendous appeal because, like "stranger danger," it presents the struggle between good and evil as the explanation for child abduction, exploitation, and abuse.

In regard to "ritualistic" abuse, today we may not be where we were with incest in the 1960s but where we were with missing children in the early 1980s. The best data now available (the 1990 National Incidence Studies on Missing, Abducted, Runaway and Thrownaway Children in America) estimate the number of stereotypical child abductions at between 200 and 300 and the number of stranger abduction homicides of children at between 43 and 147 a year. Approximately half of the abducted children are teenagers. Today's facts are significantly different from yesterday's perceptions, and those who exaggerated the problem, however well intentioned, have lost credibility and damaged the reality of the problem.

Child Sex Rings

The term child sex ring is defined as one or more offenders simultaneously involved sexually with several child victims. As a rule of thumb, a child is defined as someone who has not yet reached his or her eighteenth birthday. Legal definitions, however, of what constitutes a child may vary from situation to situation and case to case and must be considered in any criminal investigation.

Child sex rings need not have a commercial component. In one case in which a teacher was convicted of sexually molesting several of his students, I used the term child sex ring during a pre-sentence hearing. The defense attorney objected, stating that there was no evidence that his client had operated a sex ring. By definition, however, that is exactly what the teacher had operated. Just because the children were not bought and sold does not mean that it was not a sex ring.

A child sex ring does not necessarily mean group sex. Although that has happened in some cases, it is more likely that the offender is sexually interacting with the children one at a time. In a child sex ring, the offender has sex with other children before terminating the sexual relationship with prior victims. The various child victims being molested during a certain period of time usually know each other but may or may not know that the offender is having sex with the other children. Some may believe that they are the only ones having a "special" relationship with the offender. Other victims may actually witness the sexual activity of the offender with other children. Offenders may have favorite victims that they treat differently than the other victims.

Many of the nation's child sexual abuse experts have little or no experience dealing with child sex ring cases. Almost all their experience is with one-on-one intrafamilial incest cases. The investigation of child sex rings requires specialized techniques. I am convinced that the intrafamilial model for dealing with child sexual abuse has only limited application when dealing with multi-offender/ multi-victim child sexual exploitation cases.

In one case that I was asked to evaluate, a military officer had sexually molested his daughter from shortly after birth to shortly before her seventh birthday. He was convicted and sent to prison. After several years, he was released and is now living with his wife and daughter. When I describe this case during a presentation, most people operating only from the intrafamilial perspective of child sexual abuse react with disgust or outrage to the notion that the offender is back in the home with the victim. Although I am concerned about that, I am much more concerned for other young female children in the community where the offender now lives. Having reviewed and analyzed the offender's collection of child pornography and erotica, I know a great deal about this man's sexual fantasies and desires. His daughter is now too old to be a preferred sexual partner. Those who focus on intrafamilial abuse rarely think of the danger to other children in the community because, in their minds, intrafamilial offenders molest only their own children.

Dynamics of Child Sex Rings

Child sex rings have many dynamics different from "typical" intrafamilial abuse cases.

Multiple Victims. Interaction among the multiple victims is one major difference. In intrafamilial cases, the sexual activity is usually a secret that the victim has discussed with no one until disclosure takes place. In a child sex ring there are multiple victims whose interactions, before and after disclosure, must be examined and evaluated.

Multiple Offenders. Interaction among multiple offenders is a second major difference. Offenders sometimes communicate with each other and trade information and material. Offender interaction is an important element in the investigation of these cases. The existence of multiple offenders can be an investigative difficulty, but it can also be an advantage. The more offenders involved, the greater the odds that there is a weak link who can be used to corroborate the alleged abuse.

The Victim's Parents. The role of the child victim's parents is a third major difference between child sex rings and intrafamilial child sexual abuse. In intrafamilial cases there is usually an abusing and a non-abusing parent. In such cases, a non-abusing mother may protect the child, pressure the child not to talk about the abuse, or persuade the child to recant the story so that the father does not go to jail. Dealing with these dynamics is important and can be difficult.

Since parents are usually not the abusers in child sex ring cases, their role is different. It is a potentially serious mistake, however, to underestimate the importance of their role. Their interaction with their victimized child can be crucial to the case. If the parents interrogate their children or conduct their own investigation, the results can be damaging to the proper investigation of the case. It is also possible that a child sexually exploited in a sex ring also was or is sexually, physically, or psychologically abused at home.

Gender of the Victim. The gender of the victim is the fourth major difference between intrafamilial and sex ring cases. In a recent study, Dr. Gene Abel (1987) found that two-thirds of all victims molested outside the home were boys. Unlike intrafamilial sexual abuse, in which the most commonly reported victim is a young female, in child sex rings we are often dealing with the adolescent boy victim.

After years of evaluating and analyzing child sex ring cases, I have identified two major patterns or types of cases. It is difficult to label these two patterns or types. At first I referred to them as traditional and nontraditional child sex rings. The idea of referring to any kind of child sexual abuse and exploitation as "traditional," however, was distasteful to me. For a time I called them Type A and Type B child sex rings. For want of better labels, I now refer to these two types of cases as historical child sex rings and multidimensional child sex rings. These terms were first suggested to me by an unknown police officer attending a training conference in Hamilton, Ontario. After some thought and analysis, these terms were adopted because they give a descriptive name or label to each type of case without the emotion or implication of such terms as "traditional," "ritualistic," or "satanic" abuse.

Historical Child Sex Rings

The term "historical child sex ring" is now used to refer to what the author previously called a child sex ring. Dr. Ann W. Burgess (1984) set forth the dynamics of such child sex rings. This research identified three types of child sex rings: solo, transition, and syndicated. In the solo ring, the offender keeps the activity and photographs completely secret. Each ring involves one offender and multiple victims. In the transition ring, offenders begin to share their experiences, pornography, or victims. Photographs and letters are traded and victims may be tested by other offenders and eventually traded for their sexual services. In the syndicated ring, a well-structured organization recruits children, produces pornography, delivers direct sexual services, and establishes an extensive network of customers.

Some have begun to refer to child sex rings as multi-offender/multi-victim cases. A historical child sex ring can involve a day-care center, a school, a scout troop, a Little League team, or neighborhood children. It can also involve marriage as a method of access to children, intrafamilial molestation of children, and the use of family children to attract other victims.

In contrast to the confusion and lack of corroboration characteristic of multidimensional child sex ring cases, there is much we know about historical child sex ring cases. The information is well documented by law-enforcement investigation and is based on my involvement in hundreds of these cases. The investigation of these cases can be challenging and time consuming; once, however, a law-enforcement agency understands the dynamics and is willing to commit the manpower and resources, it can be easier in these cases to obtain convictions than in one-on-one intrafamilial cases. A detailed description of the characteristics of historical child sex rings can be found in my *Child Sex Rings: A Behavioral Analysis* (Lanning 1989, chapter 4).

Multidimensional Child Sex Rings

Sometime in 1983, I was first contacted by a law-enforcement agency for guidance in what was then thought to be an unusual case. The exact date of the contact is unknown because its significance was not recognized at the time. In the months and years that followed, I received more and more inquiries about "these kinds of cases." The requests for assistance came (and continue to come) from all over the United States. Many of the aspects of these cases varied, but there were also some commonalities. Early on, however, one particularly difficult and potentially significant issue began to emerge.

These cases involved and continue to involve unsubstantiated allegations of bizarre activity that are difficult to prove or disprove. Many of the unsubstantiated allegations, however, do not seem to be true or possible. These cases seem to call into question the credibility of victims of child sexual abuse and exploitation. These are the most frustrating and baffling cases I have encountered in more than seventeen years of studying the criminal aspects of deviant sexual behavior. Privately I sought answers, but said nothing publicly about these cases until 1985.

In October 1984, the problems in investigating and prosecuting one of these cases in Jordan, Minnesota, became public. In February 1985, at the FBI Academy, the FBI sponsored and I coordinated the first national seminar held to study "these kinds of cases." Later in 1985, similar conferences sponsored by other organizations were held in Washington, D.C.; Sacramento, California; and Chicago, Illinois. These cases have also been discussed at recent national conferences dealing with the sexual victimization of children. Few answers have come from these conferences. I continue to be consulted on these cases on a regular and increasing basis. Inquiries have been received from law-enforcement officers, prosecuters, therapists, victims, families of victims, and the media from all over the country. I do not claim to understand completely all the dynamics of these cases, but I continue to keep an open mind and to search for answers to the questions and solutions to the problems they pose. The following is based on my analysis of several hundred of "these kinds of cases."

Dynamics of Multidimensional Child Sex Rings

What are "these kinds of cases"? They were and continue to be difficult to define. They all involve allegations of child sexual abuse, but with a combination of some atypical dynamics. Multidimensional child sex rings seem to have the following four dynamics in common: (1) multiple young victims, (2) multiple offenders, (3) fear as the controlling tactic, and (4) bizarre and/or ritualistic activity.

Multiple Young Victims. In all the cases, the sexual abuse was alleged to have taken place or at least begun when the victims were between the ages of two and six. In addition, the victims all described multiple children being abused. The numbers ranged from three or four to as many as several hundred victims.

Multiple Offenders. In all the cases, the victims reported numerous offenders. The numbers ranged from two or three to dozens of offenders. In one recent case, the victims alleged *four to five hundred* offenders involved. Interestingly, many of the offenders (perhaps as many as 40 to 50 percent) were reported to be females. The multiple offenders were often described as being part of a cult, occult, or satanic group.

Fear as a Controlling Factor. Child molesters in general are able to maintain control and ensure the secrecy of their victims in a variety of ways. These include attention and affection, coercion, blackmail, embarrassment, threats, and violence. In all of the cases studied by the author, the victims described being frightened and reported threats against themselves, their families, their friends, and even their pets. They reported witnessing acts of violence perpetrated to reinforce this fear. I believe that this fear and the traumatic memory of the events may be the key to understanding many of these cases.

Bizarre and/or Ritualistic Activity. This is the most difficult dynamic of multidimensional child sex rings to describe. Bizarre is a relative term. Is the use of urine or feces in sexual activity bizarre, or is it a well-documented aspect of sexual deviancy, or is it part of established Satanic rituals? The ritualistic aspect is even more difficult to define. How do you distinguish acts performed in a precise manner to enhance or allow sexual arousal from those acts performed in a manner that fulfills spiritual needs or complies with "religious" ceremonies? Victims in these cases report ceremonies, chanting, robes, and costumes, drugs, use of urine and feces, animal sacrifice, torture, abduction, mutilation, murder, and even cannibalism and vampirism. All things considered, the word *bizarre* is probably preferable to the word *ritual* to describe this activity.

Scenarios

Multidimensional child sex rings typically emerge from one of four scenarios: adult survivors, day-care cases, family/isolated neighborhood cases, and custody/visitation disputes.

In *adult survivor cases,* adults of almost any age—nearly always women— are in therapy for a variety of personal problems and failures. They are frequently hypnotized as part of the therapy and are often diagnosed as suffering from Multiple Personality Disorder. Gradually, during the therapy, the adults reveal previously unrecalled childhood victimization that includes multiple victims and offenders, fear as the controlling tactic, and bizarre or ritualistic activity. The multiple offenders are often described as members of a cult or satanic group. Family members, clergy, civic leaders, police officers, or individuals wearing police uniforms are frequently described as present during exploitation. The offenders may allegedly still be harassing or threatening the victims. This type of case is probably best typified by the book, *Michelle Remembers* (1980). In several of these cases, women called breeders claim to have had babies that were turned over for human sacrifice. If and when the therapist comes to believe the patient, the police or FBI are sometimes contacted to conduct an investigation. The therapists may fear for their safety because they now know the secret. The therapists will frequently tell law enforcement that they will stake their professional reputation on the fact that the patient is telling the truth. Some adult survivors go directly to law enforcement. They may also go from place to place in an effort to find therapists or investigators who will listen to them.

In *day-care cases,* children currently or formerly attending a day-care center gradually describe their victimization at the center and at other locations to which they were taken by the day-care staff. The cases include multiple victims and offenders, fear, and bizarre or ritualistic activity, with a particularly high number of female offenders. Descriptions of strange games, killing of animals, photographing of activities, and wearing of costumes are common. The accounts of the young children do not seem to be quite as "bizarre" as the adult survivor accounts.

In *family/isolated neighborhood cases,* children describe their victimization within their family or extended family. The group is often defined by geographic boundary, such as a cul-de-sac, apartment building, or isolated rural setting. The stories are similar to those told of the day-care setting, but with more male offenders. The basic dynamics remain the same, but victims tend to be older than six years, and the scenario is more likely to include a custody or visitation dispute.

Custody or Visitation Dispute. In custody or visitation dispute cases, the allegations emanate from a custody or visitation dispute over the child victims. The four dynamics described above make these cases extremely difficult to handle. When complicated by this scenario, the cases can be overwhelming. This is especially true if the disclosing child victims have been taken into the "underground" by a parent during the custody or visitation dispute. Some of these parents or relatives may even provide authorities with diaries or tapes of their interviews with the children. An accurate evaluation and assessment of a young child held in isolation in this underground while being "debriefed" by a parent or someone else is almost impossible. However well intentioned, these self-appointed investigators severely damage any chance to validate these cases objectively.

Characteristics of Multidimensional Child Sex Rings

A problem in conducting training and research in the area of multidimensional child sex rings is the term used to define "these kinds of cases." Many refer to them as ritual, ritualistic, or ritualized abuse of children cases or satanic ritual abuse cases. Such words carry specialized meanings for many people and might imply that all these cases are connected to occult or satanic activity. If ritual abuse is "merely" severe, repeated, prolonged abuse, why use a term that, in the minds of so many, implies such specific motivation? Others refer to these cases as multi-offender/multi-victim cases. The problem with this term is that most multiple offender and victim cases do not involve the four dynamics discussed above.

For want of a better term, the author has decided to refer to "these kinds of cases" as multidimensional child sex rings. Following are general characteristics of multidimensional child sex ring cases.

Female Offenders. As many as 40 to 50 percent of the offenders in these cases are reported to be women. This is in marked contrast to historical child sex rings in which almost all the offenders are men.

Situational Molesters. The offenders appear to be sexually interacting with the child victims for reasons other than a true sexual preference for children. The children are substitute victims and the abusive activity may have little to do with pedophilia.

Male and Female Victims. Both boys and girls appear to be targeted, but with an apparent preference for girls. The most significant characteristic of the victims, however, is their youth (generally two to six years old when the abuse begins).

Multidimensional Motivation. Sexual gratification appears to be only part of the motivation for the sexual activity. Many people today argue that the motivation is "spiritual"—possibly part of an occult ceremony. It is my opinion that the motivation may have more to do with anger, hostility, rage, and resentment carried out against weak and vulnerable victims. Much of the ritualistic abuse of children may not be sexual in nature. Some of the activity may, in fact, be physical abuse directed at sexually significant body parts (penis, anus, nipples). This may also partially explain the large percentage of female offenders. Physical abuse of children by females is well documented.

Pornography and Paraphernalia. Although many of the victims of multidimensional child sex rings claim that pictures and videotapes of the activity were made, no such visual record has been found by law enforcement. In recent years, American law enforcement has seized large amounts of child pornography portraying children in a wide variety of sexual activity and perversions. None of it, however, portrays the kind of bizarre and/or ritualistic activity described by these victims. Perhaps these offenders use and store their pornography and paraphernalia in ways different from perferential child molesters (pedophiles). This is an area needing additional research and investigation.

Control Through Fear. Control through fear may be the overriding characteristic of these cases. Control is maintained by frightening the children. A very young child might not be able to understand the significance of much of the sexual activity but certainly understands fear. The stories that the victims tell may be their perceived versions of severe traumatic memories. They may be victims of a severely traumatized childhood in which being sexually abused was just one of the many negative events affecting their lives.

Why Are Victims Alleging Things That Do Not Seem to Be True?

Some of what the victims in these cases allege is physically impossible (victim cut up and put back together, offender took the building apart and then rebuilt it); some is possible but improbable (human sacrifice, cannibalism, vampirism); some is possible and probable (child pornography, clever manipulation of victims); and some is corroborated (medical evidence of vaginal or anal trauma, offender confessions).

The most significant crimes being alleged that do not seem to be true are the human sacrifice and cannibalism. In none of the multidimensional child sex ring cases of which the author is aware have bodies of the murder victims been found—in spite of major excavations where the abuse victims had claimed the bodies were located. The alleged explanations for this include: the offenders moved the bodies after the children left, the bodies were burned in portable high-temperature ovens, the bodies were put in double-decker graves under legitimately buried bodies, a mortician member of the cult disposed of the bodies in a crematorium, the offenders ate the bodies, the offenders used corpses or aborted fetuses, or the power of Satan caused the bodies to disappear.

Not only are no bodies found, but also, more important, there is no physical evidence that a murder took place. Many of those not in law enforcement do not understand that, while it is possible to get rid of a body, it is much more difficult to get rid of the physical evidence that a murder took place, especially a human sacrifice involving sex, blood, and mutilation.

The victims of these human sacrifices and murders are alleged to be abducted missing children, runaway and throwaway children, derelicts, and the babies of breeder women. It is interesting to note that many of those espousing these theories are using the long-since-discredited numbers and rhetoric of the missing children hysteria in the early 1980s. Yet, a January 1989 Juvenile Justice Bulletin, published by the Office of Juvenile Justice and Delinquency Prevention of the U.S. Department of Justice, reports that researchers now estimate that the number of children kidnapped and murdered by non-family members is between 52 and 58 a year and that adolescents fourteen to seventeen years old account for nearly two-thirds of these victims. These figures are also consistent with the 1990 National Incidence Studies.

We live in a very violent society, and yet we have "only" about 23,000 murders a year. Those who accept these stories of mass human sacrifice would have us believe that the satanists and other occult practitioners are murdering more than twice as many people every year in this country as all the other murderers combined. Many of those who accept the stories of organized ritualistic abuse of children and human sacrifice will tell you that the best evidence they now have is the consistency of stories from all over America. It sounds like a powerful argument. It is interesting to note that, without having met each other, the hundreds of people who claim to have been abducted by aliens from outer space tell stories that are also similar to each other. This is not to imply that allegations of child abuse are in the same category as abduction by aliens from outer space. It is intended only to illustrate that individuals who never met each other can sometimes describe similar events without necessarily having experienced them.

The large number of people telling the same story is, in fact, the biggest reason to doubt these stories. It is simply too difficult for that many people to commit so many horrendous crimes as part of an organized conspiracy. Two or three people murder a couple of children in a few communities as part of a ritual, and nobody finds out? Possible. Thousands of people do the same thing to tens of thousands of victims over many years? Not likely. Hundreds of communities all over America are run by mayors, police departments, and community leaders who are practicing satanists and who regularly murder and eat people? Not likely. In addition, these community leaders and high-ranking officials also supposedly commit these complex crimes leaving no evidence, and at the same time function as leaders and managers while heavily involved in illegal drugs. It is interesting to note that the best documented example of this kind of alleged activity in the United States is the Ku Klux Klan, which used its version of Christianity to rationalize its activity.

In the beginning, I was inclined to believe the allegations of the victims. But as the cases poured in and the months and years went by, I became more concerned about the lack of physical evidence and corroboration for many of the more serious allegations. With increasing frequency, I began to ask the question, "Why are victims alleging things that do not seem to be true?" I considered many possible answers.

The first possible answer is obvious—clever offenders. The allegations may not seem to be true—but they are true. The criminal justice system lacks the knowledge, skill, and motivation to get to the bottom of this crime conspiracy. The perpetrators of this crime conspiracy are clever, cunning individuals using sophisticated mind-control and brainwashing techniques to control their victims. Law enforcement does not know how to investigate these cases.

I do not deny the possibility that some of these allegations of an organized conspiracy involving the take-over of day-care centers, abduction, cannibalism, and human sacrifice might be true. But if they are true, then it is one of the greatest crime conspiracies in history.

Many people do not understand how difficult it is to commit a conspiracy crime involving numerous co-conspirators. One clever and cunning individual has a good chance of getting away with a well-planned interpersonal crime. Bring one partner into the crime and the odds of getting away with it drop considerably. The more people involved in the crime, the harder it is to get away with it. Why? Human nature is the answer. People get angry and jealous. They come to resent the fact that another conspirator is getting "more" than they. They get in trouble and want to make a deal for themselves by informing on others.

If a group of individuals degenerate to the point of engaging in human sacrifice and cannibalism, that would most likely be the beginning of the end for such a group. The odds are that someone in the group would have a problem with such acts and be unable to maintain the secret. The appeal of the satanic conspiracy theory is two-fold. One, it is a simple explanation for a complex problem. Nothing is simpler than "the devil made them do it." If we do not understand something, we make it the work of some supernatural force. During the Middle Ages, serial killers were thought to be vampires and werewolves, and child sexual abuse was the work of demons taking the form of parents and priests.

Second, the conspiracy theory is a popular one. We find it difficult to believe that one bizarre individual could commit a crime we find so offensive. Conspiracy theories about the assassination of Abraham Lincoln continue to this day. On a recent television program commemorating the one hundredth anniversary of Jack the Ripper, almost 50 percent of the viewing audience who called the polling telephone numbers indicated that they thought the murders were committed as part of a conspiracy involving the British Royal Family. The five experts on the program, however, unanimously agreed the crimes were the work of one disorganized but lucky individual who was diagnosed as a paranoid schizophrenic. In many ways, the murders of Jack the Ripper are similiar to those allegedly committed by satanists today.

Alternative Explanations

Even if only part of an allegation is not true, what then is the answer to the question "Why are victims alleging things that do not seem to be true?" After consulting with psychiatrists, psychologists, therapists, social workers, child sexual abuse experts, and law-enforcement investigators for more than seven years, I can find no single, simple answer. The answer to the question seems to be a complex set of dynamics that can be different in each case. In spite of the fact that some skeptics keep looking for it, there does not appear to be one answer to the question that fits every case. Each case is different, and each case may involve a different combination of answers.

I have identified a series of possible alternative answers to this question. I will not attempt to explain completely these alternative answers because I cannot. They are presented simply as areas for consideration and evaluation by child sexual abuse intervenors, for further elaboration by experts in these fields, and for research by objective social scientists. The first step, however, in finding the answer to this question is to admit the possibility that some of what the victims describe may not have happened. Some child advocates seem unwilling to do this.

The first possible alternative answer to why victims are alleging things that do not seem to be true is *pathological distortion*. The allegations may be errors in processing reality influenced by mental disorders such as hysterical neurosis, borderline or histrionic personality disorders, or psychosis. These distortions may be manifested in false reports of direct victimization (Munchausen Syndrome) or indirect victimization through their children (Munchausen Syndrome by Proxy) in order to get attention and sympathy. Mass hysteria may partially account for the large numbers of victims describing the same symptoms or experiences. Many "victims" may develop pseudomemories of their victimization and actually come to believe the events really occurred.

The second possible answer is *traumatic memory*. Fear and severe trauma can cause victims to distort reality and confuse events. This is a well-documented fact in cases involving individuals taken hostage or in life-and-death situations. The distortions may be part of an elaborate defense mechanism of the mind called "splitting." The victims create a clear-cut good and evil manifestation of their complex victimization that is then psychologically more manageable. Through the defense mechanism of dissociation, the victim may escape the horrors of reality by inaccurately processing that reality.

Another defense mechanism may tell the victim that it could have been worse, and so his or her victimization was not so bad. They are not alone in their victimization; other children were also abused. Their father who abused them is no different from other prominent people in the community they claimed abused them. The described human sacrifice may be symbolic of the "death" of their childhood.

It may be that we should anticipate that very young children abused by multiple offenders with fear as the primary controlling tactic will distort and embellish their victimization. Perhaps a horror-filled, yet inaccurate account of victimization is not only not a counterindication of abuse, but is in fact a corroborative indicator of extreme physical, psychological, and/or sexual abuse.

The third possible answer may be *normal childhood fears and fantasy*. Most young children are afraid of ghosts and monsters. Even as adults, many people feel uncomfortable, for example, about dangling their arms over the side of their beds. They still remember the "monster" under the bed from childhood. While young children may rarely invent stories about sexual activity, they might describe their victimization in terms of evil as they understand it. In church or at home, children may be told of satanic activity as the source of evil. Children do fantasize. Perhaps whatever causes a child to allege something impossible (such as being cut up and put back together) is similar to what causes a child to allege something possible but improbable (such as witnessing another child being chopped up and eaten).

Misperception, confusion, and trickery may be a fourth answer. Expecting young children to give accurate accounts of sexual activity for which they have little frame of reference is unreasonable. The Broadway play *M. Butterfly* is the true story of a man who had a fifteen-year affair, including the "birth" of a baby, with a "woman" who turns out to have been a man all along. If a grown man does not know when he has had vaginal intercourse with a woman, how can we expect young children not to be confused? Furthermore, some offenders may deliberately introduce elements of satanism and the occult into the sexual exploitation simply to confuse the victims. Simple magic and other techniques may be used to trick the children. Drugs may also be deliberately used to confuse the victims and distort their perceptions. This is the most popular explanation and even the more zealous believers of ritualistic abuse allegations use it, but only to explain obviously impossible events.

Overzealous intervenors, causing intervenor contagion, may be a fifth answer. These intervenors can include parents, family members, doctors, therapists, social workers, law-enforcement officials, and prosecutors. Victims have been subtly as well as overtly rewarded and bribed by usually well meaning intervenors for furnishing additional details. In addition, some of what appears not to have happened may have originated as a result of intervenors making assumptions about or misinterpreting what the victims are saying. The intervenors then repeat, and possibly embellish, these assumptions and misinterpretations, and eventually the victims are "forced" to agree with or come to accept this "official" version of what happened. However well intentioned, these overzealous intervenors must accept varying degrees of responsibility for the unsuccessful prosecution of most of these cases. This is the most controversial and least popular of the alternative explanations.

Allegations of ritualistic or satanic abuse may also be spread through *urban legends.* In *The Vanishing Hitchhiker,* the first of his four books on the topic. Dr. Jan Harold Brunvand defines urban legends as "realistic stories concerning recent events (or alleged events) with an ironic or supernatural twist" (1981). Dr. Brunvand's books convincingly explain that just because individuals throughout the country who never met each other tell the same story does not mean that it is true. Today the mass media frequently participate in the rapid dissemination of these stories. Training conferences for all the disciplines involved in child sexual abuse may also play a role in the spread of this contagion. At a recent child abuse conference I attended, an exhibitor was selling more than fifty different books dealing with satanism and the occult. By the end of the conference, he had sold nearly all of them. At another national child sexual abuse conference, I witnessed more than one hundred attendees copying down the widely disseminated twenty-nine "Symptoms Characterizing Satanic Ritual Abuse" in preschool children (see Catherine Gould's chapter in this book). Is a four-year-old child's "preoccupation with urine and feces" an indication of satanic ritual abuse or part of normal development? Do intervenors uncover ritualistic abuse because they have learned how to identify it or because it has become a self-fulfilling prophecy?

Most multidimensional child sex ring cases probably involve a *combination* of the answers previously set forth, as well as other possible explanations unknown to me at this time. Obviously, each case of sexual exploitation must be evaluated on its own merits without any preconceived explanations. All the possibilities must be explored if for no other reason than the fact that the defense attorneys for any accused subjects will almost certainly do so.

Most people would agree that just because a victim tells you one detail that turns out to be true, this does not mean that every detail in the testimony is true. But many people seem to believe that if you can disprove one part of a victim's story, then the entire story is false. One of my main concerns in these cases is that people are getting away with sexually abusing children because we cannot prove that they are satanic devil worshipers who murder and eat people.

I discovered that the subject of multidimensional child sex rings is a very emotional and polarizing issue. Everyone seems to demand that one choose a side. On one side of the issue are those who say that nothing really happened and it is all a big witch hunt led by overzealous fanatics and incompetent "experts." The other side says, in essence, that everything happened; children never lie about sexual abuse, and so it must be true.

I believe that there is a middle ground—a continuum of possible activity. Some of what the victims allege may be true and accurate, some may be misperceived or distorted, some may be symbolic, and some may be "contaminated" or false. The challenge, however, is to determine which is which. I believe that the vast majority of victims alleging "ritualistic" abuse are in fact victims of some form of abuse or trauma. After a lengthy discussion about various alternative explanations and the continuum of possible activity, one mother told the author that for the first time since the victimization of her young son she felt a little better. She had thought her only choices were that either her son was a pathological liar or, on the other hand, she lived in a community controlled by satanists.

There is a middle ground. It is the job of the professional investigator to listen to all the victims and conduct appropriate investigation in an effort to find out what happened, considering all possibilities.

Do Children Lie about Sexual Abuse and Exploitation?

The crucial central issue in the evaluation of a response to cases of multidimensional child sex rings is the statement "Children never lie about sexual abuse or exploitation. If they have details, it must have happened." This statement, oversimplified by many, is the basic premise upon which some believe the child sexual abuse and exploitation movement is based. It is almost never questioned or debated at training conferences. In fact, during the 1970s, there was a successful crusade to eliminate laws requiring corroboration of child victim statements in child sexual abuse cases. The best way to convict child molesters is to have the victims testify in court. If we believe them, the jury will believe them. Any challenge to this basic premise was viewed as a threat to the movement and a denial that the problem existed.

I believe that children rarely lie about sexual abuse or exploitation, if a lie is defined as a statement deliberately and maliciously intended to deceive. The problem is oversimplification. Just because a child is not lying does not necessarily mean the child is telling the truth. I believe that in the vast majority of these cases, the victims do not lie. They are telling you what they have come to believe has happened to them. Furthermore, the assumption that children rarely lie about sexual abuse does not necessarily apply to everything a child says during a sexual abuse investigation. Stories of mutilation, murder, and cannibalism are not really about sexual abuse.

Children rarely lie about sexual abuse or exploitation, but they do fantasize, furnish false information, furnish misleading information, leave out humiliating details, misperceive events, try to please adults, respond to leading questions, and respond to rewards. Children are not adults in little bodies. They go through stages of development that must be evaluated and understood. In many ways, however, children are no better and no worse than other victims or witnesses of a crime. They should not be automatically believed, nor should they automatically be disbelieved.

The second part of the statement—if children can supply details, the crime must have happened—must also be carefully evaluated. The details in question in most of the cases of multidimensional child sex rings have little to do with sexual activity. Law-enforcement officials and social workers must do more than attempt to determine how a child could have known about sex acts. These cases involve determining how a child could have known about a wide variety of bizarre and ritualistic activity. Young children may know a little about sex, but they may know a lot about monsters, torture, kidnapping, and murder.

Children may supply details of sexual acts using information from sources other than direct victimization. Such sources must be evaluated carefully by the investigator of multidimensional child sex rings.

Personal Knowledge. The victim may have personal knowledge of the sexual acts, but not as a result of the alleged victimization. The knowledge could have come from viewing pornography or sex education material, witnessing sexual activity in the home, or witnessing the sexual abuse of others. It could also have come from having been sexually or physically abused, but by other than the alleged offenders.

Other Children. Young children today are socially interacting more often and at a younger age than ever before. Many parents are unable to provide possibly simple explanations for their children's stories because they were not with the children when the events occurred. They do not even know what videotapes their children may have seen, what games they have played, or what stories they may have been told or overheard. Children are being placed in day-care centers for eight, ten, or twelve hours a day starting as young as six weeks old. The children share experiences by playing house, school, or doctor. Bodily functions such as urination and defecation are a focus of attention for these young children. To a certain extent, each child shares the experiences of all the other children. The odds are fairly high that in any typical day-care center there might be some children who are victims of incest; victims of physical abuse; victims of psychological abuse; children of cult members (even satanists); children of sexually open parents; children of sexually indiscriminate parents; children of parents obsessed with victimization; children of parents obsessed with the evils of satanism; children without conscience; children with a teenage brother or pregnant mother; children with heavy metal music and literature in the home; children with bizarre toys, games, comics, and magazines; children with a VCR and slasher films in their home; children with access to dial-a-porn, party lines, or pornography; or children victimized by a day-care staff member. The possible effects of interaction with such children prior to the disclosure of the alleged abuse must be evaluated.

Media. The amount of sexually explicit, occult, or violent material available to children in the modern world is overwhelming. This includes movies, videotapes, television, music, toys, and books. There are also documentaries on satanism, witchcraft, and the occult available on videotape.

The International Coalition Against Violent Entertainment estimates that 12 percent of the movies produced in the United States can be classified as satanic horror films. Cable television and the home VCR make all this material readily available even to young children. Religious broadcasters and almost all the television magazine and tabloid programs have done shows on satanism and the occult. Heavy metal and black metal music, which often has a satanic theme, is readily available and popular. In addition to the much debated fantasy role-playing games, there are numerous popular toys on the market with an occult, bizarre, or violent theme. Books on satanism and the occult, both fiction and nonfiction, are readily available in most book stores. Several recent books specifically discuss the issue of ritualistic abuse of children. Obviously, most young children do not read this material, but their parents and relatives might and then discuss it in front of or with them.

Suggestions and Leading Questions. This problem is particularly important in cases stemming from custody or visitation disputes. It is the author's opinion that most suggestive, leading questioning of children by intervenors is inadvertently done as part of a good-faith effort to learn the truth. Not all intervenors are in equal positions to potentially influence victim allegations. Parents and relatives especially are in a position to subtly influence their young children to describe their victimization in a certain way. Children may also overhear their parents discussing the details of the case. Children often tell their parents what they believe their parents want or need to hear. In one case a father gave the police a tape recording to "prove" that his child's statements were spontaneous disclosures and not the result of leading, suggestive questions. The tape recording indicated just the opposite. Why then did the father voluntarily give it to the police? Probably because he truly believed that he was not influencing his child's statements—but he was.

Therapists are probably in the best position to influence the allegations of adult survivors. The accuracy and reliability of the accounts of adult survivors who have been hypnotized during therapy is certainly open to question. One nationally known therapist personally told the author that the reason police cannot find out about satanic or ritualistic activity from child victims is that they do not know how to ask leading questions. Types and styles of verbal interaction useful in therapy may create significant problems in a criminal investigation. The extremely sensitive emotional and religious aspects of these cases make problems with leading questions more likely than in other kinds of cases.

Misperception and Confusion. In one case, a child's description of the apparently impossible act of walking through a wall turned out to be the very possible act of walking between the studs of an unfinished wall in a room under construction. In another case, pennies in the anus turned out to be copper-foil-covered suppositories. The children may describe what they believe happened. It is not a lie, but neither is it an accurate account of what happened.

Education and Awareness Programs. Some well-intentioned awareness programs designed to prevent child sexual abuse and exploitation may, in fact, be unrealistically increasing children's and parent's fears and concerns. Some of what children and their parents are telling intervenors may have been learned in or fueled by such programs. Religious programs, books, and pamphlets that emphasize the power and evil force of Satan may be adding to the problem. In fact, most of the day-care centers in which ritualistic abuse was alleged to have taken place were church affiliated centers.

Investigating Multidimensional Child Sex Rings

Multidimensional child sex rings can be among the most difficult and complex cases that any law-enforcement officer will ever investigate. The investigation of recent allegations from multiple young children under the age of six offers one set of major problems. The investigation of allegations from adult survivors concerning events ten or twenty years in the past offers additional problems. In spite of any skepticism, allegations of ritual abuse should be aggressively and thoroughly investigated. This investigation should attempt to corroborate the allegations of ritual abuse but should also attempt to identify alternative explanations for the allegations. Any law-enforcement agency must be prepared to defend and justify its actions when scrutinized by the media, politicians, courts, or any higher authorities. This does not mean, however, that a law-enforcement agency has an obligation to prove that the alleged crimes did *not* occur. This is almost always impossible to do, and investigators should be alert for and avoid this trap. The following techniques apply primarily to the investigation of multidimensional child sex rings.

Minimize Satanic/Occult Aspect. There are those who claim that one of the major reasons more of these cases have not been successfully prosecuted is that the satanic/occult aspect has not been aggressively pursued. One state has even introduced legislation creating added penalties when certain crimes are committed as part of a ritual or ceremony. I strongly disagree with such an approach. It makes no difference what spiritual belief system was used to enhance and facilitate or rationalize and justify criminal behavior. It serves no purpose to "prove" someone is a satanist. As a matter of fact, if it is alleged that the subject committed certain criminal acts in order to conjure up supernatural spirits or forces, this may very well be the basis for an insanity or diminished-capacity defense. The defense may well be very interested in all the "evidence of satanic activity." It is best to focus on the crime and all the evidence to corroborate its commission. In one case, a law-enforcement agency executing a search warrant seized only the satanic paraphernalia and left behind the evidence that would have corroborated victim statements. Even offenders who commit crimes in a spiritual context are usually motivated by power, sex, and money.

Keep Investigation and Religious Beliefs Separate. One of the biggest mistakes any investigator of these cases can make is to attribute supernatural powers to the offenders. During an investigation, a good investigator may sometimes be able to use the beliefs and superstitions of the offenders to his or her advantage. The reverse happens if the investigator believes that the offenders actually possess supernatural powers. Satanic or occult practitioners have no more power than any other human being. Law-enforcement officers who believe that the investigation of these cases puts them in conflict with the supernatural forces of evil should probably not be assigned to them. The religious beliefs of officers should provide spiritual strength and support for them, but not affect the objectivity and professionalism of the investigation. It is easy to get caught up in these cases and begin to see "evil" everywhere. Supervisors need to be alert for and monitor these reactions in their investigators.

Listen to the Victim. It is not the investigator's duty to believe the victims, it is his or her job to listen and be an objective fact finder. The investigator must remember, however, that almost anything is possible. Most important, the investigator must remember that there is much middle ground. Just because one event did happen does not mean that all reported events happened, and just because one event did not happen does not mean that all other events did not happen. Do not become such a zealot that you believe it all, nor such a cynic that you believe nothing.

Assess and Evaluate Victim Statements. This is the part of the investigative process in child sexual exploitation cases that seems to have been lost. Is the victim describing events and activity that are consistent with *law-enforcement* documented criminal behavior or that are consistent with media accounts and erroneous public perceptions of criminal behavior? Accounts of victimization that are more like books and movies and less like known criminal activity should be viewed with skepticism but thoroughly investigated. Consider and investigate all possible explanations of events. The information learned will be invaluable in counteracting the defense attorneys when they raise alternative explanations. The first step in the assessment and evaluation of victim statements is to determine how much time has elapsed since disclosure was first made and the incident was reported to the police or social services. The longer the delay, the bigger the potential for problems. The next step is to determine the number and purpose of all prior interviews of the victim concerning the allegations. The more interviews conducted before the investigative interview, the larger the potential for problems. Although there is nothing wrong with admitting shortcomings and seeking help, law-enforcement officers should never abdicate control over the investigative interview. When an investigative interview is conducted by or with a social worker or therapist using a team approach, law-enforcement officials must direct the process.

The investigator must closely and carefully evaluate events in the victim's life before, during, and after the alleged abuse. Events to be evaluated before the alleged abuse include:

- Background of victim
- Abuse of drugs in home
- Pornography in home
- Play, television, and VCR habits
- Attitudes about sexuality in home
- Extent of sex education in home
- Activities of siblings
- Need or craving for attention
- Religious beliefs and training
- Childhood fears

- Custody/visitation disputes
- Victimization of or by family members
- Interaction between victims

Events to be evaluated during the alleged abuse include:

- Use of fear or scare tactics
- Degree of trauma
- Use of magic, deception, or trickery
- Use of rituals
- Use of drugs
- Use of pornography

Events to be evaluated after the alleged abuse include:

- Disclosure sequence
- Background of prior interviewers
- Background of parents
- Commingling of victims

Evaluate Contagion. Consistent statements obtained from different multiple victims are powerful pieces of corroborative evidence—that is, as long as those statements were not "contaminated." Investigation must carefully evaluate both pre- and post-disclosure contagion and both victim and intervenor contagion. Are the different victim statements consistent because they reflect contamination or urban legends?

The sources of potential contagion are widespread. Victims can communicate with each other both prior to and after their disclosures. Intervenors can communicate with each other and with victims. Documenting existing contagion and eliminating additional contagion are crucial to the successful investigation and prosecution of these cases.

In order to evaluate the contagion element, investigators must meticulously and aggressively investigate these cases. The precise disclosure sequence of the victim must be carefully identified and documented. Personal visits to all locations of alleged abuse and to the victims' homes are essential. Events prior to the alleged abuse must be carefully evaluated. Investigators may have to view television programs, films, and videotapes seen by the victims. It may be necessary to conduct a background investigation and evaluation of everyone, both professional and nonprofessional, who interviewed the victims about the allegations. Investigators must be familiar with the information about "ritualistic abuse of children" being disseminated in magazines, books, television programs, videotapes, and conferences. Every possible way that a victim could have learned about the details of the abuse must be explored, if for no other reason than to eliminate them and counter the defense's arguments. There may, however, be validity to these contagion factors. They may explain some of the "unbelievable" aspects of the case and result in the successful prosecution of the substance of the case. Consistency of statements becomes more significant if contagion is identified or disproved by independent investigation.

Munchausen Syndrome and Munchausen Syndrome by Proxy are complex and controversial issues in these cases. No attempt will be made to discuss them in detail (Rosenberg 1987), but they are documented facts. Most of the literature about them focuses on their manifestation in the medical setting as false or self-inflicted illness or injury. They are also manifested in the criminal justice setting as false or self-inflicted crime victimization. If parents would poison their children to prove an illness, they might sexually abuse their children to prove a crime. These are the unpopular, but documented, realities of the world.

Establish Communication with Parents. The importance and the difficulty of this cannot be overemphasized. An investigator must maintain ongoing communication with the parents of victims in extrafamilial abuse cases. Once the parents begin to interview their own children and conduct their own investigation, the case may be lost. Parents must be made to understand that their child's credibility will be jeopardized when and if the information obtained turns out to be false. Further, within the limits of the law and without jeopardizing investigative techniques, parents must be told on a regular basis how the case is progressing.

Develop a Contingency Plan. If a department waits until actually confronted with a case before a response is developed, it is probably too late. Departments must respond quickly, and this requires advance planning. There are added problems for small to medium-sized departments with limited personnel and resources. Effective investigation of these cases requires planning, identification of resources, and, in many cases, mutual-aid agreements between agencies. The U.S. Department of Defense has conducted specialized training and had developed such a plan for child sex ring cases involving military facilities and personnel.

Multidisciplinary Task Forces. Sergeant Beth Dickinson, Los Angeles County Sheriff's Department, was the chairperson of the Multi-Victim, Multi-Suspect Child Sexual Abuse Subcommittee. Sergeant Dickinson states, "One of the biggest obstacles for investigators to overcome is the reluctance of law-enforcement administrators to commit sufficient resources early on to an investigation that has the potential to be a multidimensional child sex ring. The concept/purpose of these protocols is to get in and get on top of the investigation in a timely manner—to get it investigated in a timely manner in order to assess the risk to children and to avoid hysteria, media sensationalism, and cross-contamination of information. The team approach reduces stress on individual investigators, allowing for peer support minimizing feelings of being overwhelmed."

The investigation of child sex rings can be difficult and time consuming. The likelihood, however, of a great deal of corroborative evidence in a multi-victim/multi-offender case increases the chances of a successful prosecution. Because there is still so much we do not know or understand about the dynamics of multidimensional child sex rings, investigative techniques are less certain. Each new case must be carefully evaluated in order to improve investigative procedures. Because mental health professionals seem to be unable to determine, with any degree of certainty, the accuracy of victim statements in these cases, law enforcement must proceed through the corroboration process. If some of what the victim describes is accurate, some misperceived, some distorted, and some contaminated, what is the jury supposed to believe? Until mental health professionals can come up with better answers, the jury should be asked to believe what the investigation can corroborate.

Conclusions

Professionals should avoid the paranoia that has crept into this issue and into some of the training conferences. Paranoid belief systems are characterized by the gradual development of intricate, complex, and elaborate systems of thinking based on and often proceeding logically from misinterpretation of actual events. It typically involves hypervigilance over the perceived threat, the belief that danger is around every corner, and the willingness to take up the challenge and do something about it. Another very important aspect of this paranoia is the belief that those who do not recognize the threat are evil and corrupt. In this extreme view, you are either with them or against them—part of the solution or part of the problem. Any professional evaluating victims' allegations of ritualistic abuse cannot ignore the lack of physical evidence (no bodies or even hairs, fibers, or fluids left by violent murders); the difficulty in successfully committing a large-scale conspiracy crime (the more people involved in any crime conspiracy, the harder it is to get away with it); and human nature (intragroup conflicts resulting in individual self-serving disclosures would be bound to occur in any group involved in organized kidnapping, baby breeding, and human sacrifice). If and when members of a destructive cult commit murders, they are bound to make mistakes, leave evidence, and eventually make admissions in order to brag about their crimes or to reduce their legal liability. The discovery of the murders in Matamoros, Mexico, in 1989, and the results of the subsequent investigation are good examples of these dynamics.

Overzealous intervenors must accept the fact that some of their well-intentioned activity is contaminating and damaging the prosecutive potential of these cases. We—the media, churches, therapists, victim advocates, law enforcement, and the general public—must ask ourselves if we have established an environment in which victims are rewarded, listened to, comforted, and forgiven in direct proportion to the severity of their abuse. Are we encouraging needy or traumatized individuals to tell more and more outrageous tales of their victimization? Are we now making up for centuries of denial by blindly accepting any allegation of child abuse no matter how absurd or unlikely? Are we increasing the likelihood that rebellious, antisocial, or attention seeking individuals will gravitate toward "satanism" by publicizing and overreacting to it? The overreaction to the problem can clearly be worse than the problem.

Bizarre crime and evil can occur without organized satanic activity. We must distinguish between what we know and what we're not sure of.

The facts are:

- Some individuals believe in and are involved in satanism and the occult.
- Some of these individuals commit crime.
- Some groups of individuals share these beliefs and involvement in satanism and the occult.
- Some members of these groups commit crime together.

The unanswered questions are:

- What is the connection between the belief system and the crimes committed?
- Is there an organized conspiracy of satanic and occult believers responsible for interrelated serious crime (e.g. molestation, murder)?

After all the hype and hysteria is put aside, the realization sets in that most satanic or occult activity involves the commission of *no* crimes, and that which does, usually involves the commission of relatively minor crimes such as trespassing, vandalism, cruelty to animals, or petty thievery.

The law-enforcement investigator must objectively evaluate the legal significance of any criminal's spiritual beliefs. In most cases, including those involving satanists, it will have little or no legal significance. If a crime is committed as part of a spiritual belief system, it should make no difference which belief system it is. The crime is what is important. We generally don't label crimes with the religion of the perpetrators, and there is no reason to proceed differently with the crimes of child molesters, rapists, sadists, and murderers who happen to be involved in satanism and the occult.

Many police officers ask what to look for during the search of the scene of suspected satanic activity. The answer is simple: look for evidence of a crime. A pentagram is no more criminally significant than a crucifix unless it corroborates a crime or a criminal conspiracy. If a victim's description of the location of the instruments of the crime includes a pentagram, then the pentagram would be evidence. But the same would be true if the description included a crucifix.

There is no way any one law-enforcement officer can become knowledgeable about all the symbols and rituals of every spiritual belief system that might become part of a criminal investigation. The officer needs only to be trained to recognize the possible investigative significance of such signs, symbols, and rituals. Knowledgeable religious scholars, academics, and other true experts in the community can be consulted if a more detailed analysis is necessary. Any analysis, however, may have only limited application, especially to cases involving teenagers, dabblers, and other self-styled practitioners. The fact is, signs, symbols, and rituals can mean anything that practitioners want them to mean *and/or* anything that observers interpret them to mean. The meaning of symbols can also change over time, place, and circumstance. Is a swastika spray painted on a wall an ancient symbol of prosperity and good fortune, a recent symbol of Nazism and anti-Semitism, or a current symbol of paranoia and adolescent defiance? The peace sign, which in the 1960s was a familiar antiwar symbol, is now supposed to be a satanic symbol.

In spite of what is sometimes said or suggested at law-enforcement training conferences, police have no authority to seize any satanic or occult paraphernalia they might see during a search. A legally valid reason must exist for doing so. It is not the job of law enforcement to prevent satanists from engaging in noncriminal teaching, rituals, or other activities.

There must be a middle ground in this issue. Concern about satanic or occult activity should not be a big joke limited to religious fanatics. On the other hand, law enforcement is not now locked in a life-and-death struggle against the supernatural forces of ancient evil. Law-enforcement officers need to know something about satanism and the occult in order to properly evaluate their possible connections to and motivations for criminal activity. From a community-relations perspective, they must also learn to respect spiritual beliefs that may be different or unpopular but that are not illegal. The focus must be on the objective investigation of violations of criminal statutes.

Until hard evidence is obtained and corroborated, the public should not be frightened into believing that babies are being bred and eaten, that 50,000 missing children are being murdered in human sacrifices, or that satanists are taking over America's day care centers. No one can prove with absolute certainty that such activity has *not* occurred. The burden of proof, however, as it would be in a criminal prosecution, is on those who claim that it has occurred. The explanation that the satanists are too organized and law enforcement is too incompetent only goes so far in explaining the lack of evidence. For at least eight years American law enforcement has been aggressively investigating the allegations of victims of ritualistic abuse. There is little or no evidence for the portion of allegations that deals with large-scale baby breeding, human sacrifice, and organized satanic conspiracies. Now it is up to mental health professionals, not law enforcement, to explain why victims are alleging things that don't seem to be true. Mental health professionals must begin to accept the possibility that some of what these victims are alleging just didn't happen and that this area desperately needs study and research by rational, objective social scientists.

If the guilty are to be successfully prosecuted, if the innocent are to be exonerated, and if the victims are to be protected and treated, better methods to evaluate and explain allegations of "ritualistic" child abuse must be developed or identified. Until this is done, the controversy will continue to cast a shadow over and fuel the backlash against the validity and reality of child sexual abuse.

References

Abel, G. G. 1988. "Self-Reported Sex Crimes of Non-Incarcerated Paraphiliacs." *Journal of Interpersonal Violence* 2, no. 1 (March): 37-48.

Breiner, Sander J. 1990. *Slaughter of the Innocents*. New York: Plenum.

Brown, Rebecca. 1987. *Prepare for War*. Chino, Ca.: Chick Publications.

Brunvand, J. H. 1981. *The Vanishing Hitchhiker*. New York: W. W. Norton.

Burgess, A. W. 1984. *Child Pornography and Sex Rings*. Lexington, Mass.: Lexington Books.

Diagnostic and Statistical Manual of Mental Disorders. 1987. 3d ed. Washington, D.C.: American Psychiatric Association.

Lanning, K. V. 1987. *Child Molesters: A Behavioral Analysis*. 2d ed. Washington, D.C.: National Center for Missing and Exploited Children.

———. 1989. *Child Sex Rings: A Behavioral Analysis*. Quantico, Va.: National Center for Missing and Exploited Children, Behavioral Sciences Unit, Federal Bureau of Investigation.

LaVey, Anton. 1969. *The Satanic Bible*. New York: Avon Books.

Missing, Abducted, Runaway, and Thrownaway Children in America. 1990. Washington, D.C.: U.S. Department of Justice, Office of Juvenile Justice and Delinquency Prevention.

Rosenberg, D. A. 1987. "Web of Deceit: A Literature Review of Munchausen Syndrome by Proxy." *Child Abuse and Neglect* 2:547-63.

Rush, Florence. 1980. *The Best-Kept Secret: Sexual Abuse of Children*. New York: McGraw-Hill.

Smith, Michelle, and Lawrence Pazder. 1980. *Michelle Remembers*. New York: Pocket Books.

Timnik, L. A. 1985. "The Times Poll." *Los Angeles Times*, August 25-26, 41.

6
Psychological Testing and Ritual Abuse

Richard Mangen, Psy.D.

Introduction

Despite the recent reemergence of interest in the areas of trauma, dissociation, and Multiple Personality Disorder (MPD) in the scientific literature, the relationship of satanic cult abuse to these issues continues to find only limited access to a professional audience. Although journals such as *Dissociation* now carry articles (e.g., Hill and Goodwin 1989; Kluft 1989; Ganaway 1989) discussing the issue of cult abuse and its relationship to trauma and the dissociative disorders, the topic is one that remains relatively fallow in the professional literature. This is despite the fact that recent estimates of the percentage of patients with MPD who may also be victims of cult abuse are in the range of 20 percent (Braun and Gray 1986, quoted in Sachs and Braun 1987). Nonetheless, the topic of cult abuse has been generating increasing interest among mental-health professionals treating a variety of patients, as reflected in the increasing availability of a variety of local, regional, and national workshops on working with and understanding survivors of ritual abuse.

There is also a lack of literature in the area of psychological testing of cult abuse victims. The purpose of this chapter is to begin to fill this gap and to address some of the issues involved in conceptualizing and undertaking psychological testing with victims of satanic cult abuse. A critical factor in testing this population is an understanding by the examiner of the types of beliefs and practices of satanic cults as well as the types of traumas that survivors have endured. Much of the psychological material produced by these patients can be best understood in this light, so that responses based on traumatic intrusions can be separated from psychosis or other psychiatric phenomena.

Review of the Literature

A review of the psychological and psychiatric literature revealed no references directly addressing issues related to the psychological assessment of victims of

---

I take the liberty throughout this chapter to refer to patients as "she" or "her" because the overwhelming majority of these patients, in my experience, has been female.

147

satanic cult abuse. However, given that satanic cult abuse involves extensive psychological trauma leading to a variety of dissociative disorders—including MPD—the small but growing body of literature relating to psychological test results of MPD and other dissociated states is relevant. It is this set of writings, as well as several other articles of significance, which will be reviewed here.

The first reference to the psychological testing of patients with Multiple Personality Disorder was made by Milton Erickson and David Rapaport (1980) in the 1940s. They analyzed the Rorschach responses of two 'dual personality' patients, and described the test results as reflecting tendencies toward intellectualization, introversion, and "compulsive-obsessional" personality characteristics. This article is characterized by several elements that are typical of a significant amount of the testing literature with such patients. First, the paper is based on a very small sample of patients; many of the papers to follow pursued a similar method of approach. Second, there is no indication of any awareness of persistent trauma (e.g., in the form of childhood abuse) as a possible contributing factor in such cases. This lack of context involving the impact of trauma is also typical of many of the papers to follow. Rather, there is an unwritten presumption of what would be referred to, in ego psychological terms, as more or less of an "average expectable environment."

Several studies on MPD in the 1940s and 1950s (Rosenzweig 1946; Leavitt 1947; Bowers and Brecher 1955) included some references to Rorschach responses, but none in a comprehensive form. An article by Charles Osgood and Zella Luria (1954) described a blind analysis of a multiple personality patient using the semantic differential technique. Several decades later, these authors (Osgood, Luria, and Smith 1976) performed a similar analysis on another multiple personality patient. In a series of articles, Edwin Wagner and his colleagues (Wagner and Heise 1974; Wagner 1978; Wagner, Allison, and Wagner 1983) studied the Rorschach responses of MPD and other dissociative states; their work culminated in a list of tentative rules for diagnosing MPD using the Rorschach. Unfortunately, these decision rules do not definitively rule out other types of psychopathology.

Angelo Danesino, Joseph Daniels, and Thomas McLaughlin (1979) used the Rorschach test as a means of assessing the structure and psychodynamics of a single case of Multiple Personality Disorder. The authors focus on how the test responses highlight the difficulties these patients have with interpersonal relationships, identity integration, conflicts between impulses and values, and role conflicts. There is no clear reference to the role of trauma, although reference to disturbed early object-relationships is made.

Robert Lovitt and Gary Lefkof (1985) describe the use of Exner's Comprehensive System for analyzing the structural features of Rorschach responses for three MPD patients. The authors described several features that were consistent in the test results: all of the 'major' personalities vacillated in their manner of responding to the inkblots. Adult patients emphasized color over form, suggesting some difficulty in modulating the influence of affective states on their perceptions, and they also gave some indications of an inability to delay affect. In general, these patients also exhibited an adequate capacity to perceive their experience in a manner based in reality. Lovitt and Lefkof noted that the "secondary" personalities showed wide variability from the "primary" personalities in scoring features; this finding was inconsistent with John Exner's comments regarding the test-retest reliabilities of a number of his structural elements.

A pair of articles (Carr 1984; Kowitt 1985) are relevant here, although they do not address themselves to MPD or ritual abuse per se. They discuss the relationship between traumatic events and intrapsychic conflict, as reflected in Rorschach symbol formation. Arthur Carr argued that Rorschach responses involving percepts of body integrity or body damage may be specific representations of a real traumatic event, and that therefore dynamic interpretations relating to unconscious intrapsychic conflict may be inadequate and possibly misleading. Michael Kowitt expands on Carr's ideas, focusing particularly on the notion that specific traumatic events become interwoven with the subject's prevailing conflicts, wishes, and fantasies; such unconscious elements may also be reflected in the traumatic imagery of Rorschach responses.

Bessell van der Kolk and Charles Ducey (1989) focus on post-traumatic stress disorder incurred by Vietnam War veterans, although their findings may have relevance for survivors of trauma induced by ritual abuse as well. The authors note that the Rorschach records of these subjects "showed an unmodified reliving of traumatic material," and reflected the subjects' tendency to deal with their trauma in a biphasic manner: being dominated by intrusive, overstimulating, and overwhelming imagery and percepts, and/or avoiding any affective participation in their surroundings. The authors suggest that the lack of integration of the traumatic experience explains why such people are so reactive to environmental stimuli, and state that there is a need for these people to put into words and feelings the traumatic events and affects as a means of organizing and mastering the trauma.

There are a number of single case studies (Ludwig et al. 1972; Brandsma and Ludwig 1974; Brassfield 1980; Ohberg 1984) of MPD patients that use the Minnesota Multiphasic Personality Inventory (MMPI) to argue that a wide variety of diagnostic configurations—including the schizophrenic, sociopathic, depressive, schizoid, psychotic, prepsychotic, hysterical-dissociative, and conversion—were evident in the profiles of the patients and various of their alter personalities. However, Robert Solomon's (1983) paper is the first to articulate MMPI results with a number of MPD patients. Eugene Bliss (1984) and Phillip Coons and Arthur Sterne (1986) also have contributed multi-patient MMPI studies to the literature. (Bliss was the first author in this area of the literature on MPD to suggest that trauma may play a role in the etiology of MPD.) Several consistent findings emerge from this research. Invalid profiles generated by MPD patients often result from extremely high scores on one of the validity scales (i.e., the F scale), which measures the tendency to exaggerate problems or difficulties. The Sc scale—which measures experiences of social alienation, isolation, bizarre feelings and sensations, feelings of inadequacy and dissatisfaction, thoughts of external influence and peculiar bodily dysfunction—was also typically elevated. Profiles with highest elevations on the Pd and Sc scales (i.e., four to eight codetypes) were frequently found. A. M. Ludwig characterized patients with these profiles as unpredictable, impulsive, alienated, underachieving, and associated with a diagnosis of borderline personality disorder. Other scales (e.g., Hy, D, Pa, Pt) were often found elevated as well, consistent with the multiplicity of symptoms reported by such patients. These authors encouraged a cautious stance in diagnosing MPD from the MMPI; Coons and Sterne expressed a recurrent theme along these lines by stating that they found no pathognomonic signs for MPD in their MMPI results, but also stated that patients who provided an MMPI with the characteristics they noted, coupled with a history of severe childhood abuse, should raise one's suspicions about the possibility of MPD.

At this point in the evolution of the literature there is a qualitative shift, characterized by an increased interest in statistically based efforts to measure dissociation in clinical and normal populations. First among these efforts was Eve Bernstein and Frank Putnam's (1986) work with the Dissociative Experiences Scale (DES). The authors state that dissociative phenomena are best thought of as existing along a continuum, and conclude that the DES has good split-half and test-retest reliability, that it is stable, and displays both construct and criterion-related validity.

The Perceptual Alteration Scale (PAS) (Sanders 1986), drawn from items of the MMPI, is also designed to measure dissociation. Shirley Sanders's factor analysis of the scale indicated three factors that accounted for 46 percent of the variance: modification of affect—related to disturbances in identity; modification of cognition—related to disturbances in cognition; and modification of control—related to loss of control over sensations, emotions, thoughts, and behavior. Sanders concluded that the PAS appeared to be a reliable instrument for assessing dissociative experiences, but also stated that further work was necessary before it could be used as a clinical tool.

The DES and the PAS were the subjects of a factor-analytic study (Fischer and Elnitsky 1990) designed to evaluate the construct validity of dissociation. The results of this analysis, which involved statistical procedures different from those used by the authors of the scales themselves, led Fischer and Elnitsky to believe that a single factor was being tapped by both the PAS and DES, although the nature of this factor was different for each scale. For the PAS, this dimension of dissociation seemed most related to disturbances of cognition control; for the DES, the dimension of dissociation reflected disturbances of affect control. They refute the idea that the PAS and the DES reliably measure three dimensions thought to underlie the concept of dissociation, suggesting instead that the dimensions tapped by these scales are two statistically correlated but conceptually distinct aspects of dissociation.

Along similar lines is work being done by Laurie A. Pearlman, Liza McCann, and Grace Johnson (1990). This group has developed a scale—the McPearl Belief Scale—to assess areas of cognitive disruption in survivors of psychological trauma. This scale may hold promise as a means of further understanding the cognitive schemas of trauma victims including cult abuse survivors.

Kevin Riley (1988) presented a brief discussion of the Questionnaire of Experiences of Dissociation (QED), which he described as a scale with good reliability and validity designed to measure dissociation. Although Riley claims good validity results for the scale, he does not indicate the specific nature or results of any validity studies done with the QED.

Marlene Steinberg, Bruce Rounsaville, and Domenic Cichetti (1990) describe preliminary information on a structured clinical interview that allows for rating of severity of five groups of dissociative symptoms, and for the overall diagnosis of dissociative disorders. They describe good to excellent reliability and discriminant validity values.

Judith Armstrong and Richard Lowenstein (1990) articulate an approach to psychological testing with MPD patients that attempts to track "state" changes, and encourages the participation in the testing of the greatest number of personality states in order to observe the patterns of interaction and functioning of the patient. Armstrong and Lowenstein suggest that MPD patients display patterns in the testing that are significantly different from those of schizophrenic and borderline patients. They noted that the aggressive and sexual content conveyed by these patients on projective tasks does not necessarily reflect true psychotic decompensation, but rather the impact of intrusive traumatic memories. Traumatic associations were evident in all aspects of the testing process, and spontaneous "state changes" became apparent when other efforts at distancing from these intrusive experiences failed. These patients tended to present with far more complicated defensive structures than the biphasic tendencies shown by Bessell van der Kolk's (1984) sample of traumatized war veterans.

As can be seen, the literature on psychological testing of MPD patients has evolved over time. There has been an increased awareness of the ways in which trauma can impact psychological functioning and be reflected in the testing situation, and an expanded interest in developing ways of conceptualizing and measuring dissociation. Thus, the testing literature presently stands to offer an increasingly sophisticated and relevant way to help in the diagnosis and treatment of victims of trauma, including satanic cult and other ritual abuse.

Rationale for Testing

Psychological testing with victims of satanic cult abuse can contribute significantly to a diagnostic understanding of a client, and can be useful in helping develop treatment implications and recommendations for her. At the same time, however, testing these patients is an extremely challenging endeavor for several reasons. It is easy to feel overwhelmed with the intensity and the pervasive extent of the experiences the patients often describe in the testing. Faced with the task of performing a psychological evaluation of such a patient, an evaluator can initially feel as if there is almost no commonality of experience between his or her world and the patient's. Given these reactions, the examiner can easily feel helpless to provide a meaningful diagnostic service—as if the issues that might be revealed in the course of the testing are either so obvious to others as to be self-evident, or so complicated and convoluted as to be inexplicable or indefensible in any logical fashion. Furthermore, the material that is presented in the test responses is often of a profoundly "primitive" and traumatic nature, which can have the effect of traumatizing, or at least overstimulating, the examiner who hears them. Indeed, this is just one of several kinds of response that the tester is likely to experience.

The patients often respond to the task demands of the testing situation in an overwhelmed and traumatized manner, which demands interventions on the part of the examiner beyond the typical bounds of the role of the diagnostic consultant. Episodes of dissociation and/or "switching" into alter personalities, confusion, intense flashbacks, and abreactions of painful memories stimulated by the test tasks, are not uncommon. As a result, the testing often takes longer with these patients than with other patients referred for testing. The patients' test responses often sound frankly psychotic, although they are not necessarily so, and thus raise complex issues related to differential diagnosis. Although investigators are increasingly sensitive to the idea that it is important to distinguish between test responses representing psychotic processes and those reflecting post-traumatic sequelae, there are currently few, if any, formal guideposts to help distinguish between the two.

Despite these difficulties, an appreciation of the significance of the patient-examiner interactions, the patient's response process, and a familiarity with the culture and activities of satanic cults allows considerable room for diagnostic differentiation and understanding. The use of psychological test materials and task demands, coupled with the active use by the examiner of the patient-examiner relationship, allows the development and testing of a variety of hypotheses, which can lead to diagnostic impressions, treatment recommendations, and other relevant clinical data. Psychological testing can help the evaluator appreciate the particular 'texture' of the individual patient's trauma—that is, to understand the manner in which the impact of profound trauma has affected the patient's particular experience of herself and others, her way of perceiving, feeling, and acting and other relevant clinical information.

Depending on the specific focus of the referral questions generated, psychological testing can offer a window into a number of different psychological functions. A patient's current level of intellectual functioning can be assessed, including the practical impact of trauma on cognitive processes and the manner in which the patient relates to her own verbal and perceptual productions. Testing can also be helpful in identifying the presence, kind, and degree of thought disorder that may characterize a patient's present cognitive functioning. Through the use of both the formal test responses and the patient's interactions with the examiner, one can develop inferences regarding the patient's experience of herself and others. Various reactions to specific persons (e.g., mother, father) in the patient's life can be identified. An understanding of the patient's particular role demands can be developed—the ways in which the patient wishes to be seen by those around her, and the complementary roles that she may attempt to have others adopt. Transference and countertransference paradigms can be inferred from this material as well. Testing can also be useful in describing the particular strengths, weaknesses, and styles with which a patient manages various types of affects, and whether there are particular affects that are most significant for the patient. In addition, the ways in which the patient defends against anxiety and other disruptive or disorganizing psychological experiences can often be identified. Although this last issue may appear self-evident—all of these patients rely on dissociation as a major defense—in fact there is more that can be ascertained by an analysis of test data. These patients typically also use a variety of other defenses, such as splitting, projection, and projective identification, as a means of maintaining a level of psychological organization. The testing can offer insights into the conditions under which such defenses (as well as other aspects of psychological functioning) are likely to occur.

I have used a battery of tests in performing psychological evaluations with approximately twenty-five patients who were victims of ritualistic abuse in a satanic cult setting. The majority of these patients also carried a diagnosis of Multiple Personality Disorder. Typically, these evaluations were performed in the context of an inpatient treatment setting, where testing was requested to help with the broad diagnostic understanding of the patient's functioning. This battery includes the Wechsler Adult Intelligence Scale–Revised (WAIS–R); the Rorschach Inkblot Test; a story-telling task such as the Thematic Apperception Test (TAT); a human figure drawing task coupled with a number of brief projective questions; the Animal Choice Test; and a number of other brief projective tasks. The results obtained with this battery will serve as the basis for discussion in the remainder of this chapter. Taken together, these tests provide a considerable range of task demands and interaction between the examiner and the patient, while also allowing for active use of the patient-examiner relationship in assessing the patient's level of functioning. Further, these procedures all allow particular insights to be gained and hypotheses to be developed regarding the patient's experience of self and others. While there is a significant body of clinical and testing research that suggests that this perspective is a useful one in conceptualizing the work of psychological diagnosis and treatment, it is of particular relevance for these patients because of the profound impact of satanic cult abuse on the deepest levels of one's sense of oneself and one's perceptions and expectations of others. In evaluating and treating victims of ritual abuse, one must keep in mind that the traumas they have experienced have always occurred in an intensely intimate interpersonal context. Therefore, an appreciation of the patients' experience of self and others is of particular relevance for working therapeutically with them.

Special Considerations in the Testing of Ritual Abuse Survivors

A number of guidelines have emerged from working with this population. The examiner must approach the assessment task with some specific awareness about ritual abuse. First, the examiner should be open to the *possibility* that cult abuse can serve as a possible organizing theme for understanding the patient's behavior and test responses. This is not to say that one should not also maintain an attitude of cautious skepticism. However, without an attitude of openness to the possibility, one is left to use potentially inappropriate conceptual frameworks for drawing inferences and making sense of the test data. For instance, on first glance, many responses given by these patients can sound blatantly psychotic. Yet, closer scrutiny may reveal that the response reflects material from an experience of ritualized abuse and indicates a traumatized level of functioning engendered by the task demands and the patient's particular associations to the material. Further, in considering the impact of trauma on these patients, it is important to appreciate that their traumas have resulted not only from numerous episodes of torture and abuse, but also from the chronic anticipation of the next episode. Our conception of traumatized functioning must therefore be a broad one.

Second, it is helpful to familiarize oneself with the visual and verbal symbols, beliefs, customs, and holidays of the satanic "culture." This allows placing the patient's words and actions into a particular context. For example, if the examiner is unfamiliar with the meaning of an inverted pentagram, the numbers 666 or other symbols with satanic meaning, the significance of the presence of such signs in the patient's responses will go unnoticed. Many satanic cults have a complex and complicated philosophical/religious underpinning, which is translated into very specific tasks, beliefs, and values through which these patients (or at least some aspect of them) organize their lives. The more familiar the examiner is with these aspects of cult life, the more able he or she will be to consider—or discard—them in drawing inferences about a patient's functioning. Third, the examiner needs to develop an appreciation of the extent to which these patients have had to, and feel they must continue to, straddle two completely different (i.e., cult/non-cult) worlds. The values, teachings, use of language, and expectations of behavior of these two worlds are often at completely different ends of the spectrum. The role of language is particularly important here, since language is the means by which most test tasks and responses are conveyed. Survivors of cult abuse are familiar with and responsive to a "private," trauma-invoking language, which they learned as a result of their cult experience, as well as the "public" language of the non-cult society. Words can carry private—and traumatic—meaning, even when spoken in a benign public context.

Consider the meaning of "being tested" from the patient's point of view. Wonder what it must be like to have grown up in a world where no one could be trusted, where at literally any time you were vulnerable to being brutalized— emotionally, physically, sexually, spiritually—for no apparent or consistent reason. Imagine being told that such episodes were "tests" to see if you were "strong enough," or "good enough," and that these tests were for your own good and were to *help* you. Consider knowing that your life was out of your control, *totally*, but if you gave any sign of outward distress, you would only be further brutalized. Now consider what it would be like to be approached by a stranger (i.e., the examiner) who essentially says he's interested in giving you some tests in order to help you. Such a perspective can help the examiner begin to appreciate the kinds of themes that these patients carry with them into their interactions with the world.

Fourth, the examiner should attempt to appreciate that the practical goal of dissociation is to "make things invisible." Because it is in the interest of satanic cults to keep their activities secret, these patients are taught *not* to reveal themselves, and to keep many aspects of their experience hidden and secret. As a result, in many arenas of the patient's life—including therapy and the testing process—"things are not what they seem to be." From the examiner's perspective, this requires an active use of the patient-examiner relationship to "help make the invisible visible."

Fifth, an examiner needs to develop a capacity to tolerate traumatizing material, and to respond to it in a nonjudgmental manner. The examiner needs to be guided in his or her responses to the patient by the principle that the tester's interventions should always be in the service of the diagnostic process. This requires a willingness to be flexible in response to the patient's behavior, while maintaining a stance of curiosity about the interpersonal and intrapsychic meaning of the patient's actions.

Sixth, the examiner should be aware of the variety of countertransference experiences that are particularly likely to be engendered in testing these patients, and be willing to consider that such reactions may be relevant to the particular "texture" of the patient's trauma. One such countertransference reaction is to feel traumatized by the responses, memories, and associations the patient presents during the testing process. Another is to feel as if the examiner is somehow perpetrating abuse against the patient by requiring her to proceed through a testing situation that may result in gross disorganization and distress. Another type of countertransference involves becoming so fascinated with the material that the patient presents that the patient becomes "object-ified," thus possibly repeating an early interpersonal paradigm. Yet another is to idealize these patients as brilliant and courageous individuals who found a profoundly creative way to survive an impossible situation. While there may be some truth in this notion, it also serves to keep the examiner from appreciating the profound desperation of their actions, and the extent of the damage and devastation they have suffered to their sense of self.

This is certainly not meant to be an exhaustive list of countertransference possibilities. The examiner can serve the diagnostic process, however, by allowing him or herself the experience of whatever feelings may arise in relation to the patient, and then consider the significance of these feelings in the context of what the patient is trying to do or express. Such an analysis can have useful implications for treating the patient and anticipating transference/countertransference paradigms in the treatment.

These suggestions are tantamount to encouraging the examiner to be willing to enter into the patient's world and attempt to appreciate the unique nature of her experience. However, the examiner must also strive to maintain a solid foundation in his or her own frame of reference so as to not get completely lost in these patients, and lose both diagnostic stance and leverage. In a sense, the examiner must attempt to straddle the same two different worlds as the patient in order to help diagnose what is going on for the patient and what may be helpful for her healing.

The Test Situation

In testing ritual abuse patients, as with other patients, the approach that I use encourages an active participation on their part in sharing not only their responses to the specific tasks but also their thoughts, feelings, and associations to the tests and their own responses. This stance not only allows me access to the test responses per se for developing hypotheses, it also allows me to begin to assess the patient's manner of engaging in an interpersonal process for the purpose of understanding something more about themselves. This is very useful for forming hypotheses about how they will be able to work collaboratively in the therapy relationship.

During the course of the testing I also take an active stance in attempting to engage the patient in a process of self-observation. For example, after each test, I am likely to ask the patient some type of question geared to elicit their reactions or impressions to the particular task. Similarly, if the patient responds to a specific task in a curious or odd manner, I am likely to comment on that and ask the patient what she thought, felt, or was responding to. Responses to these interventions often provide useful diagnostic information. I also pay attention to the manner in which the patient deals with beginnings and endings, looking to see what appears most significant in her handling of these experiences. I also ask the patient if she had any thoughts or reactions to the test situation during the time between testing sessions, and encourage her to let me know if she does have any such thoughts at any time. I am eager to see how well the patient can engage in such a process with me, and will encourage her through example and through questions to collaborate with me.

If the patient presents with MPD as part of the clinical picture, I make no attempt to test only certain of the alters. This is because I am interested in seeing what the patterns of adaptive and defensive functions are, and the patient's need to "switch" to different personalities or states of mind is in response to those functions. In addition, it is a fallacy—and a lack of appreciation of the patient's need for defenses—to expect that the patient is always capable of consciously stopping their dissociative defenses in the face of unfamiliar settings and task demands. This is true even when there is no gross or obvious evidence of such switching.

While I use the approaches described above with all of the clients that I evaluate, they have particular relevance for ritual abuse patients and other trauma victims. This is because dissociative defenses conceal, and therefore active efforts to highlight such psychological functioning are necessary to assess when they are in effect. In a sense, then, the diagnostic process aims, in part, to reveal. Thus, I am likely to make several types of interventions with ritual abuse patients (or others where there is reason to believe that dissociative defenses are of primary importance). For example, if I have any sense that some type of dissociative episode has taken place, I will ask the patient a question geared to address this. If the patient has exhibited Multiple Personality Disorder, I might ask, "Who's response was this?" or "Was there anyone else inside who had a part in coming to that answer?" A similar question might be something like, "Tell me how you came to that answer?" At other times, dissociative episodes are quite blatant, coming in the form of a "switch" from one alter personality to another. At such times I usually ask the patient to tell me what was it that caused them to switch. The answers to such questions can lead to relevant information about the themes, affects, or other triggers to which the patient is sensitive. Repeating test questions at a later time in the testing process, and asking the patient if she remembers whether the question had previously been asked, and what her answer was, is another way to try to track dissociative episodes that may not be grossly evident.

Patients who have experienced ritual abuse respond to the testing situation in a variety of ways, depending in part on the degree to which the amnestic barriers against traumatic memories are intact, and where they are in the course of their treatment. As a result, there does not appear to be a definitive pattern or profile to the formal test results given by these patients. However, there are some similarities in the manner in which the patients respond to the testing situation. It is not uncommon, for example, for these patients to exhibit some type of traumatized reaction to some aspect of the testing. This can come in the form of an unanticipated abreaction of a traumatic event that was triggered by the patient's reactions to the test stimuli. If MPD is part of the clinical picture, switching can occur rapidly and/or without warning. It can come in response to apparently benign and familiar stimuli that nonetheless serve as triggers for memories of traumatic experiences. More often than not, the patients have a difficult time in response to the mere fact of being tested, both because the notion of being tested is a dangerous one, and also because the testing process stands as a potential threat to their equilibrium. Nonetheless, most are willing to participate in the process.

There is considerable variability in the patients' capacity to observe and reflect on these self-experiences. In the case of ritual abuse survivors with MPD, in my experience it is not common for alter personalities who are most identified with the cult experience to present themselves directly for the testing situation. Typically, the alters who have some alliance with the goals of treatment will present for the testing, although this may change in the face of the various testing task demands.

Intellectual Functioning and Formal Thought Processes

Although there is no particular pattern in how these patients do on the formal intellectual testing, almost all of the patients I have tested have been of at least average intelligence, and some have scored in the high average range of overall cognitive functioning. However, they typically show some signs of cognitive slippage and disrupted, traumatized thought processes at some points during the testing process. In keeping with the ideas of Arthur Carr (1984), Michael Kowitt (1985), and Bessel van der Kolk and Charles Ducey (1989), they display some of the characteristics of patients suffering from post-traumatic stress disorder. Cognitive efficiency can be impaired, and adherence to "reality" intruded upon, in response to any number of different task demands. Because of their exposure to secret traumas and their connection to a private language, ritual abuse victims can be triggered by even the most apparently benign test stimuli and task directions. As a result, the entire testing process involves presenting the patient with a variety of stimuli, any of which could serve as a trigger into a traumatized state. For example, these patients often react to the relatively straightforward demands of the intelligence test (the WAIS-R) in idiosyncratic and/or bizarre ways. I have observed this with each of the different subtests of the WAIS-R. On tasks dealing with general information about the world, these patients can show striking discontinuities in what they know. For instance, a woman who had an overall IQ in the high average range and who had been employed as a nurse and was quite competent to carry on sophisticated discussions regarding drug interaction effects and mechanisms for medication effectiveness, was asked

"How many weeks in a year?"; her response, after some reflection, was "forty-two."

Cognitive tasks involving numbers often evoke disorganized, frightened, or traumatized responses because of the patient's automatic associations to certain numbers (e.g., 666, 3, 9) that have satanic significance, or because they were beaten or tortured as children for not learning their math well enough or fast enough. One WAIS-R task, the Digits Backward task—which involves repeating in *reverse* order series of numbers read aloud to the patient by the examiner—can be particularly troublesome to these patients not only because of the involvement of numbers, but also because satanic cults often do things "backwards"—such as walking backwards as part of rituals, chanting words or prayers backwards, reversing the order of words, or creating new words by spelling a word backwards (e.g., "Satan" becomes "Natas") as part of their rituals. Similarly, the Digit Symbol task, which requires the matching up of a number with a particular symbol, can be disorganizing to some of these patients because of the association of the symbols used in the task to the use of various symbols of satanic significance.

Tasks involving the understanding and use of language, such as the Vocabulary, Similarities, or Comprehension subtests of the WAIS-R, frequently capture the struggle these patients confront in trying to straddle both their private and public worlds. The use of words themselves—such as simply asking to tell what a word means, or to share a piece of information, or explain the meaning of a proverb—can become fraught with danger. This can take different forms: for many of these patients, they have been inculcated with the idea that to talk about the "wrong" things could be life-threatening to them or others that they cared about. But the patients aren't always certain as to what the "wrong" thing is because they can be rewarded for talking about some things and then brutalized later for talking about the same things in the same circumstances. For some patients, the use of words as *labels*—symbols of an object or concept or action—gets lost, or perhaps is never fully developed. For example, in asking one patient to tell the meanings of some words, she experienced profound distress as she heard the word, at times writhing in her seat as the ideas came to her to describe what the word meant. In talking with her about this experience, it became clear that to her that the word and the deed were the same—the linguistic distance and symbolic meaning that words allow was simply not present for her. As she said the word, she lived its meaning. and for these patients, their meanings are often permeated with deadly messages or abusive intent on the part of others. For example, when asked to define "consume," she said: "My first thought . . . or define it? My first thought is . . . to kill . . . to devour . . . to completely devour . . . engulf . . . but I also know it means to eat . . . because of the cult I was in, I had to kill people and eat them."

The manner in which the patients respond to tasks involving physical stimuli (e.g., small cubic blocks with sides colored either all red, all white, or half-red and half-white; drawings of familiar items with an important part missing; puzzle pieces that can be put together to make a familiar object) is also striking and susceptible to the intrusion of traumatic material. For example, one patient was unable to respond to a particular item on the Block Design task. When this was explored with her she indicated that the red color of the blocks reminded her of blood, which made it hard to do any of the items. She went on to say that the shape of the particular test item she couldn't do reminded her of the ceremonial chalice that held the blood of the sacrificial victims which she had to drink. In a similar situation, another patient was unable to attempt an item from the Object Assembly task. The patient understood that the finished product would yield a figure of a man; however, when faced with an array of disconnected body parts placed in front of her, she simply froze up and couldn't do anything. When asked about what had happened when trying to do the task, it was evident from her posture and tone of voice that she had "switched" into a young alter personality; she described that she had seen bodies of people cut up, and had helped cut them up and even eaten parts of them, but she had never been told to try to put them together.

Despite the presence and frequency of such episodes it is important to keep in mind that they can occur next to instances of organized, task-appropriate, goal-directed functioning. This phenomena speaks to the possible existence of "trauma-free" and "traumatized" spheres of functioning, and raises questions about state-dependent elements of cognitive functioning. Although these patients are not always in a state of traumatized functioning, they enter such a state too readily. In Piagetian terms, the question becomes whether these patients are capable of functioning at formal operational levels of cognitive ability in some instances, while unable to function at other than pre-operational, or even sensori-motor levels of cognition, at other times. Nancy Cole (1990) has described these and other issues of cognitive phenomena in the framework of "traumatic thinking." The practical result of this type of functioning is that "things are not what they seem" with these patients.

The idiosyncratic, personalized, and often traumatized response to the testing process is often highlighted in the more projective tasks. A picture is included of a tree that was drawn by a ritual abuse survivor (see figure 6–1). Many of the principles described above can be seen in such productions. One can see the influence of traumatic events (such as witnessing an arm being chopped off) as well as specific cult symbols (e.g., 666) and various defenses (such as the split into many personalities). These productions clearly provide a wealth of clinical information.

The Rorschach Test is an excellent device for such projective material since it involves both perceptual and associational elements (Rapaport, Gill, and Schafer 1968). These mesh together as integral parts of the patient's response process as she attempts to attribute some type of meaning to the inkblots in response to the task question "What might this be?" What is striking about these patients is that the associational process is more likely to be devastated

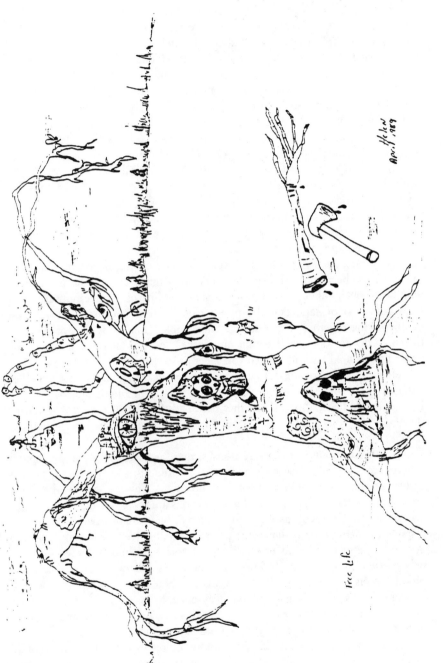

Figure 6–1.

than is the perceptual process. Thus, it is often easy to perceive at least the central elements of what these patients perceive in the inkblots. However, they often have a tendency to make associations that are far removed from what might typically be expected. For example, one patient responded to Card III by perceiving "two ladies." This is a common response to this card. However, the meaning which she attributes to them is typical of what occurs for these patients: "Two ladies . . . that look like they are murdering babies . . . cutting the baby and pulling it apart. . . . Actually, I think it's dead babies . . . because there's blood in the picture. . . . They removed the hearts of the babies." When asked to elaborate more on what she saw, she said "Here's the lady on each side. . . . There's the dead babies. . . . Here's the blood so you know they're really dead . . . it looks like blood running down . . . it starts off and ends in a pool . . . it's the color. . . . The babies, here and here, because they don't have any legs or any . . . you can't live that way . . . especially with your heart out."

Such traumatic imagery, often replete with direct or indirect references to satanic rituals and symbols, is common in the projective responses of these patients. Often, these responses are given in a bland, matter-of-fact manner, as if the affect has been drained from them. At other times, the responses are given with "too much" affect. The following is a sampling of such responses, taken from a number of patients and a number of different Rorschach cards: "Two people sitting together over a fire . . . they look human but they're not. . . . their mouths are open as if eating raw flesh," "an evil face with a grin—the upper lip is pulled back like when you sneer or something. . . . It has the colors of a clown, but it's not something nice . . . more like it's going to cast a spell of damnation on you," "an insect climbing on something moldy and rotten. . . . It's like putrid flesh," "two sheep that have had their heads cut off . . . not for slaughter, 'cuz that's not how they'd do it . . . more like as part of a ritual sacrifice."

Despite the sound of these responses, there was at least some perceptual support from the inkblots; most evident is the extent to which scenes of horror and terror are prominent in many of these protocols. This is not to say that there are not instances in which perceptual distortions are more central; in fact, these do exist in the protocols as well. For example, one patient gave the following response, which was quite difficult to follow perceptually: "It looks like a person descending into some kind of bizarre—like into somebody's body—like the pelvis—here's the pelvis. . . . These are the tubes and ovaries. . . . These are blood vessels that feed it. . . . The veins are blue. . . . They come out in a network . . . like if this part of me was gone he could just drop in from above. . . . It's a way to get inside somebody. . . . That's a real nourishing area to have babies and stuff so maybe they want to get in to get power."

However, even apparent misperceptions or distortions of the perceptual qualities of the inkblots can sometimes be understood with regard to the extent to which associational processes have been impacted. For example, if a patient were to give a response such as "this is a person with woman's breasts and a penis," an examiner might typically begin to think of the presence of some type of disordered thought process that does not allow the filtering out of incongruent elements. This might have implications for self/other differentiation and boundary and reality testing problems, among other difficulties. However, victims of ritual cult abuse have been exposed to situations in which people are presented as both male and female at the same time. In some cult activities, Satan is described as both male and female, and rituals occur in which women with penises, and men with breasts, appear to exist. In the experience of these patients, that is, they *do* exist. Thus, that which sounds psychotic cannot, in fact, automatically be presumed to be psychotic; it may, in fact, be a fundamentally accurate perception of an overwhelming and traumatic situation. It is imperative that examiners and treaters consider the implications of this type of reality for these patients.

Experience of Self and Others

Victims of satanic ritual abuse share a common bond that has many variations on a common theme. They have been brutalized in the worst imaginable—unimaginable—ways. Yet they have been told they have deserved what has been done to them, and been taught to believe that they don't deserve any better. They have been taught to enjoy what has been done to them, and what they have done to others. They have learned, and therefore know, that pain is pleasure and pleasure is pain, that good is bad and that bad is good.

Recent testing literature (e.g., Kissen 1986) elaborates the idea that a legitimate way to conceptualize some test responses—for example, human or animal responses on the Rorschach—is as reflective of core self-experiences. Daniel Stern (1985) elaborates a model of how a sense of self becomes established during the first several years of life. Stern articulates four core aspects—*self-agency, self-history, self-affectivity,* and *self-coherence*—of a healthy sense of self. *Self-agency* refers to the sense of being the author of your own actions; *self-history* refers to a sense of having a continuous and enduring past; *self-affectivity* involves experiencing patterned, consistent inner feelings that are congruent with other experiences of the self; and *self-cohesion* involves a sense of being a nonfragmented physical entity with its own boundaries. John Kurkjian (1990) has described how profoundly each of these aspects is adversely affected by the type of early and sustained trauma that victims of ritual abuse sustain.

These two general areas—the testing literature and the developmental/psychodynamic literature—converge to provide a helpful model for conceptualizing about self and other experiences in ritual abuse victims. Both the projective test responses of these patients and their interactions with the examiner yield significant data regarding their experience of themselves and others.

Consider the following response, not atypical of some of the kinds of responses given by these patients to the first Rorschach card:

> It's a bug . . . and it's in between two other bugs that are trying to eat it. . . . It's trying to get away because it has hands . . . but it can't, because they got it good. . . . They're devouring it. . . . Whatever it is, it's got wings the other things have wings and tails. . . . It's it's screeching or maybe laughing . . . and they got it pinned down.

The patient's manner of relating this response suggests that the primary focus is on the "bug" in the middle. In a simplistic way, one can wonder if the patient is expressing something like "I am a bug—caught by others who are like me, who surround me, but who want to devour me—who hold me down and keep me from getting free—I don't know whether to laugh or cry, and they don't help, they just keep trying to devour me."

Although such a response is rich with diagnostic possibilities, I wish to focus solely on a consideration of the self-experiential aspects implicit in it. In this percept one can hear the lack of self-agency—the ability to have control over one's life and one's actions, and the futility of efforts to fight or flee or to know whether to laugh or cry: "a bug . . . trying to get away . . . but it can't . . . because they got it good." One can hear the lack of self-cohesion—the lack of safety and continuity regarding a sense of bodily integrity: "a bug . . . in between two other bugs that are trying to eat it." One can hear the lack of self-affectivity—the uncertainty of whether a situation of self-destruction leads to pleasure or to pain: "a bug. . . . they're devouring it. . . . It's screeching or maybe laughing."

The TAT provides another window into these patients' experiences of self and others. Consider the following TAT story, told in response to a picture in which an older woman is sitting on a sofa close beside a girl, speaking or reading to her. The girl, who holds a doll on her lap, is looking away.

> This is a mother and daughter, and the mother just gave the daughter a doll and is trying to read her a story and be real nice . . . and the girl turns away because she knows it's not real—that mom only does and says all the right things, but she hasn't been in the room for a real long time. . . . She goes somewhere in her mind . . . and she just feels sad because she wants to believe her mother wants to be nice to her, but she knows that even when it happens it's not real. . . . You can't be nice to something you don't even like. . . . The end is she goes on always playing that part. . . . The mother is being nice to her to confuse her. . . . She has no room for any kind of emotional involvement on any level."

The sense of interpersonal estrangement and disconnection, which is a centerpiece of this story is a frequent theme—either overtly or covertly—in the stories of ritual abuse victims. Inherent in this story is the idea that "things are not what they seem." This theme also is frequently expressed in the interpersonal dynamics of ritual abuse victims. These patients do not have a stable interpersonal context from which to make sense of the world. Because of this lack of context, because of the devastating and pervasive nature of the abuses perpetrated against them, because of their apparent deficits in core elements of self, these patients have great difficulty comprehending the motives and intentions of others in relation to themselves.

In the story, it is made clear that the mother's apparent interest in the child is not only not sincere, but malicious in ultimate intent: "the girl knows that even when it happens it's not real. . . . The mother is being nice to her to confuse her." Similarly, the child's own feeling state is hidden behind a facade: "the girl does and says all the right things, but she hasn't been in the room for a real long time." The expression of feeling states is thus also affected. These patients have difficulty in trusting that what is expressed is what is meant.

Implicit in this story also is a profound and pervasive lack of safety and trust between people. Not enough can be said about the extent to which this theme is intensely active in these patients. The life-and-death quality of the danger inherent in both of these themes (safety and trust; "things are not what they seem") is captured in the following story in response to a picture in which a young man is lying on a couch with his eyes closed; leaning over him is the gaunt form of an elderly man, his hand stretched out above the face of the reclining figure.

> This boy's laying there—he's really tired, he's been all over—he meets this really nice man. . . . They talk for a long time so he feels really safe—so he falls asleep. . . . Next thing he knows he wakes up with this man standing over him, and the man has this look in his eyes—and the boy knows the man is going to kill him—and he struggles real hard and gets away and he's learned that even when it feels safe . . . don't always trust it."

In contrast to these responses, many of the projective responses are more blatantly satanic and traumatic in nature, and the patient frequently becomes overwhelmed by her own associations. References to demons, Satan, devils, darkness and hellfire, bizarre torture, sexual perversion, human and animal sacrifice, excrement, and cannibalism are not uncommon elements of these patients' test responses. Consider the following Rorschach images, taken from a variety of patients: "The yellow makes me sick to my stomach. . . . What does yellow mean? . . . something angry about yellow . . . having to drink yellow . . . urine . . . poured all over me"; "An evil demon with robes . . . crucifying someone"; "A bat . . . and it's got sucky things here to poke you for blood," "A lady . . . she's on fire. . . . Her hair is painted . . . and she's got a hole in her middle. . . . they poked her with something and they cut off her feet . . . like in a ritual—maybe tortured her before they burned her . . . maybe she told something she wasn't supposed to"; "Two very mad demons . . . here's their eyes and their mean teeth and they're bloody and their heads are chopped off"; "Two naked men . . . each of them have a dead baby they're putting it in a pot . . . and the babies are in the pot and they're turning black. . . . they're going to burn them. . . . The men have devil feet, big devil feet, and big pokey man parts . . . to poke you . . . that hurt you. . . . It's very clear—very clear."

In a similar fashion, some of their TAT stories are built around obvious satanic imagery, as the following story indicates:

> It's one of the Dark Ones in the middle of the cemetery. . . . He's one of the demons they're pulling out of the body—there's probably a child laying on a grave and they're passing the demons through her . . . and when he gets done—he'll leave the child covered in dirt and tell her she belongs to Satan—and that some demons stayed inside . . . because these nasty people put you in holes in graveyards and tell you if you talk they'll throw dirt on your face . . . and she's grateful to Satan for saving her.

These responses reflect more of the traumatized nature of these patients' experiences, their sense of passivity and helplessness, and their terror in the face of overwhelming assault. Themes of ritualized abuse and the ultimate power of Satan; expectations of sadistic and/or murderous treatment at the hands of others; confusion of thought and deed; confusion of such polarities as good/bad, love/hate; victim/perpetrator, male/female, etc; all contribute to profound identity disruption and uncertain roles and values. It is in the context of such issues that the previously discussed themes of estrangement, danger, and distrust are played out.

Affect Organization and Defensive Functioning

Victims of satanic ritual abuse generally have tremendous difficulty in integrating and modulating affective experiences. From a psychodynamic and developmental perspective, this can be understood in part as a result of the impact of early, pervasive, and prolonged psychological (and physical) trauma that disrupted and devastated their capacities for mastering emotional expression. This issue is compounded by the fact that satanic cults often actively attempt to inculcate the belief that the sadistic expression of certain affects (e.g., aggression, hatred, or rage) is to be applauded.

Most striking about the manner in which affects are experienced by these patients, however, is the extreme intensity with which they are felt. At the same time, these patients often express affects in a global, polarized, and amorphous manner. Evidence for these ideas is readily available in the testing data. As noted in the examples from the previous sections, themes of raw aggression (e.g., animal and human sacrifice, victims being tortured and/or mutilated, cannibalism) and polymorphous perverse sexuality (e.g., ritualized gang rape, sodomy, pedophilia, necrophilia) are often dominant in Rorschach percepts and TAT stories. Tender, caring, or loving feelings are usually given in only fleeting incidents, often with an underlying current of mistrust or within a context of fundamental "disconnection" between people. In fact, there is a striking paucity of more positively tinged affective experiences (e.g., love or hope) reflected in the test responses of these patients. When they are given, they are often imbued with a brittle or unbelieving quality that serves to undermine or disavow the kind of relatedness that they speak of. It is my belief that such percepts and themes typically reflect some sorts of traumatic experience or memory that has become stimulated by the task demands of the testing.

The extent of anxiety these patients experience is best considered in the context of terror. For them, feeling states can only lead to a vulnerability that keeps them traumatized. Similarly, experiences of loss—and subsequent despair—are expressed in a primitive manner. Fears of annihilation and loss of the object are more typical and prominent than higher level fears, such as loss of love of the object.

A discussion regarding the ways in which victims of cult abuse attempt to protect themselves from overwhelming internal or external experiences must, obviously, begin with dissociative defenses. In the testing situation, dissociative phenomena can, in general, be seen from two different perspectives—process and content. As a *process,* dissociation is sometimes seen in the extreme in the obvious "switches" that occur when the patient is overwhelmed by something she is experiencing. For example, in response to a TAT picture of a man standing in a graveyard, one patient first described hearing voices in her head getting increasingly loud and wanting to "praise the Hand of Glory." (Later, this patient described how, as a youngster, she had been forced to participate in cult rituals that took place at night in graveyards.) Suddenly and dramatically, she tossed the card down, curled up into a ball in her chair, began waving her arm over her head like a bird with a broken wing, and manipulated her fingers in spastic gestures that seemed like—and in fact were—some sort of private sign language. When asked, she said her name was Bobbi, and in a terrified little girl voice kept repeating: "Get out of the box," and "No kill babies." After a few minutes of talking with this alter, another alter presented; this second alter had no idea who the first alter was, or what she was doing. Thus, despite reexperiencing something of the trauma again, the patient's capacity to dissociate had made what had been visible invisible. Dissociation had allowed for an apparent escape from the life-or-death struggle with which the patient had been confronted.

Sometimes dissociation is evident in the *process* when a patient describes, in awful detail, the specifics of some traumatic personal memory—the killing of an infant, the incestuous assault on a young child, the slaughter of a family pet—but without any trace of affect. It is as if the patient were reading a weather report, or watching something on a TV screen. The memory is preserved in excrutiating detail, yet the affect is gone. One could think of this as intellectualization, or as trauma which has been mastered, but this would be incorrect. Neither of these ideas accurately reflects the extent to which the affects involved in the trauma live on, unassimilated, within the patient.

A reliance on dissociation as a defense can also be reflected in the *content* of responses. For example, in the previously noted TAT story about the mother and daughter, the patient describes how the daughter "hasn't been in the room for a real long time . . . she goes somewhere in her mind." This is as clear a description of a dissociated state as one might find.

Other brief examples of how dissociation can be expressed include a patient's TAT story of a man and woman who meet in a bar and go back to her room: "And they have sex and both fall asleep . . . and he wakes up and *realizes he didn't want to be there. . . .* So he got up and put his clothes on—and he knows she hasn't moved or said anything—and he *suddenly realizes she's dead."* This kind of sudden and unexplained shift in awareness of a character is often a reflection of the same type of process that occurs during a discrete dissociative episode in these patients. Similarly, expressions of confusion about the passage of time, or the transposition of place, or the sudden acquisition of knowledge or information—all can be descriptions of dissociative experiences that are translated into the story.

These patients also make use of other defenses, as reflected in the testing situation. Splitting, projective identification, and denial are also typically evident in their test responses. In keeping with Paul Lerner and Howard Lerner (1980), splitting is implied in test responses where affective attributes of people are polarized and/or separated from one another in some form. Thus, the following Rorschach response is reflective of splitting: "The top here looks like a devouring demon. . . . It's about to consume this bottom part that it's connected to. . . . It's all pure and goodness. . . . The evil hasn't touched it yet . . . but it's going to."

Similarly, projective identification is frequently seen in the responses of these patients. Projective identification has been described as a defensive maneuver in which parts of the self are projected onto another person in an attempt to control the frightening parts of the self by controlling the other. Lerner and Lerner (1980) operationalize this defense with regard to the Rorschach in the context of confabulatory human figure responses in which form level is problematic, associative elaboration is too extensive, and the nature of the elaboration is aggressive or sexual. These elements are very consistent in the responses of cult abuse victims; for instance: "The man here is about to kill this woman. . . . He's got knives and fire and power coming out of his eyes. . . . She's going to be his. . . . She has no choice. . . . he loves that she's so terrified!"

Denial also plays a role in the defensive functioning of these patients. More primitive forms of denial are common in the context of the patients' attempts to ward off unacceptable experiences or impulses. Thus, reality is disregarded in significant ways, or incompatible attributes are made to the same character. For example, in telling a TAT story, one patient described that the central character was pleased that he had just finished murdering a young child, and now was going to go off to his job as legal prosecutor to help find and convict the murderer. Although gross denial can be seen to play a part in this story, as with other aspects of cult victims' experiences, one must also wonder about the extent to which such responses reflect something of actual incongruous action from their environment. For example, another patient, who told a similar story, came from a family in which she eventually revealed that her grandfather—who was involved in law enforcement—did, indeed, participate in murders which he then would be assigned to investigate.

Areas for Further Consideration

Numerous areas are in need of further investigation in considering the role of psychological testing in the diagnosis and treatment of victims of satanic cult abuse. One of these involves further determining how psychological testing can best be used in helping diagnose the presence of satanic cult abuse as a particular type of trauma, when no such diagnosis has previously been made. This is an area which the testing literature has not yet addressed. The large majority of cases I have tested had already been diagnosed as victims of ritual abuse; therefore the sample that I draw from is skewed in that most—although not all—of them had already begun uncovering memories that had overt satanic implications. What about the patient who has not yet broken the amnestic, repressive, or dissociative barriers that keep such material hidden? The literature on testing MPD patients does not make me optimistic that testing can be routinely useful in diagnosing the presence of multiplicity when such a diagnosis has not yet been made. This may be related to an inherent limitation of the testing process, or the need for secrecy on the part of the patients being tested, or other considerations. At the least, the types of questions that psychological testing is best suited to help answer with these patients may be further clarified in the course of this type of investigation.

Questions concerning the possibility of "typical" profiles or characteristics of victims of ritual abuse on such tests as the Rorschach, Wechsler scales, MMPI (and MMPI-2), and TAT need to be addressed. An ongoing debate in the literature currently exists regarding the extent to which patients who have experienced significant trauma end up being diagnosed as suffering from a "Borderline Personality Disorder" (e.g., Herman, Perry, and van der Kolk 1989). Victims of ritual abuse fall into the realm of this debate as well. Underlying these issues are attempts to make conceptual sense of the manner in which people make sense of their world, and to identify the crucial elements that motivate people to grow psychologically. Victims of ritual cult abuse confound our efforts in these directions because they do not allow us to make all of the assumptions that we would like to in understanding psychological development. Most important of the assumptions that cannot readily be made is that of the "average expectable environment," which suggests that the child's caretakers will do what they reasonably can to provide an atmosphere that fosters physical, emotional, and psychological safety and growth. It is safe to state that victims of satanic ritual abuse are not the beneficiaries of any such expectation. This has significant repercussions for the manner in which we conceptualize test results. For example, responses usually conceptualized simply as representations of internally generated drive-related fantasy must now also be considered as possible representations of actual traumatic memories that may (or may not) have become condensed, distorted, or otherwise affected by the patient's efforts at maintaining psychological equilibrium.

The possibility of creating new measures, subscales, or scoring criteria remains a viable strategy in looking at this population of patients. Such an approach is reflected in Judith Armstrong and Richard Lowenstein's (1990) development of a new Rorschach subscale (the TC/R subscale) to measure traumatic associations in their work with MPD patients. Comparing the overall test results of ritual abuse victims with other groups of traumatized patients (e.g., survivors of war situations) may also be a useful step in developing a differential diagnosis regarding the impact of trauma.

Along similar lines, there is an ongoing need for further analysis of test responses to help develop increased understanding of these patients' various ego functions, including the impact of trauma on their cognitive functioning and formal thought processes, their experience of themselves and their object relationships, their capacity to manage affective states and their defensive proclivities. The issue of state-dependent functioning is relevant here. There is also a need for establishing an operational definition of 'dissociation' as reflected in test responses. Such a definition should be grounded in a solid theoretical foundation and also lend itself to the development of clinically relevant hypotheses to the examiner for use in diagnostic and treatment planning. Further, the interplay between dissociation and other defenses typically used by these patients is an area in need of further inquiry.

Application of object-relations concepts to psychological testing (as reflected in the work of Sidney Blatt and his colleagues (Blatt et al. 1976) and others (Athey 1976; Urist 1977) holds the presently unfulfilled promise of articulating the inner world of self and object representations for these patients.

Efforts in the direction of distinguishing between "malingering" and true ritual abuse have not yet been pursued. Similarly, the relationship between simulation (i.e., the patient's attempts to appear more well adjusted than is the case) and ritual abuse (particularly, the cult demands related to not drawing attention to oneself) also begs for investigation.

As should be evident, this is by no means a comprehensive list of topics for further pursuit. Ritual abuse raises an open-ended series of questions for us to follow in our attempts to understand what can be useful in healing, as well as for our efforts to understand the workings of the human psyche. Unlike many other types of patients, the catastrophic and pervasive nature of their abuse, coupled with the typically early time of onset, provides us with an unfortunate but important window into understanding how the mind works under extreme conditions.

References

Armstrong, Judith, and Richard Lowenstein. 1990. "Characteristics of Patients with Multiple Personality and Dissociative Disorders on Psychological Testing." *Journal of Nervous and Mental Disease 178*: 448–54.

Athey, George. 1974. "Schizophrenic Thought Organization, Object Relations, and the Rorschach Test." *Bulletin of the Menninger Clinic 38*: 406–9.

Bernstein, Eve, and Frank Putnam. 1986. "Development, Reliability and Validity of a Dissociation Scale." *Journal of Nervous and Mental Disease 174*: 727–35.

Blatt, Sidney, C. Brooks Brenneis, Jean Schimek, and Marion Glick. 1976. "The Normal Development and Psychopathological Impairment of the Concept of the Object on the Rorschach." *Journal of Abnormal Psychology 85*: 364–73.

Bliss, Eugene. 1984. "A Symptom Profile of Patients with Multiple Personalities, including MMPI Results." *Journal of Nervous and Mental Disease 172*: 197–202.

Bowers, M. K. and S. Brecher. 1955. "The Emergence of Multiple Personalities in the Course of Hypnotic Investigation." *Journal of Clinical and Experimental Hypnosis 3*: 188–89.

Brandsma, J. M. and A. M. Ludwig. 1974. "A Case of Multiple Personality: Diagnosis and Therapy." *International Journal of Clinical and Experimental Hypnosis 22*: 216–33.

Brassfield, P. A. 1980. *A Discriminative Study of a Multiple Personality*. Ann Arbor, Mich.: University Microfilms International.

Carr, Arthur. 1948. Content Interpretation re: Salley and Teilings 'Dissociated Rage Attacks in a Vietnam Veteran: A Rorschach Study.' *Journal of Personality Assessment 48*: 420–21.

Cole, Nancy. 1990. Paper presented at workshop on "Psychodiagnosis in Multiple Personality Disorder," Littleton, Colorado. April 7, 1990.

Coons, Phillip and Arthur Sterne. 1986. "Initial and Follow-Up Psychological Testing on a Group of Patients with Multiple Personality Disorder." *Psychological Reports 58*: 43–49.

Danesino, Angelo, Joseph Daniels, and Thomas McLaughlin. 1979. "Jo-Jo, Josephine, and Joanne: A Study of Multiple Personality by Means of the Rorschach Test." *Journal of Personality Assessment 43*: 300–313.

Erickson, Milton, and David Rapaport. 1980. "Findings on the Nature of the Personality Structures in Two Different Dual Personalities by Means of Projective and Psychometric Tests." In *The Collected Papers of Milton Erickson*, ed. E. L. Rossi. Vol. 3, *Investigations of Psychodynamic Processes*. New York: Irvington.

Fischer, D. G., and S. Elnitsky. 1990. "A Factor-Analytic Study of Two Scales Measuring Dissociation." *American Journal of Clinical Hypnosis 32*: 201–7.

Ganaway, George. 1989. "Historical Truth Versus Narrative Truth: Clarifying the Role of Exogenous Trauma in the Etiology of Multiple Personality Disorder and Its Variants." *Dissociation* 2: 205–20.

Herman, Judith, Christopher Perry, and Bessel van der Kolk. 1989. "Childhood Trauma in Borderline Personality Disorder." *American Journal of Psychiatry* 146: 490–95.

Hill, Sally, and Jean Goodwin. 1989. "Satanism: Similarities between Patient Accounts and Pre-Inquisition Historical Sources." *Dissociation* 2: 39–44.

Kissen, Morton. 1986. *Assessing Object Relations Phenomena.* Madison, Conn.: International Universities Press.

Kluft, Richard 1989. "Editorial: Reflections on Allegations of Ritual Abuse." *Dissociation* 2: 191–93.

Kowitt, Michael. 1985. "Rorschach Content Interpretation in Post-Traumatic Stress Disorders: A Reply to Carr." *Journal of Personality Assessment* 49: 21–24.

Kurkjian, Joh. 1990. Paper presented at workshop on "Psychodiagnosis in Multiple Personality Disorder." Littleton, Colorado. April 7, 1990.

Leavitt, H. 1947. "A Case of Hypnotically Produced Secondary and Tertiary Personality." *Psychoanalytic Review* 34: 274–95.

Lerner, Paul, and Howard Lerner. 1980. "Rorschach Assessment of Primitive Defenses in Borderline Personality Structure." In *Borderline Phenomena and the Rorschach Test,* ed. Jan Kwawer, Howard Lerner, Paul Lerner, and Alan Sugarman, 257–74. New York: International Universities Press.

Lovitt, Robert, and Gary Lefkof. 1985. "Understanding Multiple Personality with the Comprehensive Rorschach System." *Journal of Personality Assessment* 49: 289–94.

Ludwig, A. M., J. M. Brandsma, C. B. Wilbur, F. Benfeldt, and D. H. Jameson. 1972. "The Objective Study of a Multiple Personality, or Are Four Heads Better Than One?" *Archives of General Psychiatry* 26: 298–310.

Ohberg, H. G. 1984. "Test Results for a Blind Multiple." Paper presented at the First International Conference on Multiple Personality/Dissociative States. Chicago, Ill. September.

Osgood, Charles, and Zella Luria. 1954. "A Blind Analysis of a Case of Multiple Personality Using the Semantic Differential." *Journal of Abnormal and Social Psychology* 49: 579–91.

Osgood, Charles, Zella Luria, and Sara Smith. 1976. "A Blind Analysis of Another Case of Multiple Personality Using the Semantic Differential Technique." *Journal of Abnormal Psychology* 85: 256–70.

Pearlman, Laurie Ann, Lisa McCann, and Grace Johnson. 1990. "The McPearl Belief Scale: A New Measure of Cognitive Schemas." Unpublished manuscript.

Rapaport, David, Merton Gill, and Roy Schafer. 1968. *Diagnostic Psychological Testing.* New York: International Universities Press.

Riley, Kevin 1988. "Measurement of Dissociation." *Journal of Nervous and Mental Disease* 176: 449–50.

Rosenzweig, S. 1946. "The Dynamics of an Amnesic Personality." *Journal of Personality* 15: 121–42.

Sachs, Roberta, and Bennett Braun. 1987. "Issues in Treating MPD Patients with Satanic Cult Involvement." In *Dissociative Disorders: 1987—Proceedings of The Fourth International Conference On Multiple Personality/Dissociative States,* ed. B. G. Bennett,. Chicago, Ill. Rush University.

Sanders, Shirley. 1986. "The Perceptual Alteration Scale: A Scale Measuring Dissociation." *American Journal of Clinical Hypnosis* 29: 95–102.

Solomon, Robert. 1983. "Use of the MMPI with Multiple Personality Patients." *Psychological Reports* 53: 1004–6.

Steinberg, Marlene, Bruce Rounsaville, and Domenic Cicchetti. 1990. "The Structured Clinical Interview for DSM-III-R Dissociative Disorders: Preliminary Report on a New Diagnostic Instrument." *American Journal of Psychiatry* 147: 76–82.

Stern, David. 1985. *The Interpersonal World of the Infant*. New York: Basic Books.

Urist, Jay. 1977. "The Rorschach Test and the Assessment of Object Relations." *Journal of Personality Assessment* 41: 3–9.

Van der Kolk, Bessel, and Charles Ducey. 1989. "The Psychological Processing of Traumatic Experiences: Rorschach Patterns in PTSD." *Journal of Traumatic Stress* 2: 259–74.

Wagner, Edwin. 1978. "A Theoretical Explanation of the Dissociative Reaction and a Confirmatory Case Presentation." *Journal of Personality Assessment* 42: 312–16.

Wagner, Edwin, Ralph Allison, and Carol Wagner. 1983. "Diagnosing Multiple Personalities with the Rorschach: A Confirmation." *Journal of Personality Assessment* 37: 143–49.

Wagner, Edwin, and Marion Heise. 1974. "A Comparison of Rorschach Records of Three Multiple Personalities." *Journal of Personality Assessment* 38, no. 4: 308–31.

7

Ritual Abuse: The Experiences of Five Families

Linda Stone
David Stone

I am the mother of a ritual abuse survivor. I am also a voice speaking for other nonperpetrator parents of ritually abused children. Our pain is great and unending. Our lives are extremely difficult. Words cannot express adequately our suffering, our anger, and our frustration. My personal reason for speaking out is to increase the awareness of mental health professionals about ritual abuse and satanism, particularly about multigenerational satanism. I would like to share my experiences as a mother of ritually abused children, and as a parent who has gone through the labyrinth of child protection agencies, police investigations, the judicial system, and therapy. I would also like to share the similar experiences of five families who were caught in the same predicament. In writing this chapter I hope that all who work with ritual abuse survivors will become better educated about this area. I hope that victims of ritual abuse will be diagnosed as such, and that mental health professionals will come to approach treatment for those survivors with sensitivity, wisdom, and intelligence.

In the years since my daughter's first divulgence of ritual abuse I have spent hours and hours of research on this horrific subject. I have called and spoken to virtually every expert in the country and have also spoken with and counseled other nonperpetrator parents and survivors. I have read most of the books on satanism, incest, and multiple personality disorder. I feel I can speak with some authority on this subject. It is important to note that the real authorities on the subject of ritual abuse are not the therapists, police officers, nor other investigators or counselors. The real authorities are the survivors themselves and their nonperpetrator parents who have usually provided the survivor's principle base of support.

Professionals who work in the field of ritual abuse seldom consider the parents of survivors as authorities on anything. However, if one examines the situation closely, it usually turns out that most of the information of the so-called experts is obtained verbally from survivors and their nonperpetrator parents. When we try to provide this information directly, we often are disbelieved or are asked to provide excessive documentation. It is ironic that the "experts" are usually asked for far less "proof" when they make statements, even though these are usually based on what we have told them. There is clearly a need for as much "proof" as possible, but unfortunately the issue of hard evidence is a tricky one since the only evidence of ritual abuse that is likely to have endured is the testimony of the survivors. Physical evidence is rare. This is especially the case since victims are often traumatized to the degree that even verbal disclosure never occurs, and if it does, it is usually not until many years after the fact, when the person has managed to find a safe enough place from which to risk talking about it.

The emotional impact to a parent, upon learning that his or her child is a victim of ritual abuse is indescribable. In short, it is simply devastating psychologically, emotionally, physically, and spiritually. My own reaction ran the gamut from being incredibly outraged to being so depressed that I couldn't make myself get out of bed in the morning. Our grief cannot be healed.

The inability of a parent to protect his or her child while witnessing the ongoing symptomatic behavior that the child is exhibiting as a consequence of the ritual abuse is probably one of the most stressful circumstances that a person can experience. There are no words to describe the grief, panic, anger, and fear that a parent feels as a result of the failure of the system to believe and protect his or her children. The protective parent feels outrage at the system for questioning the child's testimony and for what often amounts to exhonorating the perpetrators through inaction. In the vast majority of ritual abuse cases with which I am familiar, especially those that involve only one perpetrating parent, the system has failed miserably. Results of extended court battles usually end in the ritual abuse never even being investigated and the final decisions being inconclusive. This is a severe blow to the victims of ritual abuse who often then conclude that no one is ever going to believe or protect them. As a society we must look at what incentive is left for a survivor to speak out. The painful trauma of divulgence does not seem worth the risk when so often the survivors are further traumatized by a system that treats them as suspect and does nothing to stop the abuses they are trying to report.

The five family cases upon which this chapter is based all involved alleged ritual abuse by the father. In each case the mother was neither a perpetrator nor a satanist. (Of course there are other cases in which the mother is involved and the father is not, or where both parents are involved.) Each of these five cases involved therapists, the police department, a child protection agency, custody evaluators, guardians *ad litem,* and the judicial system. Each case shares a common profile while maintaining its own individual variables. No case reached a satisfactory conclusion, and no agency truly served the needs of the ritually abused children.

I was contacted by each nonperpetrator parent through a loosely organized network of ritual abuse investigators. In each of the cases I spent no less than fifty hours of assessment. In one case in particular, I spent hundreds of hours reading court documents, interviewing the mother and children, attending court hearings, interviewing professionals, and working with a highly respected expert. In each case the children alleged specific accounts of ritual abuse. Based on this evidence, I concluded that in each of the five cases, ritual abuse was indeed occurring. It is very sad to report that to date the children in four of the five cases have not been protected from the alleged perpetrators. These alleged perpetrators retain unsupervised visitation rights. Unbelievably, in one case involving two children, the *non*perpetrator parent is restricted to supervised visits and monitored phone calls, while the perpetrator parent has full custody. *All* efforts by the nonperpetrator parents to protect their children have been met by resistance from the child protection agencies and the judicial system.

In reviewing the five cases it became very clear that the system currently in place to aid abused children is clearly unable to handle situations where the allegations are so horrendous. The agencies viewed all of our cases as a problem of a dysfunctional family. From such a model, all family members are co-conspirators of abuse. Unfortunately, this model does not work well when applied to ritual abuse. The belief system from which perpetrators of ritual abuse operate (eg., satanism) is usually based on a very systematic theology. These doctrines supercede any family dynamics. Particularly in situations in which there is a nonperpetrator parent, it is essential to understand satanic beliefs and practices rather than to try to fit the abuse into a model of a dysfunctional family. However, despite the fact that the family may be deemed to be dysfunctional, it is a grave error to assume that this means that the nonperpetrator parent is always actively or passively colluding with the abuse.

In the cases I have seen, the child protection agencies often view any anger by the victim toward the nonperpetrator parent as an indictment against them. In the agency's view, the anger of the victim is enough reason to suspect this parent of abuse. However, each of the five mothers in the cases reported here reports at least one child who has expressed a great deal of anger toward her. There are some clear reasons why this anger might be directed at the parent who was not a participant in the abuse. The child is often very angry that this parent did not know, did not believe them, or for whatever reason did not protect them from being hurt. This parent also may be the only safe outlet for the intense anger that the ritual abuse created. The child has usually learned that it is extremely dangerous to show any feelings of anger toward the perpetrators. Thus, it does not invariably follow that a child's anger indicates a guilty parent. Investigators must develop a more sophisticated understanding of how feelings of anger are manifested within such families.

Clearly, it is very reasonable for both parents (and any significant others) to be initially suspected when a child discloses ritual abuse. However, it is also important to realize that when one or both parents were not involved, they too need support and not just accusations and disbelief. In the cases that I examined, the nonperpetrator parents were subjected to much more suspicion and assessment than the perpetrators themselves. In none of the cases did they receive any support or help from the system. For example, many of us were asked to take psychological tests. One mother was subjected to thirteen such tests. This often felt like an attempt to discredit us so that no further investigation would be necessary. It might be more comfortable to believe that children and/or parents are just making up these stories than to truly integrate the horror of what is being described. Unfortunately, whatever the reasons, the focus on discrediting the nonperpetrator parent, instead of rigorously investigating the allegations only results in a disregard for the much-needed protection of the children involved. The protective parent and his or her children begin to despair of obtaining any help from the system. This only serves to weaken their resolve to keep fighting. Many nonperpetrator parents have personal histories that already predispose them toward feeling powerless. My experiences with these cases also suggest that many parents themselves were abused in childhood and then again in their marriages. Thus, they have never felt much personal power and can easily feel helpless when confronted with an authority that blames them while ignoring the reality of the situation. The children in these cases had often watched the nonperpetrator parent be abused and had little faith in that parent's ability to protect them. When the system then takes the same approach and believes the perpetrators while blaming the protective parent, the child only becomes more convinced that there can be no help.

The particular kinds of abuse reported in all five of the cases indicated behavior that is extremely bizarre. Professional investigators without specific knowledge of this area are often unwilling to believe that such extreme forms of abuse could have occurred. Thus, the motives of the nonperpetrator parent become the focus. For example, one social worker stated that "critical thinking" disavowed the possibility of the occurrence of ritual abuse. Clearly, such a person is not going to investigate the allegations seriously, but rather will try to explain why they are being "made up." This can result in a frightening reversal of justice. For example, in two of the cases (involving six children) permanent custody was actually awarded to the perpetrator parent because it was argued that the protective parent was "brainwashing" her children to allege things that were clearly too bizarre to be believed. In one of these cases the mother was actually relegated to supervised visitation to protect the children from this brainwashing. In all five of the cases reported here, the nonperpetrator parent was viewed as a "vindictive ex-spouse." The typical view was that this parent was trying to work out a custody battle through the judicial system by alleging such atrocities. In my own case, this attitude prevailed despite the fact that my own divorce had already occurred (seven years earlier) and that custody was not an issue at the time.

Just as we tend to blame victims for their misfortunes, it appears to be a fairly natural reaction to start with a very negative view of a nonperpetrator parent. This is true throughout the mental health system and often is expressed even by therapists who work in the area. Other survivors often assume or fear that the protective parent is a perpetrator or an infiltrator who is seeking to betray them. Indeed, there do appear to be some parents and some survivors themselves who are still fully active cult members or who have personalities that are still active in the cult. However, this does not mean that all people in any group deserve our mistrust. It is important to recognize that many nonperpetrator parents are truly struggling to end the tragedy of ritual abuse.

As a result of all this suspicion, the protective parent usually ends up feeling very isolated. Their own friends have usually placed them at a distance, either because they believe them and are overwhelmed and afraid, or else because they don't believe them, don't want to hear anymore, or just can't stand to be around such upsetting circumstances. Many professionals take the same approach. However, because they cannot decide between the denials of the accused and the testimonies of the victims, they often make the protective parents out to be the suspects, and characterize them either as co-conspirators or as malicious story tellers. It is no wonder that many nonperpetrator parents end up giving up on a system that not only fails to help their children, but points a blaming finger at them.

An understanding of the psychodynamics of my family will serve to illustrate the type of environment and level of control typically imposed on a nonperpetrator mother by a satanist father. It also illustrates the typical perspective of the government agencies that process these types of cases. My own family situation involved a paternal multigenerational satanist family. My daughter divulged the ritual abuse when she was seventeen. The details of this story are not at all atypical for the five cases that I investigated.

My ex-husband and I met in a Christian church. Our marriage lasted for eleven years. During the entire marriage, my ex-husband was continually controlled by his parents through their power, manipulation, and money. In retrospect, I can see that I too was controlled in many ways by these parents. After six years of living in an extremely manipulative and psychologically abusive environment, I reacted by developing an eating disorder. By the time our marriage ended, I felt so physically weak due to this self-abuse that I truly felt as if I were dying. My ex-husband and his parents had convinced me that I was a total failure as a human being. Like many nonperpetrator parents, my own childhood had laid the foundation for feeling worthless and full of guilt thus making it difficult for me to notice abusive cues or to feel able to protect myself or anyone else.

Like other satanist perpetrators my ex-husband and his parents were master manipulators. For example, in order to prove to my daughter that she could never be anything but a satanist, she was shown a precise geneological record of her father's family tree dating back to the fourteenth century. My ex-husband's family were particularly skilled at finding a weak spot and then bearing down on that spot until it gave way. They were also masters at manipulating society. Like many multigenerational satanists, they presented a family that outwardly looked like a group of model citizens. For example, my ex-husband's parents are influential in the community, he still calls himself a Christian, and still attends church every Sunday. Such a façade puts these people "beyond suspicion" so that their deviant behavior cannot be believed by the rest of society, even when revealed.

Fear and coercion are often used as weapons within such families. In my situation, for example, when my divorce occurred, my in-laws threatened to prove in court that I was an unfit mother to my two children unless I would go along with their demand for joint custody. I was certain that with their money and influence they could succeed at this, so I settled out of court. Part of this meant that although I had been a full-time mother and homemaker I had to leave with no money and no home. I could only afford a tiny apartment at the time. After the divorce was final I was surprised and dismayed to find that my children would not come to see me during our scheduled visitations. I could not understand this rejection by my children, with whom I had always been close. I knew that my ex-husband was trying to alienate them from me by the things he would say, but this was not sufficient to explain their turnaround. It was not until almost six years later that I learned that he had threatened the children that I would be killed if they ever tried to visit me. Thus, they actually had felt that they were protecting me by staying away. Two years after the divorce my ex-husband secretly moved the children out of state into his parents' home. During the next four years I only saw my children for four weeks at most per year. My ex-husband and his parents collaborated to keep us separated. There was always an excuse to keep my children from seeing me.

Six years after the divorce my then fifteen-year-old daughter arrived on my doorstep physically and emotionally ill. She was to remain seriously ill for the next two full years. It was obvious to me that she was deeply depressed. I suggested many times that she see a therapist but she always refused. She was angry and upset but refused to discuss the reasons behind any of her problems. By this point in time I had remarried and had a three-year-old daughter by this marriage. Through a series of events the younger daughter divulged that my son, who was still living with his father, had sexually abused her during a visit. My oldest daughter finally agreed to go to therapy, and I put my youngest in treatment as well. My ex-husband adamantly refused to put my son in treatment, but both daughters began therapy. It soon came out that my fifteen-year-old had also been sexually abused. The two well-trained and highly respected therapists that they saw confirmed this fact and after four months of therapy they reported their conclusions to the child protection agency that was now handling our case. My older daughter gave a three-hour statement to the child protection agency and to the police department. She testified that she had been sexually abused by her father and had witnessed her father sexually abuse her brother. The particular abuse involved was extremely perverse and bizarre. I spent many hours pondering what type of individual could have perpetrated that type of abuse on his own daughter. It is interesting to note that the child protection agency actually became involved because my ex-husband called them to say that I had falsely accused my son of sexually abusing his half sister. I had not planned to contact them at that point, and was really only interested in getting help for my children. The lengthy court case that ensued involved three therapists, two guardians *ad litem*, two detectives, four social workers, two judges, and two lawyers. I do not think we would have survived if not for my family's strong spiritual beliefs. It was not until months after my ex-husband had dragged our case into the system that my son was finally put into therapy. I made an appointment to speak with his therapist in order to provide information about our family background. During the session I had with him I also told him what my older daughter had remembered concerning his having been sexually abused by his father. At the end of that meeting I was told by my son's therapist that he would have to take everything that I said from the perspective of a "vindictive ex-spouse."

The "vindictive ex-spouse" theme was a catch-all phrase that we heard throughout our entire case. For this to be true I would have had to coach my children to lie about being sexually abused. This occurred despite the fact that we had two highly respected therapists who had testified that the two girls had been sexually abused. In addition to this, I had never taken my ex-husband to court during the preceding seven years, nor did I when we were divorced. It was overlooked that it was my ex-husband and not I who had involved the child protective system in the first place. Surely a mother who qualified as a "vindictive ex-spouse" would be the one who initiated the legal process or at least who had something to gain by it. I was outraged by this flagrant disregard for the facts and for being so unfairly labeled. It is interesting to note that the other mothers in the five cases were also all labeled as "vindictive ex-spouses" at some point in the process. Once again, this was in spite of the evidence that was being presented. It is important to recognize that when a parent finds out that his or her spouse (or ex-spouse) has severely abused their children, they are likely to be very upset and very angry. It is a mistake to assume that the anger came first and caused the accusations of abuse, rather than recognizing that such feelings are a natural reaction to finding out that your child has been harmed.

During the nine months that we were involved with the judicial system, the child protection agency, and the police department, I was accused of emotionally abusing my daughter. The charges of emotional abuse against me were at best, vague. The basis of these charges came from false information that was being given to the agency by my ex-husband. This tactic was also a common one for the other perpetrator parents in the current sample. At one point, because of my ex-husband's allegations, my daughter was actually taken from my home and placed with her father. She was unwilling to stay there after a few days, and I was later to learn that this was because the sexual abuse had resumed. Clearly, that abuse was completely preventable. *I will never forgive the agency involved.* Although my daughter was returned to me, I was then forbidden by court order to talk to her about the abuse that she had suffered. Imagine how bizarre that would feel as a parent. I knew that my daughter needed to talk, that she was remembering horrible incidents of ritual abuse and that no one in the system even believed her incest allegations. However, openly showing her any support could have resulted in my going to jail and her being moved back with her father. It was terribly difficult for my daughter to try to discuss any of the abuse, and the agencies did not make it any easier. For example, after describing the abuse to one social worker, my daughter asked if she was being believed. The social worker replied "I believe that you believe you were abused." This response prompted my daughter to refuse to divulge any further details to the child protection agencies. Incredibly, in all of the hearings and testimonies the subject of ritual abuse was never even raised nor questioned. My daughter gave up hope of being heard and clearly felt extremely traumatized by the system's failure to respond in her hour of need.

When the whole ordeal was over, the ruling was that the abuse was inconclusive and that the children had merely been "harmed by the divorce." My son, who was still being sexually abused was left with his father. No charges were ever filed, and the case was neatly closed without having accomplished any thing productive. This is not unusual. The system is clearly not equipped to adequately investigate this type of situation, as the experiences of all five of the families has shown.

During the next two years I listened to my daughter's memories and lived through the turmoil involved in the divulgence of ritual abuse. The experiences she endured included forced injection of drugs; forced consumption of human blood and organs; incest perpetrated by her grandmother, grandfather, father, and other relatives. She was forced to watch such bizarre acts as her grandmother sucking the menstrual pads of her first period. She was forced to watch human sacrifices. She was given as a child sex slave to the apprentice of her grandfather, the "high priest." She was impregnated and aborted at four months in a ritual setting. She experienced severe physical and psychological tortures, including the use of electric shock. This abuse was so severe that plastic surgery was needed at one point to reconstruct her face. She was even forced to lure other children into certain rituals. Clearly, these were not minor allegations. It is difficult to understand why the system is not more supportive to someone who has been so traumatized. Such allegations must be systematically investigated. Instead of disbelief and blame that only silences such reports, we need a system that is more open to them. Anyone watching my daughter go through the agony of reliving and remembering such abuse could not doubt its authenticity. However, the children's reports of such atrocities, in all of the five families, were largely ignored by a system that was hard pressed to seriously investigate even the incest allegations.

In spite of feelings of rage and grief at the perpetrators and then at the unresponsive system, I still had to care for my abused daughter. She had been sick for years prior to her divulgence. When she began to discuss the abuse, each new memory triggered a crisis for her. I spent six months talking my child out of suicide. As with other survivors, my daughter had many triggers that could set off flashbacks, as well as deliberately "programmed" suggestions that certain cues would lead to self-destructive behavior or pulls to return to the cult. It was a nightmare to get past all of this deliberate damage. During most of this period, I too felt on the brink of a nervous breakdown. Somehow we survived.

I did my best to counsel my daughter, to understand how she felt, and mostly to just be there in a supportive way. I began my own research into the subject of ritual abuse in order to understand what we were dealing with. My reading, interviews, and attendance at various lectures only served to confirm and validate what my daughter was describing. Even as I see my daughter healing, concern over the welfare of my son, who still lives with his perpetrator father, plagues me daily.

Clearly, cases involving ritual abuse are both complex and difficult to investigate. However, I would have to conclude from the cases that I have seen that the current standards and procedures used to evaluate these cases needs dramatic revision. To start, the mandate of child protection agencies to keep families together needs rethinking. For the sake of the children there are some families better off split apart. It is also clear that the professionals involved in investigating these cases need far more training in this area, even if it is only to know that such extreme forms of abuse exist.

Although not all of the experts are in agreement, my research would also clearly suggest that not all satanists are self-styled or individual practitioners. Many appear to be from multigenerational families. The multigenerational families seem to have developed the perfect societal cover. To an outsider the family looks ideal. The perpetrators are usually considered to be model citizens, civic leaders, child care workers, politicians, and so on. Secrecy is the name of their game. Although many appear to be into power, wealth, and control over others, there are few if any outward clues of what goes on in secret.

Clinicians need to learn that not all victims of ritual abuse are the same. For example, not all develop MPD. My daughter is an example. It is also important to realize that many survivors were not abused by both parents. Although this obviously can be the case, one parent may have no knowledge of the abuse at all. Clearly, it will never be easy to investigate such cases. For example, the perpetrators may confuse the issue by trying to turn the children against the other parent, or by making their own false allegations to the authorities. The children are usually terribly frightened of the consequences of speaking out. For example, most of the children in the five cases had been told that their mothers would be harmed if they spoke to anyone about the abuse. Thus, it will take an open mind, excellent assessment skills, and true caring, as well as a great deal of fortitude, patience, and dedication for investigators to get to the bottom of these cases. However, the severity of the devastation to the child from ritual abuse mandates that we rebuild our child protective system in such a way that these essential characteristics become possible.

8
Constructivist Self-Development Theory: A Theoretical Model of Psychological Adaptation to Severe Trauma

Lisa McCann, Ph.D.
Laurie Anne Pearlman, Ph.D.

Introduction

Over the past ten years, clinicians and researchers have become increasingly concerned about the relation between severe childhood physical and sexual abuse and the development of serious psychological problems, including chronic anxiety (e.g., Briere 1984), depression (e.g., Sedney and Brooks 1984), multiple personality disorder (MPD) (Braun and Sachs 1985; Kluft 1984), and post-traumatic stress disorder (PTSD) (Donaldson and Gardner 1985). As professionals in this field noted commonalities among survivors of child abuse and other traumatized populations, they developed theoretical models to conceptualize the underlying processes of adaptation to trauma. In this paper, we describe a new theory of trauma and adaptation, constructivist self-development theory (CSDT). In the following sections, we will describe the theoretical roots of CSDT, some concepts underlying CSDT, and the implications of the theory for clinical assessment and therapeutic intervention with a growing population of clients, often presenting with severe disorders such as MPD, who have been *ritually* abused.

Historical Antecedents of Current Post-Trauma Theories

In their classic work, *Theories of Hysteria,* Joseph Breuer and Sigmund Freud (1895) developed the first theory of trauma as they observed that many female patients with conversion reactions reported histories of seduction by male parental figures. They hypothesized that hysterical symptoms, such as psychoso-

185

matic blindness or paralysis, were symbolic representations of repressed memories of abuse. Due to complex social and cultural influences, Freud soon abandoned the seduction theory in favor of the fantasy theory, asserting that his patients' recollections of abuse were merely fantasies that represented unacceptable oedipal longings. The reversal in Freud's thinking, which influenced the field for much of the twentieth century, contributed to society's persistent denial of the realities of child abuse (Miller 1984). The parallels between Freud's denial of the reality of child sexual abuse and the recent controversies in the field surrounding the reality of clients' memories of satanic cult abuse are pointed out in the introduction to this volume by David Sakheim and Susan Devine.

Although the problem of child sexual abuse remained largely hidden for many years, the two world wars renewed interest in the psychological impact of extreme stress. Observing that many World War I veterans suffered nightmares and startle reactions, Freud (1920) hypothesized that these symptoms resulted from a breach in the "stimulus barrier" when the ego was overwhelmed by stimuli that it could not master. During this time, Freud first acknowledged that a trauma of a certain magnitude would affect almost all who were exposed to it.

Later in his career, again as a result of the interest in war neurosis, Freud (1939) described the tendency to repeat or reexperience a trauma as an attempt to master it, thus integrating notions of the repetition compulsion into theories of trauma. He also described the use of denial as a defense against the painful affect that accompanies repetition. This original thinking has continued to influence theories of trauma and adaptation.

Contemporary Theories of Trauma

Beginning in the mid-1970s, a renewed interest in trauma developed, largely as a result of the convergence of interest in the returning Vietnam veteran and the feminist movement's focus on violence against women. Since the inclusion of post-traumatic stress disorder (PTSD) in DSM-III (American Psychiatric Association 1980), a number of theorists have attempted to explain how trauma results in the oscillation among reexperiencing symptoms (e.g., nightmares and flashbacks), denial or avoidance (psychic numbing and repression of traumatic memories), and hyperarousal (startle responses and overreactivity).

M.J. Horowitz (1975, 1976, 1979) has had a major influence in the area of stress response syndromes. He has conceptualized PTSD from a perspective that integrates earlier psychoanalytic thinking on the role of defenses and controls with more contemporary cognitive theories. He emphasizes the impact of trauma on cognitive schemas and the role of defenses in regulating the processing of information. He proposes that until the traumatic event is integrated into existing cognitive schemas, the psychological representations of the event are stored in active memory, which allows for repeated representations of the traumatic events. Reexperiencing phenomena include intrusive thoughts and images about the trauma, often accompanied by intense and painful emotional states. Denial or avoidance often follow these states, as a defense against becoming emotionally overwhelmed. The processes of approach (or reexperiencing) and avoidance (or denial) are viewed by many as a hallmark of trauma.

Susan Roth and L.J. Cohen (1986) focus on the concepts of approach and avoidance in their review of related formulations and synthesize the literature with a view toward understanding individual differences in this dimension of response to trauma. They view approach-avoidance as a metaphor for emotional and cognitive activity moving the individual either toward or away from the threatening material. They suggest that individuals will move back and forth between the two coping styles, according to their needs at the time, rather than suggesting that people are "approachers" or "avoiders," or that all victims manage traumatic material similarly.

In recent years, a number of researchers have discussed the ways victimizing life events can disrupt or alter an individual's basic assumptions about the self, other people, and the world (Epstein, in press; Janoff-Bulman 1985; Janoff-Bulman and Frieze 1983; Roth 1989; Roth and Lebowitz 1988). In a comprehensive formulation of traumatic stress reactions, Seymour Epstein (in press) describes how trauma disrupts a person's *schemas,* or beliefs and assumptions about the self, other people, and the world. These schemas include beliefs about the world as benign or malevolent, beliefs about the world as meaningful (including predictable, controllable, and just), and assumptions about the self as worthy or unworthy.

Seymour Epstein postulates that the disruption of these schemas or conceptual systems can disrupt the entire personality, producing a state of disequilibrium and symptoms of PTSD. He suggests that the individual must develop a modified theory of reality that can assimilate the trauma in order to reestablish equilibrium. All of these theories have much in common with constructivist self-development theory.

In a description of the evolution of contemporary theories of trauma, it is important to address a controversy ongoing since World War I, namely that concerning the degree to which personal factors, such as the individual's preexisting personality (or psychopathology), and situational factors, such as the magnitude or nature of the external stressor, determine the post-traumatic response. As a variety of traumatized populations were studied, an important paradox emerged. Although it was evident that many traumatized individuals experienced many of the cardinal symptoms of PTSD, it was also apparent that not all individuals were similarly affected. In fact, there is a great degree of variability in response among people who have experienced the same traumatic life event. The question that emerged concerned the degree to which preexisting personality structure or past history affects the individual's response to trauma.

Are there certain events so extreme (such as concentration camp confinement or childhood torture) that all will be affected? On the other hand, are individuals with more vulnerable personality structures or prior psychopathology predisposed to more serious post-trauma responses? To what extent do traumatic events affect people at different developmental stages? These issues are extremely complex and deserve continued exploration through theory development and empirical research.

A number of contemporary trauma theories, including constructivist self-development theory, are basically interactionist in nature. That is, the prevailing thinking is that adaptation to trauma results from a complex interplay between the person (including personal history and personality) and the situation (the traumatic event, the social and cultural context, and others' responses to the traumatized individual). Below, we address the specific nature of this interaction in detail.

Constructivist Self-Development Theory: An Overview

Essentially, constructivist self-development theory (CSDT) integrates clinical insights from object relations theory, self psychology, and research in social cognition. Lisa McCann et al. (1988) and Lisa McCann, David Sakheim, and Daniel Abrahamson (1988) presented the first formulations of this theory, which focused on cognitive schemas disrupted by trauma, in earlier papers. Subsequent elaborations of the theory (McCann and Pearlman 1990), broadened the cognitive portion of this work to include the concept of the self, the social and cultural context, and a fuller elaboration of the imagery and verbal systems of memory. The theory has been developed in an interactive process of research and clinical work. In this chapter, we present a revised conceptualization of the self, one which encompasses the notion of identity.

Constructivist Self-Development Theory: An Outline

Assumptions:

Constructivist: Individuals construct and construe their own realities.
Developmental: The self develops over the life-span within a particular social and cultural context.

The self: The seat of the individual's identity and understanding of how he or she relates to the world and how the world works. Beliefs related to the self are termed *frame of reference* schemas.

Psychological needs: Motivate behavior; shaped through experience. Six needs particularly affected by trauma:

> *Safety:* The need to feel safe and reasonably invulnerable to harm.
>
> *Trust/Dependence:* The need to believe in the word or promise of another and to depend upon others to meet one's needs, to a greater or lesser extent.
>
> *Esteem:* The need to be valued by others, to have one's worth validated, and to value others.
>
> *Independence:* The need to control one's own behavior and rewards.
>
> *Power:* The need to direct or exert control over others.
>
> *Intimacy:* The need to feel connected to others, through individual relationships; the need to belong to a larger community.

Cognitive schemas: Beliefs and expectations about self and others which reflect indentity, world view, and psychological needs.

Self capacities: Abilities which enable the individual to maintain inner stability.

> Ability to moderate self-loathing.
>
> Ability to tolerate and regulate affect.
>
> Ability to be alone without being lonely.

Ego resources: Assets which enable the individual to meet psychological needs, to protect himself or herself from future harm, and to engage fully in the therapy process.

> *Self-protective resources:*
>
> > Awareness of boundaries between self and others.
> >
> > Ability to make self-protective judgments.
>
> *Resources important to therapy:*
>
> > Ability to introspect.
> >
> > Intelligence.
> >
> > Will-power.
> >
> > Sense of humor.

Traumatic memories:

> Verbal (statements about what happened).
>
> Imagery (closely tied to affect).

The cognitive portion of CSDT parallels the trauma theories of Seymour Epstein (in press), Ronnie Janoff-Bulman (1985, 1989), Horowitz (1986), and Roth (1989). We extend their work with CSDT by describing both distinct and overlapping schemas about self and world that are most vulnerable to disruption as a result of severe trauma. We consider psychological needs as forming the basis for these core schemas and further posit that traumatic experiences are most likely to affect schemas related to each individual's most central need areas. While Epstein takes into account the important relation between needs and schemas, the role of needs is not central to his theory.

An underlying premise of CSDT is that adaptation to severe trauma is the result of a complex interplay between life experiences (including personal history, specific traumatic events, and the social and cultural context) and the developing self (including one's identity, psychological needs, cognitive schemas about self and world, self capacities, and ego resources). Psychological development reflects the evolution of complex systems, including the self (the individual's identity, or sense of who he or she is both internally and in the world), psychological needs (which motivate behavior), and cognitive schemas (or beliefs and expectations about self and others that relate both to identity and psychological needs). This chapter will focus primarily on the relation of cognitive schemas to psychological adaptation in ritually abused clients. We refer the reader to Lisa McCann and Laurie Ann Pearlman (1990) for a description of CSDT as applied to other adult survivors.

Some major concepts underlying CSDT are derived from Jean Piaget's cognitive developmental theory (Piaget 1971). As individuals develop, their cognitive structures become increasingly complex and differentiated through the processes of *assimilation* and *accommodation*. Assimilation is the process whereby new information is integrated into the individual's existing schemas for experience. For example, when a child consistently experiences interactions with adults who are responsive to his or her basic needs, these experiences are gradually assimilated or "digested" in a way that shapes generally positive schemas about self ("my needs are acceptable") and other people ("I can depend upon others"). When the environment presents information that cannot be assimilated into existing schemas, cognitive schemas are modified or new schemas develop, a process called accommodation. For instance, when a child encounters other people who frustrate or hurt him or her, this creates a need to modify positive schemas ("most of my needs are acceptable") or develop new schemas about people ("I can't always depend upon others").

Identity, World View, and Frame-of-Reference Schemas

Trauma presents a challenge to schemas related to identity and world view (which CSDT labels "frame-of-reference" schemas), most often requiring accommodation, or a change in positive schemas. This process is psychologically painful and has a profound effect on the individual's identity, as well as his or her emotional and interpersonal life. Clinicians often hear acute trauma survivors say things like, "I'm not the same person any more," "everything has changed," "the world feels like a very different place." These are examples of frame-of-reference schemas affected by trauma. Individuals who have experienced severe abuse in early years develop frame-of-reference schemas that incorporate their traumatic experiences. They may feel as if they live in extreme psychological isolation and believe they are very different from others, that they are unique in some negative way.

Traumatic Memories

In our view, then, traumatic memories may present a painful discrepancy to the client's existing schemas about self and the world. In CSDT terms, traumatic memories can be disruptive not only because of the individual's fear of overwhelming affect but also because these memories threaten core schemas about oneself and the world. The disruption to the individual's frame of reference or conceptual framework for understanding the world is perhaps the most central experience of trauma against which individuals defend, a concept we elaborate below.

Furthermore, the emergence of traumatic memories may present an intolerable threat to other psychological needs and related schemas. For example, a client with a strong need for independence may find it extremely difficult to recall and acknowledge her helplessness when she was raped by her father. Avoidance may be essential until the self capacities for affect regulation and tolerance are strong enough to allow her to assimilate this experience. The client's avoidance of difficult material is a signal to the therapist that important groundwork must be done, and provides the time to do it. As Susan Roth (1989) points out, although the ideal therapeutic situation moves toward approach and integration, approach can produce painful affects that are psychologically disruptive unless the individual is able to "dose" herself with tolerable levels of affect. Thus, avoidance should not be challenged until the client has established the ability to confront the painful affects and meanings in therapy and the capacity to tolerate the painful affect associated with discrepancies to existing schemas, has begun to explore the impact of the traumatic experiences upon his or her identity, and has begun to develop alternative ways of meeting psychological needs. These notions represent some of the underlying premises of CSDT's understanding of trauma integration and resolution.

In the following sections, we describe guidelines for assessing disturbances in cognitive schemas about self and the world and the implications this has for therapy with ritually abused clients.

Assessing Psychological Needs and Cognitive Schemas

The client's unique experience of trauma is determined in large part by his or her psychological needs and related schemas about self and others. Although some schemas are conscious, most often they operate at a preconscious or unconscious level, becoming activated by stimuli that serve as reminders of earlier experiences that originally shaped the schemas. Traumatic experiences may reinforce negative schemas or disrupt positive schemas. In a synthesis of the literature on trauma and victimization McCann, Sakheim, and Abrahamson (1988) proposed that persons develop schemas in the areas of safety, trust, esteem, power, and intimacy. In later work (McCann and Pearlman 1990) we introduced the notion of psychological needs and expanded the needs of interest to include independence. These need areas are central to many major theories of personality. According to CSDT, the schemas are the cognitive manifestation of the needs. In addition, CSDT posits that individuals have schemas (or beliefs and expectations) about their own identity and world view (or the self). We refer the reader again to the outline of CSDT for an overview the how these constructs relate to one another.

CSDT proposes that trauma disrupts these psychological needs and related cognitive schemas, and shapes the individual's unique psychological experience of the traumatic event. Although ritual abuse is so extreme that it is likely to produce disturbances in many schema areas, the degree of disturbance in each area will vary across individuals. For example, some ritual abuse survivors may show greater disturbances within the areas of *trust* and *self-esteem* while others might be more disturbed in the areas of *safety* and *power*. Conceptualizing disturbances in these schema areas can help the clinician develop therapeutic strategies that respect individual differences. Individuals will experience greater emotional distress related to disruptions in their more central need areas. The degree of disruption or importance of the different need areas to each person may depend in part on the level of the individual's psychological development when various traumatic events occurred.

Conversely, the client will interpret traumatic experiences through the unique filter of his or her disturbed schemas. For example, a client with strong trust/dependence needs may experience abuse as evidence that men can't be trusted, while another client with strong needs for security might experience a similar traumatic event as confirmation that the world is not a safe place.

Greater psychological disruptions occur when disturbed schemas are overgeneralized and are either inconsistent with or out of proportion to the current situation. For example, one client may have developed the generalized belief that all *men* are dangerous. This belief forecloses the possibility of healthy intimacy with men. Another client, on the basis of a similar traumatic experience, may believe that all *people* are dangerous. This belief could lead to a pervasive withdrawal from the activities of the world as well as serious interpersonal problems.

Schemas develop in response to one's environment. In a cult family, a child may develop the belief that the world is a dangerous place. This belief may be adaptive if it led to vigilance that enabled the child to protect himself from harm. In new life circumstances, however, the same schemas may now be maladaptive.

A pervasive sense of danger that is no longer appropriate to the individual's adult life circumstances will inhibit him from feeling secure.

In summary, CSDT proposes that:

1. Individuals develop schemas, or assumptions and beliefs, about self, other people, and the world, within six fundamental need areas. These schemas develop over the life-span through the processes of assimilation and accommodation.
2. Schemas may operate within or outside of conscious awareness.
3. Schemas may be positive or negative and generalized or specific. Schemas are associated with various thoughts, feelings, and behaviors.
4. A traumatic event potentially disrupts core schemas about self and the world. Trauma often produces negative, overgeneralized schemas, disrupting one's identity, one's emotional and interpersonal life outside of the traumatic environment, and one's ability to meet central psychological needs.

Implications for Assessment and Treatment

The assessment of schemas about the self and the world is fundamental to the therapy process. The implications for therapy include formulating a treatment plan, working though resistances to uncovering traumatic memories, and resolving transference reactions. Implicit and explicit schemas can be assessed by listening for characteristic themes that emerge over the course of therapy. For example, themes related to feelings of vulnerability and danger may reflect disturbed safety schemas, while themes related to abandonment and betrayal may represent disturbed trust schemas. We elaborate each schema area and the related themes below. One available tool for the formal structured assessment of these core schema areas is the McPearl Belief Scale. (Pearlman, McCann, and Johnson 1990).

As disturbed schema areas are explored in therapy, it is important to understand how these schemas originally developed. Often, disturbed schemas are related to specific traumatic experiences. Furthermore, the traumatic imagery that is most distressing for an individual often reflects that individual's central schema areas. For example, traumatic imagery related to being trapped, powerless, and immobilized may reflect disrupted schemas related to independence. In exploring the personal history, one may discover memories of being overpowered, tied down, and exploited by others. As the link is made over the course of therapy between these memories and schemas, powerful feelings will emerge, including fear, rage, and sorrow, all of which must be acknowledged and worked through. Often the schemas have developed in order to protect the individual from being overwhelmed by these painful feelings. For example, a person's belief that she is at fault for the abuse that occurred may be protecting her from the helplessness, sorrow, and anger that will likely emerge once she is able to see herself as an innocent child who was hurt by trusted adults.

An important part of the therapy process is to understand the psychological implications of these disturbed schemas. An analysis of each schema area will reveal the various ways in which disturbed schemas may be both adaptive and maladaptive. Clearly, this must be understood within the context of the individual's unique life circumstances and social and cultural context. For example, for a survivor of ritual abuse who is currently involved with cult activities, it may well be adaptive to hold the generalized belief that the world is basically dangerous and that people cannot be trusted. These schemas may serve to help the individual maintain a more vigilant stance toward other people and the world, protecting her from potential harm. On the other hand, it may be maladaptive for an individual for whom the external danger is no longer present to maintain these overgeneralized negative schemas. In the current life situation, the cost of not trusting anyone may mean having few friends and living a lonely, isolated existence. Likewise, continued overgeneralized beliefs that other people and the world are malevolent and dangerous may be associated with chronic anxiety and hypervigilance that are no longer adaptive.

Disrupted schemas may also have a defensive value in that they may protect an individual both from painful emotions and traumatic memories. For example, disturbed self-esteem schemas, such as believing that one is bad, unworthy, and responsible for the abuse, may have the emotional cost of depression, suicidal feelings, and self-loathing. However, such schemas may protect the survivor from fully experiencing the overwhelming helplessness, despair, and rage that result from being violated and abused by a trusted parental figure.

These brief examples underscore the importance of fully understanding both the adaptive and maladaptive functions, or costs and benefits, of disturbed schemas for the individual's emotional and interpersonal life. It is important to remember that the therapy process itself can potentially change or create an accommodation in previous schemas. As an accommodation or change in *either* positive or negative schemas is potentially disruptive psychologically, discrepancies to schemas must be presented in "tolerable doses" so that the accompanying emotions and meanings can be assimilated gradually and integrated into the self. These issues will be elaborated in the section on treatment.

An important aspect of CSDT is the hypothesized relation between disturbed schemas and psychological adaptation. These disturbances may occur with respect to oneself and with respect to others. We first describe disruptions in frame-of-reference schemas. Then we briefly describe each need area and give examples of disturbed schemas in each.

Finally, since many victims of ritual abuse develop multiple personality disorder (MPD), we will note some of the ways that disruptions in the schema areas may be manifested in the various alters. MPD can be an extreme example of the personification of each of the major need areas or it may represent the maintenance of opposing, rigid, needs/schemas in different situations, rather than their integration. In order to maintain functioning, some alters remain unaware of traumatic life experiences and therefore have different schemas than the alters who are aware of the traumas.

Identity, World View, and Frame of Reference

The self is the seat of the individual's identity, one's sense of oneself as a knowing, active entity. Part of identity is an implicit map of how one fits into the world in terms of one's own history, future, and relations with others. Finally, an understanding of the world itself is both the context for and an integral part of identity. This includes ways of understanding why things happen as they do.

The need for a meaningful frame of reference for one's experience is viewed as fundamental within many theories of personality (Epstein 1985; Fromm 1955; Rogers 1951). Psychological trauma often disrupts one's entire frame of reference or usual ways of making sense of experience. Trauma survivors often become preoccupied with questions such as, "Why did this happen to me?" (Figley 1983; Janoff-Bulman 1985). Disturbed frame-of-reference schemas may be reflected in an obsessive need to understand why one was abused along with a generalized belief that nothing makes sense. MPD clients evidence severe disruptions in identity and a variety of frame-of-reference schemas, with child alters being most confused about what happened to them and why. Different alters have different perspectives on why things happen. Often, attributions of causality for the abuse may reflect magical thinking or self-blame. Therapeutically, these attributions must be respected and thoroughly explored before they are challenged, an issue we discuss below.

A fragmented or discontinuous identity is nowhere more apparent than in the case of MPD, where different alter personalities live entirely different existences. Many ritual abuse survivors report personalities for dealing with the world of the cult and another group of alters for dealing with the outside world. This double or secret life causes radical discontinuities in the sense of how the world operates and what is real or unreal. In such cases, there may be a pervasive sense of confusion and disorientation in which the world of people and the inner world make little sense. This disruption is only resolved as individuals are ultimately able to approach their memories of abuse and understand how the abuse shaped their experience of reality and frameworks for understanding themselves and the world.

Safety

The belief that one is safe and reasonably invulnerable to harm is fundamental to psychological well-being and is a central need area often disrupted by traumatic life events. Examples of positive safety schemas include beliefs that one can protect oneself from physical and emotional harm, injury, or loss, and that the world is fundamentally a safe place. Survivors of situations of extreme danger and terror generally experience a serious disruption in this area. Themes of unique vulnerability to future harm; chronic, generalized anxiety about potential dangers in the world; and concerns about being unable to find a safe place within oneself or the world reflect disturbed safety schemas. While a natural disaster may temporarily disrupt safety schemas and result in anxiety reactions, often these schemas are more circumscribed and specific. That is, the individual may become anxious upon exposure to stimuli that symbolize the trauma, such as heavy rains, as in the case of a flood victim. For survivors of ritual abuse, there may be so many stimuli associated with danger that safety schemas become overgeneralized and pervasive. Those behaviors that were originally adaptive as a defense against danger may persist into adulthood, with serious costs that interfere with current functioning.

Clients with disturbed safety schemas often express beliefs that they are unable to protect themselves, that the world is a dangerous place, and that other people are threatening or harmful. In MPD, often one or more alters are especially vulnerable to disruptions in this area, while this area may be less salient for others. The feeling states that often accompany such disturbed schemas are fear, anxiety, phobias, panic, and so forth. Creating a safe therapeutic environment is particularly important, and may be particularly challenging, for clients with seriously disrupted safety schemas.

Dependency/Trust

Dependency refers to the need to have others prevent frustration and satisfy basic needs (Rotter 1954), and to be treated with understanding, kindness, and support (Gordon 1976). This need is closely related to trust schemas. Positive self-trust schemas are reflected in the belief that one can rely on one's own perceptions and judgments, while positive other-trust schemas involve the belief that one can rely upon the word or the promises of other people. There is ample evidence in the clinical literature that severe trauma often disrupts both self and other schemas in the area of trust. Ritual abuse survivors, as well as other survivors, who were forced to participate in horrific acts while being told it wasn't really happening are likely to have extreme difficulty trusting their own perceptions. Likewise, extreme betrayals and violations by early caretakers makes trust an extraordinary developmental task for many survivors.

Just as trust schemas are developed through early childhood interactions with others, severe disruptions in trust may reflect early childhood trauma. Individuals with overgeneralized negative trust schemas often maintain a suspicious, guarded stance toward other people and the world as a way of protecting themselves from future violations. Disturbances in the area of trust/dependency can be assessed by listening for themes of betrayal, abandonment, being made a fool of, being disappointed by other people, or being reluctant to ask for help or support from others.

Within MPD, various alters may be more or less vulnerable to disruptions within the area of trust. Some may be distrusting in more circumscribed areas of life, such as only distrusting men, while others may experience a more generalized distrust of all people. These alters, while deeply wishing for support and care, may need to test the possibility that they can depend on others. They will most often put the therapist through "trust tests" throughout the therapy process. The dilemma created for the therapist is that in passing such trust tests, the therapist creates a discrepancy (and corresponding emotional upset) for such an alter. These discrepancies then become material to process in the therapy.

The feeling state most often associated with disturbed self-trust schemas is self-doubt, while feelings of disappointment, betrayal, or bitterness are common when other-trust schemas are impaired. Behaviorally, clients with disturbed self-trust may find themselves paralyzed by indecision or making poor judgments of other people that put them in difficult positions (e.g., failing to be alert to specific signals of harm from abusive men, because of the inability to differentiate trustworthy from untrustworthy men). Likewise, clients with disturbed trust related to other people are likely to avoid close relationships, and to be suspicious, resulting in chronic interpersonal difficulties.

Independence

Independence refers to the need to control one's own behavior or rewards (Gordon 1976; Rotter 1954). The belief that one can control one's own thoughts, feelings, and behaviors is a reflection of positive independence schemas. Disturbed independence schemas are often revealed in themes of humiliation, shame, or disappointment in oneself for appearing to be weak, vulnerable, or helpless, as well as an unwillingness to ask others for help. In relation to ritual abuse survivors with MPD, we have observed that some of the more protective adult and adolescent alters can be fiercely independent. They may repudiate any signs of weakness or vulnerability within themselves and will often fear becoming too dependent on the therapist. Among some alters, independence and trust/dependency are closely linked. Disturbed schemas in these areas may include an extremely strong need to be in control of one's thoughts, feelings, and actions at all times or an unwillingness to tell others when one is in pain or needs help. Clients with extremely strong needs for independence tend to overinterpret any signs of emotional vulnerability as a personal flaw and resist crying or being emotional with anyone because it feels too shameful. Such beliefs can often be traced directly back to early experiences of being punished severely for emotional expression. Again, it is important to respect these needs and, very gradually, to begin reframing emotional expression as a sign of strength rather than weakness. Behaviorally, these individuals may be rigid and overcontrolled, making it difficult to process emotional experiences.

As the therapy experience encourages a fuller range of emotional expression, these disturbed schemas can gradually be modified.

Power

The need to direct or exert control over others is another fundamental human need (Gordon 1976; Rotter 1954) that is often disrupted in severe trauma. Positive power schemas may involve the belief that one can affect or control future outcomes in interpersonal relations or take a leadership role in group projects. Disturbed needs for power are often reflected in interpersonal conflicts related to aggression and assertiveness.

There are two ways in which power schemas may be disturbed. The first manifestation of this disturbance is the belief that one is helpless to control forces outside oneself or that one has no influence or control in relationships. The feeling states associated with the first type of disturbed power schemas are weakness, helplessness, and depression. Here one may observe a learned helplessness pattern, a concept originally conceived by Seligman (1975) and later applied to victims of domestic violence (Walker 1978).

Another manifestation of disturbed power schemas is the belief that one must control and dominate others in order to avoid being dominated. Behaviorally, these individuals may be aggressive, controlling, or abusive, as a way of protecting themselves against being weak and helpless.

Specific alters of ritually abused persons may show either type of pattern. Typically, hostile or aggressive alters are manifesting the second type of disturbed power schemas. Understanding this behavior as a protection against fear, helplessness, and vulnerability is often necessary before these schemas can be reshaped. Often these individuals will ultimately reveal strong, unmet needs for safety and dependence that previously have been split off within the personality.

Esteem

The basic human need for recognition or validation is reflected in esteem schemas. Positive esteem schemas refer to the belief that oneself and others are valuable and worthy of respect (Gordon 1976; Rotter 1954). Disturbed esteem schemas related to the self are often reflected in themes concerning self-blame, unworthiness, or badness, and, with regard to others, feelings of contempt for or disillusionment about other people.

Disrupted self-esteem schemas include the belief that one is bad, flawed, or damaged and that others with whom one has contact will be contaminated, harmed, or doomed. Often these disturbed schemas are reflected in the transference relationship and in descriptions of both past and current relationships. An example of this is a client who believed it was her fault when the therapist was out sick, which reflected a belief that she was "poison" to those she loved.

Damaged other-esteem schemas are reflected in the belief that people are malevolent or that people are out for themselves. Disturbed self-esteem schemas are often associated with feelings of self-loathing, worthlessness, despair, and futility. A diminished belief in the value of other people is likely to be associated with cynicism, anger, or contempt. Behavioral manifestations may be antisocial life patterns or a general withdrawal from the world.

With regard to MPD and ritual abuse, certain alters may engage in self-punishing behaviors, with suicide being the ultimate destruction of the damaged or bad self. Alters may internalize cult beliefs about being evil or about deserving punishment. However, there may also be certain alters who possess more positive esteem schemas, particularly when they are involved in activities that enhance feelings of pride and mastery. This can be very helpful during treatment. For example, during the therapy of a ritual abuse survivor, one personality who had previously self-mutilated during times of self-loathing was helped internally by another alter who had the capacity to feel good about herself when she was able to sing. As with the other schema areas, however, if the individual is ultimately to reframe the meanings of the abuse in ways that are more adaptive to the current life situation, the therapy will need to help the client to recall the situations which shaped the disrupted schemas and experience the feelings related to the early trauma.

Intimacy

Human beings have a fundamental need for connection or attachment to other human beings (e.g., Bowlby 1969). Positive schemas in the area of self-intimacy may include the belief that one can be alone without being lonely or empty, that one can be a friend to oneself, and with regard to other-intimacy, that one can connect with others in a meaningful, positive way. Disturbed intimacy schemas related to self are often manifested in panic when one is alone or in an overreliance on drugs, alcohol, sex, food, self-mutilation, vomiting, spending money, or other addictive or compulsive behaviors as sources of inner comfort and calm (Horner 1986). Intimacy schemas with respect to others are reflected in the individual's internalization of other people or the world in general. The "reality" of the person's interpersonal world is less important than his or her internalization of this world. Thus, a client may report having friends and other supports but nonetheless chronically feel alone and alienated. With regard to MPD, certain alters may experience different disturbances within this area, with some able to maintain human connections, while others may have never had a genuine relationship with others outside the internal world.

The feeling states associated with these disturbed schemas are a pervasive sense of emptiness, loneliness, alienation, or estrangement. In essence, these individuals have given up on the interpersonal world and can find little comfort in human connection. With regard to therapy, these clients may repeatedly express feeling disconnected from the therapist and other people.

As with the other areas, it is important to understand the adaptive significance of disturbed intimacy schemas as well as the ways in which they are linked to other schema areas. For example, some survivors will reveal fears that if they allow themselves to feel connected to others, that others will die, go away, or otherwise abandon them. This may relate to beliefs that other people are basically unreliable or that the individual is unworthy of loving and care. Other survivors' fears of intimacy may relate to an inability to set boundaries between self and others and the related fear of being overwhelmed or of dissolving if they become too close to another person.

Conveying Respect for Central Needs and Disturbed Schemas

The therapist must convey an attitude of respect for the client's central needs and schemas, without prematurely challenging those that appear maladaptive. It is important to remember that even the most disturbed schema serves some protective or defensive function, even if it is no longer adaptive in one's present life. The healing process takes place first through providing a therapeutic climate that is respectful of central needs and schemas and then gradually presenting tolerable doses of discrepancy to disrupted schemas through corrective experiences within the therapy relationship.

It is important to create the therapy frame in a way that meets these needs in adaptive and respectful ways. For example, clients with strong needs for recognition and disturbed self-esteem schemas are likely to need empathetic validation and positive mirroring (Kohut 1977) within the therapy before they can talk about their more shameful, humiliating memories. Clients with strong needs for independence or self-control may not be ready to delve into painful memories until their fears of vulnerability and loss of control are resolved. Others with strong security needs and concerns about safety will need to feel that the therapy setting is a safe place, and to learn, through imagery or active coping techniques, that they can create a sense of safety in their world. Clients with strong dependency needs and trust issues will need to test out their fears that the therapist will disappoint, betray, or abandon them before they can risk needing the therapist. Clients with disturbances in the area of intimacy may need to work through their fears around loss and closeness before the next stage of work can begin. Finally, clients who have severely damaged frame of reference schemas will need to make sense of the abusive experiences in ways that can be assimilated gradually.

With respect to MPD, the therapist must consider the developmental level of each alter in relation to how these needs and related disturbances in schemas will be addressed therapeutically. For example, needs for safety will have a very different meaning for a child alter than for a competent adult alter. The therapist might allow the child alter to hold a teddy bear during therapy in order to feel safe, while an adult alter might be encouraged to talk about how he can regulate the closeness/distance in the therapy relationship in order to feel safe. Over time, the therapist gradually encourages meeting needs in increasingly adaptive, developmentally appropriate, ways.

Gently Challenging Disturbed Schemas

When a clinician is faced with extremely distorted schemas, it is tempting to challenge these disturbed beliefs directly within the therapy. This must be handled very delicately because a premature challenge to core schemas will be psychologically disruptive and potentially traumatic. For example, a prematurely challenging interpretation might be to say, "You were not to blame for what happened. Your father was responsible for the abuse." A more gentle way of challenging these schemas might be to say, "What do you imagine it would feel like if you were not at fault?" The therapist must always remember that these schemas developed originally as a way of making sense of painful or incomprehensible situations and may have adaptive value for the individual. As stated above, these schemas often serve to protect the individual from some emotion or experience that she views as dangerous. Thus, it is important to first explore how these schemas are adaptive for the individual or, in the case of MPD, within a particular subsystem. This can be accomplished by exploring how the schemas are helpful and what the client imagines it would be like to change her beliefs. The exploration of schemas as valued defenses will thus be an integral part of the healing process.

In general, disturbed schemas are gently challenged through the therapy relationship itself. Many survivors of ritual abuse as well as other interpersonal traumas believe that the therapist will hurt, betray, violate, abandon, overpower, or otherwise revictimize them. The specific transference themes will usually be linked to the disturbed need areas that are most salient for that individual.

One way to explore the defensive value of disturbed schemas is to explore repeatedly the question, "What would it be like if you could imagine allowing yourself to trust, to feel safe, connected, etc., in here with me?" With regard to disturbed safety schemas, clients will often express the conviction that these schemas enable them to remain vigilant and watchful. They may fear that letting down their guard will make them vulnerable to repeated violation. In the words of one client who had seriously disturbed safety schemas, "I would feel defenseless, like a turtle without a shell. What if I got too careless and the same thing happened again?" Likewise, clients with disturbed trust/dependence schemas are often protecting themselves from being betrayed and violated by others. The possibility of trust within the therapy may be perceived as dangerous because of the threat of making themselves too vulnerable again. Learning to trust is a process that must take place gradually. Disturbed self-esteem schemas may protect clients from fully assimilating the reality that their "loving" mother or father cruelly betrayed or hurt them. Clients with disturbed independence schemas are often fearful that they will lose control of their emotions and behaviors. The experience of being emotional, vulnerable, or dependent is terribly frightening as it has been associated with being helpless, out of control, and/or victimized. Clients with disturbed power schemas who believe they cannot control others or the environment may fear a painful loss of a relationship or the possibility that others will punish them if they were to become more assertive. Likewise, the angry or aggressive client may be fearful that giving up this form of power will result in repeated victimization. Clients with disturbed intimacy schemas may fear that being close to others emotionally will open them up to the potential for traumatic losses. Intimacy and attachment, having been associated with intense pain and hurt, may be far more threatening than enduring chronic feelings of alienation and estrangement. Finally, disturbed frame-of-reference schemas, such as the belief that one is to blame for everything bad that happens to oneself, may feel adaptive in that they provide an illusory sense of control over events in one's life. Conversely, these disturbed attributions may protect the survivor from overwhelming feelings of rage toward the perpetrator.

In summary, an important early goal of therapy is to understand, acknowledge, and explore the adaptive significance of these disturbed schemas. First, the therapist should explore what it would mean to the individual if she were to change these beliefs as well as what would be frightening about allowing herself to trust, feel safe, be intimate, and so forth. Next, the therapist very gradually challenges these disturbed schemas by gently pointing out the costs of these schemas for the client's present emotional and interpersonal life. For example, one might talk about how not trusting anyone previously served an important purpose but now serves to keep the individual from feeling supported and cared for by others. In this way, the therapist gradually presents "tolerable doses of discrepancies" to disturbed schemas in ways that enable the individual ultimately to assimilate the full meanings and emotional implications of this change.

As the therapist explores with the client the various coping strategies available to the client, it is important to acknowledge that *all* coping techniques have costs and benefits. For example, self-mutilation such as cutting may serve the purpose of relieving accumulated tension or punishing the bad parts of the self. However, the cost is that the client loses control, experiences physical injury, and feels despair and shame afterwards. "Adaptive" coping strategies also have costs and benefits. Calling the therapist or other supports when the client feels like cutting may provide an opportunity to release feelings in a way that is not hurtful. However, the cost of this is that the client may feel needy and dependent. Over time, as the costs and benefits of various coping strategies are discussed and explored, the client may be able to make more fully conscious choices about actions as he or she is able to test new, more adaptive ways of managing painful memories and affects.

Restoring Positive Schemas

Over the course of therapy, the therapist helps the client gradually develop more positive schemas in the areas that are most central and disturbed. Exploring what it would take to feel safe, to trust, to feel in control, and so forth, and how the client might test this in current relationships is an important part of the therapy. Specific interventions focused on building positive schemas will depend upon which schema area is disrupted. For instance, positive safety schemas can be developed through such varied techniques as finding a safe place in one's mind, transforming images of danger in fantasy, and employing systematic desensitization or other behavioral anxiety-reducing techniques. More positive trust schemas are often first developed within the context of the therapeutic relationship as well as through testing how one might begin to trust other people, in small steps. Clients who need to develop more adaptive independence schemas will need to learn gradually that vulnerability and emotionality are not always equated with helplessness and loss of control and that there are more adaptive ways of achieving a sense of personal control. Clients who manifest disturbed power schemas through aggressiveness will need to learn that this pattern is a protection against underlying feelings of vulnerability. They may need to know that the therapist will not challenge their sense of power, but rather will work with them to find more adaptive ways of meeting these needs. Severely disturbed self-esteem schemas are often most deeply entrenched and thus most difficult to overcome, largely because these belief systems result from serious early psychological injuries to the self. Cognitive-behavioral techniques such as learning to spend nurturing time alone, to be aware of and acknowledge one's positive attributes, and to talk lovingly to oneself can be helpful in certain instances. However, in our experience, it is often more important to explore fully the meanings and affects associated with self-loathing and ultimately see the connection between these feelings and particular traumatic experiences. Clients with disturbed intimacy schemas may need first to experience a sense of connection with the therapist while simultaneously working through their fears of loss and abandonment. Finally, clients with disturbed frame of reference schemas may need to test alternative attributions of causality and ultimately separate responsibility for what happened from responsibility for the solution (Shaver and Brown 1986).

Summary

We have presented a new theory of adaptation to trauma that can provide a map for understanding and ultimately resolving severe disruptions to the self that result from psychological trauma. We have applied these concepts to understanding the unique psychological experience of clients who have been ritually abused, although the theory has applicability to all trauma survivors. We hope this theory will help clinicians and researchers alike better understand the richness and complexity of human adaptation to trauma and victimization.

References

American Psychiatric Association. 1987. *Diagnostic and Statistical Manual of Mental Disorders*. 3d ed. Washington, D.C.: American Psychiatric Association.

Bowlby, John. 1969. *Attachment and Loss*. Vol. 1, *Attachment*. London: The Hogarth Press.

Braun, Bennett G., and Roberta G. Sachs. 1985. "The Development of Multiple Personality Disorder: Predisposing, Precipitating, and Perpetuating Factors." In *Childhood Antecedents of Multiple Personality*, ed. R. P. Kluft, 38–64. Washington, D.C.: American Psychiatric Press.

Breuer, Joseph, and Sigmund Freud. 1895. "Studies in Hysteria." Reprinted in *The Standard Edition of the Complete Psychological Works of Sigmund Freud*, ed. James Strachy. Vol. 2, 1–19. London: The Hogarth Press, 1955.

Briere, John. 1984. "The Effects of Childhood Sexual Abuse on Later Psychological Functioning: Defining a Post–Sexual Abuse Syndrome." Paper Presented at the Third National Conference on Sexual Victimization of Children. Washington, D.C., April.

Donaldson, M. A., and R. P. Gardner, Jr. 1985. "Diagnosis and Treatment of Traumatic Stress among Women after Childhood Incest." In *Trauma and Its Wake: The Study and Treatment of Post-Traumatic Stress Disorder*, ed. C. R. Figley, 356–77. New York: Brunner/Mazel.

Epstein, Seymour 1985. "The Implications of Cognitive-Experiential Self-Theory for Research in Social Psychology and Personality." *Journal for the Theory of Social Behavior*, 15, 283–310.

Epstein, Seymour. In press. "The Self-Concept, the Traumatic Neurosis, and the Structure of Personality." In *Perspectives on Personality*, ed. Daniel Ozer, J. M. Healy, Jr., and A. J. Stewart. Vol. 3, *Perspectives on Personality*, 63–97. Greenwich, Conn.: JAI Press.

Figley, C. R. 1983. "Catastrophes: An Overview of Family Reaction." In *Stress and the Family: Coping with Catastrophe*, ed. C. R. Figley and H. I. McCubbin. Vol. 2, 3–20. New York: Brunner/Mazel.

Freud, Sigmund. 1920. "An Autobiographical Study." Reprinted in *The Standard Edition of the Complete Psychological Works of Sigmund Freud*, ed. James Strachy. Vol. 18, 3–64. London: The Hogarth Press, 1924.

———. . 1939. "Moses and Monotheism." Reprinted in *The Standard Edition of the Complete Psychological Works of Sigmund Freud*, ed. James Strachy. Vol. 23, 3–137. London: The Hogarth Press, 1964.

Fromm, Erich. 1955. *The Sane Society*. New York: Rinehart.

Gordon, L. V. 1976. *Survey of Interpersonal Values: Examiner's Manual*. 2d ed. Chicago: Science Research Associates.

Horner, Althia. 1986. *Being and Loving*. Northvale, N.J.: Jason Aronson.

Horowitz, M. J. 1975. "Intrusive and Repetitive Thoughts after Experimental Stress." *Archives of General Psychiatry* 32:1457–63.

———. . 1976. *Stress Response Syndromes*. New York: Jason Aronson.

———. . 1979. "Psychological Response to Serious Life Events." In *Human Stress and Cognition: An Information-Processing Approach*, ed. Vernon Hamilton, and D. M. Warburton, 235–63. New York: John Wiley & Sons.

———. . 1986. *Stress Response Syndromes*. 2d ed. New York: Jason Aronson.

Janoff-Bulman, Ronnie. 1985. "The Aftermath of Victimization: Rebuilding Shattered Assumptions." In *Trauma and Its Wake: The Study and Treatment of Post-Traumatic Stress Disorder*, ed. C. R. Figley, 15–25. New York: Brunner/Mazel.

———. . 1989. "Assumptive Worlds and the Stress of Traumatic Events: Application of the Schema Construct." *Social Cognition* 7, no. 2:113–46.

———. , and I. H. Frieze. 1983. "A Theoretical Perspective for Understanding Reactions to Victimization." *Journal of Social Issues* 39, no. 2: 1–17.

Kluft, R. P. 1984. "Aspects of the Treatment of Multiple Personality Disorder." *Psychiatric Annals* 14:51–55.

Kohut, Heinz. 1977. *The Restoration of the Self*. New York: International Universities Press.

McCann, Lisa, and Laurie Ann Pearlman. 1990. *Psychological Trauma and the Adult Survivor: Theory, Therapy, and Transformation*. New York: Brunner/Mazel.

McCann, Lisa, Laurie Ann Pearlman, D. K. Sakheim, and D. J. Abrahamson. 1988. "Assessment and Treatment of the Adult Survivor of Childhood Sexual Abuse within a Schema Framework." In *Vulnerable Populations: Evaluation and Treatment of Sexually Abused Children and Adult Survivors*, ed. S. M. Sgroi. Vol. 1, 77–101. Lexington, Mass.: Lexington Books.

McCann, Lisa, D. K. Sakheim, and D. J. Abrahamson. 1988. "Trauma and Victimization: A Model of Psychological Adaptation." *The Counseling Psychologist* 16, no. 4: 531–94.

Miller, Alice. 1984. *Thou Shalt Not Be Aware: Society's Betrayal of the Child*. New York: Farrar, Straus, and Giroux.

Pearlman, L. A., I. L. McCann, and Grace Johnson. 1990. "Assessing Disturbed Cognitive Schemas within Constructivist Self-Development Theory." Paper presented at the annual meeting of the American Psychological Association. Boston, Mass., August. 10.

Piaget, Jean. 1971. *Psychology and Epistemology: Toward a Theory of Knowledge*. New York: The Viking Press.

Rogers, C. R. 1951. *Client-Centered Therapy*. New York: Houghton Mifflin.

Roth, Susan. 1989. "Coping with Sexual Trauma." Unpublished manuscript.

———. , and L. J. Cohen. 1986. "Approach, Avoidance, and Coping with Stress." *American Psychologist* 41: 813–19.

———. , and L. P. Lebowitz. 1988. "The Experience of Sexual Trauma." *Journal of Traumatic Stress* 1:79–107.

Rotter, J. B. 1954. *Social Learning and Clinical Psychology*. Englewood Cliffs, N.J.: Prentice-Hall.

Sedney, M. A., and Barbara Brooks. 1984. "Factors Associated with a History of Childhood Sexual Experiences in a Nonclinical Female Population." *Journal of the American Academy of Child Psychiatry* 23:215–18.

Seligman, M.E.P. 1975. *Helplessness: On Depression, Development, and Death.* San Francisco: Freeman.

Shaver, K. G., and Debra Brown. 1986. "On Causality, Responsibility, and Self-Blame: A Theoretical Note." *Journal of Personality and Social Psychology* 50, no. 4: 697–702.

Walker, L.E.V. 1978. "Learned Helplessness and Battered Women." *Victimology* 2:499–509.

9

Diagnosis and Treatment of Ritually Abused Children

Catherine Gould, Ph.D.

R itual abuse is a brutal form of abuse in which the victim is assaulted at every conceivable level, usually by multiple perpetrators of both sexes, over an extended period of time. The physical abuse is so severe that it often involves torture and killing. The sexual abuse is typically sadistic, painful, and humiliating. The psychological abuse relies upon terrorization of the victim, mind-altering drugs, and mind-control techniques. The spiritual abuse causes victims to feel that they are so worthless and evil that they can only belong to Satan (or a similar deity) whose evil spirits further terrorize and control them (Ritual Abuse Task Force 1989).

These forms of abuse are perpetrated by a cult in a highly systematic way, utilizing ceremonies and symbols, in an attempt to indoctrinate the victim into the cult's antisocial, life-destructive belief system. While such cults are not always satanic, most survivors state that their ritual abuse took place at the hands of satanic cult members. Through an elaborate process of abuse and indoctrination, the cult attempts to gain absolute control over their victims' minds in order to transform them into members who will function in whatever way the cult demands. To forge a new member who is maximally useful to the cult, the process of abuse and indoctrination must begin when the child is very young. In this chapter, I will speak to the difficult task of diagnosing and treating the child victims of ritual abuse.

The information offered in this chapter is derived from four sources: from my clinical experience with over twenty victims of ritual abuse, no more than any two of whom were involved in the same case; from direct clinical experience with eight adult survivors of ritual abuse; from contact with over one hundred adult survivors whom I have interviewed over the past five years, either in person or on the telephone; and from the dozens of ritual abuse cases, both child and adult, on which I have consulted.

Thus, while these findings hardly represent a controlled study of ritual abuse victims, they do represent a sample of over 150 survivors, ranging in age from two to sixty-five. Some were abused in Canada, some in Mexico and Central America, and a few in Europe. The majority of this group were abused in various parts of the United States.

The information represented here is largely consistent with the few formal research studies of ritual abuse victims that have been conducted (e.g., Brown 1990; Young, Sachs, and Braun 1988). However, because the purpose of this chapter is not academic but clinical, my focus will not be on the presentation of statistics, or formal tests of hypotheses, but on helping the reader to understand the exceedingly difficult process of diagnosing and treating ritual abuse in children.

Diagnosis of Ritual Abuse in Children

The first impediment to accurate diagnosis of which the reader must become aware is that ritually abused children very seldom disclose any part of their abuse spontaneously. Several aspects of the abusive situation combine to make this so. First, ritually abused children are nearly always drugged before the assault occurs, precisely so they will be unable to consciously recall the abuse. Second, in the trance-inducing drugged state, hypnosis is often used to implant the suggestion that victims will be unable to remember what has taken place, and that if they do remember, they will have to harm or kill themselves. Third, the acts that children are forced to endure, witness, or participate in during the course of the ritual abuse are so intolerable that dissociation typically results. In other words, victims must split off the extremely traumatic events from awareness and encapsulate them psychologically in order to survive their horror. The dissociation-producing traumas are then used by the cult members to terrorize victims into silence about the abuse. They are told, "If you ever remember or tell about this, the same thing will be done to you."

These conditions, taken together—drugging, hypnosis, dissociation-producing trauma, and terrorization of the child, combine to produce a dissociative barrier truly daunting to the clinician. It appears that such dissociative barriers can be effectively erected with virtually any child who is ritually abused under the age of six. That is to say, the immature personality structure in the child less than six years old cannot prevent amnestic barriers from being erected in response to the abuse. The older child, with his or her more fully developed psyche, has more intellectual as well as emotional resources with which to deal with the abuse, and is somewhat less likely to forget it entirely, unless the abuse began before the age of six.

The implications of this finding are quite staggering for the clinician, for it must be assumed that no matter how bright or verbal a given child might be, a history of ritual abuse beginning before age six is extremely unlikely to be remembered by the child or spontaneously disclosed to anyone. As a result, most of the children encountered for evaluation or treatment who are in fact ritually abused have never made a disclosure to this effect, and the clinician who has no knowledge of how to evaluate a symptoms picture for ritual abuse is likely to overlook this aspect of the child's history entirely.

In a small percentage of cases, the child may disclose only a single aspect of the ritual abuse, usually a sexual molestation by one of his or her perpetrators. Without training in the diagnosis of ritual abuse, the clinician is likely to make the assumption that he or she is working with a child who is the sole victim of a single perpetrator. Even if the clinician does not think to ask whether other children were hurt, or other adults hurt the child, or additional abuses took place, the ritually victimized child is unlikely to recall these other elements of the assault consciously. In other words, while one abusive event may be recalled and reported by the ritually abused child, many others are likely to remain concealed behind dissociative barriers.

It is my contention that the evaluating or treating therapist has a compelling ethical responsibility to evaluate each child in his or her practice for any history of abuse, especially ritual abuse, as the long-term consequences of this most massive form of victimization are so severe. David Finkelhor and his colleagues (1988) found in their nationwide study of children sexually abused in day care that ritually abused children suffered the most serious psychological impairments. This finding is consistent with my clinical observations of the extreme damage suffered by young victims of ritual abuse.

In the light of the finding that ritually abused children suffer serious psychological impairments, it might seem logical to conclude that the evaluating therapist would not need to screen higher functioning children for a history of ritual abuse. Unfortunately for the evaluator, the severe impairments suffered by ritually abused children do not always manifest in the kind of florid symptom picture that would immediately lead him or her to suspect that some form of extreme trauma existed in the child's background. In particular, children who evidenced high levels of adjustment prior to the ritual abuse may show few obvious symptoms, and yet be deeply scarred by their victimization. Rather than becoming overtly symptomatic, these children often manifest developmental failures in later stages of childhood, ranging from emotional stunting to interpersonal failures to intellectual development that falls short of their potential.

Therefore, it behooves clinicians who work with children to learn how to evaluate for possible ritual abuse, and to initiate such an evaluation in order to rule out the condition in all children who present for clinical services. In some cases, making the determination that a child has been ritually victimized will lead to the discovery that the abuse is current and ongoing. The therapist may then be able to facilitate the removal of the child from the abusive situation, thereby limiting the damage to that child. In other cases, the ritual abuse will prove to have taken place in the past. Whether the ritual abuse is past or present, psychotherapy cannot be truly effective in the child's recovery until the history of victimization is uncovered.

When gathering information to screen a given child for a history of ritual abuse, the clinician must obtain data from several sources. *The first source of information will always be the child's parents.* The clinician often has no way to know for sure whether the parents of a child who turns out to have been ritually abused are involved in the abuse. However, it is reasonable to assume that parents who have voluntarily sought help for the child are or were *not* involved in the child's victimization. The vast majority of child ritual abuse cases encountered in clinical settings have been perpetrated outside the home, usually in day care. Occasionally, a parent who has an undiagnosed multiple personality disorder resulting from his or her own early history of ritual abuse will seek clinical services for a child who has been abused by a cult in which the parent is unwittingly still active. In cases of this type, there is a healthy and caring part of the parent who is seeking to rescue the child from a situation that may be almost impossible to escape without extensive professional help for the whole family.

Table 9-1
Signs and Symptoms of Ritualistic Abuse in Children

1. Problems associated with sexual behavior and beliefs:

_____A. Child talks excessively about sex; shows age-inappropriate sexual knowledge; uses words for sex and body parts which are not used in the family.

_____B. Child is fearful of being touched or of having genital area washed; resists removing clothes for baths, bed, etc.

_____C. Child masturbates compulsively or publicly, tries to insert finger or object into vagina or rectum.

_____D. Child pulls down pants, pulls up dress inappropriately.

_____E. Child touches others sexually, asks for sex, interacts in an inappropriately sexualized fashion. Child is sexually provocative or seductive.

_____F. Child complains of vaginal or anal pain or burning when washed, pain when urinating or defecating.

_____G. Semen or blood stains are evident on child's underwear.

_____H. Child "hints" about sexual activity, complains someone is "bothering" him/her.

_____I. Child refers to sexual activity between other children, or between him/herself and another child, in the abusive setting.

_____J. Child states someone removed his/her clothes.

_____K. Child states someone else exposed self to him/her.

_____L. Child states someone touched or penetrated his/her bottom, vagina, penis, rectum, mouth, etc.

_____M. Child states (s)he was made to touch or penetrate someone's bottom, vagina, penis, rectum, mouth, etc.

_____N. Child states that sharp objects were inserted in his/her private areas.

_____O. Child states (s)he witnessed sex acts between adults, adults and children, adults or children and animals, etc.

_____P. On examination by a pediatrician specially trained to diagnose sexual abuse in children, child relaxes rather than tenses rectum when touched; relaxed anal sphincter, anal or rectal laceration or scarring.

_____Q. On exam, blood or trauma around genital area; enlargement of vaginal opening, vaginal laceration or scarring in girls; sore penis in boys.

_____R. On exam, venereal disease.

_____S. Female child refers to being married, states that she is married, is going to have a baby; or, child states she will never be able to have a baby.

2. Problems associated with toileting and the bathroom:

_____A. Child avoids bathroom; seems fearful of bathrooms, becomes agitated when has to enter a bathroom.

_____B. Child avoids or is fearful of using toilet; has toileting accidents because (s)he puts off going; develops chronic constipation.

_____C. Child of toilet-training age is fearful and resistant to being toilet trained.

_____D. Child avoids wiping self because it is "too dirty"; child's underwear is soiled because (s)he will not wipe, or due to relaxed anal sphincter.

_____E. Child avoids bathtub; fears bathing; resists being washed in genital area.

_____F. Child is preoccupied with cleanliness, baths; changes underwear excessively.

_____G. Child is preoccupied with urine and feces; discusses it compulsively or at meal times; becomes agitated while discussing it. Child uses words for bodily wastes that are not used at home, especially "baby" words. Child compulsively discusses or imitates passing gas.

_____H. Child acts out in toileting behavior, eliminating in inappropriate places, handling urine or feces, dirtying an area or sibling with bodily wastes, tasting or ingesting wastes.

_____I. Child draws nude pictures of self or family members urinating or defecating.

_____J. Child talks about ingesting urine or feces, having it put on his/her body or in his/her mouth, being urinated or defecating upon, or having any of these things happen to someone else.

3. Problems associated with the supernatural, rituals, occult symbols, religion:

_____A. Child fears ghosts, monsters, witches, devils, dracula, vampires, evil spirits, etc.
_____B. Child believes such evil spirits inhabit his/her closet, enter the house, peer at the child through windows, accompany the child, torment or abuse him/her or watch to make sure (s)he keeps secrets, inhabit the child's body, and/or direct the child's thoughts and behavior.
_____C. Child is preoccupied with wands, sticks, swords, spirits, magic potions, curses, supernatural powers, crucifixions, and asks many or unusual questions about them. Child makes potions, attempts magic, throws curses, calls on spirits, prays to the devil.
_____D. Child sings odd, ritualistic songs or chants, sometimes in a language incomprehensible to the parent; sings songs with a sexual, bizarre, or "you better not tell" theme.
_____E. Child does odd, ritualistic dances which may involve a circle or other symbols. Child may costume him/herself in red or black, take off his/her clothes, or wear a mask for such dances.
_____F. Child is preoccupied with occult symbols such as the circle, pentagram, number 6, horn sign, inverted cross, etc. Child may write backwards, inverting all the letters and/or writing right to left.
_____G. Child fears such occult symbols, becomes agitated or upset in their presence.
_____H. Child fears attending church, becomes agitated or upset in church, fears religious objects or people, refuses to worship God.
_____I. Child states that (s)he or someone else prayed to the devil, threw curses, made potions, performed ritualized songs or dances, called upon spirits, did magic. Child states that (s)he or someone else wore ghost, devil, dracula, witch etc. costumes, used ceremonial wands or swords, had their body painted (usually black).

4. Problems associated with small spaces or being tied up:

_____A. Child fears closets or being locked in a closet.
_____B. Child fears other small spaces e.g., elevators, becomes agitated if forced to enter one.
_____C. Child closes pets or other children in closets, or otherwise attempts to entrap or confine them.

_____D. Child states that (s)he or someone else was confined in a closet.

_____E. Child expresses fears of being tied up, states that (s)he or someone else was tied up.

_____F. Child expresses fears of being tied (usually by one leg) and hung upside down, states that (s)he or someone else was hung upside down.

_____G. Rope burns are evident on the child.

_____H. Child attempts to tie up other children, pets, parents, etc.

5. Problems associated with death:

_____A. Child is afraid of dying; states (s)he is dying, or fears (s)he will die on his/her sixth birthday.

_____B. Child states that (s)he is "practicing" to be dead, or is dead.

_____C. Child is afraid parents, sibling, other family members, or friends will die.

_____D. Child talks frequently of death, asks many questions about illness, accidents, and other means by which people die. Questions may have an overly anxious, compulsive or even bizarre quality.

6. Problems associated with the doctor's office:

_____A. Child fears, avoids visits to the doctor, becomes highly agitated in or on the way to the doctor's office; refers to "bad doctors," or otherwise expresses mistrust of the doctor's motives.

_____B. Child is excessively fearful of shots; may ask if (s)he will die from the shot.

_____C. Child is excessively fearful of blood tests; ask if (s)he will die from blood tests or whether someone will drink the blood.

_____D. Child fears taking clothes off in the doctor's office; asks whether (s)he will have to walk around naked in front of others.

_____E. Child behaves in a sexually seductive way on the examining table, appears to expect or "invite" sexual contact.

_____F. Child states (s)he or someone else received "bad shots," had to take clothes off or have sexual contact with others, drank blood, or was hurt by a "bad doctor."

7. Problems associated with certain colors:

_____A. Child fears or strongly dislikes red or black (sometimes orange, brown, purple); refuses to wear clothes or eat foods of these colors, becomes agitated in the presence of them.

_____B. Child states that black is a favorite color, for peculiar reasons.

_____C. Child refers to ritualistic uses of red or black that are inconsistent with what (s)he has experienced in church.

8. Problems associated with eating:

_____A. Child refuses to ingest foods or drinks because they are red or brown (e.g., red drinks, meat); becomes agitated at meal times.

_____B. Child expresses fears that his or her food is poisoned; refuses to eat home cooked food because (s)he fears the parents are trying to poison him/her; refers to poisons of various types.

_____C. Child binges, gorges, vomits, or refuses to eat.

_____D. Child states that (s)he or someone else was forced to ingest blood, urine, feces, human or animal body parts.

9. Emotional problems (including speech, sleep, learning problems):

_____A. Child has rapid mood swings, is easily angered or upset, tantrums, acts out.

_____B. Child resists authority.

_____C. Child is agitated, hyperactive, wild.

_____D. Child displays marked anxiety, e.g., rocking, nail biting, teeth grinding.

_____E. Child feels (s)he is bad, ugly, stupid, deserving of punishment.

_____F. Child hurts self frequently, is accident prone.

_____G. Child is fearful, withdrawn, clingy, regressed, babyish.

_____H. Child's speech is delayed or regressed, speech production drops, speech disorder develops.

_____I. Child has "flat" affect, fails to respond in emotionally appropriate ways.

_____J. Child has frequent or intense nightmares; fears going to bed, cannot sleep, has disturbed sleep.

_____K. Child has poor attention span, learning problems.

10. Problems associated with family relationships:

_____A. Child fears the parent(s) will die, be killed, or abandon him/her.

_____B. Child fears (s)he will be kidnapped and forced to live with someone else.

_____C. Child is afraid to separate from parents, cannot be alone at all, clings.

_____D. Child fears the parents(s) no longer love him/her, are angry and wish to punish him/her, or want to kill him/her.

_____E. Child seems distant from parent(s), avoiding close physical contact.

_____F. Child "screens out" what the parents say, failing to retain information they give.

_____G. Child becomes excessively angry or upset when told what to do or "no" by the parents(s), tells them "I hate you" or "I want to kill you"; threatens them with bodily harm, physically attacks them.

_____H. Child talks about "my other mommy," "my other daddy," or "my other family" (in the cult).

_____I. Child expresses fears that a sibling or pet will be killed, kidnapped, molested.

_____J. Child physically attacks, initiates sexual contact with, confines, puts excrement on or threatens a parent, sibling, or pet.

_____K. Child states someone said his/her parents would die, be killed, abandon or try to hurt the child. Child states someone said (s)he would be kidnapped.

11. Problems associated with play and peer relations:

_____A. Child destroys toys.

_____B. Child acts out death, mutilation, cannibalism, and burial themes by pretending to kill play figures, taking out eyes, pulling off heads or limbs, pretending to eat the figures or drink their blood, and burying them.

_____C. Child's play involves theme of drugging, threats, humiliation, torture, bondage, magic, weddings and other ceremonies.

_____D. Child is unable to engage in age-appropriate fantasy play, or can do so for only brief periods.

_____E. Child hurts other children, sexually and/or physically.

_____F. Child's drawings or other creative productions show bizzare, occult, sexual, excretory, death or mutilation themes.

_____G. Child is extremely controlling with other children, constantly plays "chase" games.

_____H. Child talks to an "imaginary friend" who (s)he will not discuss, or who (s)he states is a "spirit friend."

12. Other fears, references, disclosures and strange beliefs:

_____A. Child fears the police will come and put him/her in jail, or states a "bad policeman" hurt or threatened him/her.

_____B. Child is excessively afraid of aggressive animals, e.g., crocodiles, sharks, large dogs, or poisonous insects; states (s)he was hurt or threatened with such animals or insects.

_____C. Child fears the house will be broken into, robbed, or burned down, or states someone threatened that this would happen; may wish to move somewhere else.

_____D. Child fears "bad people," "robbers," "strangers," or states (s)he had contact with such people; watches out the window for "bad people."

_____E. Child discusses unusual places such as cemeteries, mortuaries,

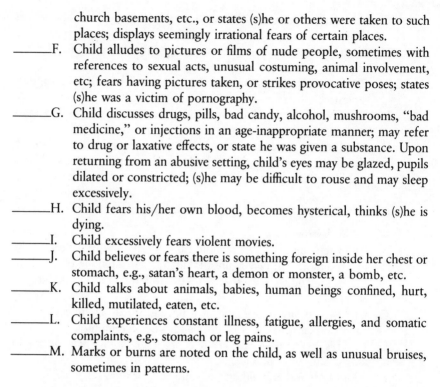

church basements, etc., or states (s)he or others were taken to such places; displays seemingly irrational fears of certain places.

_____F. Child alludes to pictures or films of nude people, sometimes with references to sexual acts, unusual costuming, animal involvement, etc; fears having pictures taken, or strikes provocative poses; states (s)he was a victim of pornography.

_____G. Child discusses drugs, pills, bad candy, alcohol, mushrooms, "bad medicine," or injections in an age-inappropriate manner; may refer to drug or laxative effects, or state he was given a substance. Upon returning from an abusive setting, child's eyes may be glazed, pupils dilated or constricted; (s)he may be difficult to rouse and may sleep excessively.

_____H. Child fears his/her own blood, becomes hysterical, thinks (s)he is dying.

_____I. Child excessively fears violent movies.

_____J. Child believes or fears there is something foreign inside her chest or stomach, e.g., satan's heart, a demon or monster, a bomb, etc.

_____K. Child talks about animals, babies, human beings confined, hurt, killed, mutilated, eaten, etc.

_____L. Child experiences constant illness, fatigue, allergies, and somatic complaints, e.g., stomach or leg pains.

_____M. Marks or burns are noted on the child, as well as unusual bruises, sometimes in patterns.

The table suggests questions that should be asked, of both parents if possible, when evaluating a child for possible ritual abuse. Ideally, the child's teacher should also be contacted, in order to gather information pertaining to the child's interpersonal behavior and the themes he or she includes in drawings and stories done at school. If the child is attending a preschool suspected of ritually abusing the child, the facility should *not* be called while the evaluation is in progress, because the perpetrators will usually escalate their victimization of any child being evaluated, in order to ensure that he or she does not disclose the abuse. Whenever possible, a child who appears to be ritually abused should be removed from any facility or childcare situation until the source of the abuse is discovered. This not only increases the probability that the child is safe, it also may make the child safe enough to begin to disclose his or her abuse.

Finally, the clinician must evaluate the child in person. It has been my experience that direct questions about possible abuse make many children who have been ritually abused exceedingly anxious and resistant. Even conscious memories of the abuse are not readily shared, because the child has been made by his or her perpetrators to suspect everyone of being a cult member. Ritually abused children usually need to build a relationship of trust before they can begin to disclose their victimization to the evaluator. This is not to say that direct questioning of the child has no place in an evaluation for possible ritual abuse, only that it must be done in a careful and timely manner.

The stage for evaluating the child should always be set with appealing, age-appropriate, therapeutically relevant toys. At a minimum, the clinician who evaluates a child for a possible history of ritual abuse should have available scissors, string, markers, and paper (including large paper), *Playdoh* or other clay that is easy to manipulate, blocks, marbles, a doctor kit, play dishes, stuffed animals (and/or puppets, dolls of both sexes, dogs, rabbits and chickens), a dollhouse with furniture (including bathroom fixtures), and small cars, trucks, and airplanes. A police car and fire engine can be useful additions. Whenever possible, the small figures should have hats, masks, costumes, and weapons of various types with which ritually abused children can symbolically reenact their abuse. Small monster-type figures are similarly useful. A sand tray allows ritually abused children to play out themes of burial, caves, tunnels, basements, dirtiness, and hiddenness to name just a few. Anatomically correct dolls can be useful, but recently have proven problematic in cases that go to court.

Many clinicians who find themselves with the difficult task of evaluating a child for possible ritual abuse are faced with a painful conflict between the requirements of the judicial system should the case end up in court and what children may need from their evaluators to be able to disclose their victimization. Whereas the judicial system usually requires disclosures to be made by the child in response to only the most neutral and open-ended questions, it is this writer's experience that ritually abused children seldom disclose in this kind of a format. Frequently they require a structure for disclosure to take place which the judicial system would consider to be "leading." It is my contention that the clinician's most compelling ethical responsibility is to the discovery of any underlying victimization so that the child might heal. If this need for accurate diagnosis and effective treatment ultimately makes the case difficult or impossible to prosecute, the needs of the child must take precedence over the requirements of the courtroom.

The clinician will be faced with the task of organizing material gathered from the child as well as from the child's parents and teachers. Signs and symptoms of ritual abuse can be checked off on the symptom list at table 9–1. If the child's symptom picture is suggestive of ritual abuse, but the child has not disclosed that ritual abuse occurred, the evaluator may have no way of knowing when or where the abuse might have taken place. Since the evaluator's first responsibility to a child who may be a victim of ritual abuse is to do everything possible to ensure current safety for the child, it is often wise to construct a time line on which the child's symptomatology can be considered. To do so, the clinician must look at the time when each of the child's various symptoms first became apparent to the informant in light of events occurring in the child's life at that time.

If, for example, a nondisclosing child has a new stepparent at age two, starts preschool at three, and got a new babysitter at four, the clinician who felt that the child's symptoms indicate ritual abuse would want to evaluate when the child became symptomatic in order to develop some idea about who the child's perpetrators might be. If many of his symptoms became apparent within a few months of starting preschool, the evaluator might suggest to the parent that the child be removed from the preschool until further evaluation has clarified the source of his distress.

Removing the child from the situation most closely linked in time to the onset of ritual abuse symptoms not only heightens the chances that the child will be made safe, it also increases the likelihood that the child who has previously been terrorized into silence about his abuse will feel safe enough to begin to disclose it. The clinician who suspects ritual abuse of a nondisclosing child must be able to tolerate a high degree of ambiguity and anxiety about the child's situation in order to be effective in evaluating and protecting that child. In such a situation the evaluator must also be willing to tell the parents that until the child discloses, there is no way to know for sure whether the abuse occurred or who might have perpetrated against the child, but that until disclosures are made, it is imperative that the parents take every possible precaution to ensure the child's safety. The clinician must be clear in his or her own mind, and must convey to the parents that ensuring the child's safety takes precedence over securing "proof" of whether the child was abused, or who perpetrated against that child.

I will now turn to a discussion of the symptom picture of the ritually abused child. To date, no quantified data exist that would allow us to examine statistically how symptoms might cluster if ritually victimized children's symptom profiles were factor analyzed, or which combinations of symptoms must exist to know with a high degree of certainty that ritual abuse has occurred. Such research will eventually add to our ability to accurately diagnose a history of ritual abuse in children. For the time being, we need to utilize a clinical, nonquantitative approach to making this diagnosis. This presentation will include information on how much weight the clinician should assign to any given symptom, as well as how to conceptualize symptom clusters that may emerge.

The reader can refer to table 9-1 as symptoms are presented and discussed. Until a more rigorous diagnostic schema for ritual abuse is constructed, this table should be used as a guideline in the clinical evaluation of all children to rule out any possible history of ritual victimization.

The first symptoms I will address are those which indicate a possible history of sexual abuse in the child. While sexual abuse does not always include ritual abuse, ritual abuse virtually always includes sexual abuse. If the clinician has reason to suspect sexual abuse (and even if he or she does not) other possible symptoms of ritual abuse should be explored. However, if after a thorough evaluation the child *only* shows symptoms of sexual abuse, the clinical may conclude that no ritual component to the abuse exists.

In each of the categories of symptoms, the reader can think in terms of an avoidance cluster and an acting-out cluster. Many children have a noticeable style of displaying symptoms, tending toward either acting-out or avoiding, although a mixture of acting-out and avoidance symptoms will be seen on occasion. The sexually abused child is most likely to be identified as such if he or she acts out sexually.

Excessive discussion of sex and age-inappropriate knowledge about sex (especially about sexual perversions) can be symptoms of sexual or ritual abuse. Some children will discuss sex excessively because they are sexually abused, whereas others will do so because they live in environments that, while inappropriately sexualized for the child's development, are not actually abusive. Similarly, age-inappropriate sexual knowledge on the part of the child can result from sexual abuse or from living in an overly sexualized environment. The evaluator must be familiar with the ways in which nonabused children of various ages normally discuss sex in order to accurately determine whether a child talks excessively about sex or shows knowledge of sexual matters that is age-appropriate. Once it is determined that the child shows one or both of these symptoms, the evaluator must seek to establish the source of the symptom.

The use of words for sex, elimination, and body parts that are not used by the child's family may also be a symptom of sexual or ritual abuse. At its most benign, the child's use of sexual words not used by the family may simply reflect terminology picked up from peers or adults in the child's environment; however, it can also result from the child's having been exposed to these words while being sexually abused. This symptom has particular significance in the context of ritual victimization, because cult members often use "baby" words for sexual and bodily functions as they abuse the child. Words like "peepee" and "boobies" are commonly used by cult members in the context of ritual abuse. This is probably because so many ritual abusers have multiple personality disorders stemming from their own early abuse, and when their "young child" alters perpetrate, they use language consistent with the age of that alter personality. Children whose language signals possible ritual abuse often tend to become agitated or regressed when using such language. The evaluator, or parent who is reporting to the evaluator, may sense a lewd quality to the language atypical of a young child. Such qualitative aspects of the child's use of sexual language will give the evaluator important additional information about its origins.

Fearfulness or avoidance of being touched is another symptom of possible sexual or ritual abuse. Even a child who is sexually assaulted by a single perpetrator has had his or her trust in adults severely jeopardized, and may be afraid to be touched by anyone. Children who have been sexually assaulted by multiple perpetrators, especially perpetrators of both sexes, are even more likely to resist physical contact with caretakers. Children whose sexual abuse took place in the context of ritual abuse are the most likely to resist close contact with others, since touch has been associated not only with the violation of trust in which sexual abuse results, but with the extreme physical pain and total loss of control experienced in ritual abuse. Parents of ritually abused children often complain that their young child no longer wishes to cuddle or to sit on the parent's lap. It is vitally important that the evaluator know what constitutes a normal degree of physical contact in children of different ages in order to ascertain when a child is avoiding touch abnormally.

Sexually and ritually abused children often resist being washed in their genital area. Such contact with the genitals may trigger traumatic memories of sexual assault for the sexually victimized child. The evaluator must be sure to distinguish children who are resistant to bathing because they would rather play from children who are afraid to remove their clothes or afraid to be washed between the legs. A child who is fearful due to a history of abuse is often distinguished by agitated behavior or a rigidly "frozen" posture, sometimes accompanied by a glazed facial expression and blank look to the eyes. This facial expression is characteristic of a child who is dissociating from intolerably painful internal experiences.

Public or compulsive masturbation, inappropriate exposure by the child of his or her body to others, and sexualized behavior toward others are all signs of a sexualized child who has probably been sexually victimized, and may have been ritually abused as well. The symptoms the child presents usually give the evaluator a clue to what has happened to that child. For example, children who masturbate compulsively or publicly usually do so because they have been so sexually stimulated that they are attempting to find relief from a kind of stimulation with which they are physiologically as well as psychologically unprepared to cope. Alternatively, compulsive or public masturbation can also signal that the child has been traumatically exposed to a masturbating adult, or has been masturbated by someone. Similarly, children who insert fingers or objects into their anal or vaginal openings have probably either witnessed or been subjected to such acts. Children who force, seek out, or submit to sexual acts with other children may be reenacting sexual contact perpetrated by adults, or they may be acting out sexual contact with other children into which they were coerced by adults.

Children who are sexually abused, whether ritually or not, may act out sexually in a variety of ways. They may identify with a coercive abuser and sexually assault another child. They may identify with a seductive perpetrator, and seduce another child into sexual contact. Or, they may identify as a victim and allow themselves to be perpetrated against or seduced by another child. Just as the original sexual assaults may be dissociated for the child, his or her sexual acting-out may be dissociated as well. That is, the child may have no conscious awareness of his or her sexual acting-out. The more massive and traumatic the original sexual assaults, the more likely both those original assaults and any subsequent sexual acting-out to be dissociated by the child.

The ritually abused child is more likely to act out sexually than are other sexually abused children, and the sexual acting-out is more likely to have a coercive, perpetrating quality to it. This greater degree of sexual trauma, perpetrated against the child in an extremely coercive and brutal fashion, and the child's subsequent dissociation of that trauma, all contribute to the tendency on the part of ritually abused children to become overtly symptomatic and to express their distress through a similarly coercive and brutal kind of sexual acting-out. A second and perhaps even greater contributor to the tendency of ritually abused children to act out sexually in a brutal or coercive way is the indoctrination they received in the cult. These children have usually been forced to perpetrate against other children as well as against adults during the course of their abuse. The cult responds to perpetrating children by telling them that now they too are bad. The cult may deliberately create alter personalities within the child whose function it is to sexually assault others, so that during a sexual ritual the cult can call on that alter to participate. The ritually abused child who acts out sexually may have a multiple personality disorder. The cult-created alter is doing what it was created to do—sexually assault others.

The sexual assaults suffered by the child in the context of ritual abuse are more physically painful and humiliating than those suffered by most other victims of sexual abuse. Because the primary purpose of the abuse is to break down the child in order to make him or her subservient to the cult, the sexual victimization often involves insertion of objects, including sharp objects, weapons, and religious artifacts, into the anus or vagina. The ritually abused child who acts out sexually may attempt to perpetrate against other children in a similar fashion.

Other signs of sexual or ritual abuse about which the evaluator should inquire include vaginal, anal, or genital pain. Even in girls, sexual assaults in the context of ritual abuse often involve anal penetration with either body parts of the perpetrator or objects. Such penetration can cause trauma to the child's tissue resulting in pain with defecation. Insertion of pins and the like into the urethra can cause pain with urination, and sometimes blood in the urine. Trauma to the genitals can cause burning with urination or pain when the child's genital area is washed. Semen or blood stains on the (prepubescent) child's underwear are nearly always signs of sexual abuse.

Children who hint that someone is "bothering" them should be questioned about possible sexual abuse. Disclosures about sexual contact between children, or between the child being evaluated and other children, should be taken as serious indicators of possible sexual or ritual abuse. Any disclosure of sexual assault or of an act often associated with sexual assault should be taken very seriously by the evaluator. A child who stated someone removed his or her clothes should be evaluated very carefully for possible sexual abuse. Statements that someone exposed him or herself to the child, that someone touched or penetrated the child's bottom, vagina, penis, rectum, or mouth, or that the child was made to touch or penetrate someone's bottom, vagina, penis, rectum, or mouth usually prove to be true, even when they are later retracted by a frightened or dissociated child.

The nature of the sexual acts the child reports may give the evaluator some clue whether the assault is ritual in nature. Sexual assaults involving groups of adults and children, women as well as men, religious artifacts, insertion of objects or weapons, ritualized behavior such as chanting or prayer, murder, and the use of blood or dismembered body parts all indicate possible ritual abuse. Reports of having witnessed sex acts between adults, adults and children, and people and animals are also indicators of possible ritual abuse. A female child who reports that she is married, about to have a baby, or will never be able to have a baby may also have been ritually abused. Ritually abused girls often undergo a ceremony in which they are "married" to Satan or to a cult member. The sexual assault they undergo in connection with this ceremony is sometimes paired with the message that the girl is now pregnant, and that the child she will eventually bear belongs to Satan and the cult. Alternatively, some girls sexually assaulted in a ritual context are told that their reproductive functions have been destroyed, and they will never be able to bear a child.

Children in whom sexual or ritual abuse is suspected should be referred for medical examination to a pediatrician with special training in the diagnosis of sexual abuse in children. Most pediatricians lack such training, and will fail to diagnose existing physical signs of sexual abuse. While the majority of sexually abused children will show no medical signs of abuse, the examination is nonetheless important. For one thing, it allows a traumatized child to be reassured that he or she is physically intact. A proper screening involves tests of all sites for venereal disease—mouth, genitals, and anus in both boys and girls. Thus, the examination is important for the diagnosis and treatment of venereal disease. Finally, cases in which medical evidence of sexual abuse is discovered have a greater chance of being criminally prosecuted. Medical findings of sexual abuse may also have clinical significance in the treatment of a child who has dissociated all memories of the sexual assaults.

Ritually abused children also have avoidance symptoms associated with toileting and the bathroom. For perpetrators, the bathroom may be the room of choice for abuses ranging from smearing urine and feces on the victim to the ritual killing of animals and human beings, because it is the easiest room to clean up and thus to get rid of evidence of the crimes the cult has committed. Ritually abused children often fear the bathroom because it reminds them of the intolerable horrors that have taken place there.

Ritually abused children may often avoid using the toilet because toileting threatens to bring to conscious awareness dissociated memories of having urine and feces smeared on their bodies and placed in their mouths. As one ritually abused two-and-a-half-year-old who adamantly resisted his (nonabusing) mother's attempts to toilet train him put it, "If I use the potty am I going to have to eat it, Mommy?"

The child who chronically resists using the toilet will, of course, have frequent toileting accidents. It is important that the clinician closely evaluate an eneuretic or encopretic child to determine the source of the problem. Too often, evaluators make the assumption that the child who soils must be responding to an overly rigid and controlling approach to toilet training, and the parents are advised of simply shifting their attention away from the symptoms to other matters in which the child's own sense of mastery and autonomy are emphasized. When the soiling is in fact a symptom of ritual abuse, diverting attention from it will certainly hinder the discovery of an extremely serious underlying problem.

Ritually abused children may soil because having a bowel movement in the toilet is terrifyingly reminiscent of the abuse. Similarly, they may avoid wiping because it brings them too close to touching the excrement and thus reminds them of the disgusting experience of having it smeared on their body. They may also soil because the anal muscle over which a child develops control during toilet training has been damanged by anal penetration to such an extent that there is periodic leakage of fecal matter. Soiling due to either toileting avoidance or physiological damage should be distinguished from the kind of acting out wherein the ritually abused child defecates or urinates in inappropriate places. The latter symptom and its dynamics will be discussed in the section on the acting-out cluster of symptoms pertaining to toileting and the bathroom.

Ritually abused children have many reasons for avoiding the bathtub. Like other sexually abused children, removing their clothes and being washed, especially between the legs, may be painfully reminiscent of the sexual abuse. In addition, many ritual abuses take place in the bathroom in general, and the bathtub in particular. Not only may the bathtub remind the child of the horror of bloody slaughter or the shame of being dirtied and defiled, it may also have been the site of traumatic near-drownings. Children who have endured this form of abuse often fear bodies of water in all forms. Finally, the bathtub is usually the place where the child is bathed after a ritual assault. Thus it comes to symbolize the transition from the ritual to the nonritual world, which is not traumatic per se, but is nonetheless extremely disorienting for the child. As children move back into the nonritual world, they must achieve a dramatic shift of consciousness, which requires reestablishing massive amnestic barriers against memories of the assault.

While some ritually abused children avoid the bathtub, others become preoccupied with cleanliness and bathe as often as their parents will allow. These children are responding to overwhelming feelings of dirtiness, which can result from their bodies being traumatically dirtied by urine, feces, semen, blood, or other substances. This form of assault is intended to tear down the child's sense of dignity and body integrity, and is typically magnified by degrading insults from cult members to the effect that the child is dirty, disgusting, beneath contempt, and the like. Compulsive bathing represents an attempt by the child to be emotionally and physically cleansed.

Acting-out around assaults of defilement ranges from the verbal to the overtly behavioral. While many young children discuss toileting functions frequently, in ritually abused children these discussions have a more compulsive and less innocent quality. Ritually abused children are often anxious and agitated as they talk about matters related to toileting. Because of the trauma they endured when bodily wastes were put in their mouths, these children often discuss toileting in the context of eating. Additionally, they may use words for bodily wastes and functions learned from their abusers, that are not used within the family.

More overt forms of acting-out in response to assaults of defilement include eliminating in inappropriate places, handling urine or feces, dirtying an area or sibling with bodily wastes, and tasting or ingesting wastes. Traditionally, Freudian therapists view some of these behaviors as normal aspects of the anal stage of development. Some therapists view this kind of acting-out as an expression of anger on the part of the child. Still others see these behaviors as indicators of psychosis. In the experience of this therapist, such acting-out most often signals a history of trauma around toileting, and represents the child's reenactment of events experienced in the context of ritual abuse. While assaults of defilement are known to exist in nonritual abusive contests, they are most commonly perpetrated within the framework of ritual abuse.

Certainly a child who makes a disclosure about an assault of defilement should be taken very seriously. As is the case in disclosures of sexual abuse, children rarely invent such stories. Children who talk about being made to ingest urine or feces, having bodily wastes put on their bodies or in their mouths, being urinate or defecated upon, or witnessing the perpetration of such acts against someone else probably have indeed been the victims of such assaults. In most cases, the clinician will discover that such children have also been subjected to many of the other kinds of assaults common in ritual abuse.

The third category of symptoms I address involves problems with the supernatural, rituals, occult symbols, and religion. The reader will recall that ritual abuse involves not only sexual, physical, and emotional assaults, some of which have already been discussed, but spiritual abuse as well. By spiritual abuse, I mean that ritually victimized children are made to feel that they are continually controlled and assaulted by spiritual entities who serve Satan or some similar deity. I do not intend to imply here that evil spirits either do or do not exist, only that in the context of the ritual abuse the child has experienced trauma and terror that have been attributed to the influence of such spirits.

Not only are ritually abused children made to feel that evil spirits assault and control them, they are also made to believe that they themselves are so evil and worthless that God could never love them. Once their sense of personal worth and goodness is sufficiently damaged, the cult is able to convince them that they belong to Satan. Some of the ceremonies conducted by satanic (or similar) cults are constructed to indoctrinate children into the belief that they belong to Satan. In the satanic birthing ritual, for example, the child is "reborn" to Satan. In the satanic wedding ceremony, the child is "married" to Satan or some representative of him. In addition, ritually abused children are often made to take a vow of allegiance to Satan, which includes promising to carry out his work under a veil of total secrecy. This vow includes a promise to serve the cult in whatever way its leaders demand.

Certainly most clinicians are unaccustomed to examining a child's relationship to a spiritual realm when conducting an evaluation. Material pertaining to religious beliefs and practices is usually considered outside the purview of clinical evaluation and treatment. Until ritual abuse became the serious problem it is today, this separation of psychological intervention and religious orientation was probably in most cases appropriate. However, given the fact that a central component of ritual victimization and coercive indoctrination into life-destructive cults is spiritual abuse, clinicians must not ignore the symptoms that arise from abuse of this kind.

It is normal for young children to exhibit some fears of ghosts, monsters, and the like. Between the ages of three and six, these fears are quite common. They are usually experienced when the child goes to bed at night and must sleep alone in the dark. However, unless the child is quite troubled, he or she can usually be soothed by the parent and go to sleep. In the morning, thoughts of frightening supernatural entities have disappeared. The ritually abused child, on the other hand, often experiences virtually constant terror of not only the traditionally feared ghosts and monsters, but also of witches, devils, Dracula, vampires, and/or evil spirits, depending on the precise belief system of the cult within which he or she was abused. Ritually abused children may lie awake at night for hours in desperate fear of being assaulted by such entities.

Ritually abused children are usually told by the cult that one or more evil spirits spy on them constantly. Most typically, the child is made to believe that a spirit inhabits his or her closet. Ritually abused children are also told that spirits can enter the house even when the doors and windows are locked. Spirits not only can move through walls but can hear through them as well, according to the cult teachings, so ritually abused children often feel unsafe physically as well as unable to disclose the abuse to anyone for fear of being overheard by spirits. These children feel that the spirits act as emissaries of the cult, spying on them and reporting back about their every activity.

Part of the ritual abuse often involves a "magical surgery" in which the child is made to believe that a spiritual entity has been put into his or her body. As a result, many ritually abused children believe that a monster, demon, or something similar lives inside of them, usually in their chest or stomach. The perpetrators impress upon the child that this spirit will henceforth guide the child's thoughts and behavior in a fashion consistent with the requirements of the cult.

Ritually abusive activity involves a great deal of paraphernalia. While the paraphernalia varies from cult to cult, it most typically involves costuming (often including masks or hoods), ceremonial knives, special containers for blood and potions, candles, an altar, and crucifixes. Ritually abused children often become entranced with cult paraphernalia, and include it in their play. These abused children may also exhibit in their play the cult activities associated with black magic, such as the making and drinking of potions, throwing curses, calling on spirits, and praying to the devil. These symptoms of ritual abuse are usually distinguishable from normal childhood play about magic of the sort that is encountered in fairy tales.

Songs, chants, rhymes, and dances are an integral part of ritual abuse. They constitute both a religious expression and an indoctrination of the child into the antisocial, life-destructive system of beliefs and practices subscribed to by the cult. Some of the rhymes ritually abused children may recite are merely perversions of recognizable nursery rhymes, such as "Twinkle, twinkle little star, you're a naked booby star." It may be difficult for the evaluator to distinguish these from rhymes that children invent on their own, so the evaluator may need to ask the child where the rhyme comes from. More easily recognizable are rhymes that emphasize cult principles of secrecy, punishment for transgression, enjoyment of sexual abuse and perversion, and the like. One example is "Tell, tell, go to jail, don't forget your panties." The ritually indoctrinated child's recitation of this rhyme reinforces the belief that telling about the cult abuse will result in being put in a "jail" as punishment. "Don't forget your panties" suggests that the child has been disrobed, presumably as part of a sexual ritual, and is responsible for making sure his or her underwear is put back on in order to cover up any evidence of the assault.

Songs and chants with deeper ritualistic meaning may be recited either in the child's native language or in a language unrecognizable to the evaluator. In the latter instance, the foreign language is often archaic, and derives from the place and time of the cult's origins. The ritually abused child may sing these cult songs or recite the chants. He or she may also engage in ritualistic dances, often involving a circle or other symbols. Songs, chants, and dances associated with ritual abuse are often discernible from those which children invent or learn from peers by their furtive quality. Children who are reenacting songs, chants, and dances learned in cult rituals may costume themselves in red or black clothes, take their clothes off, or wear masks.

When confronted with symptomatology or other clinical data that seem to reveal information about the symbology, ceremonies, language, or system of deities to which the cult subscribes, the clinician may be tempted to spend a good deal of time and energy researching the subject. It is the opinion of this writer that too much emphasis on making precise distinctions between one cult and another often distracts helping professionals from the important job at hand—the accurate diagnosis and effective treatment of the victim.

In addition to the paraphernalia, songs, rhymes, chants, and dances that characterize abusive rituals, such cults place heavy emphasis on symbols. As a result, the ritually abused child is often either preoccupied with or fearful of occult symbols. The most typical symbols to which ritually abused children react are the circle, the pentagram, the number 6, the horn sign, and the inverted cross.

As part of an inverted system of values and beliefs, the ritually indoctrinated child is often taught to do "mirror writing." Whereas most young children will sometimes make their letters and numbers backwards, the "satanic" writing of ritually abused children is striking in that all the letters are reversed. Additionally, the child may write from right to left.

Ritually abused children often fear church and are afraid to worship God. The reasons for this are several. First of all, they have been made to take vows to Satan (or some similar deity) in the course of the cult abuse and indoctrination. They are usually taught that Satan is strong and God is weak, and that those who worship God will be hurt by the cult members. Secondly, many of the symbols and costumes employed by the cult have their roots in Christianity, so that when ritually victimized children see a cross, an altar, or candles in church, they are often reminded of the abuse and become terrified. Christian clergy are often difficult for ritually abused children to distinguish from cult members dressed in black ceremonial robes. The sight of clergy in the context of candles, altar, crucifix, and other Christian symbols can trigger terror in the child who is reminded of his or her ritual abuse. Finally, some children report that they have actually been ritually abused in churches. For these children, the church itself is a frightening place.

Clearly, children who disclose that they or someone they have witnessed has prayed to the devil, thrown curses, made potions, performed ritualized songs or dances, called upon spirits, done magic, used satanic paraphernalia, worn satanic costumes, or had their bodies painted in a ceremonial fashion should be taken quite seriously. There are cultural settings in which ritualistic behaviors may take place without being accompanied by abusive acts and coercive mind control. However, it is the responsibility of the clinician to actively rule out an abusive component to ritualism that involves the child, by conducting a thorough evaluation.

The fourth category of symptoms involves problems associated with small spaces and being tied up. Ritual abuse usually involves one or more types of confinement of children in order to break their will and make them compliant with the demands of the cult. For example, ritually abused children may be locked in "jails," closets, or boxes and told that they will be left there to die of hunger, thirst, or lack of oxygen. Sometimes these children are told that there are snakes, poisonous insects, or dangerous animals in the enclosed place with them, which further magnifies their terror. One particularly traumatic ritual engaged in by many life-destructive cults is the "burial" ritual, in which the child is put in a coffin, often with a dead body, and lowered into the ground. The child is made to believe that he or she is being buried alive and will be left there to die. As a result of these trauma of confinement, ritually abused children often have symptoms that could be described as claustrophobic. They may fear closets, elevators, or other small spaces. They may express terror of being locked in a closet, box, or jail. Conversely, they may act out the confinement trauma by attempting to lock a pet, sibling, or even the therapist in a closet or other small space. They may reenact the trauma by lying down when they enter a small space. Finally, the ritually abused child may report that he or she, or someone else, was locked in a closet, jail, box, coffin, or other enclosed space.

Ritually abused children are often tied up as part of the perpetrators' attempts to terrorize them into subservience to the cult. The child may be suspended by one or both arms, or by one or both legs. Sometimes he or she is suspended in a pit which contains a dead body. As a result of being tied up or suspended in a traumatic way, ritually abused children may express fears of being tied up or suspended. They may act out such trauma by attempting to tie up or suspend another child, a pet, or even an adult. Finally, children who have been traumatized in this fashion may make disclosures that they have been tied up or suspended. Rope burns on a child should be investigated, as they may signify that the child has been tied or suspended.

Ritually abused children may experience problems associated with death. Ritual abuse usually involves not only sexual assaults, physical torture, and terrorization, but animal and/or human killing as well. Simulated as well as actual murders teach cult members of all ages that the power of the cult is absolute, and that whoever fails to comply with the demands of the cult faces a similar fate. Murder also constitutes the ultimate evil the cult can perform, and is believed by many satanic (or similar) cults to provide an avenue to harnessing the spiritual forces of evil for the cult's purposes. Ritually abused children have usually both witnessed death and been threatened with death. The child may be told that he or she will be killed on a particular date or birthday, most typically the sixth birthday. Threats to the child's family are often made in the context of the ritual abuse as well. Many ritually victimized children comply with cult demands for secrecy out of a fear that disclosure will cause their family members to be killed.

Ritually victimized children's problems with death follow logically from abuses of this kind. These children are often afraid of dying, and may experience many problems as their sixth birthday approaches. They may feel that they are dying, that they must "practice" to be dead, or even that they are already dead. In the later case, the child has been told that he or she was killed and that Satan or a similar deity allowed the child to be resurrected in a new form. Ritually abused children may express fears that parents, siblings, other family members, pets, or friends will die. They may talk frequently or ask many questions about death, illnesses, accidents, or other means by which people die. Their questions are distinguishable from the questions of nonabused children by their anxious, compulsive, or bizarre quality.

Ritually abused children may experience problems when they visit the doctor. Their abuse often involves drugging by injections, which are given in the most painful manner possible. Frequently, the child is told that he or she will die from the injection. As a result, when ritually abused children must receive an injection at the doctor's office, they may become fearful and highly resistant, believing that the shot will either be extremely painful or it will kill them. Blood tests may be similarly feared by a child who has been traumatized by needles. Not only do ritually abused children often fear that they will be tortured or killed by the needle used for the blood test, they may also fear that someone will drink their blood once it is taken, since they have witnessed or been made to participate in such activity at rituals.

Having to remove their clothes and be looked at or touched by the doctor can trigger memories of sexual assault in abused children. Ritually abused children may resist taking their clothes off in the doctor's office, for fear that they may be made to parade naked in front of others, to have pornographic pictures taken, or to be sexually assaulted. Some sexually or ritually abused children will behave seductively on the examining table, appearing to expect or "invite" sexual contact.

Given that many different aspects of a child's visit to the doctor may trigger memories of trauma, it is not surprising that ritually abused children often fear the doctor or the doctor's office. This fear may manifest in resistance to seeing the doctor, agitated behavior on the child's part, or evidence that the child is dissociating. The child may refer to the doctor as "bad" or otherwise convey mistrust of the doctor's motives. A child who discloses that at some time he or she received "bad shots," was made to drink blood, had clothes removed and experienced sexual contact with others, or was hurt by a "bad doctor" should be taken very seriously. Such disclosures strongly suggest that the child has been ritually abused.

Ritually victimized children may experience problems with certain colors. Cults differ in the colors they wear when engaged in abusive rituals, but the color most commonly worn is black. Red and purple are also worn frequently. Some cults wear white, brown, or orange. Ritually abused children are most likely to respond aversively to black. They may become fearful, agitated, negativistic, or dissociative in the presence of black. For some ritually abused children to establish a relationship of trust with the clinician, it is important that he or she not wear solid black clothes. These children may refuse to wear black as well. Ritually abused children who are more cult-identified may state that black is their favorite color. Under normal circumstances it is very unusual for young children to express a preference for black. Finally, the clinician should be attuned to any references made by the child to ritualistic uses of red or black that are inconsistent with what he or she would have experienced in a religious setting such as church.

Ritually abused children often develop one or more problems with eating. During the course of the ritual abuse, the child victim is typically made to ingest many extremely revolting substances, including excrement, urine, semen, blood, and body parts. Any child who discloses that he or she or someone else had to ingest any such substance should be taken very seriously. Foods that remind the child of such trauma are likely to provoke rejection, agitation, or dissociation. The foods most commonly rejected by ritually victimized children are red drinks, which remind them of blood, and meat, which reminds them of human flesh. The mere anticipation of a meal causes some ritually abused children to become agitated or oppositional.

Ritually abused children are often told that the "potions" they are made to drink (which may have as ingredients blood, urine, and the like) will make them die. They may also be told by their perpetrators that their parents are trying to kill them by poisoning their food. For these reasons, some ritually abused children express fear that their food is poisoned, and may refuse to eat food cooked at home.

Because of the many traumas around eating ritually abused children endure, they frequently develop some form of eating disorder. Vomiting and food refusal are common sequelae of ritual victimization. In the course of their abuse, child victims are usually deprived of food and drink and told that they will be left to die of hunger and thirst. This trauma causes some ritually victimized children to become compulsive overeaters, who binge or gorge.

Ritually abused children often suffer from emotional problems of some kind. Throwing tantrums and acting-out are common expressions of rage in the ritually victimized child; they may also reflect the indoctrination to behave in an antisocial manner that the child has received from the cult. These children may resist the authority of parents and teachers, both because their trust in adults has been seriously violated and because they have been indoctrinated to reject legitimate authority in favor of the dictates of the cult.

The angry episodes characterizing the ritually abused child are often distinguishable by their sudden onset and surprising degree of intensity. The child may make threats to kill or otherwise physically harm the person at whom he or she is angry. Physical attacks by the ritual abuse victim are also common, and may do a degree of damage to the object of the attack, which suggests that the child has actually received training in how to hurt a person. Because of the agitated behaviors and sudden outbursts they may exhibit, in conjunction with the attentional deficits characteristic of dissociative children, ritually abused children are sometimes misdiagnosed as hyperactive and medicated accordingly. This diagnostic error may have particularly grave psychological consequences for a child who has suffered extreme trauma in connection with the drugs he or she has been forced to take in ritual abuse situations.

Ritually abused children may display marked anxiety in the form of rocking, nail biting, teeth grinding, and the like. They are often fearful, withdrawn, clingy, or regressed in their behavior. They frequently turn their anger inward, blaming themselves not only for the bad things that have been done to them, but also for the horrendous crimes they have been made to commit against others. Shame and guilt may cause the ritually abused child to feel bad, ugly, stupid, and deserving of punishment, qualities which the cult has attributed to the child as well in an attempt to undermine his or her self-esteem. Self-blame coupled with indoctrination by the cult to self-abuse should the child fail to comply with cult demands may result in hurting him or herself in ways that seem more deliberate than accidental. If such incidents become frequent, the child may be considered accident-prone.

Ritually abused children may develop a variety of speech disorders in response to their abuse. The quality and quantity of the child's speech may regress as part of an overall regression resulting from the extreme abuse which he or she has suffered. In addition, the child's speech may become delayed or regressed as a way to cope with the cult's prohibitions against telling what has happened to him or her. Some ritually abused children become unintelligible or mute as a way to protect the secret they believe must be kept in order to safeguard them and their family's safety.

Ritually abused children often develop problems having to do with going to bed and sleeping. They may resist letting down their defenses to sleep out of fear of having nightmares or night terrors of their abuse. They have usually been told that their perpetrators will come in the night to kill them or take them for rituals or that evil spirits will come at night to abuse them, so they may try to stay awake to guard against this happening.

The ritually abused child may exhibit "flat" affect and fail to respond to people and events in appropriate ways. These children often do not cry when hurt, nor do they express joyful excitement when they receive a special gift. Such emotional inhibition is partly a function of dissociation. The severely traumatized child tends to dissociate not only what happened, but the emotions connected with the events as well. When the abuse is especially severe or protracted, the child may experience a blunting of emotions even about things that have nothing to do with the abuse. Ritually abused children's emotional expressions are affected not only by trauma and dissociation, but also by cult punishments for emotional displays. The cult teaches all prospective members to respond stoically to even the most horrific abuses.

Ritually abused children often exhibit attentional deficits that may result in learning problems. So many of the child's internal resources are required to maintain amnestic barriers against memories of the abuse that often the child lacks the resources necessary for attention and learning. The cult teaches the child to live in two worlds simultaneously, the everyday world and the ritual world. Living this "double life" also takes its toll on the child's energies and may make learning difficult. Finally, a significant (though as yet undetermined) percentage of ritual abuse victims have multiple personality disorders. Learning and academic performance problems arise for MPD children when only one or a few alter personalities attend to the material in school. Incomplete learning and erratic performance often result.

Ritually abused children experience a whole range of problems associated with family relationships. In abusive situations taking place outside of the home and family, cult members work to make the child believe that he or she belongs to them by undermining that child's bond with his or her parents. The child is terrorized with threats to the parents' lives. He or she is told that they will die, be killed, or abandon the child. Children are told that they will be kidnapped or otherwise separated from their parents, and made to live with members of the cult instead. Because of this well-orchestrated assault on the child's faith in the parents' ability to care for or protect him or her, that child may distance itself emotionally from parents perceived as untrustworthy or undependable. Ritually abused children may express fears that their parents will die, be killed, or abandon them. They may express fears that they will be kidnapped. They may experience intense separation anxiety, clinging to their parents not only out of fear that cult members will get the child if the parents are not present to protect him or her, but also out of fear that bad people will do away with the parents, and the child will never see them again. The cult often makes similar threats against siblings and pets, causing some ritually abused children to express fears that a sibling or pet will be killed, kidnapped, or molested.

Ritual abusers seek not only to undermine their young victims' faith in their parents' ability to protect and care for them, they also make the children feel that their parents represent an endangerment to them. It is quite typical for cult members to dress up like the parents and abuse a child who is so drugged and terrorized that he or she can be convinced that the assault is actually being perpetrated by the parents. Young victims are often told that the parents no longer love them, are angry and wish to punish them, or are trying to kill them. As a result, ritually abused children may express fears of being unloved, brutally punished, or even killed by parents who are in fact quite loving and nonabusive. They may avoid close physical contact with their parents because the cult has succeeded in making the children afraid of them. They may "screen out" what their parents say, as a way of distancing from parents who seem unsafe or unreliable, and whose authority the cult has taught them to resist.

Ritually abused children may become excessively angry when told what to do by the parents, or when the parents do not allow them to do what they want. They may respond by telling parents that they hate them or want to kill them, and in some cases will physically attack parents and even try to kill them. These responses to parental authority represent more than the young victims' rage at their abusers displaced onto the parents. Such responses may also constitute the enactment of programming implemented by the cult, in which the child has been instructed (under the mind-altering conditions of drugging, pain, terror, and hypnotic suggestion) to release rage originally induced by cult abuse onto the parents when they attempt to exercise authority over the child. Angry, violent responses to parental authority on the part of the child contribute to the breakdown of the bond between parent and child.

As the bond between parent and child erodes, the cult attempts to firm up the child's allegiance to its members. A female cult member will often tell the child that she, not the child's mother, is the "real" mother. In this fashion the child who is ritually abused outside of the family will be taught that his or her real mother, real father, and real family are among the cult members. Therefore, when a child with a possible history of ritual victimization discloses an abusive incident by his or her mother or father, it behooves the evaluator to gain clarification about who the child is referring to. Similarly, a child who talks about his or her "other mommy," "other daddy," or "other family" may be referring to cult members who are in fact that child's perpetrators.

Any child who states that someone said that his or her parents would die, be killed, abandon, or try to hurt the child should be taken very seriously and evaluated for possible history of ritual abuse. Any child who states that someone said that he or she would be kidnapped should be similarly evaluated. Any child who violently attacks, initiates sexual contact with, confines, puts excrement on or threatens a parent, sibling, or pet should also be evaluated for a possible history of ritual abuse.

Ritually abused children experience problems with play and peer relationships. Because they have been taught by their abusers to behave destructively, ritually victimized children often destroy toys. Their play and drawings frequently contain themes of ritual abuse—death, mutilation, cannibalism, burial, drugging, threats, humiliation, torture, bondage, magic, and various ceremonies with occult overtones. Their play and drawings have bizarre, occult, sexual, or excretory overtones. Themes in the child's play are often the evaluator's best clues whether or not the child has been ritually abused.

Some ritually victimized children will engage immediately in play that expresses their ritual abuse. Others, however, will resist play altogether, because unconsciously they fear divulging the secret of their abuse, even in such an indirect fashion. It is the evaluator's responsibility in such cases to get the child to play, by providing appealing toys, structuring the play in a way that will draw the child out, or using rewards. Rewards should be used to induce the child to engage in the process of symbolizing his or her experience through play and other creative productions. As long as rewards are given for process and not content, the clinician will not need to worry that the child is being led to give responses that do not accurately reflect his or her experiences.

Still other children will draw or play, but in an overly conventional or stereotyped fashion. A highly defended ritually abused child may, for example, wish to draw nothing but hearts and rainbows in the clinical setting. It is the clinician's responsibility when evaluating such a child to intervene in this defensive presentation, using rewards or other inducements to get the child to symbolize in a less defended manner. Play that is truly reflective of the child's emotional condition will vary and deepen from one session to the next. It will involve elements of motivation, affect, action, and human or anthropomorphized figures of some kind. Children who have great difficulty symbolizing through play will need the clinician to actively involve him or herself in the process with the child. For example, the clinician can draw a picture that the child receives a reward for finishing. Or, the clinician makes a "snowman" figure out of clay with a facial expression reflective of an affect frequently experienced by the child, and asks the child a series of questions about what the snowman feels and why. The ability to symbolize through play and other creative productions will prove vital to the diagnosis and especially the treatment of the ritually abused child. It therefore behooves the clinician to spend a good deal of energy developing and nurturing the child's capacities in this area.

The tendency of ritually abused children to act out in a physically or sexually aggressive fashion with their peers has already been discussed. Often ritually abused children are exceedingly controlling with other children as well. Such domineering behavior represents an attempt to repair the effects of extreme loss of control that they suffered in connection with the ritual abuse.

Frequently, ritually abused children talk to or state that they have one or more "imaginary friends." This can be a symptom of multiple personality disorder in children (even when their abuse history does not contain ritual elements) who often characterize alter personalities as "friends" or "people who live inside of them." Ritually abused children's imaginary friends have usually been created deliberately by the cult as part of the process of indoctrinating the child into cult membership. These alter personalities may be perceived by the host personality of the child as people who belong to the cult or believe in its doctrines, or as spiritual entities possessing occult or satanic characteristics. The child may describe a perceived spiritual entity as a "spirit friend" or "spirit guide." He or she is likely to have a ritualized way of calling upon the perceived spiritual entity for help in carrying out cult directives.

Ritually abused children may exhibit a variety of other fears or strange beliefs, or make unusual references. Characteristically, ritually victimized children fear the police will come to put them in jail, or state that they have been hurt or threatened by a "bad policeman." Sometime in the course of the ritual abuse and indoctrination, a cult member may dress up like a police officer and abuse the child, threatening to put the child in jail if he or she should ever disclose the abuse to anyone. The reasons for this are twofold. First, the perpetrators attempt to destroy within the child any hope of being rescued from the cult's control. Since children look to police officers and parents to provide protection, cult members devote a good deal of attention to convincing their young victims that these sources of security are untrustworthy. Children who come to believe there is no one to whom they can turn for protection from their abusers are more likely to bond to the cult and adopt its belief in the desirability and inevitability of coercive control and violence. Second, by having a "bad policeman" abuse the victim, the cult seeks to prevent a child whose amnestic barriers against memories of the abuse have failed from making disclosures to police officers. Because of indoctrination to make the child believe that the police are secretly working for the cult, many children who are able to recover memories of their abuse and make disclosures to their therapists are nonetheless unable to disclose to the officer who is investigating the case. Many investigations of ritual child abuse break down for this reason. A good deal of therapeutic work is often required for children to be able to disclose ritual abuse to a police officer.

Ritually victimized children often exhibit fear of aggressive animals or poisonous insects. Ritually abusive cults often use frightening animals or insects to further terrorize the victim. Snakes, large dogs, and insects that the child is told are poisonous are commonly used against the child. In addition, children may be threatened with harm by animals they never actually see. For example, cult members may tell them they will be thrown to a school of sharks or fed to lions if they fail to internalize cult teachings.

Ritually abused children commonly fear that their house will be broken into, robbed, or burned down. One of the ways in which ritual perpetrators indoctrinate their victims into the belief that there is no way in which they can be protected from the cult's control is to convince them that the house in which they live is vulnerable to intrusion or attack. Thus, ritually abused children are often told that cult members will break into their house, rob the family, kidnap the child, or burn the house down. Some ritually victimized children become so fearful of intrusions into or assaults on the house that they ask the parents to move the family to a new location.

Ritually victimized children may refer to "bad people," "robbers," or "strangers" when discussing their perpetrators. Ritual abusers sometimes use this or similar terminology when referring to themselves, causing their young victims to refer to them in the same way. Because these children have often been told that cult members spy on them continually, they may watch out the window for bad people to walk or drive by. During the course of their abuse, young victims are often given disinformation about how to recognize a cult member. They may be told that any man wearing a blue jacket, or anyone driving a red or black car is a member of the cult. Since there are many men in blue jackets and many red and black cars on the road, children who have been taught that these are signs of cult membership come to believe that the cult surrounds them and can indeed monitor their behavior at all times.

Ritually abused children may discuss unusual places such as cemeteries, mortuaries, or church basements, or appear irrationally afraid of such places. When cult members are able to arrange to keep their activities from becoming known to the authorities, these are preferred locations for rituals. Ritually victimized children may mention such places or express fear of them because they have been abused there.

Ritually victimized children may talk about pictures or films of nude people, and make references to sexual or violent acts, unusual costuming, or animal involvement in that context. They may fear having their pictures taken, or act out feelings of specialness associated with being the subjects of pornography by striking sexually provocative poses. Pornography is a very common component of child ritual abuse. Some of it is made for sale and profit, but much of it is used simply to humiliate and blackmail the child. Child pornography victims are commonly told that if they fail to comply with cult demands, pictures of them in compromising situations will be shown to their parents (if the abuse is extrafamilial) or to the police.

Ritually abused children may discuss drugs, pills, bad candy, alcohol, mushrooms, potions or other liquids, "bad medicine," or injections in a manner that is not normal or age-appropriate. They may refer to drug or laxative effects, or may state they have been given a substance. Drugging of the child comprises a virtually ubiquitous aspect of ritual abuse, and serves many functions within the cult. Most important, drugs are administered that have particular mind-altering properties. They cause the child to dissociate in such a way that the cult member charged with that child's cult training can effectively compartmentalize the indoctrinating experiences. Feelings associated with the abuse will be reposited in one dissociated part of the child (or alter personality), information about cult beliefs and practices in another part, physical pain in another, and so forth. Such compartmentalization makes retrieval of memories by the child exceedingly difficult because drug-induced amnestic barriers exist not only between the child's conscious awareness and each part of the memory, but also between the memory fragments themselves. Because ritually victimized children usually cannot access memories of their abuse, they often cannot disclose their victimization and thus be rescued from it.

The compartmentalization of memories of abuse and indoctrination made possible by the use of particular drugs also contributes to the control the cult is able to achieve over the young victim's mind and behavior. The victim is typically programmed to have a certain word, color, name, piece of music, hand signal, series of taps, or voice elicit a particular memory fragment. Thus, by knowing just where within the cult-created internal system each memory fragment is reposited and how it can be accessed, the cult can call up particular dissociated bits of memory and indoctrinated parts of the personality—one of which receives the telephone message about an upcoming ritual, another decodes the message to understand where to go to attend the meeting, another puts on the requisite ritual costume, another takes the drug that is administered before the ritual begins, and so forth.

Children who have been drugged during the course of ritual abuse and indoctrination will sometimes show behavioral signs of their condition when they are returned from the abusive setting. Evaluators should routinely ask parents or other informants whether the child's eyes have ever appeared unusually glazed, and whether the pupils were ever observed to be abnormally dilated or constricted. A child who is difficult to rouse and seems to sleep excessively upon return from a particular setting may be sleeping off drug effects. Children should also be asked whether they have ever been given any pills, drugs, "bad medicine," or the like. Whereas memories of abusive activities that take place after the drugging has occurred are often very difficult for the child to retrieve because of the dissociative properties of the drugs used, the drugging itself usually takes place when the child is still in a normal state of consciousness and is therefore the aspect of the abuse that the child is most likely to be able to recall. Careful questioning can be done after trust has been established, with the clear understanding of the part of the evaluator that even if the young ritual abuse victim does recall an aspect of the abuse such as drugging, he or she is no doubt terrorized by the prospect of cult retaliation if disclosure is made.

Finally, many cults give drugs that have laxative effects, so that excrement can be made available to use for ritualistic defilement of the child. Ritually abused children may refer to pills, "bad candy," or some other substance that was given to make them defecate.

Ritually abused children often fear the sight of their own blood. They may become hysterical over even a small scrape that bleeds, and feel that they are dying. Bleeding may remind ritually abused children of cult victims who were mutilated and killed in a bloody and horrifying way. It may also remind them of their own physical vulnerability and the death threats made to them by their perpetrators. Ritually abused children may respond to violent movies or television programs with a similarly excessive degree of fear, because such shows tap into dissociated memories of cult violence.

Ritually abused children experience many somatic complaints, the most common of which is stomach pain. In part, these complaints can be understood in the conventional sense of a child who "somatizes" an abusive event by experiencing it as a body pain in order to defend against awareness of the memory and the emotional pain associated with that memory. However, the somatic complaints of ritually abused children have other causes as well. These children have endured nearly intolerable pain to various parts of their bodies, often administered by electric shock or some other means that leaves no obvious physical signs. What appear to be physical complaints with no medical basis may in fact be body memories of severe physical abuse. Such physical abuse is not perpetrated randomly by the cult, but is incorporated systematically into the cult-created dissociative internal system of the victim. The traumatized stomach for example, will become the repository not only of the physical pain it has endured, but of a particular aspect of cult indoctrination. If, in conjunction with the pain administered to the stomach, the child is told that a bomb has been placed in his stomach and will go off if he remembers the abuse, the stomach aches he subsequently endures become constant unconscious reminders to him that he must never recall or disclose his victimization.

Ritually abused children often suffer from extreme fatigue. If the abuse is ongoing, the fatigue reflects drug effects and the children's efforts to recover from the physical and emotional traumas to which they are continually subjected. If the abuse is in the past, many recovering children exhibit deep fatigue as they recontact experiences of abuse that took a great physical and psychological toll on them. Enormous psychological resources are required both to maintain amnestic barriers against memories of the abuse, and to disassemble those barriers. Thus, children with a past history of ritual abuse may suffer from exhaustion whether they are amnesiac to their abuse or are dealing with their memories.

Ritually abused children often suffer from allergies and illnesses as well, particularly when the abuse is ongoing. These children are made to ingest a variety of drugs as well as excrement, urine, and human and animal blood and flesh, among other substances. It is not surprising that they often become ill or develop allergies, both in response to the substances ingested and to the overwhelming stress engendered by the abuse.

Although most of the physical and sexual assault perpetrated on children during the course of ritual abuse leave no physical evidence, occasionally the abuse will leave marks. One of the more common forms of physical evidence of ritual abuse is bruising. Sometimes the child will be bruised in a deliberately patterned way which has some kind of ritual significance. Another kind of physical evidence of ritual abuse that is sometimes seen in rope burns. Children who have been suspended by one or both wrists or ankles may show rope burns on those parts of their bodies.

In order to effectively diagnose ritual abuse, the evaluator must be skilled at developing rapport with children and their families. He or she must employ appealing, therapeutically relevant toys in a manner that maximizes the quality and quantity of projective material generated by the child. The evaluator must have a strong background in normal childhood development as well as a clear understanding of the effects of trauma on children in order to accurately interpret the material the child produces. He or she should also know a good deal about dissociative responses to overwhelming trauma in childhood. Even with such a substantial base of understanding, the clinician who is called upon to evaluate a ritually abused child for the first time will have to make a significant "paradigm shift" to understand the context of dissociation, mind control, and negative spirituality in which the child's symptoms and clinical material present. The clinician facing his or her first case of ritual abuse should seek consultation from a colleague who is experienced in the evaluation and treatment of ritually abused children.

Treatment

A good beginning for a presentation of the treatment of ritually abused children is a brief discussion of some of the misconceptions about psychotherapy with this admittedly difficult population. Many therapists seem to have fallen prey to the notion that disclosure of the particulars of the abuse constitutes the bulk of the child's healing process. Since most therapists who treat abused children also treat adults who were abused as children, they know the working through of the feelings and attitudes associated with the abuse is at least as crucial for their adult patients' recovery as is the surfacing of memory content. But when therapists attempt to help their child patients work through feelings and attitudes associated with the abuse by trying to develop the kind of dialogue they would have with their adult patients, they often make little progress. Not knowing how else to achieve the working through with their young patients except by trying to elicit a style of talk therapy in which these children are often too young to engage, many therapists conclude that they must settle for a less ambitious treatment that focuses primarily on disclosure.

Conversely, many therapists feel that a child who is known or suspected to have been abused (ritually or otherwise) is not engaged in a significant process of recovery if he or she is not making disclosures of the abuse. Treatments of abused children that do not lead to disclosure are often terminated, or allowed to lapse into perennial "relationship building" with the therapist, in which the therapist allows the child to select most or all of the session's activities whether or not they are therapeutically relevant. This "child-centered" approach to treatment is usually predicated on the notion that if the child is able to build a trusting relationship with the therapist, he or she will eventually disclose any history of abuse. Therapists are frequently disappointed when, after many sessions spent with the child in this manner, no disclosures of the abuse are made.

In order to successfully treat child victims of ritual abuse, it is imperative that the therapist master play-therapy modalities. Play therapy allows severely abused children to symbolize their victimization in powerfully healing ways. Children who are able to disclose part or most of their abuse still face the extremely challenging task of working through the feelings and attitudes engendered by that abuse. Play therapy constitutes the primary mechanism by which such working through occurs for children who have not yet reached puberty. Even children who are never able to consciously recall or disclose their abuse can achieve a great deal of recovery through skillfully conducted play therapy. The nondisclosing child's recovery grows out of therapeutic work in which the events, feelings, and beliefs associated with the abuse are brought to preconscious awareness and worked through in the context of the child's play.

Therapists treating their first case of child ritual abuse should seek consultation on the case, regardless of how much prior experience they have had treating child victims of other forms of abuse. There are several reasons why the treatment of ritually abused children is so much more difficult and complex that the treatment of children who have been abused in other ways. Chief among these is the fact that the dissociative barriers against awareness of the abusive events are extremely difficult to penetrate. Unless the events, feelings, and perceptions associated with the abuse can be accessed (i.e., either consciously remembered or preconsciously represented through the symbolization of play) little recovery will be made. Because ritual abuse frequently constitutes such a massive victimization, the therapist is confronted at every stage of the ritually abused child's treatment with uncertainty about how much of the abuse and its sequelae may still remain behind amnestic barriers. It is very difficult for the therapist to ascertain how much of the child's abuse has surfaced and been dealt with at any given point in treatment because he or she cannot be sure what or how much material remains dissociated. There is a tendency to terminate treatment when the child stops remembering new material, when the child's level of adjustment has improved a certain amount, or when the child or parents (or the therapist) tires of the treatment process.

When a ritually abused child's therapy is terminated before most or all of the abuse has been brought to conscious or preconscious awareness and worked through, that child is gravely at risk. Among the risks to the incompletely recovered child are those with which therapists experienced in the treatment of adults abused as children are familiar—depression and suicidality, drug abuse and alcoholism, violent and sexual acting-out against others (including children), to name only some of the long-term sequelae of childhood abuse. Ritually abused children, and the adults they eventually become, suffer not only from these incidental effects of extreme abuse in childhood, they also suffer from the effects intended by the cults that abused them. As was discussed in an earlier section of this chapter, ritual child abuse is intended to undermine the victim's free will to such an extent that the cult can establish control over that individual for its own purposes, and exploit him or her over the course of a lifetime. The physical, sexual, emotional, and spiritual abuse of the ritually abused child merely comprises the foundation upon which the cult builds the structure of mind control that is its true purpose.

When the treatment of the ritually abused child fails, or is terminated prematurely, that child may remain vulnerable to cult recontact and revictimization, in adulthood if not before. We know from adult survivors that once the mind control is in place, the child or adult can go on being cult-involved (both victimized by and perpetrating on behalf of the cult) with little or no conscious awareness of that involvement. Thus, the unrecovered ritually abused child is at risk for developing a cult-involved dissociative disorder. Victimization thus compounds tragically over time, as the child participates, often without conscious awareness or the exercise of free will, in murder, child sexual assault, and other forms of perpetration typically engaged in by members of satanic and other similar kinds of cults.

In order to be successful, treatment must address not only the whole complex of the post-traumatic stress disorder that results from the child's ritual abuse, but the mind control as well. Mind control of the victim is established bit by bit each time that abuse is inflicted. Each abusive ritual is designed to create a degree of pain, terror, and trauma intolerable to the child, so that he or she will dissociate in response to it. Cult members who possess the skill to be "trainers" are then able to manipulate the child's dissociative response to intolerable pain, terror, and trauma in such a way that a dissociated part of the child is created which is imbued with a particular function in relationship to the cult.

For example, the child will be drugged, terrorized, physically and sexually tortured, and made to witness or participate in the perpetration of similar abuse of someone else, all of which combine to create an altered state of consciousness in which he or she dissociates and becomes willing to do, think, or believe anything that will cause the pain to stop. A hypnotic induction may then be used to deepen the victim's psychological openness to directions from the trainer.

When the child is maximally dissociated and vulnerable to psychological manipulation, the trainer will instruct the child in how to split off a new part of him or herself and the role which that part will play. Instructions are given on how that part will be accessed by the cult. Often the part is given a name so that "he" or "she" can be called out by the cult at will. The part may also be reposited in a particular place within the child's body, and can be called out by touching that place on the body while other prespecified cues are given simultaneously.

It is hoped that this brief description of the extremely complex process of achieving mind control over the ritual abuse victim will help the reader to understand what is involved in treating a child who has been victimized in this manner. Not only must the victim's post-traumatic stress disorder be treated, the dissociative psychic structure created by the cult to establish control over the child must be surfaced and treated as well. It should be acknowledged at this point in our discussion that the model for the treatment of ritual abuse presented here is certainly incomplete, and will no doubt be expanded and abridged as we gain more experience treating ritually abused children. For the moment, I propose a three-part treatment model. First, the ritually abused child's post-traumatic stress disorder must be treated through a combination of disclosure and abreactive play therapy. Second, the dissociative internal system must be identified and worked with. Third, the indoctrinating messages given to the child during the dissociation-producing abusive rituals must be surfaced and worked through.

The treatment of the child's post-traumatic stress disorder has already received some discussion. Most of the work in this area of recovery will be done through play therapy structured by the therapist to help the child abreact as much of the trauma associated with each abusive incident as possible. Braun's (1985) BASK model should be born in mind when the therapist is engaged in play therapy with the ritually abused child. The "B" stands for "behavior," or what happened during the abuse. The therapist structures the therapeutic work in such a fashion that the child is able to represent through play what it was that happened to him or her. Therapists who treat ritually abused children often discover the need for a wider variety of toys than they previously found necessary. The better the toys symbolize the ritually abusive situation, the more effective the child is likely to be in representing the abuse through play. Cages and coffins, ropes, knives and guns, policemen and police cars, doctor kits with medicine bottles and syringes, figures of insects and aggressive animals, toy cameras, chalices, crucifixes, pots for potions, and occult type figures such as witches, devils, monsters, and the like all constitute equipment important for ritually abused children to have available as they attempt to act-out through play the things that happened to them.

The "A" in BASK stands for affect, or what the child felt emotionally during the abuse. The therapist may inquire what the little character who is the victim of the abuse in the play is feeling as the abusive situation is being reenacted by the child. Many ritually victimized children play out horrificly abusive scenarios with no overt expression of affect or agitation, because the emotional component of the experience is dissociated. Sometimes inquiry about the character's feelings will begin the vitally important process of reuniting the affective component of the experience with the events themselves, but usually the therapist must help to provide expressions of affect as the child plays out the abuse. This should be done in a way that reflects how children actually express themselves. For example, as the child is locking the little character in jail and telling her that she will never be allowed to come out, the therapist may loudly protest being locked up, by saying something like "Stop it! I hate being locked in here. It is really dark and scary! I want my mom! Let me out of here!" This naturalistic expression of emotions is more genuinely abreactive for the child and thus more healing than the conventional practice of "talking about" the character (or child) feeling sad, angry, or lonely.

Therapists who employ this technique of providing expressions of affect within the context of the play often find that as the link between affect and cognition is reestablished, the child comes in contact with more pieces of the memory and extends the play therapy scene accordingly. As the therapist protests on behalf of the character who is being locked up, for example, the child may introduce a policeman who threatens to put the child in jail forever if she ever divulges the abuse. For both adult and child survivors of ritual abuse, recovery often involves this kind of step by step process of retrieving part of a memory of an abusive event, and experiencing the emotions connected with the event that had to be dissociated at the time it actually occurred in order to survive it. Once this link between the partial memory and the affective response has been made, another piece of the memory can surface. A purely cognitive acknowledgment of how the abuse felt is not usually sufficient to integrate the dissociative split between the event and the victim's emotional response to it. The affect must be experienced and expressed for deep healing to occur. Ritually abused children do not seem to be able to recall and abreact their experiences of abuse the way adult survivors can. They have a tremendous capacity to symbolize the abusive events in their play, but they usually require active participation by the therapist in the manner described above to integrate their dissociated emotional responses.

The "S" in BASK stands for sensation. In order to heal as completely as possible, the ritual abuse survivor must surface, identify, and experience the body trauma caused by the abuse. Body memories are most productively resolved when they are experienced in the context of events and affects within which the trauma to the body originally occurred. When ritually abused children act out their victimization through play, they usually dissociate the body trauma component of the memories. For example, the character will be pummeled, strangled, or even killed in the course of the play, and the child will never have him moan, scream, or express any signs of experiencing physical pain. The therapist will usually need to fill in this gap for the child. The therapist does this by having the abused character say something like "Ouch! That hurts! My leg is really hurting! Stop it! Stop it!!" These expressions of physical suffering should be as genuinely representative as possible of how children normally respond to overwhelming physical pain.

During the course of therapy, ritually abused children who are working through their body memories are likely to experience physical symptoms some might consider psychosomatic. It behooves the therapist to interpret these aches and pains to the child and the child's parents (assuming the abuse was extrafamilial) as signs that the child is working very hard in therapy and that his or her body is remembering the bad and painful things that happened to it. The parents can be appraised that a child who is undergoing body memories of sexual assault may begin to masturbate compulsively or publicly, and will need extra support from the parents to know that this confusing upsurge of sexual feelings does not mean that he or she is no longer loved by them. The therapist can help the parents assist the child in containing the sexual feelings in ways that are appropriate and do not involve sexual acting-out against other children.

The "K" in BASK stands for knowledge, or the meaning of the abusive event to the child and to the perpetrator. The therapist can participate in the child's play in such a way that the reasons for the abuse are elucidated for the child and pathological attitudes engendered by it are corrected. For example, the child whose therapeutic work includes having the character who represents the child put in jail can be told by the therapist, "Wait a minute! Children don't go to jail. No matter what they do, children cannot be put in jail." The corollary belief, that the child is responsible for the crimes that cult members forced him or her to commit, needs to be addressed as well. The therapist can ask questions such as, "If bad grown-ups make a child do bad things, whose fault is it? Is it the child's fault or the grown-up's fault?" The child should be given opportunities to hear therapeutic messages and answer therapeutic questions such as these repeatedly and in a variety of contexts. Repeated discussion of the fact that the child is not responsible for the evil acts he or she was made to commit, and that young children are not jailed for committing crimes, can go a long way toward reducing the ritually abused child's guilt and terror. As the child comes to understand that blame and punishment will not ensue from the discovery of what he or she has done in the context of cult activity, the groundwork is laid for that child to feel safe enough to disclose his or her ritual abuse.

Other messages typically communicated to children by ritually abusing cults, and which the therapist needs to address both in and out of the context of the play therapy, include the following. "You are bad, ugly, stupid, etc." should be rebutted by the therapist and parents not only by telling the child that he or she is good, attractive, and smart. In the context of the play, the therapist should also confront the perpetrating figures with their motives for undermining the child's self-esteem. The therapist can say something like, "You just want me to think I'm bad so I will be on your team and help you do bad things. Well I am not bad! And I don't want to be on your team!"

At the same time that the therapist joins the play therapy to expose the motivations of the perpetrators and to help the child defiantly reject their attempts to entrap him or her into cult membership, the therapist must be careful to address both sides of the child's ambivalence about belonging to the cult. While ritual abuse is painful, humiliating, terrorizing, and guilt-inducing, the child is also likely to have experienced intense feelings of specialness and empowerment during his or her involvement with the cult. To successfully treat ritually abused children, the therapist must be able to genuinely appreciate the attraction that the cult can hold, and to articulate that attraction within the context of the play therapy. For example, when the bad people in the play come to take the child character to a cult meeting, the therapist may want to have the child character say something like, "I must be very special that they want me to go with them! And I'm only four years old. Maybe they'll let me hold the sword this time and do things with it. All the grown-ups will watch and tell me I am great!" Another character can be introduced to present the opposing viewpoint, saying something to the child character like, "But they'll make you hurt somebody with the sword! You don't want to hurt anybody. There's nothing special about that."

Other cult-created beliefs the therapist needs to address repeatedly with the child both in and out of the context of the play therapy include the idea that the parents wish to harm the child and that the "true" parents are cult members; the notion that the child's parents will soon be killed by the cult or will otherwise abandon him or her; the idea that the parents are angry with the child because of the bad things he or she has done, no longer love the child and plan to punish him or her; the notion that the parents know about and approved the child's abuse by the cult; the idea that the parents are secretly cult members also; the idea that there are large numbers of cult members and their spiritual counterparts who surround the child and monitor his or her every move; the notion that the child and his or her family are powerless to stay safe from cult members and their spiritual counterparts; the idea that because the child has taken part in ceremonies intended to make him or her a cult member who worships the cult's deity and carries out cult commands, the child has no choice but to continue to belong to the cult and worship Satan (or a similar deity); the idea that only Satan could love the child after the things he or she has done; the notion that the cult is strong and the parents are weak, or that Satan is strong and God is weak; the idea that a spiritual entity lives inside the child and forces him or her to carry out the wishes of Satan and the cult; the notion that if memories of the abuse begin to surface, the child must hurt himself; the idea that the cult will know if the child discloses the abuse and will harm the child or the family in retaliation for disclosing.

The distinction between cult-created beliefs and actual programming is not an easy one for the therapist to make. One of the signs that the therapist is dealing with a program is that it is relatively impervious to the kinds of therapeutic intervention described above. For example, the point in therapy may be reached where the child understands many of the ways in which he or she was tricked into feeling that cult membership was unavoidable, and through the therapy the child has come to believe that everyone should have choices about groups to which they belong. Yet the therapist discovers that the child still believes that if someone tapped on the bedroom window in a particular way, he or she would have to go with whoever delivered this signal.

When the therapist discovers that there is a program in place, he or she must structure the play therapy in such a way that the child is able to reenact and abreact the entire set of conditions under which the program was created. Drugging, terror, physical pain, humiliation, and hypnotic induction are all likely to be components of the programming scenario. Once the child can recall through play the entire constellation of abuse that set the stage for the programming to take place, the therapist must ask for "the words which were said" by the trainer or programmer. The child provides the words which the bad character in the play says to the child character. These words may be in the form of a chant or rhyme. It is important that the therapist write these words down verbatim, so that they can be processed and discussed both in and out of the play therapy context. As this material is worked on over time, the therapist can ascertain the degree to which the child has been freed from the programming by asking whether the child character in the play is now able to maintain conscious awareness when he or she is triggered, and whether or not that character can resist responding to the trigger. The therapist should help the child understand that factors such as stress, fear, hunger, fatigue, and the like may affect the character's and the child's ability to resist responding to a programmed trigger.

It is not known what percentage of ritually abused children have multiple personality disorders, or how many hours or days of ritual abuse are required to split the child in such a way that multiple personality disorder will result. It is clear that some significant percentage of children ritually abused in out-of-home settings suffer at least from incipient multiple personality disorder. Therapy that does not address the child's dissociative internal system and the programming associated with it may improve the child's level of functioning, but will leave him or her vulnerable to recontact and ongoing exploitation by the cult.

Play therapy can be adapted to explore possible multiplicity within the ritually abused child. For example, the therapist can draw a snowman and ask the child whether the snowman had another snowman inside him or her. The name, age, feelings, and functions of this "other snowman" can be explored if the child says that the snowman does indeed have somebody else inside. The child should be encouraged to show where in the snowman's body the other snowman lives. Over time, the internal system of the child who turns out to be multiple can be mapped using techniques such as this one.

As alter personalities are discovered within the child, their memories can be explored and worked on. The therapist and child can work together on a map that shows what each alter remembers of the abuse. Issues of co-consciousness and cooperation between alters are especially important. The relationship that each alter has with the parents, the therapist, and various cult members also constitute important therapeutic issues. The therapist will usually discover that some of the cult-created alters do not relate to the child's mother as their mother. In fact, these cult alters may not even know who the parents are because they have only been "out" at rituals. It behooves the therapist to work on the relationship between each of the alters and the parents. It is also important that each alter develop a relationship with the therapist, and understand that the therapist considers all of the alters important to the internal system as well as to the process of recovery. Integration of alters should not be attempted until their memories and programming have been thoroughly abreacted and worked through.

It is very important that the ritual abuse victim's family also receive treatment. Some family members of the child who is the victim of extrafamilial ritual abuse may require individual treatment. Whether or not these family members exhibited psychopathology prior to the occurrence of the abuse, the impact of the abuse on the family is so great that one or more of its members is likely to need help coping with it. The mother, or whoever in the family is the child's primary caretaker, is likely to be the most profoundly affected and therefore to have the greatest need for therapeutic support. The child's therapist will rely upon her heavily to make weekly reports about the child's behavior at home, as well as to receive disclosures and symbolic material that the child has shared with the therapist. Mothers of ritual abuse victims often need help integrating their awareness of the abuses to which their children have been subjected. As the mother works through her denial of what has happened to her child, the child is able to accept his or her own memories of the abuse as real. To the extent that the parents deny or dissociate awareness of their child's abuse, the child's recovery process is delayed and undermined.

The parents, and especially the mother, not only need to achieve a cognitive understanding of what has happened to their child, they need to experience and express the emotions parents feel when their child is violated. Rage and grief are chief among these emotional responses, and the ability of the parents to experience and express them will to a large extent determine the degree to which the ritually abused child will be able to heal the dissociative split between memories of the abusive events and the emotions associated with them. During the course of the ritually abused child's treatment, the parents will also need to learn about the many cognitive, emotional, and spiritual sequelae in which the abuse has resulted for the child. Most parents require therapeutic support to deal effectively with, for example, the belief on their child's part that they knew about the abuse before they enrolled their child in the abusive preschool, or the belief that they are secretly planning to murder the child.

It is my experience that handling the parents' process of working through their denial of experiencing and expressing rage and grief over the massive victimization perpetrated against their child, and of sorting out the whole complex of attitudes and beliefs the abuse has engendered in their child, is too much for the therapist who is treating the child to cope with alone. To treat the ritually abused child effectively, the therapist must develop and maintain a deep appreciation of the extreme suffering the child has undergone in the course of the abuse. To effectively treat the parents of the ritually abused child, the therapist must be able to empathize with their denial of what has happened to the child, and even with their anger at the child for being a victim and making their role as parents so much more difficult than it would have been had the abuse not occurred. Many therapists may find that they are unable to function with maximal effectiveness as both the child's primary therapist and the therapist to the other family members.

When choosing someone to whom to refer one or more family members of the ritually abused child for treatment, it is important for the child's therapist to consider not only that clinician's qualifications for taking on such a complicated case, but also how effective the therapeutic collaboration between the two therapists is likely to be. It is important that the therapies involving the various family members be very well coordinated. It is also useful for the child's therapist to try to find a peer support group for the parents of the ritually abused child. Although the parents may be able to work through their guilt about having enrolled their child in an abusive preschool or day-care setting, they are nonetheless likely to feel inadequate and responsible when their child sexually assaults a younger sibling, or threatens to kill the parents, or suddenly starts failing in school. Contact with other parents who are dealing with similar behavioral problems can provide the parents with the support they need to handle these difficult situations effectively.

Termination of the child's therapy can begin to be considered when the therapist feels that most or all of the trauma associated with the abuse has been surfaced and dealt with through play therapy, cognitively, emotionally, sensorily, and in terms of the attitudes and beliefs engendered by it. The therapist who is considering termination of the child's treatment should feel confident that the child's internal dissociative structure has been explored and treated, and that the programming has been adequately dealt with as well. As we have discussed, it is not necessary that this work be done through talk therapy or that memories be consciously acknowledged. Play therapy is the most powerful modality for children's recovery from ritual abuse. Whereas the child's improved functioning is not sufficient reason to terminate the therapy, evidence that the child's play has become normal is an indicator that much healing from abuse has been achieved.

In summary, the child can heal through a combination of play therapy and disclosure of the abuse to the therapist and the parents (when the abuse is extrafamilial). The therapist must participate actively in child's treatment, structuring therapeutic activities and providing rewards that motivate the child to engage in psychotherapeutic work that he or she might otherwise avoid. All four components of each traumatic incident must be addressed and abreacted by the child in play therapy for maximal healing to occur. The child's therapeutic work must address not only what happened, but how it felt emotionally, what physical sensations accompanied the experience, and what messages were given to the child by the cult in conjunction with the experience.

Successful psychotherapy with child victims of ritual abuse includes not only treating all components of the trauma, but also identifying and healing the dissociative system the cult has deliberately created within the child. Some child ritual abuse victims will be found to suffer from multiple personality disorder. In such cases, various alter personalities are often programmed with a particular function that serves the purposes of the cult. When working with child victims of ritual abuse suffering from multiple personality disorder, the therapist must surface and work with each alter so that no part of the child remains under the control of the cult. After the programming has been undone, integration of alters can take place. Support and treatment for the family of the child victim of ritual abuse is also crucial to that child's recovery.

References

Braun, B.G. 1985. "Dissociation: Behavior, Affect, Sensation, Knowledge." In *Dissociative Disorders 1985: Proceedings of the Second International Conference on Multiple Personality/Dissociative States,* ed. by B. G. Braun, Chicago, Rush University.

Brown, Dee. 1990. "The Worship of Evil." Unpublished manuscript.

Finkelhor, David, L. Williams, and N. Burns. 1988. *Nursery Crimes: Sexual Abuse in Day Care.* Beverly Hills, Ca.: Sage.

Ritual Abuse Task Force, Los Angeles County Commission For Women. 1989. *Ritual Abuse: Definition, Glossary, and the Use of Mind Control.* Los Angeles, CA.

Young, W. C., R. G. Sachs, and B. G. Braun. 1988. "A New Clinical Syndrome: Patients Reporting Ritual Abuse in Childhood by Satanic Cults." Unpublished manuscript.

10

Recognition and Treatment of Survivors Reporting Ritual Abuse

Walter C. Young, M.D., F.A.P.A.

Introduction

The clinical tasks of recognizing and treating patients reporting ritual abuse are complicated for two reasons. First, patients reporting ritual abuse are exceedingly complex both in their presentations and in the treatment issues that they confront. Often they present with elaborate dissociative defenses that prevent access to memories and experiences. Further, the unfolding process of treatment often results in extreme hyperreactivity or emotional withdrawal. Emerging memories of abuse are often so severe that they may activate abreactions in which the patient experiences behavioral, affective, and cognitive recall of events with such vivid intensity that she may become suicidal, dangerous, or decompensated.[1] The emergence of "forbidden" material often leads to a dangerous escalation in self-destructive behavior. Thus, the patient and therapist must constantly balance having material blocked and handling the unpleasant symptoms this creates against unearthing past traumas and handling the overwhelming affects this creates. The second major reason these patients present problems is that many observers in the field of dissociative disorders disagree about whether ritual abuse actually occurs. Opinions range from total disbelief in to total acceptance of ritual abuse as a clinical entity (Young et al. 1991; Ganaway 1989; Hill and Goodwin 1989; Van Benschoten 1990; Noll 1989). George Greaves presents an excellent overview of the complex issues involved in this debate in Chapter 3.

However, clearly the **phenomena** of patients reporting ritual abuse is real, and increasing numbers of clinicians report patients talking about these issues. It must also be recognized that ritual abuse is not limited to a single group of beliefs. The reports described in this chapter are primarily asso-

Dr. Young wishes to acknowledge the editorial assistance of Kathleen Adams, M.A., in the preparation of this chapter.

[1]The vast majority of patients in the author's caseload are female; hence, the female pronoun is used throughout this chapter to refer to patients. The author acknowledges that males also suffer from ritual abuse.

ciated with satanic cults, but clearly there are other kinds of ongoing, prolonged, or formalized torture and abuse that could also be considered "ritual abuse."

This chapter addresses ritual abuse from the standpoint of those patients who report ongoing abuse since early childhood at the hands of satanic cults, not only in formalized ceremonies but also on a day-to-day basis within the family. "Satanic cults" are herein defined as and limited to intrafamilial, transgenerational groups that engage in explicit satanic worship to include the following criminal practices: ritual torture, sacrificial murder, deviant sexual activity, and ceremonial cannibalism (Young et al. 1991). The word "ritual" has been specifically chosen over "ritualistic" to emphasize that these patients are reporting abuse that occurs in the context of specific rituals and to avoid any implication that the abuse was merely "ritual-like" (Young et al. 1991; Hill and Goodwin 1989).

Many of the principles discussed in this chapter may be pertinent to survivors of other types of cults and other forms of indoctrination (Clark 1979; Tennant-Clark, Fritz, and Beauvais 1989; Lifton 1989; Hassan 1988). However, this chapter does not attempt to address other groups that display satanic or cult-like behaviors, such as teenage "dabblers" who have become seduced and enter satanic cults at an older age. It does not deal with children coming out of day-care centers who report exposure to satanic activity, nor does it address the treatment of those individuals who may be outcasts and loners in their criminal activity and are not associated with more formalized generational satanic groups.

This chapter outlines the presentation and recognition of patients who report ritual abuse and examines the complex treatment issues involved in their rehabilitation. It is likely that much of what is said will be modified and improved as our understanding of the scope, nature, and validity of this information is clarified with further research. This is only a beginning at systematizing approaches to the treatment of adult survivors of satanic ritual abuse.

Recognition of Ritual Abuse

Characteristics of Ritual Abuse

Patients reporting ritual abuse describe numerous forms of continued and ongoing abuse that occurs not only within their immediate families but also frequently with various members of the extended family. Occasionally, patients report being accessed by satanic cults outside the family. While reports of types of torture and abuse vary enormously, a number of specific abuses have been reported with some degree of regularity. Walter Young et al. (1991) have reported on the characteristic abuses found in a series of thirty-seven cases; this list is by no means exhaustive or definitive. The abuses repeatedly found include:

- A history of sexual abuse beginning in childhood
- Witnessing and receiving physical abuse and torture
- Witnessing animal mutilations and killings
- Death threats
- Forced drug usage
- Witnessing and forced participation in human adult and infant sacrifice
- Forced cannibalism
- Purported ceremonial "marriage" to Satan
- Buried alive in coffins or graves
- Forced impregnation and sacrifice of own fetus/child

Initial Presentations for Treatment

Although patients may already be diagnosed as having a history of ritual abuse and therefore be referred to special centers or therapists, in most cases they have little idea of the presence of ritual abuse and enter treatment with a variety of prior diagnoses. Most patients will present with highly developed dissociative disorders of varying complexity, frequently including Multiple Personality Disorder (MPD).

One patient, whom we shall call Anna,[2] presented initially with a history of marital problems and sexual difficulties with her husband. Gradually, Anna came to the revelation that she had been raped in college. As she worked with these memories, however, the sexual difficulties in her marriage did not improve. It became apparent, as treatment progressed, that Anna had been sexually abused by her father on repeated occasions. Efforts to deal with these findings did not relieve her depression and difficulty with sexual functioning.

It gradually became clear that Anna had a dissociative condition, and a diagnosis of multiple personality disorder was eventually made. Over time, the definition of the dissociative features, the variety of dissociative symptoms and the functions that they played were clarified. Anna began to improve.

Then she began to make allusions to satanic cult scenes, "seeing blood, chainsaws, broken babies, and people in black robes," and she "inadvertently"

---

[2]All patient names are fictitious, and case studies are composites from the author's case load.

left a crucifix in the therapist's office. Anna had been in outpatient psychotherapy for over five years before reports of ritual abuse spontaneously began to emerge.

Another patient, Brenda, was referred to inpatient treatment for "multiple personality disorder with no cult involvement." Hypnotic techniques and spontaneous recall were used in the initial stages of hospital treatment. Suddenly Brenda began having flashbacks of people in robes and scenes of torture and sacrifice. These memories increasingly led to reports of activities consistent with those reported by patients describing satanic ritual abuse. Brenda had already presented dissociative defenses and multiple personality, but the issues of ritual abuse emerged only subsequently, despite the fact that the therapist was convinced that there had been no cult involvement.

Some patients are referred for treatment who have either worked with a therapist familiar with ritual abuse or who already have memories of ritual abuse. Carla, diagnosed with multiple personality disorder, had at least one alter personality that continued to be involved in ritual activities. Carla stated that when she dissociated into that particular altered state, she would periodically return to satanic activity and sexual victimization, although she claimed that she did not participate in criminal activity. Nonetheless, she was amnestic for these episodes and only knew of her continuing involvement through the reports of other alter personalities.

These three examples demonstrate the wide spectrum of awareness that patients may have as they present for treatment. This is similar to patients presenting with dissociative and multiple personality disorders who have absolutely no awareness of multiple personality. The increased efficiency of trained observers in making a diagnosis of MPD and dissociative disorders, however, has accelerated the recognition of classic dissociative symptoms. Likewise, those working with patients reporting ritual abuse are much more likely to recognize dissociative disorders because they are familiar with the symptoms and have reason to suspect their presence in ritual-abuse cases.

There is no one pattern of experience for patients reporting ritual abuse. Some were involved in satanic cults for several years during childhood, and then the groups disbanded or the child was allowed to move away from cult activity. Other patients may report ongoing activity until adulthood, with an occasional patient coming into treatment with ongoing activity that she may not be aware of. In most instances, patients are actively seeking ways to deal with their dissociative symptoms; those who are still involved are typically looking for ways of safely extricating themselves.

Psychiatric Sequelae Specific to Patients Reporting Ritual Abuse

Walter Young et al. (1991), in a study of dissociative patients reporting ritual abuse, describe a set of psychiatric sequelae specific to patients reporting ritual abuse. These are severe post-traumatic stress disorder; dissociative states with satanic overtones; survivor guilt; indoctrinated beliefs; unusual fears; sexualization of sadistic impulses; bizarre self-abuse; and substance abuse.

Post-traumatic stress severe enough to meet the requirements for DSM-III-R (American Psychiatric Association 1987) diagnosis was found in all the cases in this study. Although the symptoms might be significantly different in nondissociative survivors of ritual abuse, all of the patients evidenced dissociative states with satanic overtones. It should be noted that the development of dissociative states and even multiple personalities may be encouraged within the cult settling when "demons" or other functional states are "called forth" while a child is being ritually abused. This encourages a situation in which the development of dissociative states becomes a survival tool that the child develops not only through her own defenses but also as a means of compliance with the perpetrators' demands.

The blending of these sequelae create complex diagnostic and treatment challenges. Marjorie, for example, acted out the confusion of sexual and sadistic impulses by eroticizing self-mutilation. When she was severely distressed, she would insert razor blades in her vagina and masturbate. In a scenario common to many patients, Nancy experienced sexual arousal as she recalled and described episodes of torture or self-mutilation. This arousal was accompanied by overwhelming shame at her inability to "control" her state of arousal.

Indoctrinated beliefs, some so bizarre that they may sound psychotic, frequently occur with patients reporting ritual abuse. Patients report that they have been surgically implanted with a device that communicates their thoughts and feelings to the cult, or that they are a "child of Satan" or a "soldier of Satan" and have been specially bred for the purpose of doing Satan's work. Closely aligned with indoctrination are irrational fears or phobias around specific calendar dates, foods, animals, or other external stimuli.

Survivor guilt and other classic symptoms of post-traumatic stress disorder are common, and often the overwhelming internal pain is managed by self-mutilation or externalized to the abuse of animals or other people. Attempts at self-medication with drugs or alcohol to manage anxiety or numb feelings is also common.

Dissociation and Multiple Personality Disorder

Any patient who presents with multiple personality disorder or other significant dissociative disorders should evoke a high index of suspicion for the possibility of ritual abuse. Most such patients will have large gaps in their memories during the early, formative years. They may have memories of abuse at the hands of various family members or other adults. It is only after the emergence of these early memories that memories of ritual involvement seem to occur; there appears to be a layering of memories of abuse beginning with the least traumatic memories and progressing to memories of satanic ceremonies.

Considerations for Recognition of Ritual Abuse

Reluctance to talk about abuse. Most ritual abuse patients are very reluctant to share information about the abuse. Generally, they indicate that they feel endangered if they give information. They are clearly different from hysterical patients who derive a large secondary gain by producing fantastic and wild stories. In contrast, ritual abuse patients appear to be genuinely frightened, and as information emerges they often act out in suicidal or self-mutilating ways. This often reflects efforts to reenact perpetrators' threats that they would be injured or killed for disclosing.

Satanic symbols. Patients who self-mutilate may carve upside-down crosses, triple sixes, pentagrams, or other satanic symbols upon their bodies, reflecting a preoccupation with and perhaps a reenactment of activities seen or experienced during periods of ritual abuse. These or similar symbols may be sketched, painted, sculpted, or molded in art therapy or sandtray productions.

Assessing authenticity of patient reports. Much is yet to be learned about the difference between patients who are confabulating and distorting memory from those who, in fact, may have experienced severe ritual abuse. This is discussed in detail in Chapter 3. In general, a guideline may be that memories that can spontaneously be elicited without leading questions and which develop increasingly clearer definition are more likely to be reports or facsimiles of actual ritual abuse. Further, the stories are more elaborate and coherent. As patients work these memories through, they appear to improve, become more cohesive in their overall organization, feel more understood, and have improved perspectives about their experiences.

Conversely, patients who continually report vague, inconsistent abusive patterns and satanic rituals and whose stories remain fragmented or logistically impossible may be fabricating or confabulating. As clinicians continue to work with survivors, a set of guidelines, questions, and techniques must be developed to help sort out memories that are reflective of actual ritual abuse from situations that represent confabulation, distortion, malingering, or the unconscious absorption of memories heard from others. As yet the differentiation often must be based on the overall consistency of the patient's clinical presentation, her "believability," the consistency with which her symptoms seem to find increasing organization, and her subsequent clinical improvement. Patients who continuously report new layers of memories, who seem to make no progress in therapy or whose symptoms are vague and inconsistent may have such dominant defensive functioning that it may be harder to tell whether ritual abuse has actually occurred.

Diagnostic tools. A number of diagnostic tools are helpful. Psychological testing, which Richard Mangen discusses in Chapter 6, is increasingly being used. For example, ritual abuse survivors will frequently make reference to a great deal of blood and scenes of torture and chaos when presented with unstructured materials, such as the Rorschach.

Art therapy and sandtrays can be particularly useful. Artistic productions may reflect satanic cult scenes with people in black robes, dismembered bodies, inverted crosses, and other symbols compatible with the patient's later verbal productions. The artwork may precede overt memories.

Use of a sandtray, where miniature toys and objects can be manipulated in a box of sand, allows those who are not artistic or are afraid to use artistic media to construct what appear to be clear-cut scenes of torture, ritual sacrifice, and other characteristic scenes of abuse.

Journal entries may reflect evidence of ritual abuse activity that the patient has not been able to make sense of and can be a useful assessment tool.

The use of direct hypnotic inquiry with ideomotor signals may reveal a presence of ritual abuse before the patient is consciously aware of it.

Treatment

Since the issue of ritual abuse remains controversial, opinions on its effective treatment cannot be expected to be uniform. The best guideline for treatment is simply this: Any therapist treating a patient with a dissociative condition and/or suspected ritual abuse must be open to a variety of possibilities that might account for the report, including the possibility that the report reflects reasonably accurate memories. Most patients come into treatment expecting to be considered "crazy" and to be ostracized and disbelieved. Additionally, patients may have an internal censor that threatens punishment or even death if they reveal forbidden secrets. Generally, patients are terrified and will require ongoing reassurance and support to piece together their stories.

A variety of structural ego defects may make it difficult for patients to assimilate new material, accurately assess reality, and interpret their own or others' motives. Like anyone who has been severely abused, these patients have skewed world views and tend to perceive the world as threatening and ominous; additionally, survivors frequently expect "the world" to compensate them for their early suffering. Such victim roles and patterns are likely to extend into adulthood. There are often a variety of ego defects in the area of object relations; the resultant damage to the ability to trust is universally a major obstacle to treatment. Patients may have defects in their impulse control, making the course of treatment quite stormy with frequent attempts to self-mutilate, self-destruct, or assault those who are intruding into their compartmentalized experiences. The disruption caused by traumatic flooding of memories or shifting dissociative states may render a patient unemployable and therefore financially inaccessible for treatment. There is often a tendency to distort information to fit internal schemas, so that when a patient appears to be understanding an interpretation or event she is, in fact, reframing it as abusive or hearing it in some other context.

General Considerations

Any patient for whom ritual abuse is suspected should be thoroughly informed about the difficulties of treatment. The therapist should explain that the course of treatment will be difficult; there will likely be periods during the course of treatment in which the patient will feel worse before she feels better; and the return of memories dissociated or repressed for traumatic reasons will often result in increased stress, anxiety, and impulsive behavior. It should be explained to patients that it is not possible to predict what kinds of information may be recalled or what impact it may have on the patient's functioning and family. Patients should be given the option of having supportive treatment in which the primary focus is learning to live with the symptom complex currently in place. The clinician should be aware of the difficulty of giving informed consent to patients whose primary symptoms consist of amnesia and dissociation of painful experience.

For those patients who lack financial or personal resources, or for whom hospital backup would present a problem, it may be necessary to postpone definitive treatment. A precipitous rush into treatment may decompensate the patient who does not have an adequate set of personal and financial resources available to help her through the difficult periods ahead.

Phases of Treatment

Treatment for patients reporting ritual abuse generally consists of several phases:

- Developing a therapeutic alliance
- Evaluation and assessment
- Clarifying the system
- Discovering repressed information and dissolving dissociative barriers
- Reconstructing memory and reframing beliefs
- Countering indoctrinated beliefs
- Desensitizing triggers and cues
- Coming to terms with the past and finding new meaning and purpose in life

Although these stages are similar to the stages of treatment for a patient suffering from severe dissociation or multiple personality disorder, the addition of the psychiatric sequelae specific to ritual abuse survivorship increases the complexity.

A variety of victim roles and reenactments may take place during the course of treatment, not only between alter states within a dissociative patient but also between the patient and the therapist as they reenact scenes that help to clarify the dilemmas that the patient experienced during the periods of her abuse. Pacing and the timing of interpretations and reconstructions are key factors. When the patient is under severe stress or when external circumstances require that she slow down the therapeutic work, the therapist may wish to help the patient focus on life-management issues dealing with the present.

Developing the therapeutic alliance. It is crucial to develop an early therapeutic alliance and a sense of consistency and trust. This requires regular treatment times in a consistent setting by a willing therapist. It is advisable to establish ground rules regarding session frequency and length early in the treatment. It is almost certain that such limits will be tested during the course of treatment. Because ritual abuse patients have experienced their worlds as chaotic, disenfranchised places with little stability and structure, containment of the treatment within a predictable setting helps to show the patient that her world can be stable and predictable. David Sakheim and Susan Devine discuss boundary issues in Chapter 11.

It is critical that the therapist maintain a clear perspective on the difference between the patient's subjective, internal reality and objective, external reality. A patient whose internal experience is one of chronic unsafety in the world can project this belief onto the therapist, who inadvertently colludes by also fearing for the patient's safety. One patient, for example, lived in a state of perpetual terror that members of the cult had plans to kidnap her and return her to cult life. Rather than interpret this back to her as a place of frozen disempowerment and assist her in practicing positive choice-making skills, the therapist helped her make arrangements to move out of state!

It is absolutely essential that the therapist make clear that no assaultive or dangerous behavior will be tolerated within the course of outpatient treatment. Hospitalization and hypnotic interventions may be needed. However, if a safe outpatient environment cannot be maintained, the patient may need to terminate treatment until she can safely function in a treatment setting.

Evaluation and assessment. Following the development of a therapeutic alliance, general assessment of the patient should be undertaken. Psychological testing can be obtained and, if she can tolerate it, the patient should have a good physical examination. If the patient has children, it is recommended that they be evaluated to screen for the possibility that the children may be abused when the patient is in a dissociated state. In many instances children do remarkably well, despite the often extreme disorganization of the parent. At other times, children may need supportive therapy to help with the demands of living with a dissociative parent.

As previously mentioned, specific awareness of ritual abuse is frequently not uncovered until well into the patient's treatment. Keeping the psychiatric sequelae for ritual abuse firmly in mind will increase the clinician's ability to respond proactively as assessment data emerges.

In addition to a thorough assessment of the patient's social, financial, psychological, physical, emotional, and cognitive readiness for treatment, the therapist should assess the patient's support systems and coping strategies. The first leg of the treatment process may involve building a container of techniques to help the patient manage anxiety and cope with the trauma of treatment. When the patient is taught self-hypnotic techniques, relaxation exercises, journaling tools, and other life-management skills before any uncovering of traumatic memories, she is better equipped to effectively deal with the inevitable anxiety that results from a difficult therapeutic process. Referrals to low- or no-cost support groups can also be made at this time.

Clarifying the system. A dissociative patient is likely to be amnestic both for the presence of other personality states and for the memories of the cult abuse that they contain. Gradually, the identification and functioning of the various altered states can be understood and their adaptive value recognized.

For example, a promiscuous alter may represent an adaptive solution for a patient who has been sexually abused or exposed to child prostitution or pornography. By using counterphobic defenses, this alter has turned sexual trauma into a mastery situation in which she sees herself as sexually molesting, or using men for her own means; by being "in control" of the situation, she believes herself **not** to be a victim. As adaptive as this may have been, it is also important to recognize that there is little in the way of intimacy or meaning in this kind of defensive solution.

The dissociative phenomena frequently involve cultlike or satanic identifications. Nearly every MPD patient reporting ritual abuse has one or more "satanic" alters. Names such as High Priestess, natas, the Enforcer, or Keeper of the Secrets may reflect dissociative states that hold memories and experiences of the cult.

The patient may develop characteristics of her abusers and attack other people or herself as a reenactment of the abuse. Self-mutilation through cigarette burns, lacerations, or suicide attempts may be internal reenactments of experiences that the patient went through during her own abuse. However, on closer evaluation, all such activities have a protective function. For example, self-abuse can serve to keep certain alters from revealing cult secrets that would result in overwhelming affect or in feared retribution from the cult. It is essential to recognize that each alter personality in a dissociative system has a functional value to the survival of the patient's system as a whole. This is sometimes difficult to understand: There is a natural tendency to devalue and try to get rid of the "satanic" or self-destructive personalities. However, when patients can understand that such alters are helpful adaptations in their survival, they may begin to accept aspects of themselves that they previously needed to disavow and deny. It is important to come to understand the defensive functions of each alter, as well as to evaluate if some of the more extreme approaches can be revised or changed now that the patient is in a noncoercive environment. Such understanding and compromises between alters are a major part of this stage of treatment.

Often there are specific alters that can be very helpful with this process since they have access to information about the whole system of personalities. They can help to clarify treatment impasses, give information about overlooked dangers, or explain the purposes of alters.

Discovering repressed information and dissolving dissociative barriers. The next major phase of treatment consists of discovery and the gradual dissolution of dissociative defenses. Once trust and an alliance have been established, the patient needs to come to terms with the experiences that required dissociation and exclusion from consciousness in the first place. Through dreams, flashbacks, and talking with altered states, the patient gradually becomes aware of more and more information. Initially this will likely come as disconnected and fragmented memories that have very little connection with one another. The patient may have an upsurge of anxiety but simultaneously experience the memories as unreal. As cult memories emerge of traumatic abuses such as torture and sacrifice, the patient may become increasingly disorganized. There is a strong possibility of attempts at self-harm during this stage as the patient may feel compelled to act out against herself for revealing the information.

It is important to help the patient understand that all of the personality states represent efforts to solve an intolerable dilemma in which the only available solution was to turn inward and develop dissociative states. In other words, the patient chose survival over death, at the cost of an integrated personality.

Gradually, dissolution of dissociative barriers occurs through increasing awareness of memories via dreams, writings, artistic expressions, internal dialogues, the use of hypnosis for memory retrieval, flashbacks, and other forms of communication among altered states. In this way, previously repressed information begins to emerge. The dissolution stage is likely to be a painful and difficult time, and escalation and abreactions are common. With caution and pacing, however, the patient gradually assimilates material and is able to make more cohesive sense of her experiences. The memories gradually separate and congeal into recollections that feel more valid and have more clarity.

Sometimes there is a massive breakthrough of memory. Although this occasionally occurs as an attempt by an alter personality to punish the patient, in general it reflects a rapid breakdown in dissociative defenses; the flooding passes, and the patient assimilates the new information.

The dissolution state often results in a crisis which may require a brief period of hospitalization and the use of hypnotic or medical interventions to help the patient maintain stability. R. P. Kluft (1983) provides an excellent description of hypnotic strategies for crisis intervention.

The patient's personal resources, ideally, will be available to help her through these crises. There will be periods in which the patient has not had access to enough pieces of a memory to reframe it or place it in perspective, and she may at times drop into dissociated states in which the psyche's ability to objectively assimilate and integrate memories is hindered. Susan, upon sudden recollection of being forced to kill a child in a cult ritual twenty-five years before, called the local police and confessed to the crime before she was able to realize that the larger context of the situation was that she was the victim of adults who forced her to participate.

The therapist should encourage the active participation of an observing ego function or personality that can assimilate information gathered from a variety of dissociative states so that the patient may organize information clearly and piece it together in a way that makes increasing sense.

Inevitably, the patient can expect periods of depression before she is fully able to cope effectively with the emergence of new traumatic material, particularly that which is specific to cult activity and ritual abuse.

Reconstructing memory and reframing beliefs. The next phase of treatment is one in which the reconstructed memories and fragments are gradually placed into a framework that the patient can comprehend as abuse.

One task of this phase is to help the patient understand that she was the victim of abuse when she was forced to participate in the torture or killing of others. Since the patient's common experience is to think of herself as a perpetrator or criminal, she needs clear and direct help in understanding that this was part of her victimization. Even a sense that she does not deserve treatment and should be punished, or that she is not entitled to further care, is an aspect of the victimization and should be interpreted as such to clarify the patient's reality testing. Reconstruction and interpretation of the experience gives the patient a current perspective of her victimization at a time when she was unable to understand that her world was manipulated and controlled by adults over whom she had no control. She must also come to understand that information she received was erroneous and misleading; beliefs were learned during states of extreme duress, torture, fatigue, overstimulation, or deprivation. In other words, the patient's ability to realistically perceive the world is severely damaged, and perspectives about her past, present and future must be restructured.

Countering indoctrinated beliefs. As skill develops in challenging outmoded beliefs, a progression can be made to countering clearly irrational, but very powerful, beliefs instilled in the patient at a young age by cult members.

Desensitizing triggers and cues. Behavior modification and phobic desensitization techniques can be used to help the patient recognize that she can exercise control of her life and choose a different response to triggers and cues.

Coming to terms with the past and finding new meaning and purpose in life.
Gradually, the patient needs to accept the experiences that have occurred to her
as true and real, but no longer immediate. The observing ego's task is to manage
and assimilate this information, reframe it, reconstruct it in an orderly fashion,
and develop a perspective on it. The patient can then work through the
information and convert the experiences into memories from the past rather
than realities in the present.

Abreactions and Dissociated Memories

Memories often return as experiences of reliving, or abreactions, in which
patients may have somatic pain, behavioral reenactments, and hallucinations
compatible with the original experience. Typically, the patient may experience
an entire event or a portion of an event as though it is current. The patient's
tasks are to gain increasing mastery over the ability to recognize that such a
flashback experience is a reliving of a past memory, and to assimilate it, allowing
the memory to become part of her personal past rather than part of her
dissociated present. These events must occur repeatedly until abreactions are
worked through. Some patients may be able to exercise control over memories
and remember them more gradually so that the intensity is more manageable.
However, this is one of the most difficult aspects of treatment to modulate.

Bodily sensations known as "somatic memories" or anxiety attacks with no
specific memory may be precursors to the retrieval of information that the
patient needs in order to complete a particular memory. For example, a patient
may experience pelvic pain prior to the entire recollection of an abuse. One
woman experienced fiery burning in her vagina. Subsequently she became aware
of a cult ceremony in which she was ritually abused and raped by a number of
men. This led to increased somaticization in which she experienced labor pains;
later, she connected them to an induced abortion.

It should be noted that processing memories is exhausting work. It may be
most productive to alternate periods of intensive memory/abreactive work with
consolidation periods, in which the patient's ego strength and self-esteem can be
built and information synthesized. The consistent hammering away at memories,
even though it brings information, may seriously damage a patient's self-esteem.
The skillful therapist will interweave gaining new perspectives about life with
going back into memories. As the therapist and client form their alliance, the
most helpful balance will emerge.

The "working through" process of discovery, reconstruction, and developing perspectives and acceptance is gradual and has to repeat itself a number of
times, both within a given memory and over the course of a variety of memories.
One aspect of the task is to address the variety of ways in which the patient
understands and continues to experience herself in life as a disempowered
victim. Another is to gradually experience herself as personally empowered,
increasingly in charge of her life. Still another is to internalize that she is the

predominant initiating force in her own life, and the perpetrators no longer have power over her.

Hypnotic Techniques and Phenomena

Because dissociative individuals are generally highly responsive to hypnosis, it is a useful therapeutic intervention, and the therapist may want to be aware of hypnotic techniques and phenomena (Kluft 1982, 1983; Putnam 1989; Braun 1986).

Often, dissociative patients will present a variety of clinical pictures compatible with events that can be seen in hypnosis. Such patients have the capacity for deep absorption in their mental experiences. They are suggestible and tend to lack critical judgment when in hypnotic or dissociative states.

These characteristics make it imperative that therapists work cautiously and judiciously with patients when they are in a state of dissociation or under hypnosis to prevent the iatrogenic contamination of the patient's memories. Questions and directives should be open-ended and nonleading, such as, "What is happening now?" or "Describe what you are experiencing."

Therapists should also be aware that hypnosis itself does not guarantee that information provided is true (Orne 1979; AMA 1985; Pettinati 1988). Hypnosis may provide a capacity for increased recall, but it may also allow the production of increased errors in recall, which may be conscious or unconscious, and which may serve internal defensive functions or may be present simply to please the examiner. Sometimes, increased suggestibility leads a patient to "recall" phenomena introduced as a leading question by a therapist. It has long been established that there is increased reporting of both valid and invalid information in patients who are pushed to give more information than they initially report. From this standpoint, information retrieved in dissociative states may be expected to be a mixture of information that is true, confabulated, distorted, or condensed from a variety of sources. Therefore, an absolute validation of any patient's memory is not likely to be possible without independent verification.

Nonetheless, cautious and judicious use of hypnotic exploration assists in the breakdown of dissociative barriers. The access to deeply dissociated information can be worked with until it achieves a form that the patient feels confident about; clinical improvement is generally the outcome.

More specific uses of hypnosis may unfold in the course of treatment. Ideomotor signals can be introduced early on (Kluft 1982, 1983). The patient should be given the choice whether she pays attention to what her fingers are communicating; in this way, she is not forced to accept or recognize information before she is ready. Using finger signals, the therapist can communicate with the patient's entire dissociative system without contacting each personality separately. With finger signals, the patient may be able to communicate whether there are additional alters, additional memories, obstacles in the course of the current work, or other information that needs to be dealt with that is being missed.

These signals may also give indications for the presence of particular diagnostic data that may be important.

Examples of questions which may be answered with finger signals include:

- Are other personalities present?
- Is there more information about a given memory that needs to be discussed?
- Are sufficient suicidal tendencies present that the patient should be hospitalized or watched carefully?
- Can the patient reliably enter into a safety contract?

An innovative therapist can find a variety of ways to effectively utilize ideomotor signals or other such hypnotic techniques.

As in any other aspect of treatment, the patient should be given complete permission and encouragement to signal "stop" whenever information is too upsetting or alarming, or when it would be best to approach the line of query from another direction. The patient's control of the process is essential for it to be safe enough to succeed.

The patient's ability to predict and control her own behavior is often very much enhanced when hypnotic techniques are used and she is taught to give contracts in which she will notify someone if destructive behavior is about to emerge. The request for a contract under hypnosis should usually include an embedded suggestion that the contract covers any "loopholes" that are not specifically verbally contracted for. However, it is equally important with any suggestion to first see if any alters have objections. Suggestions work far better when such problems or objections are resolved and internal compromises are reached.

Expressive Therapies

Expressive modalities, such as journal therapy, art therapy, and sandtray, have proven successful in treating dissociative patients and those reporting ritual abuse.

Journal therapy. The use of reflective or therapeutic writing has many benefits. First, an ongoing journal provides a container for memory work and allows for cohesion and organization of data. Second, the journal can be an invaluable communication link among parts of the dissociated system and can leave a "paper trail" of the events and happenings of periods for which the patient may be amnestic. Next, the constant availability of the journal helps patients learn to become self-reliant during times of emergency or emotional crisis. "Writing through" a memory or process can be empowering as well as validating. Last, the written record of the healing process can be reviewed at key stages of therapy and can serve as a testament to the progress being made (Adams 1990).

It is not unusual for patients reporting ritual abuse to be very reluctant to write down memories or experiences, out of fear of retribution or punishment. These patients can be encouraged to warm up to the journal process by writing here-and-now experiences, including any pleasant or positive experiences the patient may be having. Also, a second journal may be used exclusively for memory work. This helps to alleviate the patient's fear that she will be inadvertently triggered by rereading a report of a painful or traumatic event, and it may give the patient a sense of increased mastery and control over her environment.

It is imperative that the patient be assured that her journal will remain entirely private and that she will not be asked to share her writings unless she wishes to do so.

The therapist may offer suggestions for journal tasks to assist the patient in becoming focused. It is especially helpful to suggest ways in which the seeming mountain of material can be broken down into manageable pieces.

Art therapy. Art therapy and sandtrays are valuable parts of ongoing treatment and are particularly helpful in allowing patients to begin working through material that is still held at the unconscious or nonverbal level. Symbolizing events or memories in art also allows patients to achieve distance and objectivity.

Images, intrinsic to the traumatic experience, can be managed, understood and explored through art and sand. Nonverbal expression through artwork can be a safe place to tell the story of the memory or abuse; the form, content, color, intensity, and organization can all be interpreted as reflective of the inner world. Artwork is also satisfying for patients, who can take pride in a sense of mastery over the art media and pleasure in the creative process involved. Artistic avenues can also be an excellent outlet for feelings with patients who have limited abilities to be verbally expressive.

Sandtray. Sandtray, more commonly associated with children's play therapy than art therapy, is a powerful vehicle for recreating and reenacting memories in a safe and controlled environment (Sacks 1990; Braun 1986). Especially for child alter personalities, sandtray work represents a safe place to "tell" stories that the patient has been forbidden to divulge. The tangible quality of three-dimensional objects often leads to increased memory detail and connection to affect. Additionally, sandtray is highly effective with patients for whom the use of art media is difficult, either because of their inhibitions or because they are disorganized.

Medications

The pharmacological approach to ritual abuse remains empiric. The syndrome is essentially one of traumatic stress with the primary trauma reported to be at the hands of satanic cults; therefore, the pharmacological approach to post-traumatic stress disorder (PTSD) with severe depressive and anxiety syndromes is an appropriate starting place.

Decisions made around medications will be based upon several key questions:

- Does the patient primarily suffer from post-traumatic stress disorder?
- If so, is the patient primarily in the overstimulated phase or the withdrawal/numbing stage of the PTSD cycle?
- Does the patient have a significant amount of anxiety that should be treated independently?
- Is there a pervasive biological depression that needs chemical intervention?

The traditional medications used for these conditions consist of tricyclic antidepressants, minor tranquilizers, and, in some instances, monoamine oxidase inhibitors (MAOI) when tricyclics do not provide results.

One of the basic problems with dissociative patients is monitoring compliance; they may stockpile medications for suicide attempts, refuse to adhere to MAOI diets, or abuse mood-altering medications. Many of these patients have also been abusing a variety of substances since early childhood in the cult. Additionally, chronic pain syndromes may reflect physical illnesses or even psychosomatic pains that represent "body memories." An unwitting therapist may find him/herself in the midst of a pharmacological nightmare with the use of many different drugs for a variety of symptoms. General caution is in order, and the clinician should remember that it is easier to introduce medications than it is to terminate them. Since little empirical data is yet available, all medications should be used cautiously and treated honestly as being experimental. Brief uses for acute symptoms probably make the most sense. Attention to substance-abuse issues is also important; many patients have developed chemical dependencies as a way of managing excessive anxiety in traumatic states. Referral to Twelve-Step programs is often helpful.

R. J. Lowenstein (1988) has demonstrated the efficacy of clonazepam in doses of five to seven milligrams with multiple personality disorder patients who have symptoms characteristic of PTSD. It should be noted that this instance represents a use of the drug not approved by the FDA; the patient should give informed consent for the use of this potentially addictive medication and must be followed closely. Many patients appear to respond to this drug when they are in states of hyperstimulation and agitation. However, potential drawbacks include oversedation, which may inhibit the production of memories, and addiction, which can clearly cause unnecessary additional problems.

Recent investigations in post-traumatic studies (van der Kolk 1987) have indicated that fluoxetine hydrochloride is useful not only in the treatment of depression but in relieving PTSD symptoms as well. This drug has activating properties in some patients and therefore is best given in the morning. It may also act to suppress appetite. Patients who are withdrawn or have a tendency towards overeating and obesity may do well with fluoxetine hydrochloride. Caution is indicated, however, as anecdotal reports have suggested that in some instances fluoxetine hydrochloride may increase suicidal or self-mutilating impulses. Recent allegations that the use of fluoxetine hydrochloride caused a decrease in inhibitions with subsequent acting-out clearly need further investigation, but nonetheless should serve as a caution to its use with such a potentially volatile population.

For overwhelming anxiety and flashbacks, the use of mild tranquilizers may be appropriate. Increased dosages may be necessary so that the patient can function well enough to proceed in therapy. Longer-acting agents provide more stable levels and thus may be preferable. PRN doses during crises are often necessary. Many patients report difficulty in sleep patterns and may need assistance to avoid excessive fatigue. Keep in mind, however, that nightmares and flooding may be useful sources of information, and sleep medication may suppress dream recall.

Any drug for which there exists the possibility of psychological or physiological dependence must be monitored closely and discontinued if symptoms are not significantly improved. Also, patients should be encouraged and assisted in developing tolerance for a certain level of anxiety.

The use of antipsychotic drugs has generally been discouraged, as they frequently create a feeling of depersonalization and have been reported to have poor clinical effects on patients with dissociative conditions. There are, however, exceptions; some patients have utilized doses of chlorpromazine and other antipsychotic agents with surprising success. When these drugs are used patients should be informed and closely monitored for signs of extrapyramidal reactions, neuroleptic malignant syndrome, and other complications of major tranquilizers.

While published studies of the efficacy of propranolol in dissociative disorders and ritual abuse treatment have not been forthcoming, anecdotal evidence suggests that in selected cases the use of propranolol in dosages ranging from two hundred to a thousand milligrams per day have been reported to reduce rapid cycling or "switching" behavior in dissociative patients (Braun 1990; Barkin, Braun and Kluft 1986). Propranolol may also have a calming effect and contribute to a sense of increased mental organization. It has been reported that beta blockers can be effective in treating rage attacks and anxiety disorders.

Since this is not currently an approved utilization for propranolol, informed consent is necessary, and there should be no contraindications to the use of beta blockers.

Other drugs that have been utilized in post-traumatic stress syndromes with variable success rates include clonidine, lithium carbonate, and carbamazepine (van der Kolk 1987).

Pain medications are especially tricky. Chronic headaches and somatic pain both appear to be associated with repressed memory. A good rule of thumb is to avoid narcotic medications whenever possible in the treatment of memory-related or somatic pain. True migraine headaches may require the use of higher doses of non-narcotic medication, and there may be instances when short-term narcotic use may have some benefit, as long as dosage and usage is monitored carefully.

In the long-term healing process, it is important that the patient recognize the physical pain so that she may learn its relationship to the rest of her overall experience, rather than simply medicating away symptoms that may be crucial for long-range understanding.

Unfortunately, the psychopharmacological treatment of dissociative disorders and traumatic stress reactions is in its infancy. Thus, flexibility and close monitoring is key in any approach to pharmacological intervention. Clearly, further research is needed in this area.

Hospitalization

In general, the indications for hospitalization are the same as those for most patients in psychiatric care: danger to self or others, inability to function, failure to improve in outpatient therapy, or the need for a comprehensive psychiatric evaluation in an equipped setting.

Hospitalization of the ritually abused patient, however, has a number of potential difficulties. Patients may feel misunderstood, particularly if staff members are unwilling to accept ritual abuse as a potential reality and thus depreciate or deny the validity of the patient's symptoms.

Ritual abuse patients tend to have more difficulty with impulse control and therefore may act out more than other patients. Whether the patient's safety needs can be satisfactorily met is an important consideration in selecting an inpatient program. During the discovery process of treatment, the patient's behavior can be expected to escalate due to increased levels of anxiety, abreactions, and internal pressure for retribution. Useful interventions include hypnotic techniques in which the patient can be asked for safety contracts, medication, or a brief "time-out" in a seclusion or quiet room. Patients who are abreactive but not in danger do not necessarily need to be secluded or separated unless their actions are frightening or triggering to other patients. Sometimes talking with the patient and helping her process memories is the only intervention needed.

Hospital staff should be aware that patients reporting ritual abuse may have an adverse effect on the overall milieu. They may acquire a special status that is either envied or agitating to other patients. They may be scapegoated by other patients because their stories of torture and horror are difficult to hear. They may invoke countertransference and disbelief among staff members that may undermine the team effort. Clear communication between staff and primary clinician is imperative for a therapeutic milieu.

Hospitalization raises many issues for these patients, especially around issues of control. Their early experiences involved coercive control by others, and the hospital rules and limits can easily feel like a replication of this. However, if the patient requests controls to help with her healing, they can feel very different. This is a difficult balance for most hospitals to achieve. Coercive controls **are** revictimizing, while agreed-upon limits can be very helpful. The use of restraints is an excellent example. Involuntary restraint can replicate past abuses and be extremely traumatic to the patient. However, voluntary uses of restraints can allow a furthering of treatment, especially if other approaches, such as the use of hypnotic techniques, have failed.

Voluntary Restraints

The use of voluntary restraints—after appropriate and well-documented informed consent—can be very helpful when the patient or staff feels that there is a potentially dangerous escalation close at hand or when abreactive work is expected to be especially violent, aggressive, or self-destructive (Young 1986; Braun 1986).

A voluntary restraint session is optimally either scheduled in advance with the primary therapist or requested by the patient as behavior begins escalating. The patient is taken to a seclusion or other private room, securely restrained, and attended to be at least two people.

The optimum voluntary restraint position is a three-point restraint with the legs together, so that the patient does not feel vulnerable or stranded in a four-point, spreadeagle position. A rest sheet, Posey vest, or some other external controlling device may further protect the patient from injuries or strains while going through violent abreactions.

She may then be guided in the use of hypnotic techniques to enter into the memory work; alternatively, the abreaction may be allowed to take its natural course. As with any abreactive or hypnotic session, the therapist should ask that there be an observing ego function and internal self-helper present to see that the patient does not injure herself. It is also useful to ask for an internal "organizing function" to assist in structuring the information as it emerges.

Patients should be encouraged to remember only that part of a voluntary restraint session that they feel ready to know; this gives the patient control over how much information she wishes to assimilate at any given time. Staff should be aware that flashbacks, resurgence of abreactions, or "punishment" by a persecutory alter for revealing taboo information is common following a session.

It is a common belief that voluntary restraint sessions may reenact early abuse in which the patient was overpowered by force. However, it is the author's experience that by far the majority of patients who have given informed consent on voluntary restraint sessions experience the procedure as safe and protective. The containment of voluntary restraints allows patients to look at angry, violent or sadistic sides of themselves that they may otherwise feel afraid to encounter (Young 1986; Braun 1986).

Other Types of Voluntary Restraints

A patient who repeatedly attempts to self-mutilate may be able to function in the milieu if she is voluntarily placed in wrist-to-waist restraints during times when she is unable to maintain safety contracts; this may avoid the need for involuntary seclusion and/or restraints or one-to-one staff observation.

Finally, the voluntary use of hypnotic suggestion that a patient will be able to control her behavior without restraints—for instance, by perceiving herself as confined to a bed or chair from which she cannot rise without falling back into a trance—is an advisable first alternative. The therapist may also wish to suggest a cue word that could be used to purposefully induce a trance state or to bring forward a helping alter personality. It would be interesting to study whether a cue word could be used by the patient herself to become intentionally dissociated until a more controlled state can emerge.

Specific Problems of Specialized Treatment Settings

Specific problems emerge in a specialized treatment setting, when there is more than one patient on a unit who is dissociative and/or reports ritual abuse. Should the patients be encouraged to talk among themselves of ritual abuse experiences and memories with the goal of offering support and hope to each other? Should patients be discouraged from discussing ritual abuse topics to minimize the possibility of cross-contamination through absorption of each others' memories and experiences?

There is no convincingly established precedent for these issues, and each hospital unit and staff will need to assess them in the context of the overall milieu and to learn from their experiences. At my treatment center, patients are not discouraged from talking about ritual abuse issues; for patients who are stable enough to handle the material, there are structured groups that are considered "open forum" for discussion and process around cult experiences and issues. The patients are relieved to have a forum in which they can talk about material that had previously been prohibited; they consistently report that they feel more "understood."

Of course, there is the danger that familiarity with each others' symptoms may result in confusion and unconscious identification with the reports of others. There is also the possibility that patients who are dissociative but who have not experienced ritual abuse may come to expect emergence of cult memories. However, patients who are not allowed to discuss their cult backgrounds with one another, whether informally or in groups, frequently report feeling frustrated and rejected because they are denied the sense of validation or "belonging" that would come from sharing their experiences with others who can relate to them. Such denial also may negatively serve to reinforce the sense that information about ritual abuse is secretive, unacceptable, and to be suppressed.

Contagion effects. When dissociative patients are treated together on specialized units there is always a possibility of "contagion" effects. This may happen in one of two ways. In the first, there may be unconscious identifications between or among patients, in which one patient learns of a peer's memory or experience and subsequently perceives it as something that she, too, experienced. The experience becomes absorbed without conscious awareness. For example, one patient's emerging memory of being suspended in a cesspool precipitated two other similar reports within only a few group therapy sessions. It must be recognized, however, that many of these patients independently report similar experiences, and one patient's description could, in fact, trigger similar memories for others.

The other contagion effect is considerably more conscious—although perhaps not entirely so—and may involve an attempt at joining or belonging within the peer group. One patient may utilize voluntary restraint sessions, sparking a milieu-wide interest in voluntary restraints as the best way to work with abreactions.

The contagion effect may also be an attempt to compete or derive a secondary gain from being as sick or sicker than others. In one remarkable example, an eating-disordered patient refused to eat and vomited what little she ingested. She was placed on an intravenous feeding tube for hydration and nutrition. Almost immediately, several other patients also began having difficulty taking food and fluids and requested IV intervention. These reactions reflect the problem experienced by dissociative patients, due to their poor psychic boundaries, suggestibility, and tendency to lack critical judgment.

Another type of contagion effect in specialized milieus occurs before and during satanic or cult holidays and often around the patients' birthdays. Behaviors and anxiety levels begin to escalate, and there is frequently an attempt to reenact or recreate certain rituals or mutilations. Patients seem to be especially prone to being triggered by the abreactions of their peers during times of satanic holidays.

In many ways working with ritual abuse survivors who have dissociated states parallels the treatment strategies of MPD (Putnam 1989; Braun 1986; Bliss 1986; Ross 1989).

Special Treatment Issues

Working with Satanic Alter Personalities

"Satanic alters" often present themselves during the treatment of patients reporting ritual abuse. These alters often act and behave in a hostile fashion, are frequently abusive to the patient physically and psychologically, and often appear to be major obstructive forces in the course of treatment.

A "satanic" alter, like any other altered state that the patient may present, reflects a survival function. The function of this particular alter is to maintain identification with the original abusers, a form of identification with the aggressor. Through dissociation into a "satanic" alter state, the patient was able to perform and participate in the satanic rituals that were forced upon her. Additionally, "satanic" alters felt bonded with cult members and derived power and self-esteem from the strength it required to survive the rites of passage demanded in cult settings.

A useful therapeutic approach is to understand the experience of the "satanic" alter and educate it about other ways it could utilize its power and determination. When these altered states eventually recognize that they too were part of the victimization and also suffered, then the patient can come to appreciate that "satanic" alters were essential adaptations to childhood trauma and that they contain a great deal of strength and power that can be utilized for healing.

The role and function of "satanic" alters is to align with the perpetrators. This should not confuse the therapist into reacting to them as devils and expecting exorcism or religious derision to be a treatment modality. These alters, like any others, need the development of a gradual alliance, interpretation of their functions, and erosion of the defenses that have distanced them from their own suffering.

Survivor Guilt

Massive survivor guilt is common once the patient begins to recall that she was forced to participate in satanic criminal activity. Such activity may have taken the form of forced participation in the torture and killing of children, babies, or animals. She may have been forced to participate in perverse acts not only as a victim but also as a perpetrator, under the threat of being tortured or killed if she did not cooperate. She may have witnessed the murder of others; she may have developed dissociated altered states that performed these functions. Subsequently, the patient holds herself accountable as though there were no extenuating circumstances.

I tend to approach survivor guilt in two ways. First, I assist the patient in recognizing that she was a victim and did not operate out of choice. Patients report being presented with many forced-choice scenarios. For example, Sharon was given a choice of killing her own baby or witnessing the sacrifice of a series of other babies, which could only be stopped if Sharon relinquishing her own baby for sacrifice. When she then killed her own child, she was told that she "chose" to murder her infant. Nancy was told to sacrifice herself or pick someone else. Anna was forced to choose one of several children for torture, then assured that she was truly "one of them" because she had made the "right" choice. No matter what response the child made, it was interpreted to her as a matter of voluntary participation. Giving the patient the perspective to see her own victimization is a key element in dealing with survivor guilt.

Second, I often find it possible to help the patient find ways in which she resisted despite the fact that she was forced to participate. The dropping of a knife, the hesitation, the silent internal baptism of a child whom she externally dedicated to Satan, may all represent ways in which the child attempted to frustrate the cult on one level while having to participate on another. A common mechanism is to internalize a representation of the sacrificed babies or children as dissociated identifications in an attempt to "save" the children from Satan. Patients report killing a baby swiftly rather than torturing it to death, as the cult expected them to do. These are all examples of how the child maintains the only resistive stance she could take in a situation that was simultaneously unconscionable and unavoidable.

These communications can be used to reinforce the fact that the patient was not a "child of Satan" and therefore evil, but rather a victim of abuse who fought back in the only ways available. Through this perspective, patients may begin to perceive themselves as decent and worthy persons who battled with circumstances over which they had no control. This interpretation is crucial to the development of the self-esteem so essential to recovery.

Survivor guilt is even more complicated and excruciating if the patient begins to realize, as many do, that an aspect of herself may have learned to enjoy inflicting abuse and found some acts of violence pleasurable. In many instances, these sadistic pleasures can be considered defenses; at other times, they may be feelings cultivated within a closed cult system. Traumatic bonding with the perpetrators often occurs as a result of surviving the "rites of passage" continually presented. As difficult as it may be for the patient to realize, she must come to regard her pleasure as an adaptive attempt to bond, join, and belong—an attempt at a sane response to an insane environment.

Programming and Indoctrination

A cult is a tightly closed information system; children who are exposed to cult activity are deliberately not taught the discernment or reasoning skills that would assist them in forming independent judgments about cult life. Further, the information system is often dissociated from consciousness; therefore, the ability to deal with the closed system through reality testing or changes in thinking patterns is frequently severely impaired (Lifton 1989; Hassan 1988).

Additionally, cults thrive on hierarchies headed by charismatic, powerful leaders. The absolutist philosophy of Satanism is imbued with a magical, omnipotent quality. Cult leaders are promoted as being hand-picked and specially trained disciples of "Satan," with all his authority.

There is much to be learned about the whole area of mind control, thought reform, programming, and indoctrination. It is certain that we are at the frontier of our experience in trying to understand these mechanisms. By no means do we have advanced, documented knowledge in these areas, and if new theory is to be developed it is incumbent upon treatment professionals to share observations and learnings as we identify them.

The information that follows is an attempt to share what I have very tentatively identified as phenomena common to this patient base. Its accuracy is yet to be determined.

Mind control and thought reform can be the results of an intense educational process in which a person is actually trained or conditioned to think and believe a certain way. They are complex conditioned responses best understood through learning theory paradigms and best approached with behavior modification techniques.

Programming and indoctrination. A "program" is a highly complex and specific indoctrinated stimulus/response pattern which has been instilled and then reinforced through repeated trauma by cult members. "Indoctrination" is the broader training process of inducing the programming itself, without specificity as to content. The environment for indoctrination is most conducive when there is low resistance, impaired reality, and limited availability of cognitive discrimination because of the effects of factors such as torture, fatigue, the use of drugs, intimidation, fear, hyperstimulation, and sensory deprivation. The result is the passive acceptance of what is being taught.

Patients report feeling "programmed" to return to the cult at a certain age, to self-mutilate if secrets are told, or to commit suicide. Marjorie, for example, reported "programming" that caused her to believe that an alter personality whose sole function would be to self-destruct would be activated if she left the cult.

These reported indoctrinations have been sequestered and harbored in dissociated states; they have not been available for integration into conscious thinking and therefore for conscious modification. The most useful treatment approach is to help the patient recognize the messages and indoctrinated statements that were given to her *in the context in which they occurred*. The coercive and intimidating circumstances under which the programming took place is another way of being victimized, and the patient can gradually include these messages as part and parcel of the overall trauma from which recovery is sought.

Triggers. A "trigger" is any generalized stimulus that produces an intense and irrational emotional response. The triggering event or vehicle may or may not be directly related to the patient's experience. Anna, for example, had a strong aversion to any sort of tomato-based sauce and became nauseated whenever she dined with anyone who served or ordered a dish such as spaghetti. Triggers can be so pervasive and intense that they can seriously impair the patient's ability to function in the world.

The first treatment task is to help the patient identify the unconscious association with the trigger. Through hypnotic recall and artwork, Anna realized that red sauces reminded her of blood-letting and ceremonial cannibalism.

The second stage is desensitization and helping the patient become reacquainted with the benign aspects of the triggers so that anxiety is reduced. When Anna could accept that her previously traumatizing experience was not being carried over to her present reality, she became able to manage her anxiety in the present.

Cues. A "cue" is a specific conditioned stimulus or message intended to elicit a specific programmed reaction. Unlike triggers, cues are reportedly deliberate and have been programmed into the individual, sometimes years or even decades earlier. Receiving a single rose, for instance, could be a cue to make a phone call to a cult leader, come to a cult meeting, self-mutilate, or commit suicide. Certain phrases may also be cues. Karen's cult-involved mother closed all of her letters with, "We're praying for you." Karen felt that this phrase was a cue to return to the cult; she also associated the word "pray" with "prey." She experienced herself as the "prey" of her parents.

Because of their specific conditioned stimulus/response nature, desensitization to cues may be more difficult than to triggers. The most effective treatment approach is to help the patient recognize that she may exercise free choice in refusing to respond to the cue. Behavior modification techniques may also be useful.

Deceptive Practices

The use of deceptive practices is another complex component of indoctrination and programming. From patient reports, children in a cult are subjected to a wide variety of deceptive practices ranging from outright trickery to lies and fabrications for the following reasons:

The production of illusions suggests that the cult members have extraordinary powers that the child cannot possibly confront or challenge. For instance, Nancy reported that as an adolescent, she saw a woman stab herself with a collapsible knife filled with fake blood. The woman fell shrieking to the ground, convulsed in "death throes," and then "magically" came back to life when "Satan" called her.

The deception creates in the child a sense that she has witnessed or participated in more brutality or supernatural activities than have actually occurred. Patients routinely report having been drugged and otherwise sensorially manipulated. They are told that an eye has been surgically implanted and can see every move they make, or a sensor has been installed within them that reads anti-cult thoughts. Combined with dissociative defenses, this deception creates an environment in which the child cannot discriminate between the actual and the staged.

The child may believe that she observed or participated in murders that were, in fact, trickery. Jennifer reported that as a young girl she observed a ritual in which another child was "smothered" with a pillow. She later learned that the child had been drugged with barbiturates and was not dead but only unconscious.

The child's confidence in her own perceptions of what is real and what is false is severely eroded. She is subject to accepting as fact things that are taught by the cult; reality testing is seriously impaired, and "magical thinking" is common.

The child believes that she must overcome powers of a supernatural religious force and is overwhelmed at the idea of battling an entity such as Satan. The patient is, in many cases, incapable of recognizing that the task of treatment is to recover from tricks and brutal indoctrinations perpetrated by sadistic humans, not evil "deities."

However deceptive practices are conceptualized, it is useful to view all of the resultant functioning as survival mechanisms that are psychological in origin. The tendency is often to get lost in a "Manchurian Candidate" syndrome of complex programming or implantation, which can create a sense of helplessness and victimization in the therapist. It is helpful to remember that the general task, in working with indoctrinated beliefs and deceptive practices as well as in dissociative defenses in general, is to gradually reduce the dissociative defenses, allow information that has been dissociated to be retrieved into the psyche, and counter the conditioned responses through self-awareness.

Non–Multiple Personality Disorder Survivors

There is an increasing awareness of survivors who have not developed multiple personality disorder. These patients may not conform statistically to the sequalae found in dissociative patients. The author knows of three nondissociative patients reporting ritual abuse who completed treatment without hypnotic intervention and where no "satanic" entities were dissociated.

These patients may be easier to work with than those with severe dissociative disorders. However, the steps are still the same: They must develop a therapeutic alliance; they will deal with many of the same issues of working through, managing memories, experiencing abreactions. The major difference is that a patient not dominated by dissociative defenses will become aware of her experience in the more traditional ways in which repressed memories surface. She, too, will go through a period of developing a new perspective about life, a sense of decontaminating herself from the effects of cult activity, and finding new purpose and meaning for her own life. Non-MPD survivors, rather than having alternate personalities, may have a number of maladaptive self-representations and identifications that must be dealt with.

The ultimate task, for non-MPD patients as well as dissociative ones, is to move beyond victimization and mere survival to a position of empowerment and participation in life.

Conclusion

As clinicians, we must recognize that we are in an early phase of our understanding of ritual abuse and its sequelae, and yet patients with severe dissociative disorders continue to present with reports of ritual abuse. Regardless of the extent or prevalence of the phenomena, regardless of its accuracy, inaccuracy, or distortion, these patients are suffering from an internal experience and deserve to be treated with as much care and respect as patients reporting any other type of psychological disorder or emotional pain.

It is clear that what is unknown in the treatment of patients reporting ritual abuse is much greater than what is known. We are likely to hear many variations on the themes of programming, indoctrination, deceptive practices, and actual cult activities. The methodology of cults from region to region or group to group will also not necessarily be the same.

This entire area will no doubt remain highly controversial for some time to come, and as clinicians we must be prepared to continually revise and challenge our own thinking and treatment strategies when working with this complex patient population.

References

Adams, Kathleen. 1990. *Journal to the Self: 22 Paths to Personal Growth*. New York: Warner Books.

American Medical Association. 1985. Report of the AMA Council on Scientific Affairs: Scientific Status of Refreshing Recollection By the Use of Hypnosis. *Journal of the American Medical Association*, 253: 1918–1923.

American Psychiatric Association. 1987. *Diagnostic and Statistical Manual of Mental Disorders*. 3d ed. Washington, D.C.: American Psychiatric Association.

Barkin, Robert, B. G. Braun, and R. P. Kluft. 1986. "The Dilema of Drug Therapy for Multiple Personality Disorder." *Treatment of Multiple Personality Disorder, ed. B. G. Braun. Washington, D.C.: American Psychiatric Press.

Bliss, Eugene. 1986. *Multiple Personality, Allied Disorders, and Hypnosis*. New York: Oxford University Press.

Braun, Bennett G. 1990. Unusual Medication Regimens in the Treatment of Dissociative Disorders: Part I: Noradrenergic Agents. *Dissociation*, 3: 144–150.

Clark, J. G. 1979. "Cults." *Journal of the American Medical Association* 242:279–81.

Ganaway, George. 1989. "Historical Truth Versus Narrative Truth: Clarifying the Role of Exogenous Trauma in the Etiology of Multiple Personality and Its Variants." *Dissociation* 2, no. 4:205–20.

Hassan, Steven. 1988. *Combatting Cult Mind Control. Rochester, VT.: Park Street Press.

Hill, Sally, and Jean Goodwin. 1989. "Satanism: Similarities between Patient Accounts and Pre-Inquisition Historical Sources." *Dissociation* 2, no. 1:39–44.

Kluft, R. P. 1982. Varieties of Hypnotic Interventions in the Treatment of Multiple Personality. *American Journal of Clinical Hypnosis, 24:* 230–240.

Kluft, R. P. 1983. "Hypnotherapeutic Crisis Intervention in Multiple Personality." *American Journal of Clinical Hypnosis* 26: 73–83.

Lifton, R. J. 1989. *Thought Reform and the Psychology of Totalism*. Chapel Hill: University of North Carolina Press.

Lowenstein, R. J. 1988. "Open Trial of Clonazepam in the Treatment of Post-Traumatic Stress Symptoms in Multiple Personality Disorder." *Dissociation* 1:3–12.

Noll, Richard. 1989. "Satanism, UFO Abductions, Historians, and Clinicians: Those Who Do Not Remember the Past. . . ." in "Letters to the Editor." *Dissociation* 2: 251–53.

Orne, M. T. 1979. "The Use and Misuse of Hypnosis in Court." *International Journal of Clinical and Experimental Hypnosis* 27:311–41.

Pettinati, H. M., ed. 1988. *Hypnosis and Memory*. New York: Guilford Press.

Putnam, F. W. 1989. *Diagnosis and Treatment of Multiple Personality Disorder*. New York: Guilford Press.

———. , G. K. Ganaway, Richard Noll, and Sherrill Mulhern. 1990. "Satanic Ritual Abuse, Critical Issues, and Alternative Hypotheses." Panel Presentation at the Seventh International Conference on Multiple Personality/Dissociative States. Chicago, Ill. November 11. (Presentation available through Audio Transcripts, Ltd., 335 S. Patrick St., Suite 220, Alexandria, Va. 22314.)

Ross, C. A. 1989. *Multiple Personality Disorder Diagnosis, Clinical Features, and Treatment*. New York: John Wiley and Sons.

Sachs, R. G. 1990. "The Sandtray Technique in the Treatment of Patients with Dissociative Disorders: Recommendations for Occupational Therapists." *American Journal of Occupational Therapy* 44, no. 11 (November): 1045–1047.

Tennant-Clark, C. M., J. J. Fritz, and Fred Beauvais. 1989. "Occult Participation: Its Impact on Adolescent Development." *Adolescence* 24, no. 96 (Winter): 757–772.

Van Benschoten, S. C. 1990. "Multiple Personality Disorder and Satanic Ritual Abuse: The Issue of Credibility." *Dissociation* 3:22–30.

Van der Kolk, B. A. 1987. *Psychological Trauma*. Washington, D.C.: American Psychiatric Press.

Young, W. C. 1986. "Restraints in the Treatment of Patients with Multiple Personality." *American Journal of Psychotherapy* 40, no. 4: 601–606.

———. , R. G. Sachs, B. G. Braun, and R. T. Watkins. 1991. "Patients Reporting Ritual Abuse in Childhood: A Clinical Syndrome." *International Journal of Child Abuse and Neglect* 15: 181–189.

11

Bound by the Boundaries: Therapy Issues in Work with Individuals Exposed to Severe Trauma

David K. Sakheim, Ph.D.
Susan E. Devine, R.N., M.S.N.

M ost therapists who work with patients suffering from multiple personality disorder or other severely abused patients find themselves becoming intellectually isolated from their colleagues and uncertain about how to describe what it is that they do in their therapy sessions. Many of the usual boundaries in the therapy (e.g., length of sessions) become more flexible, and therapists find themselves much more active and supportive than with their other patients. There is often a feeling that what is occurring will not be accepted by other therapists, which is often the case. A way of understanding what is essential and helpful in this type of work is clearly needed.

The essential ingredient in psychotherapy with someone who has experienced severe abuse is the provision of safety. A sufficiently safe setting must be created and maintained for the patient to experience and work through the aspects of the trauma that were previously too overwhelming to integrate. It is our experience that if such a setting is provided, the patient's memories and feelings will emerge on their own. We do not endorse an active model of therapy where the therapist is the expert and does something to the patient to make this happen. Neither do we endorse a passive stance for the therapist. We believe that the therapist's role is to help to facilitate a safe and secure setting in which he or she is experienced as "being with" the patient, and that this will allow the material that needs to be explored to emerge (Winicott 1986).

Safety obviously has many aspects. This chapter focuses on the therapeutic environment and the relationship between therapist and patient. However, we do not deny the importance of stability and safety in other areas of the patient's life as well. These other areas are often insufficiently addressed in theory and practice, but can be extremely important in a patient's ability to explore the difficult material from the past. Financial problems, relationship difficulties, occupational instability, health issues, poor physical self-care, substance abuse, absence of a support system, an insecure living situation, and minimal relaxation/self-soothing strategies all should be addressed in the early phases in order to help the patient create a stable and safe environment in which to do the work of therapy. Our experience has been that supporting the emergence of difficult material before these areas have been sufficiently addressed will only retraumatize the patient. To feel safe and secure is a basic human need (Maslow 1970) and an essential component of self-esteem (Sullivan 1940). Attempting to work on frightening material in an unsafe place is setting the treatment up to fail.

Judith Herman (1990) suggests that treatment for sexual and physical abuse should help the patient to reconstruct care, connection and meaning, empowerment, and the creation of new connections. She suggests that this process consists of three stages. These are the creation of a safe environment, resolution of the trauma, and then reconnection to the world. The therapist's role is described as that of a consultant, ally, and witness for the patient. An important facet of this simple but elegant outline is the therapist's role in providing an environment that can serve as a safe container for the patient's feelings and memories. However, this is not always a simple matter with this population, as what is safe for one individual will not always feel safe to another. For many ritually abused patients safety is not a familiar concept and much more effort must be expended to create a secure working alliance than would be the case for work with other patient groups.

Traditional approaches to dynamic psychotherapy stress the importance of boundaries and neutrality in the therapeutic setting. The basic notion is that only in a bounded and neutral situation can the therapist interpret to the patient how he or she reacts and projects his or her own expectations and feelings. In such a setting transference reactions can be clearly seen as belonging to the patient and not to the situation nor to the therapist. However, this approach presumes the establishment of a working therapeutic alliance in which the patient feels sufficiently secure and trusting to be able to hear and process an interpretation.

Such an approach has even been applied to severely disturbed patient groups who are more inclined toward "acting-out." J. F. Masterson's (1976) work with borderline patients is a good example. When such a patient replicates in therapy a "no win" dilemma, rather than play into it, the therapist can simply point out the dilemma itself. For example, if a patient brings in an expensive gift and asks the therapist to keep it, the traditional response would not be to act, but rather to explore the meanings of keeping the gift and the meanings of not accepting it. The goal would be that the patient could be helped to see that while he or she might, for example, feel gratified if the therapist accepts the gift, he or she might also feel exploited and angry. On the other hand, if the therapist refuses it, although the patient might feel less obligated, he or she might also feel rejected and uncared about. Thus, the patient could come to recognize that no matter what action the therapist takes, the patient would be likely to have certain types of reactions, the strength and types of which usually would have more to do with past experiences and expectations than with the therapist's actions themselves. The focus is on the patient's understanding how he or she experiences events, rather than on playing them out in treatment.

Clearly, helping a patient to realize how he or she creates, replicates, and reacts to problematic interpersonal situations is a major goal of all treatment. Unfortunately, the appealing clarity and simplicity of the above approach is not always possible, especially when working with severely abused populations. It is also important to recognize that therapeutic neutrality is not always possible and certainly does not always equal inaction.

A clinical example may help to clarify this point. One of the authors was confronted with this issue early in his practice. He had been well schooled in the notion that interpreting the "no win" aspects of a situation rather than reacting either way was the clear therapeutic solution when confronted with "border-line" dilemmas. However, on meeting with his first dissociative patient this rule of thumb lost its value. The patient sat down in the first session, began to discuss her early years, and in explaining how her mother used to burn her for "punishment," the patient took out her cigarette lighter, lit it, appeared to go into a trance, and continued to hold the lighter under her hand. The therapist remembered the ban on action from his training. However it seemed crazy to sit there and point out how he was being placed in a "no win" situation. He could have noted that his pushing her hand from the fire might feel infantalizing, or that his inaction might feel like a lack of caring, yet the very time taken to discuss this meant ignoring that the patient's hand was burning. Despite the truth of such an interpretation the costs of making it would have been too great. The therapist instead chose to act, first asking the patient to stop and then pushing her hand from the fire. He understood that there probably would be negative aspects to acting-out but these were felt to be outweighed by the serious costs of inaction.

The above example points out that a therapist may need to act in certain situations. Such a therapeutic decision can only be made after a cost/benefit analysis rather than by following a simple rule such as "never act." In the above example the patient did, in fact, feel annoyed, confused, and somewhat infantalized at the moment. It also had the potential of setting up a dangerous precedent that the therapist would or could "rescue" the patient in future times of crisis. Fortunately, in this instance it was possible to discuss these issues and to explore her past history and its role in creating such situations. The patient's ability to see more direct ways of approaching the issues involved, and her remembering the triggering abuse more clearly, was only possible after it had been so dramatically played out in therapy. The situation was utilized many times in the course of treatment as an example of her replicating problematic interpersonal patterns as well as an example of a memory intruding into current situations. The patient's primary reaction to it was an example of someone refusing to calmly sit by while she got hurt (as had occurred in her family). It is difficult to see that such discussions or understandings could have occurred while the patient was in the process of burning her hand!

Clearly, the fact that the patient in the above example was in a trance or partial flashback made a more usual therapy approach impossible. However, even if she hadn't been in a trance, much of the above would still apply. In part this is because many patients who have been severely abused don't trust words. They have been lied to too often to believe anything but actions. Thus, much of the early course of treatment involves "trust tests" of varying types. Many of these tests involve more fluid boundaries between therapist and patient than would occur in traditional psychotherapy. Again, the therapist must weigh the benefits and the costs of changing the boundaries (or of leaving them unchanged).

A typical example in working with multiple personality disorder patients would be if the patient tells the therapist that he or she wants to allow a child alter to emerge, but that the child alter remembers being abused in a chair, and therefore could only come forward to talk if the patient and therapist sit on the floor. Again, the choice to change the usual boundaries will not be without repercussions. Clearly, the patient may feel safer. In fact, without complying with the request the child alter (and the abuse memory) may have to stay suppressed, slowing the treatment and leaving the patient with unpleasant symptoms. On the other hand, other alters may be frightened by such a change in the rules, fearing that if this boundary is changeable so are others, including ones that had been providing some feelings of safety. For example, if this boundary can change does that mean that "rules" about no sexual interactions are also flexible? In other words, no therapeutic action is without varied and complex consequences, and these meanings are very important to ascertain. However, the notion that "no action" avoids this complexity is a myth. It only provides the therapist with a false sense that he or she is protected from sending messages to the patient. R. R. Greenson (1971) points out that even in traditional analysis

> Everything we do or say, or don't do or say, from the decor of our office, the magazines in the waiting room, the way we open the door, greet the patient, make interpretations, keep silent, and end the hour, reveals something about our real self, and not only our professional self . . . the whole school of analysts which believes that psychoanalytic treatment consists of "only inter-preting" is guilty of using transference interpretations as a defense.

The point here is that there is no such thing as "neutrality," and a pretense that it exists can be very destructive, especially in work with this population. Inaction in the face of certain patient needs or actions is not "neutral." However, once a therapist acknowledges stepping into the realm of action then he or she must begin the very difficult task of analyzing the costs and benefits of such actions.

Clearly, boundaries in therapy provide much of what makes the situation safe in the first place. Knowing that feelings can be expressed without being acted upon is one of the features that allows therapy to be different from other relationships. Many of the boundaries of therapy have developed from years of experience and the wisdom of generations of patients and therapists. Bans on sexual intimacies and physical abuse, for example, have protected many individuals from getting hurt. It is not the purpose of this chapter to suggest that "anything goes" so long as it can be rationalized. However, it is equally problematic to be rigidly inflexible with areas that could be beneficial if modified. Although it is easier for a therapist to have clear rules to follow, this is not always the best therapy.

What makes this still more difficult is that the patient's past experiences with boundaries have not usually been healthy ones. Thus, the requests that are made for changes in boundaries need to be very carefully evaluated. For instance, a patient may proposition the therapist because he or she believes that this is what must occur to be cared about by someone else. When such a request is examined, the expectations behind it can be made more clear. On the other hand, a patient's request to hold a teddy bear while remembering frightening childhood abuse may have few costs and important benefits. The best guideline for developing or changing the boundaries in therapy is to try to ascertain with the patient if the change in question will increase or decrease the safety and comfort of the therapeutic alliance in both the short and long term. This is not always an easy matter, but that is not reason to avoid it.

In traditional analysis the patient is asked to lie on a couch without the ability to see the therapist. This can often help the patient to relax physically, as well as to enhance transference projections. It is important to note, however, that this style of therapeutic frame is not at all neutral. It clearly capitalizes on the meanings and associations that most people have to lying down. If analysis were being developed today, the same types of arguments would arise about moving from therapist and patient sitting facing each other to allowing the patient to lie down and relax on a couch. Why allow such a change in the frame? Couldn't this be experienced as seductive or too gratifying? Isn't it a form of acting-out? Why not just discuss the patient's wish to be more free from distraction or more comfortable? Clearly, these questions are good ones. However, the paradox lies in the fact that it may be easier to get at these issues for the patient when the frame is such that the patient can feel safe and secure as well as having minimal external interpersonal and/or other distractions to his or her associations. Clearly, some of the above problems may come up. A patient may experience difficulties after such a change in the frame. However, for most people, the costs of these problems are outweighed by the benefits of the increased safety and decreased distraction. In summary, for most people lying down is not a neutral event, but rather one that is associated with relaxation, sleep, and safety. This makes it a very useful adjunct to treatment, since it is only in such a secure environment can any person trust enough to explore difficult personal material.

In contrast to the above situation, most severely abused patients would not associate such a context with safety, but rather would be terrified at being so vulnerable, exposed, and unable to see the other person in the room. This comes from his or her past experiences as well. If one has been raped in a bed or on a couch, it does not seem reasonable to expect that person to be able to relax, lower defenses, and become insightful in a physically similar situation. In other words, the typical therapy situation is far from neutral for anyone. For the usual patient it capitalizes on associations of lying down with safety and comfort to enhance the treatment. One would be missing this important understanding about each person's unique construct system to expect all patients to feel safe under identical circumstances. There is nothing magical about the usual therapy frame. It must be designed to enhance the healing aspects of treatment. This means creating a setting that will enable each patient to feel safe and secure. Clearly, this does not mean always doing the same things or utilizing the same therapeutic framework. What is safe to one person can be terrifying for another. The therapist must work with the patient continuously to discover what will help to accomplish such a basic sense of security. This can be no small task for the severely traumatized patient, and may in fact take a very long time.

Usually this process will help the patient and therapist identify may of the things that frighten the patient, and that information will often be very helpful later in treatment. However, before the patient can truly understand why such reactions occur, the setting must be secure enough to allow the related memories to surface. A good example of this occurred with a ritual abuse survivor who was trying to draw during an early therapy session. When the therapist brought out pencils, pens, crayons, and markers the patient became very frightened of the crayons. She had no idea of why this was, but could not tolerate even looking at them. The therapist tried in vain to explore the meanings of this fear and even tried some desensitization attempts. However, after seeing that this was not helpful, but rather was only serving to make the patient more agitated and frightened, the therapist simply removed the crayons. The patient then was able to draw. Months later, this same patient remembered an abuse incident many years earlier at a day-care center that involved insertion of crayons into her vagina. Once she remembered this, she no longer felt panic upon seeing crayons or other such cues. However, the memory only emerged after she had felt safe enough to draw (with a pencil) about the various pieces of the experience. It is certainly possible that the memory could have emerged anyway, or that continued discussion of the crayons and/or approaches to desensitize the fear might have helped. However, our experience has been that the relevant memories are best able to come forward when the patient feels safe enough to tolerate them. The patient is usually the best guide as to how to create the degree and type of safety that is required.

It is much easier for a therapist to have clear and rigid rules for how to act or not to act. Allowing for boundary changes makes this considerably more complex. This is especially true for severely abused patients since they tend to present with such difficult and affect-laden material. The therapist must try to sort out all of the patient's feelings about the boundary in question, as well as his or her own. There is no question that this also allows more of the therapist's countertransference feelings to disrupt the treatment. However, when pursued honestly, with an eye on all that's involved, and with the patient as a participant in the decision, such an approach can truly move the treatment forward.

Much of the writing about therapeutic neutrality is geared toward creating an environment that is best suited for a patient to be able to hear an interpretation. However, a patient who is terrified or untrusting can not hear nor benefit from interpretation, never mind allow free rein to his or her associations and memories. Thus, before the therapy can move to that level a great deal of work must take place involving the development of a secure and trusting therapeutic relationship. Alice Miller describes this process in which the therapist must strive to "take the patient's part . . . as much as is humanly possible" by being understanding, respectful and nonjudgmental, as well as by being willing to acknowledge errors and fallibility. She points out that the patient must come to find out "often for the first time in his life what it means to have someone on his side, an advocate." Only through such a supportive connection can the patient discover "that the analyst is interested in the history of his childhood and is searching for messages and reenactments of repressed traumas in everything occurring . . . and that he is attempting to learn with the patient the language of the latter's repetition compulsion." Thus, the analyst must strive to help the adult patient understand his or her early traumas through the safety of the therapeutic connection. Alice Miller poetically describes this as "being guided by the child, who is not yet able to speak" (1984, 54–63). Greenson (1971) also points out that severely traumatized patients "require preparatory therapy which consists essentially of *building* an object relationship." As has been discussed above, in many instances, especially in the early phases, this work requires a language of action.

Unfortunately, other than being guided by the patient's lead and by an attempt to maintain a secure containment environment, there are no simple rules or formulas for pursuing this task. Each situation, therapist, patient, and therapeutic relationship is different and needs to be treated as such. A good example of how this operates in practice involves the use of physical contact between patients and therapists.

Physical contact between a therapist and patient is traditionally considered taboo. Although this taboo probably has served a useful function in protecting some patients and therapists from acting out sexually, it too is not a universal rule. Most therapists who work with severely abused patients know that some patients can benefit from physical contact, but that just as it can be nurturant, grounding, or supportive, it can also feel frightening and hurtful. As with all such boundary issues analyzing the costs and benefits of the specific situation is needed.

Patients going through an abreaction can be helped tremendously by such contact and will often report feeling less alone, more supported, more connected to the safety of the present, less "untouchable," and so forth. Holding a patient's hand during such a memory would be a typical example. In many such instances the benefits may far outweigh the costs. However, it would be a mistake to assume that this is always the case. One must be guided by the patient's lead, the point in treatment, and the feelings and needs involved.

It is not always a simple matter to sort out how best to proceed. The art of therapy is being able to balance all of the factors involved in a way that ultimately proves helpful to the patient. A therapist's staying in touch with his or her own feelings, getting supervision or peer consultation, while trying to stay open to the patient's feelings is essential. Some examples with differing outcomes regarding physical contact between a patient and therapist may help to clarify this point.

An excellent therapist working with a patient diagnosed with multiple personality disorder struggled with this issue in her supervision with one of the authors. Her patient had asked that she hold his hand during an abreaction and she found herself uncomfortable with the request. She knew that her patient was scared and that such contact could help him to stay more in touch with the present. She also knew that the safety of his contact with her probably would be required for him to be able to risk remembering. However, she was ambivalent about such touch, especially because when she had brought it up in a staff meeting at her clinic some of her peers had strongly advised her against physical contact with any patient. However, upon examining this further, the therapist was able to see that she believed that the touch would be helpful for the patient, but scary for her. She was able to see that beside the beliefs of her peers, her reluctance was primarily based on her own sexual feelings toward this patient and her own unconscious fears of eliminating a "no contact" rule. Her fear of such contact "getting out of control" did not feel realistic once she was able to be conscious of the feelings involved. In realizing this, she also was able to see that this was not the patient's issued, but rather her own, and one that once realized, she felt much more comfortable handling. In fact, the physical contact turned out to be a very significant support for the patient who was amazed that someone was willing to "be there" for him and that someone understood how little and scared he felt during the abreaction, despite his normal presentation, size, and appearance. In this instance, there were few if any negative repercussions.

On the other hand, one of the authors worked with a very psychotic hospitalized patient who repeatedly asked to be hugged. The therapist's feeling was that this was primarily a sexualized request rather than a need for nurturance, and each time he refused to act on it, but instead tried to discuss its meaning. Although the patient was not willing to discuss it, she appeared calmer with each refusal. After the third request and refusal the patient revealed that she had been a prostitute when she was younger, and then stood up and said, "Please may I give you a hug and a kiss because you have helped me so much."

The therapist again stated that they could talk about such feelings but would not act on them. At that point, the patient began to sob, and without any psychotic disruptions, she described a long history of childhood incest and other abuse. When she had tried as a child to report this, the person she told had also abused her. Thus, she needed to know that the therapist would not act in any way sexually with her before she could reveal her history. Her "knowing" this required more than reassuring words. It needed to be seen through the actions (in this case, inaction) of the therapist.

The two examples raise the important question of how to know when to act and when not to do so. Had the therapist hugged the second patient, it clearly could have been destructive to the treatment. On the other hand, had the first therapist not been able to resolve her own difficulties with physical contact and had not held the patient's hand, it likely also would have impeded the therapeutic process. It would obviously be much easier if there were a simple rule, but clearly this cannot be. A therapist must do his or her best to weigh what is said, what is felt, what is known about the patient, the diagnosis, the history, the transference and the countertransference, and work with the patient to decide accordingly. This must be done with the knowledge that errors will inevitably be made, and that even when a good decision occurs, it too may have negative side effects. The correct action is an approach that attempts to minimize the costs and maximize the benefits for the patient's growth while being willing to talk about all of the feelings that arise from whatever action is taken. Making an error is not a terrible thing if it is safe to acknowledge and learn from it. The therapist must recognize that he or she is not an all-knowing expert but rather an ally to the patient in navigating the therapy process.

Boundaries as they exist in traditional therapy are not only for the protection of the patient. A therapist who allows an examination and flexibility of boundaries must deal with his or her own feelings and anxieties about such a situation. This should probably happen in all therapy, but in this type of work one is forced to confront such feelings on a much more regular and intense basis. The patients have not known boundaries in their early years that were designed for their needs. They may have been exposed to rigid parental rules or to chaotic and changing ones, usually designed to meet the needs of the parent or perpetrator. Setting rigid boundaries in therapy can replicate this phenomena. This is especially true if the boundaries are, in fact, there for the security or protection of the therapist at the expense of the patient and are not acknowledged as such. As each aspect of the therapeutic relationship is challenged and tested, it is much more helpful to the patient to be honest if a limit is for his or her protection, for the therapist's, or for the benefit of the relationship. For example, in negotiating an initial treatment plan with a patient, some therapists state that frequent crisis calls cannot be a part of the treatment. However, it is rarely clarified for whom such a rule is designed. In fact, it is often stated or implied that it is for the patient's benefit. It would be much more honest and helpful to acknowledge that such a limit does not mean that the patient will not have crises, nor that such calls might not be helpful. Rather, that for the protection of the therapist's private life there is a limit to the time that he or she is willing to make available and that this particular service is not a part of what is being offered. Then, if the patient feels that such crisis availability is something that he or she will need, the therapist can help him or her to find a different provider, or to explore other possible resources where such calls could be made. It is very unfair and confusing to ignore this issue or to pretend that it is for the patient's benefit when it is not the case. There is nothing wrong with boundaries that are designed to protect the therapist. It is only important that they be recognized as such.

Nurturance as expressed by a therapist is clearly another boundary issue in treatment. It is not unusual for therapists who work with MPD patients to find themselves being more nurturant than their peers or than they are with other patients. This is sometimes justified as "reparenting" or is criticized as being a countertransference problem. What makes this area difficult is that both views have some validity. Nurturance can be a very significant part of the healing process, and it can equally prove very destructive. Some of the previous examples such as holding a patient's hand during an abreaction or sitting on the floor with a child alter demonstrate the safety-enhancing aspects of being nurturant. This can be critical in enabling the patient to feel safe enough for important material to surface. However, nurturant approaches can also give patients the very false belief that the therapist will be able to make up for the past losses or neglect in their lives. It is very presumptuous to believe that one can "re-parent" someone else and in a few hours each week, somehow fill the voids that he or she feels. It is also a denial that the patient, is or can be a competent, capable adult. Some therapists however, try to do this, and there are even the extreme instances of therapists taking patients into their homes to live or in other ways involving them in various intimate aspects of their lives and families. A lack of study of such approaches notwithstanding, it is probably safe to say that such attempts to redo a patient's childhood are likely misguided, and at the very least are something that most therapists are not willing to offer.

However, in less extreme ways nurturance can be critically important. The difference probably has something to do with the concept implicit in the notion that it is better to teach a man to fish than to just give him a fish. The first way will keep him fed for life, while the second is only briefly satisfying. However, if one's primary experiences with seafood have been numerous instances of food poisoning, one will likely first need to learn that fish is a good food when properly prepared before one would ever want to receive a fish in the first place, never mind learning to become a fisherman! Therapeutic nurturance can be viewed in this way. Clearly, the ultimate goal should be for the patient to learn to nurture him or herself, as well as to be able to find and accept such caring from others. It is also the case that simply providing nurturance can make a patient feel dependent on the therapist. Unless the therapist is willing to devote him or herself forever to such an endless job, it will probably be of only transitory benefit. In fact, it may end up creating serious problems for the patient when the therapist inevitably "burns out" or leaves, or for whatever reason can no longer continue to offer it. However, for some patients, nurturance is a relatively unknown commodity. Like the man in the above example whose primary experiences with fish had been food poisoning, a person whose primary experiences with others have been cruelty, is unlikely to wish to have more such exposures. In other words, before a person can accept nurturance, never mind learn to give it to him or herself, he or she must understand it as something worthwhile. Many severely abused patients have such histories and need to have positive experiences in the relationship with the therapist before they will want to learn to accept such support from others or to support themselves. Eric Erikson (1963) describes the development of trust as one of the most basic tasks of early development. The child normally comes to learn that "you can trust the world, in the form of your mother, that she will come back and feed you the right thing in the right quantity at the right time" (Erikson, quoted in Evans 1969). However, if this developmental task has not been accomplished because the patient's significant caretakers did none of those things, then that patient must experience such attentive nurturance to begin to develop a more healthy balance of trust and mistrust.

These points not only relate to external nurturance, but to the patient's ability to nurture him or herself. Due to their abusive and chaotic early years many severely abused patients do not initially understand self-soothing. A good example that arises with most ritually abused or other MPD patients involves the internal relationships between alters. Initially, these relationships typically mirror the cruelty and mistrust that was present in the patient's early years. A therapist can model (as well as discuss) different ways to handle such conflicts. If, for example, it is determined that a self-destructive alter needs to be "away" between sessions to keep the body safe, a typical "solution" by the other alters would be to try to kill her off, lock her in a dungeon, or expose her to painful feelings/memories if she tries to emerge. The therapist can instead model a more nurturant compromise solution such as using hypnosis to create a safe and comfortable place that this alter can stay between meetings. Initially, the therapist may have to come up with this type of suggestion since it has likely never been a part of the patient's experiences. P. A. Dewald (1969) points out how attitudes and feelings toward oneself develop from an internalization of early parental attitudes toward the child. Heinz Kohut (1977) describes how self-soothing becomes possible because these self-representations can become stable and cohesive structures through the internalization of responsive, empathic others. Alice Miller (1984) describes that through the therapist's respect and caring "an empathic inner object is established that enables the patient to experience sorrow but also curiosity concerning his own childhood . . . the patient becomes more and more interested in his past, and at this point, if not sooner, his depression and suicidal thoughts disappear" (55). With dissociative patients this process usually results in changes in how the system of personalities function as the alters see how well cooperation and caring can work. Some alters may even model themselves after the therapist, trying to help others internally. The patient gradually comes to see how much energy has been spent internally warring, and how much safer and effective it is to treat each alter's wishes and feelings with respect. Instead of having life decisions based on whoever internally is most powerful at the moment, they can be based on a consensus of all alters' feelings and needs.

It is difficult for someone to recognize this fact if it has never been a part of his or her life. For most of these patients might has always meant right while compromise and caring were uniformly absent. Thus, the therapist's demonstration of respect, compromise, and caring become a very significant first step in the process of learning about these phenomena.

A clinical example that helps to demonstrate this process involves a patient diagnosed with MPD who came to treatment unable to calm herself without external means (drugs, cutting, vomiting, etc.) whenever she would begin to feel overwhelmed. She first learned that talking to her therapist on the phone could help at such times. However, as she appeared to be more able to handle these situations, her therapist began to set limits on the number of such crisis calls and she had to find some other solutions. She came up with the idea of "taking [the therapist] home with" her in the form of a taperecorded voice and a small object from his office. She had been having great difficulty in falling asleep at night due to intrusive abuse memories. She recalled how helpful and soothing the phone contacts had been, and asked that the therapist make her a tape that she could listen to before bed. The tape described safe and soothing images of a beautiful relaxing place that she and the therapist developed together. It also contained suggestions about being able to sleep comfortably and safely. Parenthetically, a particularly helpful component turned out to be the suggestion that all dreams would be sufficiently disguised so as not to become nightmares nor to wake her, yet would still be able to help her to continue working on whatever themes or memories needed dream work. Clearly, such a tape and even the crisis calls represent a violation of the usual boundaries. However, the patient used this tape for months, instead of resorting to frequent crisis calls, large amounts of alcohol and benzodiazapines, or the self-destructive behaviors. The next step was to help the patient discover that she could create "safe places in the mind" herself. After a particularly gruesome memory had been relieved in therapy, one alter "took care" of the child alter who had remembered it by "playing therapist" and describing a peaceful and healing "space station" where the upset child alter could be cared for. As time has gone on, this patient has developed numerous such strategies for self-soothing and no longer utilizes any medications. Crisis calls are now few and far between. In fact, this patient recently returned the object that she had borrowed, stating that she no longer needed it to remind herself of the secure feelings from therapy since she could now picture the therapist in her mind and could imagine on her own what calming things he might say to her. Clearly, there has been a gradual process of internalizing the soothing aspects of the therapist. First by utilizing sessions, then phone calls, then the transitional object (the taperecording and small object), and finally by trying it out herself. It is a therapeutic parallel to what Althia Horner (1986) describes about this phase for the developing child: "After a time, the young child develops within himself, at a symbolic level, inner resources for the kind of comforting he derived from external supports. It is like having a loving mother within the self" (89). Had the therapist never provided such nurturance it seems unlikely that the patient would have been able to change these constructs. On the other hand, had the therapist always been available and attempting to meet all of her needs all of the time, the patient never would have had reason to begin to take over the process herself. Both parts are important to remember. We should aim to make ourselves less and less essential. However, MPD patients are often learning about nurturance for the first time in treatment. That means that the therapist has the difficult task of balancing giving them some nurturance without acting in a fashion that will keep them from learning to obtain it for themselves.

No matter how well this balance is achieved, the therapist will have to face the patient's fears, wishes, and disappointments about nurturance. The patient may wish that the therapist could re-parent him or her. In fact, this is often very directly expressed by a child alter who may ask if the therapist will be his or her mother or father. Other alters may feel entitled to such care because of all that has been endured. Accepting that this is not going to occur in the way desired is usually a real loss that needs to be faced. Angry alters may berate the therapist for not giving enough, setting limits, encouraging the patient to learn self-soothing before they feel ready or able, and so on. Other alters may express fears that accepting nurturance will mean obligation or future abuse, still others may fear abandonment and hurt if they allow themselves to trust or be cared for. The point is not to try to avoid these feelings and others, but rather to help the patient work through them, sorting out the fears and expectations that served as defenses in the past and are no longer useful. The process involved over the course of treatment is a developmental one much like that with a parent and developing child. In fact, this often occurs in a very literal way with the developing child alters. The issues that arise are similar to those that arose for all of us as we developed, starting with safety and trust and moving all the way through separation, individuation, and autonomy (Mahler 1965). In that respect the process is a sort of "re-parenting" or better stated a parallel to parenting. However, that does not in any way mean trying to "make up for" or fill the voids created by hurt and neglect, which is impossible. It is rather a process of showing the patient how their past has shut them off to some valuable intra and interpersonal experiences, and helping them to become more open to these.

However, it is very important to note that this does not mean infantalizing the patient by failing to acknowledge and appreciate their adult parts simultaneously. Unfortunately, many therapies end up denying either the adult or the child facets of the patient by attempting to "re-parent" or by only focusing on the "here and now." Such limited approaches only serve to further invalidate the patient's full internal and external experience.

Many traditional therapists object to the lack of typical boundaries that often characterizes work with dissociative patients. Instead, it might be more beneficial to learn from this work and even to assess the application of its principles to work with other populations. C. L. Field (1990) suggests that many negative therapeutic reactions in traditional therapy occur precisely because the therapist fails to recognize the traumatic background of such patients and to change the treatment approach accordingly. In most instances, with patients who have not experienced severe trauma and the corresponding difficulties with safety and trust, the balance will probably swing toward maintenance of the more usual boundaries for the purpose of protecting the consistency and "neutrality" of the treatment setting. However, even with neurotic patients, the "real relationship" is more important than is often realized. For example, a colleague described the final termination session of her eight-year-analysis. She and her analyst had done a great deal of work together, and both felt that the analysis was complete. On leaving the office for the last time the patient hugged her therapist goodbye. She described feeling surprised and hurt that her therapist stood rigidly and did not hug her back. That is not "neutrality." As Greenson (1971) points out, being a good therapist for any patient means being a caring human being first. It is our belief that this is a major part of what is curative in all treatment.

In order to pursue the necessary risks to achieve self-knowledge and awareness, the patient must experience the therapist's genuine caring and respect in their working alliance. The therapist in this role as consultant and ally must be educated about and sensitive to the possible ramifications of boundary changes as they arise in treatment. It would probably make sense for every therapist who pursues this work to read the writings of Robert Langs (1973, 1974) on the dangers of boundary violations. Not so that he or she will strive to never alter any boundaries, as Langs espouses, but rather to become more fluent with the types of themes and issues that are likely to emerge around any particular boundary change. Such knowledge and experience then can be used to inform the patient of issues and problems that could emerge from any such changes. As in all psychotherapy, the goal is to help bring into awareness what was unconscious or unavailable to the patient so that more fully conscious choices about actions can occur. Boundary issues are no exception. If the therapist and patient are sensitive to the possible costs and benefits of boundary alterations, a conscious, informed choice can occur. Of course, there must also be a willingness to acknowledge errors and/or unforseen ramifications with a corresponding willingness to return to a previous therapeutic frame when indicated. If the patient and therapist are working together as a team to find the safest and most effective means of approaching painful materials, such an approach can work effectively.

One patient described the therapy process as walking through a dangerous war zone in order to rescue a severely injured child part of herself that had been left behind. Her need for a therapist was not to tell her how to do this, nor to do it for her. It was to have someone with whom she could stay connected while she risked pursuing this "rescue mission." A virtually universal fear for someone pursuing this work is that he or she will be unable to return after actually "re-connecting" with the pain of past abuse. A therapist's genuine caring and concern can help the patient to navigate back from the war zone once such a "rescue" has occurred.

References

Dewald, P. A. 1969. *Psychotherapy: A Dynamic Approach.* New York: Basic Books.

Erikson, E. H. 1963. *Childhood and Society.* New York: W. W. Norton.

Evans, R. I. 1969. *Dialogue with Eric Erikson.* New York: Dutton.

Field, C. L. 1990. *"Working with Trauma Survivors Who Form Negative Therapeutic Reactions."* Paper presented at the 98th Annual Convention of the American Psychological Association. Boston, Massachusetts.

Greenson, R. R. 1971. In *The Unconscious Today,* ed. Mark Kanzer, 213–32. (Ed). New York: International Universities Press.

Herman, J. L. 1990. *The Treatment of Trauma: Incest As a Paradigm.* Paper presented at *Psychological Trauma.* Sponsored by Harvard Medical School. Cambridge, Massachusetts, May 31–June 1.

Horner, Althia 1986. *Being and Loving.* Northvale, N.J.: Jason Aronson.

Kohut, Heinz 1977. *The Restoration of the Self.* New York: International Universities Press.

Langs, Robert 1973. *The Technique of Psychoanalytic Psychotherapy.* Vol. 17. New York: Jason Aronson.

———. 1974. *The Technique of Psychoanalytic Psychotherapy.* Vol. 2. New York: Jason Aronson.

Mahler, M. S. 1965. "On the Significance of the Normal Separation-Individuation Phase." In *Drives, Affects, Behavior,* ed. M. Schur, 161–69. New York: International Universities Press.

Maslow, A. H. 1970. *Motivation and Personality.* New York: Harper and Row.

Masterson, J. F. 1976. *Psychotherapy of the Borderline Adult: A Developmental Approach.* New York: Brunner/Mazel.

Miller, Alice 1984. *Thou Shalt Not Be Aware: Society's Betrayal of the Child.* New York: Farrar, Straus, and Giroux.

Sullivan, H. S. 1940. *Conceptions of Modern Psychiatry.* New York: W. W. Norton.

Winicott, D. W. 1986. *Home Is Where We Start From.* New York: W. W. Norton.

Conclusion

S atanic ritual abuse is not yet well defined. The chapters in this volume should illustrate that many survivors have experienced very severe forms of abuse. However, the parameters of how, where, when, and why this abuse occurs are still unclear. Thus, almost every facet of this phenomenon warrants further research and support.

There is an urgent need for a centralized, cogent system to screen, evaluate, and pool the data that is appearing so that a more organized and systematic approach to this problem can emerge. At this stage of understanding it is premature to attempt to provide definitive answers to questions about the treatment of ritual abuse survivors, particularly in light of the fact that the patient grouping itself is still a heterogeneous one. However, a realistic first step might be to focus on basic descriptive studies that identify who these patients are and what can be made of their allegations. This would provide a data base from which to proceed toward greater understanding within this topic area.

In order to facilitate these goals it is critical to publish and disseminate the data collected and the results of investigations. This could be accomplished through the creation of a journal specifically devoted to this topic. In addition, a multidisciplinary coordinated research unit could provide more empirical data by which to assess allegations of adults and children from all over the country. It could utilize the resources of police, lawyers, social service workers, therapists, survivors, parents, and clergy for their mutual benefit in evaluating, understanding, documenting, investigating, and clarifying all aspects of these cases. Examples of the usefulness of interdisciplinary cooperation include such things as being able to develop non-leading interviewing techniques that would protect the interests of the victims without limiting any later legal uses for their testimony. Therapists could share data from anonymous patient reports to help investigators better understand what they are evaluating and determine potential risks to their safety when they investigate ritual sites. In addition, increased awareness of police findings (or lack thereof) would help therapists to better understand how to view what their patients are attempting to describe. Collaborative efforts through an academic journal or research clearinghouse of information would allow the collection of data on such critical aspects as the incidence and prevalence of ritual abuse, data on the various perpetrating groups, information about practices (rituals, symbols, holidays, locations, and beliefs), data on the validity of allegations and on the results of investigations and court preoceedings, as well as much needed data on the survivors themselves. A centralized empirical data base would also allow a more streamlined approach to understanding this area, as well as facilitating the reporting of findings. Eventually, it would be possible also to obtain data on the various subgroups of patients and document most appropriate approaches to treatment for each.

As more information is collected, it will eventually be possible to do research on the treatment process itself. This will allow more definitive answers to issues that currently remain speculative. For example, some clinicians currently argue against uncovering extreme abuse in therapy, while others believe that removing all dissociative barriers is the only way to achieve health. Until more empirical data exists, such discussions are only hypothetical. In the meantime, the publication of clinical case reports would be helpful in addressing some of the above questions, particularly such clinical issues as the effect of varying the frequency and length of sessions, successes and failures using various treatment approaches, how substance use, acting-out, and hospitalizations, have been addressed, as well as exploring issues central to this population such as working with "programming," mind control, or the uncovering of specific tortures. Hopefully, as more becomes known about this area there will be clinical data available about uncovering and "sealing over" approaches to treatment, short-term and long-term strategies, what medications appear to be helpful for what symptoms at what points in treatment, as well as information about the different subtypes of patients. Only then will patients and clinicians be better able to make informed decisions about how to proceed. Once it becomes clear what is essential and what is unnecessary in treatment more coherent treatment approaches can be developed.

Despite the fact that there is a great deal that we don't know, the findings from work with severely traumatized patients are having a major impact on all aspects of psychiatry. Traditional notions are being challenged, even in such established areas as approaches to diagnosis and treatment. Patients with such extreme abuse histories are providing new insights for the mental health field even about such age-old controversies as the respective roles of nature and nurture in creating symptoms. Many problems previously believed to be of biological origin (e.g., allergies) are being found to be etiologically related to trauma for at least some patients (Braun 1983; Putnam 1984).

As the writers in this book attest, ritual abuse provides an example of how people respond to the extremes of human cruelty. The mental health field has a great deal to learn about the types of defenses that are available to people in such situations. However, what has already come to light suggests that new conceptualizations of many aspects of diagnosis and treatment are probably in order (Sakheim 1990; McCann, Pearlman, Sakheim, and Abrahamson 1988; Pelcovitz 1990).

Understandings about ritual abuse and dissociation as well as the current explosion of literature on various other types of victimization have made clear that many forms of psychopathology can come about through a person's reactions to stress and trauma (Putnam 1989; Kluft 1985). Many types of previously confusing psychopathology become clear (e.g., the symptoms no longer appear psychotic) when one is aware of their traumatic origins (McCann, Sakheim, and Abrahamson 1988). However, this insight causes major problems for a diagnostic system such as the DSM-III-R that currently is based on observable symptoms rather than etiology. As we come to know more about such disorders as borderline personality, PTSD, ritual abuse, the dissociative disorders, brief psychotic reactions, adjustment disorders, some eating disorders, and paraphilias, it seems clear that there needs to be more of a direct recognition of the impact of trauma in the formation of these later symptoms. The need for a diagnostic category (such as "Disorders of Extreme Stress") that more specifically reflects the impact of traumatic etiology is becoming increasingly apparent (Sakheim 1990; Pelcovitz; 1990).

Currently, DSM-III-R, in an attempt to increase diagnostic reliability and validity, has tried to utilize observable symptoms rather than unobservable motives, defenses, assumed etiologies, or dynamics. However, since it has become clear that trauma is responsible for certain types of responses, it makes sense to have a category that reflects this knowledge. One advantage of starting out with a purely observational system is to start to see patterns from research and clinical experience that can then help organize thinking about etiology, course, and prognosis. Since the field is now at that point with this area, it should be reflected in the diagnostic categories that are utilized.

Pulling together the descriptions throughout this volume about the impacts of severe trauma make it clear that no current diagnostic grouping accurately reflects these experiences. There is a need for a category that would allow for notation of how the injurious events disrupted various aspects of the person's functioning. With such a category, a clinician could note how the trauma affected the patient's interpersonal relationships (some of which is included in the DSM-III-R concept of Borderline Personality Disorder), how the person distanced him or herself from the trauma (e.g., by using a dissociative defense), what types of physiological reactions he or she currently has (such as hyperreactivity or increased startle reflex), what were the resulting physical problems (such as broken bones, arthritis, immune system disorders, etc.), and how the trauma affected such areas as sexuality, sleep, expression of impulses, modulation of affect, and the person's thought processes. It could also be noted if the trauma was recurrent, when it occurred developmentally, and what types of support were available at the time. As Lisa McCann and L. A. Pearlman make clear, any system for assessing the impact of trauma should also note the ways in which the experience disrupted a person's expectations, especially in the areas of safety, trust, esteem, independence, power, and intimacy. Future research and clinical work with severely traumatized patients will continue to elucidate how such a new diagnostic classification should be structured.

There are major implications for both research and treatment to understanding more about traumatic etiology. For example, therapists react very differently with patients diagnosed as having "Borderline Personality Disorder" when they are only made aware of the problematic interpersonal patterns of the patient, than if they have become aware that many of the inter-and intra-personal symptoms directly reflect the impacts of childhood physical and/or sexual abuse. Seeing that someone flees from closeness because they were hurt produces a very different level of empathy than does just noting that the patient flees from closeness. Thus, there is a need to stop overlooking data about traumatic etiology even if it means not being in keeping with other DSM categories (where observational data probably is still most indicated).

The importance of acknowledging ritual abuse is clear in psychiatry. However, the issue also arises in other fields. For example, it is common practice to "sanitize" court cases so that bizarre forms of ritual abuse are left out of the allegations (see Kinscherff and Barnum, Chapter 4). This has many implications. It may well be true that leaving out such extreme and unbelievable stories helps make a more credible case for a jury, but it also furthers the general view that such abuses do not exist since one rarely sees prosecutions nor convictions. There are no simple answers here, but the legal field will have to attend to the issues involved.

Patients with severe abuse histories can also teach a great deal about aspects of the interconnection of mind and body as well as the extremes of human capability. For example, most patients with such backgrounds report various types of special abilities from ESP to the ability to heal rapidly from injuries. Our understanding of these areas is not even in its infancy. We need to explore such phenomena despite our usual tendencies to discount them. For example, if rapid healing does in fact occur, it clearly would be very valuable to understand and perhaps learn possible applications for this process in the general population. We hope that this work will stimulate an increased focus on and investigation of the area of ritual abuse. From work toward the prevention of such severe abuse, to the competent assessment and treatment of those who have been injured, virtually every aspect of this field warrants further development and attention. Integration of information from the various disciplines involved in this field, combined with a respect for the input of survivors themselves, will enable mental health practitioners to develop a cogent understanding of this compelling and important area.

References

Braun, G. B. 1983. "Psychological Phenomena in Multiple Personality and Hypnosis." *American Journal of Clinical Hypnosis* 26, no. 2:124–37.

Kluft, R. P., ed. 1985. *Childhood Antecedents of Multiple Personality.* Washington, D.C.: American Psychiatric Press.

McCann, Lisa, L. A. Pearlman, D. K. Sakheim, and D. J. Abrahamson. 1988. "Assessment and Treatment of the Adult Survivor of Childhood Sexual Abuse." In *Vulnerable Populations,* ed. Suzanne M. Sgroi. Vol. 1, 77–101. Lexington, Mass.: Lexington Books.

McCann, Lisa, D. K. Sakheim, and D. J. Abrahamson. 1988. "Trauma and Victimization: A Model of Psychological Adaptation." *The Counseling Psychologist* 16, no. 4: 531–94.

Pelcovitz, David 1990. "The Effects of Extreme Stress: A Proposed DSM-IV Diagnosis." Paper Presentation to the Conference: Disorders of Extreme Stress. Hartford Hospital, Hartford, Connecticut. October 19, 1990.

Putnam, F. W. 1984. *Diagnosis and Treatment of Multiple Personality Disorder.* New York: The Guilford Press.

Sakheim, D. K. 1990. "The Dissociative Disorders: Implications for Diagnosis and Treatment." Paper Presentation to the Conference: Disorders of Extreme Stress. Hartford Hospital, Hartford, Connecticut. October 19, 1990.

Index

About the Contributors

Richard Barnum, M.D., is a clinical instructor in psychiatry at Harvard Medical School. He is the director of the Boston Juvenile Court Clinic and is the senior child psychiatrist for the Division of Forensic Mental Health of the Massachusetts Department of Mental Health. Dr. Barnum is the author of a variety of publications in the area of forensic psychiatry.

Catherine Gould, Ph.D., currently maintains a private practice in Encino, California. She is the author of the 1988 publication, *Signs and Symptoms of Ritualistic Child Abuse,* as well as a primary author of the *Los Angeles County Commission for Women Ritual Abuse Task Force Report* in 1989. Dr. Gould is internationally known as a valuable educational resource in the areas of diagnosis and treatment of child and adult victims of ritual abuse.

George B. Greaves, Ph.D., is in private practice in clinical and forensic psychology in Atlanta, Georgia. He is an adjunct professor in psychology at Georgia State University. Dr. Greaves is a founder and past president of the International Society for the Study of Multiple Personality and Dissociative Disorders.

Martin H. Katchen, M.A., received his masters degree in religious studies from the University of Denver and is currently pursuing a doctorate in religious studies at the University of Sydney, Sydney, Australia. He is a member of the Cult Awareness Network and is pursuing research on differential patterns of hypnotizability and dissociation in ex-cult members.

Robert Kinscherff, Ph.D., is an instructor in psychology at Harvard Medical School. He is a past president of the New England Society for the Study of Multiple Personality and Dissociative Disorders and a Consultant and Supervising Psychologist in Forensic Psychology for the Division of Forensic Mental Health, Massachusetts Department of Mental Health. Dr. Kinscherff has consulted and lectured widely about ritual abuse of children.

Kenneth V. Lanning is the supervisory special agent for the Behavioral Sciences Unit at the FBI Academy in Quantico, Virginia. He has specialized in studying the sexual victimization of children. In his role with the Behavioral Sciences Unit, Mr. Lanning has researched, published, lectured, and consulted widely regarding the sexual victimization of children and the characteristics of sexual abuse perpetrators.

Laurie Anne Pearlman, Ph.D., is the research director of the Traumatic Stress Institute in South Windsor, Connecticut. Dr. Pearlman's research focuses on the unique psychological experiences of adult trauma survivors. She is the coauthor of a book on the psychological impact of trauma on adult survivors. At the institute's clinical division, the Center for Adult and Adolescent Psychotherapy, Dr. Pearlman does psychotherapy and clinical supervision.

Richard Mangen, Psy.D., is the director of research and training at the National Center for the Treatment of Dissociative Disorders in Denver, Colorado. He is a clinical affiliate at the University of Denver School of Professional Psychology and an associate clinical professor at the University of Colorado Health Sciences Center. In addition to research and teaching, Dr. Mangen has a private practice in the Denver area specializing in psychotherapy, psychological assessment, and clinical supervision.

Lisa McCann, Ph.D., was the founder and clinical director of the Traumatic Stress Institute and its clinical division, The Center for Adult and Adolescent Psychotherapy in South Windsor, Connecticut. She has published and lectured widely about the psychological effects of trauma. Dr. McCann recently coauthored the publication, *Psychological Trauma and the Adult Survivor: Theory, Therapy, and Transformation.*

Linda and **David Stone** are the pseudonyms of the mother and stepfather of ritual abuse survivors and they prefer to maintain their anonymity. The Stones are advocates for ritual abuse survivors and their nonperpetrator parents.

Walter C. Young, M.D., is the medical director of the National Center for the Treatment of Dissociative Disorders in Denver, Colorado. He is a cofounder and past president of the Colorado Society for the Study of Multiple Personality and Dissociation. Dr. Young is a charter member and fellow, as well as the immediate past president, of the International Association for the Study of Multiple Personality and Dissociative Disorders. He is nationally known as a presenter of seminars, workshops, articles, and papers on the subjects of multiple personality, dissociation, and ritual abuse.

About the Editors

David K. Sakheim, Ph.D., is in private practice in both South Windsor, Connecticut, and Springfield, Massachusetts. Dr. Sakheim has served on the adjunct faculties of Tufts University, Antioch College, and Union College. He has published, consulted, and lectured widely about the conceptualization and treatment of multiple personality, dissociation, and ritual abuse, as well as provided clinical supervision to therapists.

Susan E. Devine, R.N., M.S.N., received her training from Yale University School of Nursing in New Haven, Connecticut and has been involved in work with childhood trauma for many years. She has supervised inpatient psychiatric services and has experience in forensic settings as well. She is currently a consultant for the New Haven Court Clinic and the Yale Law and Psychiatry Program.